Holt MUSIC

TEXAS TEACHER'S EDITION Grade 7

Eunice Boardman Meske
Professor of Music and Education
University of Wisconsin—Madison
Madison, Wisconsin

Barbara Andress
Professor of Music Education
Arizona State University
Tempe, Arizona

Mary P. Pautz
Assistant Professor of Music
  Education
University of Wisconsin—Milwaukee
Milwaukee, Wisconsin

Fred Willman
Associate Professor of Music and
  Education
University of Missouri—St. Louis
St. Louis, Missouri

Special Texas Edition Contributor
Jack Noble White
Texas Boys Choir
Forth Worth, Texas

© 1988 by Holt, Rinehart and Winston, Publishers

All rights reserved.
Printed in the United States of America
ISBN 0-03-014054-4
78901 032 987654321

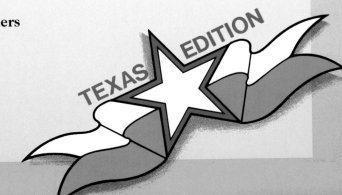

Holt Music

The Program To Count On When Performance Counts

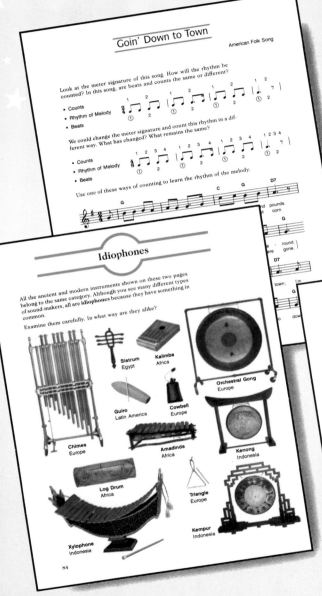

★ Holt Music presents a perfectly orchestrated program of teaching materials to help you meet the unique requirements of the Texas Essential Elements.

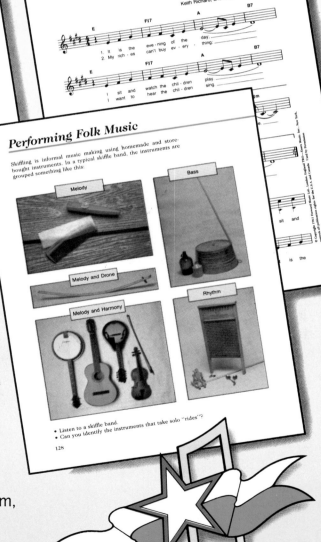

★ Comprehensive coverage of every major aspect of basic music theory, from notation, symbols, and terms to pitch, rhythm, and dynamics

★ The highest-quality song program on the market today, featuring a broad assortment of engaging music from every era, in every style

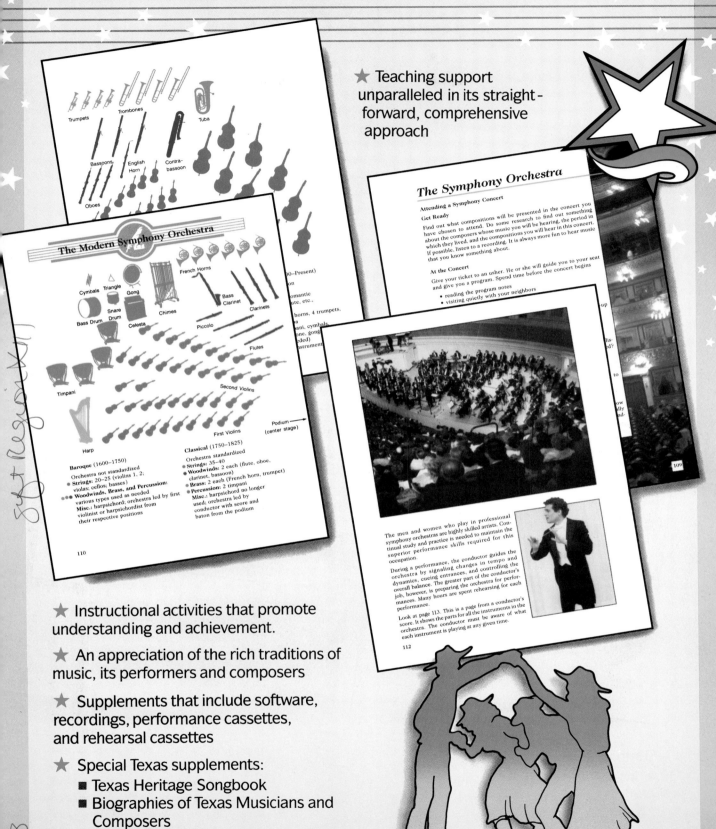

★ Teaching support unparalleled in its straight-forward, comprehensive approach

★ Instructional activities that promote understanding and achievement.

★ An appreciation of the rich traditions of music, its performers and composers

★ Supplements that include software, recordings, performance cassettes, and rehearsal cassettes

★ Special Texas supplements:
- Texas Heritage Songbook
- Biographies of Texas Musicians and Composers
- Unit Tests designed for the Texas Essential Elements
- Music Evaluations correlated to the Texas Essential Elements

Pupil's Edition

Exciting Songs And Activities

Quality songs from every era form the basis for developing true understanding of music theory.

Pages and pages of fun-to-do activities help students develop their vocal and instrumental skills.

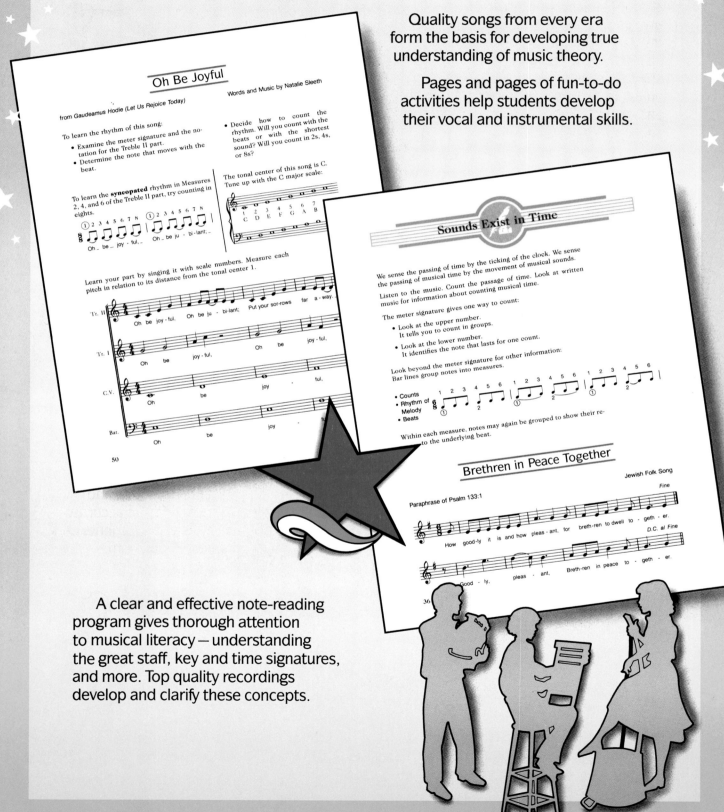

A clear and effective note-reading program gives thorough attention to musical literacy — understanding the great staff, key and time signatures, and more. Top quality recordings develop and clarify these concepts.

Listening lessons help students to recognize the unique sounds of a variety of instruments. Many of them also ask students to apply critical thinking skills in analyzing music, comparing and contrasting, and choosing alternatives.

Activities are exciting, involving, and fun for individual students, small groups, or the entire class.

The Washtub Bass

You may decide to make a washtub bass for the same reason that this instrument became popular in the early 1900s—its cost! Although people could order musical instruments from catalogues, at that time a string bass would cost well over $20.00! So people turned to materials at hand and created their own instruments. A well-constructed and well-played washtub bass sounds very much like a string bass.

To produce different bass notes on this washtub bass, you need to change the tension of the string. You can do this by pulling back on the stick with one hand as you pluck with the other to create a "walking-bass" accompaniment or by fretting the string to make an "oompah-bass" accompaniment.

Listen to "Deep Fork River Blues."

Which method is the performer using?

Root bass

Walking bass

There are many "tricks of the trade" that you will pick up as you practice. For example:

- Put your foot on the tub's edge to keep it from "dancing" away.
- Wear a glove on your hand to prevent blisters and sore fingers.
- Prop up one side of the tub with a block of wood to allow more sound to escape.

38

Language and Music of the Wolves

Wolves howl to identify themselves, to maintain contact with the pack, and to indicate the boundaries of their territory.

LISTENING

Wolf Eyes
by Paul Winter

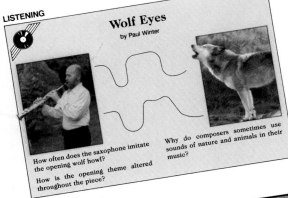

How often does the saxophone imitate the opening wolf howl?

How is the opening theme altered throughout the piece?

Why do composers sometimes use sounds of nature and animals in their music?

124

An attractive blend of instructional photographs and illustrations provides an accurate representation of instruments and proper ways to play them.

Teacher's Edition

Coming Through With More For You

Unit Openers make lesson planning easy by identifying — with page references — the Texas Essential Elements taught in the units.

In the first lesson of each lesson group, a special logo highlights Essential Elements to be taught.

Lesson Focus pinpoints the concept about to be covered. The program offers a full introduction to music theory.

Materials include recordings with first-quality selections from every major musical period.

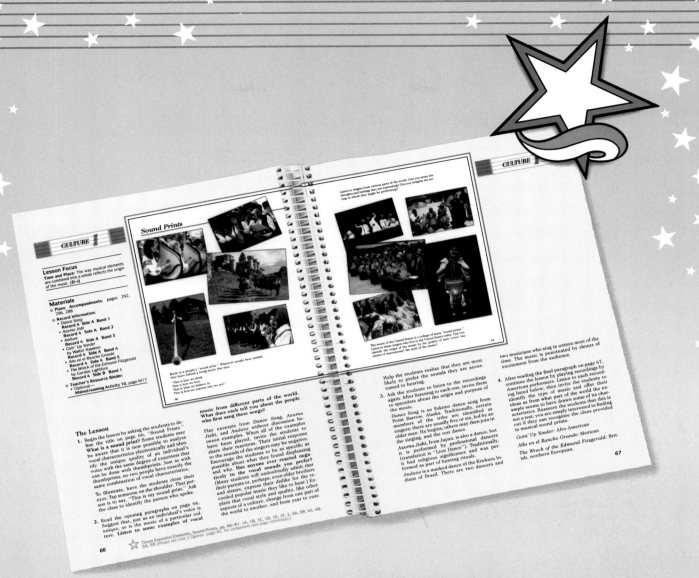

Lesson plans are rich with suggestions for individual, small-group, and large-group performances. Activities provide both instrumental and vocal applications.

Hands-on experience enables students to become familiar with the characteristics and sounds of a wide variety of instruments.

Opportunities abound for students to truly develop their singing ability — with step-by-step teaching help in guiding their breathing, diction, and tone production.

Optional activities enable students to further enrich their musical skills as performers and as audience.

Supplementary Materials

Tailor-Made For Texas Needs

Texas Heritage Songbook

You'll find a wealth of music to spark enthusiasm and pride in every student in your class. The collection includes a host of contemporary and traditional songs that truly reflect the diversity of the Lone Star State.

The Teacher's Resource Binder, Texas Edition

The Texas TRB features eleven supplemental booklets, including these special Texas components:

★ **Tests for the Texas Essential Elements** a complete set of tests designed to meet the objectives of the Texas Essential Elements

★ **Correlated Music Evaluations** Checkpoints, Reviews, and Musical Progress Reports correlated to the Texas Essential Elements

★ **Biographies of Texas Musicians and Composers** four biographies of celebrated Texas composers and musicians

The Lesson Cycle

HOLT MUSIC helps music educators fulfill their teaching goals by providing teaching strategies that correspond to those steps contained in the Lesson Cycle.* The result is quality planning, teaching, and learning.

A **Planning and Focus on Objective** — to solicit student attention; to generate and motivate learner interest

B **Explanation/Check Understanding** — information presented through a variety of formats

C **Guided Practice to Check Mastery** — an opportunity for students and teacher to evaluate together how well the lesson has been comprehended so far

D **Independent Practice** — an opportunity for students to evaluate independently how well they have comprehended the lesson

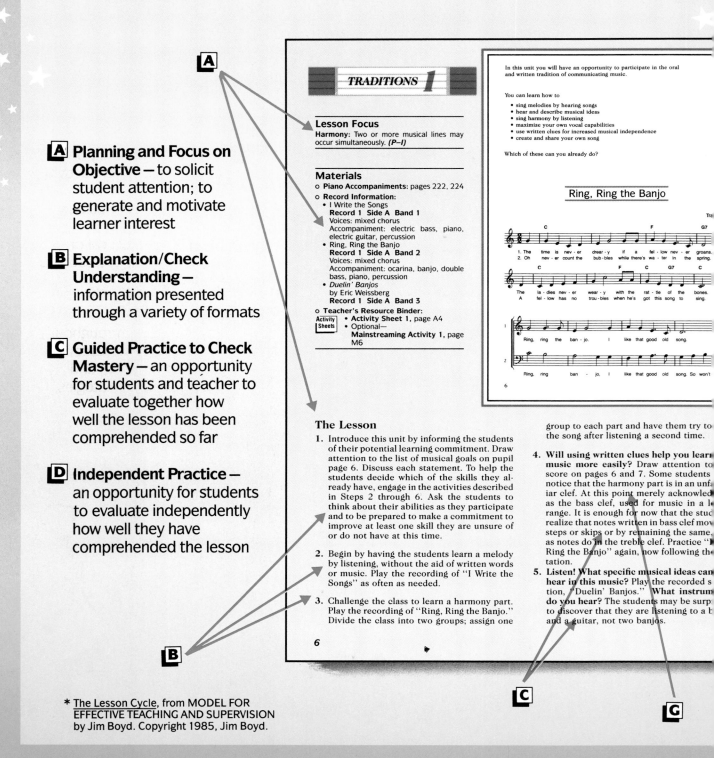

TRADITIONS *1*

Lesson Focus
Harmony: Two or more musical lines may occur simultaneously. *(P–I)*

Materials
o **Piano Accompaniments:** pages 222, 224
o **Record Information:**
 • I Write the Songs
 Record 1 Side A Band 1
 Voices: mixed chorus
 Accompaniment: electric bass, piano, electric guitar, percussion
 • Ring, Ring the Banjo
 Record 1 Side A Band 2
 Voices: mixed chorus
 Accompaniment: ocarina, banjo, double bass, piano, percussion
 • *Duelin' Banjos*
 by Eric Weissberg
 Record 1 Side A Band 3
o **Teacher's Resource Binder:**
 Activity Sheets • **Activity Sheet 1,** page A4
 • Optional—
 Mainstreaming Activity 1, page M6

In this unit you will have an opportunity to participate in the oral and written tradition of communicating music.

You can learn how to

• sing melodies by hearing songs
• hear and describe musical ideas
• sing harmony by listening
• maximize your own vocal capabilities
• use written clues for increased musical independence
• create and share your own song

Which of these can you already do?

Ring, Ring the Banjo

The Lesson

1. Introduce this unit by informing the students of their potential learning commitment. Draw attention to the list of musical goals on pupil page 6. Discuss each statement. To help the students decide which of the skills they already have, engage in the activities described in Steps 2 through 6. Ask the students to think about their abilities as they participate and to be prepared to make a commitment to improve at least one skill they are unsure of or do not have at this time.

2. Begin by having the students learn a melody by listening, without the aid of written words or music. Play the recording of "I Write the Songs" as often as needed.

3. Challenge the class to learn a harmony part. Play the recording of "Ring, Ring the Banjo." Divide the class into two groups; assign one

6

group to each part and have them try to the song after listening a second time.

4. **Will using written clues help you learn music more easily?** Draw attention to score on pages 6 and 7. Some students notice that the harmony part is in an unfa iar clef. At this point merely acknowled as the bass clef, used for music in a l range. It is enough for now that the stud realize that notes written in bass clef mov steps or skips or by remaining the same, as notes do in the treble clef. Practice "R Ring the Banjo" again, now following th tation.

5. **Listen! What specific musical ideas can hear in this music?** Play the recorded s tion, "Duelin' Banjos." **What instrum do you hear?** The students may be surp to discover that they are listening to a b and a guitar, not two banjos.

*The Lesson Cycle, from MODEL FOR EFFECTIVE TEACHING AND SUPERVISION by Jim Boyd. Copyright 1985, Jim Boyd.

Come a-gain my true love. Oh where you been so long?

come a-gain my true love? Where you been so long?

LISTENING

Duelin' Banjos
by Eric Weissberg

Listen to these two performers as they try to outdo one another. Can you hear when one instrument is imitating the other? What two instruments are playing?

7

TRADITIONS 1

For Your Information

This unit is to help the students

- grasp the importance of the oral tradition as a legitimate means of communicating musical ideas
- discover that written clues can provide greater independence in communicating musical ideas
- gain experience in reading a variety of musical styles at both the ikonic and symbolic levels
- grow in an understanding of personal development, especially with regard to changing vocal range
- continue the development of performance skills

I Write the Songs

Words and Music by Bruce Johnston

I've been alive forever,
And I wrote the very first song.
I put the words and melodies together;
I am music, and I write the songs.
I write the songs that make the whole
    world sing.
I write the songs of love and special things.
I write the songs that make the young girls
    cry.
I write the songs; I write the songs . . .

E **Closure** — summary of lesson with student activity; lesson brought to an appropriate conclusion

F **Extension** — vertical or lateral learning of lesson's emphasis

G **Monitoring and Adjustment** — throughout all aspects of the lesson, praise, prompting, and other teaching strategies to further student participation

Distribute Activity Sheet 1 (Listening Guide Sheet). Use this as a listening guide as the recording is played again. The selection begins with an introduction of broken chords; full chords rhythmically strummed and echoed follow. The imitative play begins with the guitar playing eight brief melodic ideas that are echoed exactly or with slight variations by the banjo player. (Segments 1–2–4–5–6–7 are the same. In Segment 3, fewer pitches are echoed; in Segment 8 the banjo accompanies the guitar. The music continues with a lively tune played by both instruments and the return of the imitation game. The piece ends with a banjo solo followed by both instruments playing a final strum.

Play the selection, inviting the students to follow the guide sheet. They are to mark whether the first imitative-play ideas are the

same or varied. The students are to decide if the imitation is exactly the same or varied for each segment and mark their answers in Column 2. (Segments 1–2–4–5–6–7 are the same. In Segment 3 fewer pitches are echoed; in Segment 8 the instruments divided into two parts and clear, unaccompanied imitation ceases.)

7. Explain that during this unit the students will be involved in many activities leading to the improvement of the skills they have engaged in today as well as the other skills listed on page 6. At this time you may wish to ask them to make a commitment toward improving one or two of those skills.

7

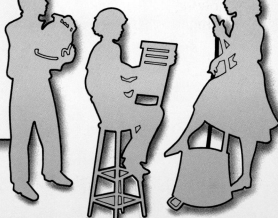

Texas Essential Elements For Music

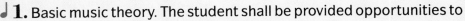

♩**1.** Basic music theory. The student shall be provided opportunities to
  - a. know and use the great staff
  - b. know and use pitch and rhythmic notation
  - c. know and use musical symbols and terms
  - d. know and use common keys and time signatures
  - e. recognize intervals
  - f. use dynamics

♩**2.** Singing techniques. The student shall be provided opportunities to develop and use the singing voice, including basic principles of proper breathing, diction, and tone production.

♩**3.** Study of instruments. The student shall be provided opportunities to
  - a. learn about the history and development of musical instruments
  - b. recognize the instruments by sight and sound

♩**4.** Music history and literature. The student shall be provided opportunities to
  - a. hear and discuss works from all major musical periods, including the music of contemporary life
  - b. learn about the lives and works of selected composers

♩**5.** Performance activities. The student shall be provided opportunities to
  - a. participate in individual, small ensemble, or large-group performances of vocal or instrumental music
  - b. practice audience etiquette

Helping You Do Your Professional Best

Texas Essential Elements Planning Guide

Unit	Lesson Groups	Essential Elements	PE Pages	TE Pages	TRB Pages
1	Exploring Musical Traditions (pp. 5–11)	1A		6; 11	E2; K2; M8; I2–3
		1B		6; 11	O2; E2; K2; M8; I2; I4–8
		1C	8–9	6; 8; 11	O2; K2; AS4; M6
		1D		11	K2; I2; I4–8
		2	8–9	6; 8–11	E2; M8
		3B	7	6	E2; AS4; I2
		4A		10	
		5A	8–9	6; 9–11	O2; I2; I4–8
		5B		10	AS6
1	The Oral Tradition (pp. 12–27)	1A	14–19; 22–24; 26	14–17; 26	O2; E5; K2; K5
		1B	14–19; 21; 23; 26	13–18; 20–21; 23; 26	O2; E5; K2; K5; AS10; AS11; M10
		1C	13–24	13–18; 20–23; 26	O2; K2; K5
		1D	13; 18–19; 22–24	13; 25	K2; K5
		2	12–19	12–15; 17; 19; 21–23; 26	O2; K2; K5; AS11
		3B		13; 25	O2; K5; AS13
		4A	12	12	E5; AS8; AS12; AS14
		5A	12–19	12–15; 17; 19; 21–23; 26	O2; K2; K5; AS11; M10
		5B	12	12	
1	The Written Tradition (pp. 28–64)	1A	29–31; 33–39; 41–43; 47–57; 63	28–29; 32; 42; 48–52; 54; 56–57; 59	EV3; EV5; O7; O14; O22; E5; E8; K8; I9–13
		1B	28–29; 32–43; 46–51; 56–58	28–30; 32–35; 38–40; 42; 46; 48–52; 54–61; 63	EV3; EV5–6; O7; O10; O14; O18; O22; E5; E8; K8; K11; AS15; AS16; AS18; AS19; AS20; AS21; AS22; M12; M14; M17; I9–13
		1C	28–29; 32–33; 36–40; 42; 46; 48–51; 54–55	28–29; 32–42; 48–52; 55–56; 59	EV3; EV5; O7; O14; E5; O18; O22; E8; K8; B3
		1D	36–43; 46–50; 56–57	36–42; 46–50; 56–57; 59	EV3; EV5–6; O7; O10; O22; E5; E8; K11; AS18; AS19; AS20; AS21; AS22; M15; I9–13
		1E	33–34	33–35	
		1F		59	E5
		2	33–34; 37; 39; 46; 48; 50–51; 55–57; 59	30; 32; 34–35; 37; 42; 46; 50; 52; 54–56; 58–59; 63	O7; O10; O14; O18; O22; K8; K11; I9–13
		3B	39; 45; 53; 62	30; 34–35; 39; 60	EV2; O10; O14; O18; O22; E5
		4A	40–41; 59	40–41; 56; 59–61	B1; B3
		4B	40–41; 59	41; 59–61	B1; B3
		5A	33–34; 37; 39; 46; 48; 50–51; 55–57; 59	30; 32; 34–35; 37; 39; 42; 44; 46; 50; 52; 54–56; 58–61; 63	O7; O10; O14; O18; O22; E5; E8; K8; K11; M15; M17; I9–13
		5B	41; 60–61	34	
2	Sound Prints (pp. 66–81)	1A	74	68; 72; 74; 76–78; 80–81	K14; I14
		1B	68, 73–74	68–69; 72–74; 76–78; 80–81	K14; I14

Unit	Lesson Groups	Essential Elements	PE Pages	TE Pages	TRB Pages
		1C	66; 68; 74; 76–78	66; 68–69; 74–81	K14; AS23; I14
		1D	74	68–69; 72; 76–78; 80–81	K14; I14
		1E	94		
		1F	68	69; 73; 78	AS23
		2	68–69; 72–73	68–69; 72–81	K14; I14
		3A			E13
		3B		79	E13
		4A	72–73	72; 74; 76	E13; B5; M17
		4B			E13
		5A	68–69; 72–73	68–69; 72–81	I14
		5B	67; 72	66–67	M17
2	Instrumental Sound Prints (pp. 82–97)	1A	95		O14; E13
		1B	88–89; 94–97	89; 94	O14; E13; K19; AS24
		1C	82–87; 90–93; 96	82–87; 90–93; 96	O14; E13
		1D	95		O14; E13
		2		95	O14; K19
		3A	96–97		
		3B	82–87; 90–93; 96	82–87; 90–93; 96	O14; E13; K19; AS24; AS25–28; M18
		4A	88–89; 96–97	88–89; 96–97	
		4B	96–97	96–97	B7
		5A	88–89; 94–95	88–89; 94–95	O14; E13; K19; AS25–28; M18
		5B	84–93	84–87	
2	Rhythm and Melody (pp. 98–105)	1A	99; 101; 103–105	101	O10; O18; E16; K11
		1B	98–105	98–101	O10; O18; E16; K11
		1C	98–105	98–105	O18; E16; AS24; AS29; AS30
		1D	99; 101; 104–105	99–101	O10; O18; E16; AS24
		1F	105		O18; AS29; AS30
		2	99; 104–105	101; 105	O10; O18; K11
		3B	102	102	O10; O18; E16
		4A	99; 101–105	102–103	
		4B	102–103		
		5A	99; 101; 104–105	101; 105	O10; O18; E16; K11
		5B	99; 101–103; 105	99; 101–103; 105	
2	Musical Texture (pp. 106–108)	1A	106–108		
		1B	106–108	106–107	
		1C	106–108	106–109	EV9–11; AS30
		1D	106–108	107	
		1F			AS30
		2	106–108	106–108	
		5A	106–108	106–108	
2	The Symphony Orchestra (pp. 109–116)	1A	113–114		
		1B	113–114	114–115	
		1C	114–116	114–115	
		1D	114	114–115	
		3A	110–111; 116	110–113	

Unit	Lesson Groups	Essential Elements	PE Pages	TE Pages	TRB Pages
		3B	109–114; 116	110–113; 115	EV9–11
		4A	114–116	110–113; 115–116	EV11
		4B	114; 116	110–113; 115	
		5B	109; 114; 116	109; 114–115	
3	**Playing Folk Instruments** (pp. 117–127)	1A	119–123; 125–127	120–123; 125–126	K17; AS35–37
		1B	119–123; 125–127	119–123; 125–126	K17; AS35–37; M18; M21
		1C	119–127	118–126	K17; AS32–34; M18
		1D	119–123; 125–127	125–126	K17; AS35–37
		1E		125; 137; 158	
		1F	119	120	
		2		125	K17
		3B	119; 120; 124	119–126	AS37; M21
		4A	119–123; 125–127	119–124	K17; AS31; A32–34; B13
		4B	119–123; 125–127	121–124	K17; AS32–34
		5A		125–126	K17; AS35–36; M18; M21
		5B	119	118–124	
3	**Performing Folk Music** (pp. 128–143)	1A	129–143	129; 132; 136–137; 142	M21
		1B	129–143	129; 130; 132; 136–138	E16; M21; M23
		1C	128–143	128; 134; 136–138; 140; 142	AS43
		1D	129–143	129; 130; 132; 136–137; 140	M21; M23
		2	131; 134	129; 131; 133–135; 137; 139; 141	
		3A	137–138	132; 138; 141	
		3B	128; 130; 132; 134; 137–142	128–142	E16; AS39–42; M21; M23
		4A		137	
		5A	131; 134; 142	129; 131; 133–135; 137; 139; 141; 142	E16; AS38; AS43–44; M21; M23; I15–19
		5B	128; 130	128–142	
3	**Playing the Guitar** (pp. 144–161)	1A	160	146; 148; 154; 158; 160	AS51–53
		1B	144–146; 150; 152; 160	146; 148; 154; 158–160	E17; AS46; AS51–53
		1C	144; 152; 160	150; 152; 154; 158; 160	AS51–53
		1D	144–146; 160	146; 148; 154; 160	E17; AS51–53
		2	144–146; 153; 155	145–146; 150–152; 154; 158	E17
		3B	144–146; 149–150; 152–155; 160–161	144–146; 154; 160–161	E17; AS45; AS49
		5A	144–146; 150; 153–155	145–146; 148; 150–154; 156; 159–161; 167	E17; AS45–49
		5B	149; 151–153; 160		
3	**Composing Commercial Music** (pp. 162–168)	1A	162–63	162–165	EV14–16; E17; AS54
		1B	162–163	162–165	EV14–16; E17; AS54; AS55–65
		1C	163	162–165; 168	EV14; EV16; E17; AS54;

Unit	Lesson Groups	Essential Elements	PE Pages	TE Pages	TRB Pages
					AS65
		1D	162–163; 168	162; 165	EV14; EV16; E17; AS54; AS65
		1F	163; 168	163; 168	EV16; AS54
		2			EV15; E17
		3B	166	162; 165	AS54
		4A	162–163	168	EV16
		5A		162–163; 165	EV15; E17; AS54
4	Choral Singing (pp. 169–219)	1A	172–173; 185–189; 217	170; 172–173; 175; 177; 178; 181–183; 185–186; 188; 192; 194–197; 199–201; 203–204; 206–207; 210–212; 214; 217	EV19; EV22; O7; O22; K19; AS67; M25; I20–21; I22
		1B	172–173; 185–189; 206–209; 217	170; 172–173; 175; 177–179; 181–183; 185–186; 188; 190; 192; 194–197; 199–201; 203–204; 206–207; 210–212; 214; 217–218	EV19; EV21; O7; O22; E19; K19; AS66; AS67; M25; I20–21; I22
		1C	172–173; 185–189; 206–209	172–173; 175; 177–179; 181–183; 185–186; 188; 190; 192; 194–197; 199–201; 204; 206–207; 211–213; 214–215; 217	EV19; EV21; O7; O22; E19; K19; AS67; I22
		1D	172–173; 186–189	170; 175; 177; 178; 181–182; 185–186; 188; 196; 199; 203; 210–211; 214; 217	EV19; O7; O22; K19; AS67; M25; I20–21; I22
		1E		175; 177–179; 195; 196	
		1F	200	170; 173; 195; 200–201; 214	EV14; O22; K14; I22
		2	170–173; 185; 200–202; 217	170; 172–173; 175; 177–179; 181–183; 185–186; 188; 191; 192; 194–197; 199–201; 204; 207; 211–212; 214; 217–218	EV19; O7; E19; K14; K19; M23
		3B		173–175; 178; 182–183; 190; 194; 197; 200; 203; 214; 217–218	O7; O22; AS67
		4A		211–212; 215	
		4B			B15
		5A	170–173; 185; 200–202; 217	170; 172–173; 175; 177–179; 181–183; 185–186; 188; 191; 192; 194–197; 199–201; 204; 207; 211–212; 214; 217–218	O7; O22; E19; K14; K19; AS67; M23; M25; I20–21; I22
		5B		186; 190; 192; 201; 204; 206; 213; 214; 218	K14

Holt MUSIC

TEACHER'S EDITION Grade 7

Eunice Boardman Meske
Professor of Music and Education
University of Wisconsin—Madison
Madison, Wisconsin

Barbara Andress
Professor of Music Education
Arizona State University
Tempe, Arizona

Mary P. Pautz
Assistant Professor of Music
  Education
University of Wisconsin—Milwaukee
Milwaukee, Wisconsin

Fred Willman
Associate Professor of Music and
  Education
University of Missouri—St. Louis
St. Louis, Missouri

Holt, Rinehart and Winston, Publishers
New York, Toronto, Mexico City, London, Sydney, Tokyo

Acknowledgments for previously copyrighted material
and credits for photographs and art begin on page 405.
ISBN 0-03-005319-6
7890 032 987654321

HOLT MUSIC

It's the leader of the band!

CONSIDER THE ADVANTAGES . . .

- *Dozens of the world's finest songs in each level—the songs your students want to sing!*

- *Exciting activities that enable students to interact with the music and acquire musical knowledge.*

- *Exceptionally motivating listening lessons that really get students involved in learning.*

- *Flexibly organized Teacher's Editions, rich with background information and no-nonsense teaching strategies.*

- *A wealth of supplementary materials that enhance, extend, and enrich.*

Music That Motivates

Every song in HOLT MUSIC builds on the natural enthusiasm that students have for singing, dancing—expressing themselves in creative ways! You'll find hundreds and hundreds of authentic songs that students really *want* to sing—songs with built-in appeal.

Choose from a rich variety of songs: contemporary, traditional, American and European folk, classical, holiday music, and more.

Just look at some of these favorites:

Bo Diddley
As Tears Go By
Fiddler on the Roof
America from *West Side Story*
The M.T.A. Song
Put Your Hand in the Hand
Song Sung Blue
Getting to Know You
Tie Me Kangaroo Down
Go Down, Moses and Joshua
    Fought the Battle of Jericho

Lively, colorful photographs and illustrations provide the perfect visual accompaniment.

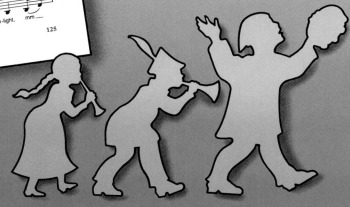

Music to Learn From

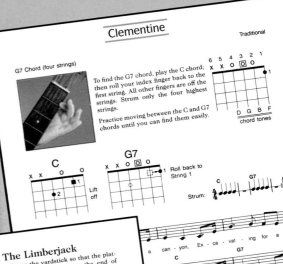

Songs throughout HOLT MUSIC develop note-reading skills and apply them as a basis for instrumental accompaniment and vocal exploration.

Each song provides a point of departure for creative involvement in learning.

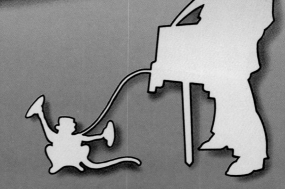

Special graphic aids reinforce note—reading skills and enhance the students' understanding of rhythm, melody, and harmony.

Music to Interact With

Engaging activities help students understand, relate to, and interact with music right from the start. These activities are more than entertaining—they're truly *instructive*, designed to strengthen and enhance musical understanding.

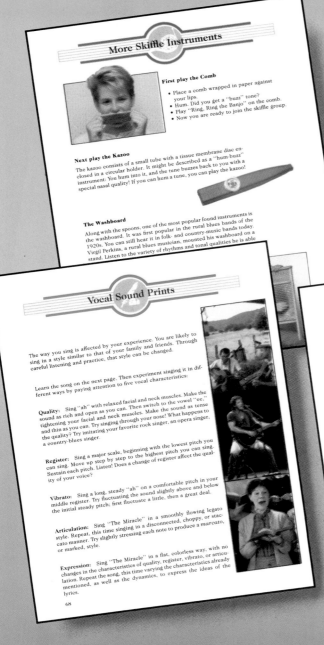

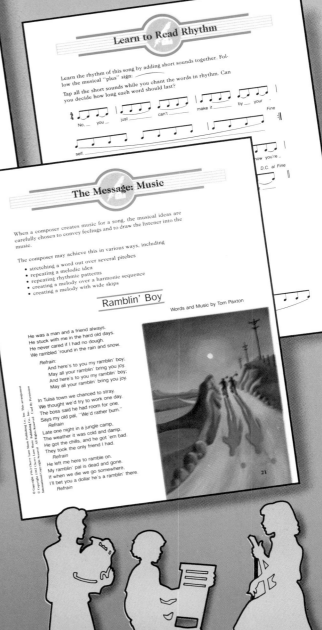

Irresistible activities inspire singing, clapping, making up melodies and rhymes, and more— the true exhilaration of musical expression. Many activities involve poetry or related arts.

Short instrumental experiences begin at Kindergarten, employing readily available instruments.

Music Worth Listening To

Many activities call upon students to move to rhythms and melodic patterns or to listen critically and make judgments about mood, instrumentation, melody, and form.

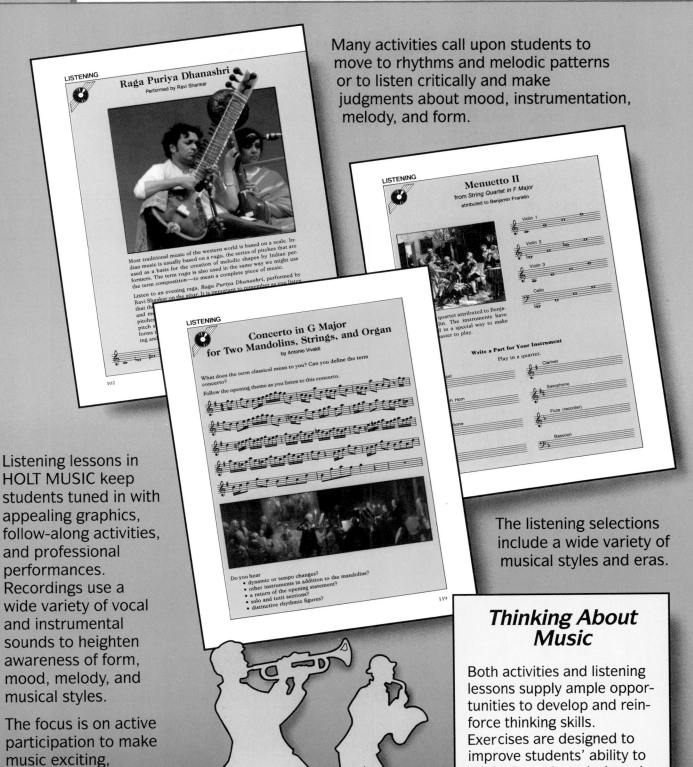

Listening lessons in HOLT MUSIC keep students tuned in with appealing graphics, follow-along activities, and professional performances. Recordings use a wide variety of vocal and instrumental sounds to heighten awareness of form, mood, melody, and musical styles.

The focus is on active participation to make music exciting, involving, and fun!

The listening selections include a wide variety of musical styles and eras.

Thinking About Music

Both activities and listening lessons supply ample opportunities to develop and reinforce thinking skills. Exercises are designed to improve students' ability to think, through analysis and evaluation, comparison and contrast, choosing alternatives, and more.

Music That's Realistic to Teach!

Whatever your musical background, you'll find all the backup help you need in HOLT MUSIC Teacher's Editions: concrete information, strategies you can rely on, and solid, flexible lesson plans with many optional suggestions. Every page is designed to bring musical understanding and appreciation within reach of all your students.

Each lesson begins with a clear objective and a complete list of program materials, including a detailed summary of recordings and the voices and instruments used.

A special logo signals when activity sheets are available for the lesson.

Each lesson begins with a motivating activity that leads naturally into the lesson content.

Step-by-step teaching instructions ensure that the lesson objective is met. Commentary and questions to the student are highlighted in boldface type.

TRADITIONS 2

Lesson Focus
Melody: Individual pitches, when compared to each other, may be higher, lower, or the same. *(P–S)*

Materials
○ **Piano Accompaniments:** pages 224, 226
○ **Record Information:**
  • Ring, Ring the Banjo
    (Record 1 Side A Band 2)
  • Lonesome Traveler
    Record 1 Side A Band 4a (Verses 1 and 2)
    Band 4b: Verses 3 and 4
    Band 4c: complete song
    Voices: mixed chorus
    Accompaniment: harmonica, acoustic guitar, electric guitar, double bass, percussion
○ **Teacher's Resource Binder:**
  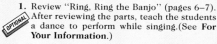
  • **Activity Sheet 2**, page A5
  • Optional—
    Enrichment Activity 1, page E2
    Instrumental Arrangements 1–3, pages 11–14
    Kodaly Activity 1, page K2
    Mainstreaming Activity 2, page M2
    Orff Activity 1, page O2

Your Singing Voice

To enjoy singing, it will be helpful if you know more about your voice and how it changes from time to time. Begin by finding your singing range. Sing "Lonesome Traveler."

Girls: Most of you will find this a comfortable singing range. You can sing melody or harmony parts. These parts will be called **Treble I** and **Treble II.** Each of you will want to learn Treble I on some songs and Treble II on others.

Lonesome Traveler

Words and Music by Lee

Rhythmically

1. I am a lone - ly and a lone - some trav - el - er
2. I trav - eled here and then I trav - eled yon - der, well

I am a lone - ly and a lone - some trav - el - er
I trav - eled here and then I trav - eled yon - der, well

I am a lone - ly and a lone - some trav - el - er;
I trav - eled here and then I trav - eled yon - der, well

I've been a trav - el - in' on.

8

The Lesson

1. Review "Ring, Ring the Banjo" (pages 6–7). After reviewing the parts, teach the students a dance to perform while singing.(See **For Your Information.**)

2. Help the students check their singing voices. Follow the instructions on pupil pages 8–9. Ask the girls to sing the song as written. Explain that their vocal range will be identified as Treble I or II. Their range is such that they may perform either part.

3. Next ask the boys to sing, explaining that while they are singing you will tap some of them on the shoulder. This means they are to drop out and not sing for the moment. Begin the song in the key as written. As they continue to sing, move among the group listening for those who are singing an octave lower than the others. Tap these singers on the

shoulder. Upon completion of this sorti tell the students who were tapped that th are Baritones as they were singing very lo They will sing a special part of the melody octave lower than written.

4. Ask the remaining boys to sing the mel again. Change the key of the song to A mir (Start the melody on E.) Repeat the pro dure. This time move among the group listen for voices that can easily sing in range. (Some will sing an octave lower.) the students who sing at pitch and later id tify them as the Treble I or II voices. Th are the boys whose voices are unchang Avoid identifying these students as boy pranos. Rather, place them in either the 7 ble I or II group.

5. The remaining boys will be those singe whose voices are in the process of changi

x

Freedom of choice is truly yours—the Junior High texts are designed for maximum flexibility. Each book is divided into four self—contained units. Units 1 and 2 allow students to explore ways of participating in music, as well as music of different traditions and times. Units 3 and 4 provide a wealth of materials for instrumental and choral performances.

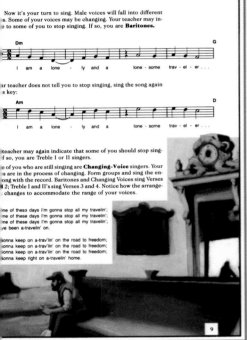

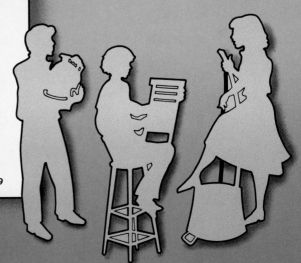

The lesson closes with an activity in which the students apply what they have learned.

Optional steps are labeled with a logo.

"For Your Information" provides a quick, convenient reference for background information about lesson contents.

Now it's your turn to sing. Male voices will fall into different ...s. Some of your voices may be changing. Your teacher may in-... to some of you to stop singing. If so, you are **Baritones.**

I am a lone - ly and a lone - some trav - el - er...

...r teacher does not tell you to stop singing, sing the song again ...f so) key:

I am a lone - ly and a lone - some trav - el - er...

...teacher may again indicate that some of you should stop sing-... ...f so, you are Treble I or II singers.

...e of you who are still singing are **Changing-Voice** singers. Your ...s are in the process of changing. Form groups and sing the en-...ong with the record. Baritones and Changing Voices sing Verses ... 2; Treble I and II's sing Verses 3 and 4. Notice how the arrange-...changes to accommodate the range of your voices.

...ine of these days I'm gonna stop all my travelin'; ...ine of these days I'm gonna stop all my travelin'; ...ine of these days I'm gonna stop all my travelin'; ...ve been a-travelin' on.

...ionna keep on a-trav'lin' on the road to freedom; ...ionna keep on a-trav'lin' on the road to freedom; ...ionna keep on a-trav'lin' on the road to freedom; ...ionna keep right on a-travelin' home.

TRADITIONS 2

For Your Information
It is important for both boys and girls of this age to understand that their voices are going through changes. An objective approach to this natural phenomenon will help the students become less self-conscious about overt signs such as cracking voices.

Dance instruction for "Ring, Ring the Banjo": Couples form a double circle, facing their partners.

VERSE I   **Phrase I:** Do-si-do right side of partner.
  Phrase II: Do-si-do left side of partner.

REFRAIN   **Phrase I:** Hold partner's hands; skip in a circle.
  Phrase II: Right hand swing; end with girl making a fancy twirl under partner's arm.

VERSE II   **Phrase I:** Hand-clapping patterns with partner, in time with beat—own hands, partner's right, own, partner's left, own, partner's both (three claps).
  Phrase II: Repeat as in Phrase I.

REFRAIN (Repeat as before)

Place them into a third group—Changing Voices.

. Change the seating arrangement in the room to accommodate the groupings you have just formed: Treble I and II, Changing Voices, and Baritones. Record the results on Activity Sheet 2 *(Ranges)*.

. "Lonesome Traveler" has been specially recorded to accommodate the voice ranges of these three groups. Perform the four verses with the record, featuring the groups as follows: Verses 1 and 2 (key of D minor)—Baritones and Changing Voices singing an octave apart; Verses 3 and 4 (key of A minor)—Treble I's and II's. Draw attention to the instrumental interlude between Verses 2 and 3. This interlude "takes the melody" to a new key that accommodates the vocal range of the treble voices. The song may be performed

with the recorded accompaniment alone by adjusting the balance on the record player.

Music That's Manageable

The **Teacher's Resource Binder** makes classroom management uncommonly convenient. Blackline masters help teachers structure the course to match individual preferences.

Teachers who use the **Kodaly** approach will find creative teaching ideas and fun-filled student charts— all correlated to HOLT MUSIC.

The **Orff** activities will delight your class with chants, games, and lively instrumental arrangements.

The **Biography** series brings music personalities to life.

A complete set of **Evaluations** provides a comprehensive testing program for HOLT MUSIC.

Students who are especially interested in music or who are academically gifted will find plenty of challenges in the **Enrichment** ideas.

Students will love working with the call charts, games, puzzles, costume patterns, and other idea-packed **Activity Sheets.** These blackline masters are designed to supplement, extend, and enrich the basic lesson plans.

Mainstreaming activities ensure that involvement in music learning is an important part of every child's day.

Instrumental Accompaniments provide simple arrangements of songs in the series for student instrumental performance.

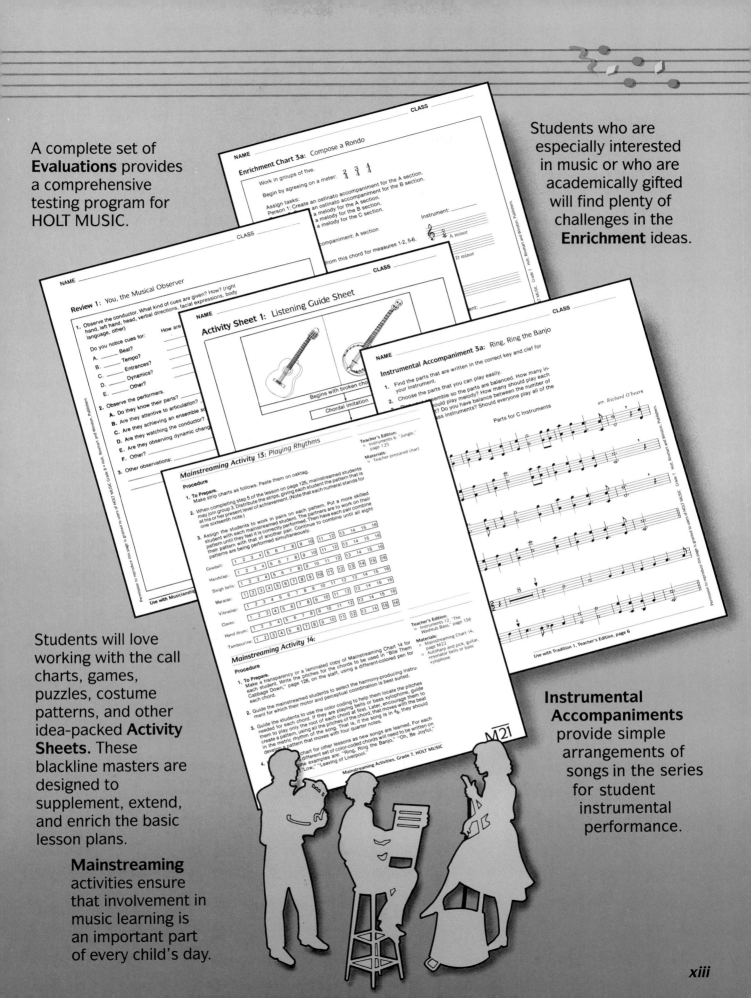

Music to Play

Recordings

A set of first-quality recordings serves a dual purpose: to give students a model for performance and to provide a valuable instrumental and vocal resource. Dual-track stereo allows separation of recorded voice and accompaniment.

A sturdy carrying case includes an index cross-referenced to lessons in the Teacher's Edition.

Song and listening selections appear in lesson order.

Extra Feature!

Each record package includes two performance cassettes. These cassettes contain instrumental tracks of songs from the program. They are specially edited to produce optimum sound for public performance.

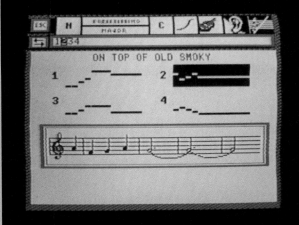

Supplementary Items

Software uses songs from HOLT MUSIC to encourage active experimentation. Students can rearrange phrases, shift tempo, or alter rhythm and print out the new musical scores to save and share with classmates. There are three separate programs: grades K–2, 3–5, and 6–8.

The *Holiday Song Book* includes lyrics and piano accompaniments for an additional 50 songs celebrating a year's worth of holidays— Mother's Day, Columbus Day, the Fourth of July, and more.

COMPONENTS CHART

	K	1	2	3	4	5	6	7	8
Pupil Book		✓	✓	✓	✓	✓	✓	✓	✓
Jumbo Book	✓	✓							
Teacher's Edition	✓	✓	✓	✓	✓	✓	✓	✓	✓
Recordings	✓	✓	✓	✓	✓	✓	✓	✓	✓
Teacher's Resource Binder	✓	✓	✓	✓	✓	✓	✓	✓	✓
Holiday Song Book	✓	✓	✓	✓	✓	✓	✓	✓	✓
Computer Software	✓	✓	✓	✓	✓	✓	✓	✓	✓
Performance Cassettes	✓	✓	✓	✓	✓	✓	✓	✓	✓

HOLT MUSIC offers you a total package for your classroom needs. A list of components is given in the chart at the left.

TABLE OF CONTENTS

UNIT 1 Exploring Musical Traditions...5

Meet the Authors xxii
Holt Music Field Test xxiii
A Guide to Holt Music xxiv
To the Classroom Teacher xxv
The Generative Approach to Music
  Learning xxvi
Scope and Sequence for Grade 7 . . . xxviii
To the Student 4

TRADITIONS 1 HARMONY 6
I WRITE THE SONGS
RING, RING THE BANJO
Duelin' Banjos (LISTENING)

TRADITIONS 2 MELODY 8
Your Singing Voice (ACTIVITY)
LONESOME TRAVELER

TRADITIONS 3 MELODY 10
No Reaction Recording (LISTENING)
BO DIDDLEY

The Oral Tradition 12

TRADITIONS 4 EXPRESSION 12
I WALK THE LINE
EASE ON DOWN THE ROAD

TRADITIONS 5 HARMONY 14
MAMA DON'T 'LOW

TRADITIONS 6 MELODY 16
Fiddler on the Roof (LISTENING)
KNOW WHERE I'M GOIN'
MEMPHIS, TENNESSEE

TRADITIONS 7 HARMONY 18
You Are My Sunshine (LISTENING)
AS TEARS GO BY

TRADITIONS 8 EXPRESSION 20
The Message: Words (ACTIVITY)
A PLACE IN THE SUN
The Message: Music (ACTIVITY)
RAMBLIN' BOY

TRADITIONS **9** EXPRESSION **22**
LEAVING OF LIVERPOOL
Your Own Message (ACTIVITY)

TRADITIONS **10** EXPRESSION **24**
The Message Transmitted: The
    Performer (ACTIVITY)
JUST A CLOSER WALK WITH THEE

TRADITIONS **11** HARMONY **26**
DELTA DAWN

The Written Tradition .. 28

TRADITIONS **12** TIME AND PLACE **28**
ARE YOU SLEEPING?

TRADITIONS **13** FORM **30**
FIDDLER ON THE ROOF

TRADITIONS **14** RHYTHM, MELODY **32**
Learn to Read Rhythm (ACTIVITY)
Learn to Read Melody (ACTIVITY)
YOU JUST CAN'T MAKE IT BY
    YOURSELF

TRADITIONS **15** MELODY,
    RHYTHM **34**
BAMBOO

TRADITIONS **16** EXPRESSION **36**
Sounds Exist in Time (ACTIVITY)
BRETHREN IN PEACE TOGETHER
Sounds Exist in Space (ACTIVITY)

TRADITIONS **17** RHYTHM, MELODY **38**
GOIN' DOWN TO TOWN

TRADITIONS **18** RHYTHM **40**
Interpreting Notation (ACTIVITY)
Gymnopédie No. 3 (LISTENING)
Waltz from Les Patineurs (LISTENING)
Wedding March from A Midsummer
    Night's Dream (LISTENING)

TRADITIONS **19** RHYTHM **42**
More Help From the Meter Signature
    (ACTIVITY)
SIXTY-SIX HIGHWAY BLUES

TRADITIONS **20** RHYTHM **44**
AMERICA

TRADITIONS **21** MELODY **46**
Read a Melody in a Major Key (ACTIVITY)
JACOB'S LADDER

TRADITIONS **22** MELODY **48**
Read Melodies Based on Different
    Scales (ACTIVITY)
GET THY BEARINGS
THE CRUEL WAR

TRADITIONS **23** MELODY, RHYTHM **50**
OH BE JOYFUL

TRADITIONS **24** HARMONY **52**
IT'S A LONG ROAD TO FREEDOM
Accompany Your Song (ACTIVITY)

TRADITIONS **25** HARMONY **54**
FIVE HUNDRED MILES

TRADITIONS **26** HARMONY,
    RHYTHM **56**
KID STUFF
WILLIAM GOAT
LONDON BRIDGE
PAW-PAW PATCH

TRADITIONS **27** EXPRESSION **58**
I AM FALLING OFF A MOUNTAIN

TRADITIONS **28** EXPRESSION **59**
Create a Choral Piece (ACTIVITY)
stinging gold swarms (POEM)
Circles (LISTENING)

TRADITIONS **29** TIMBRE........ **60**
Microtimbre I for Amplified Tam-Tam
    (LISTENING)

TRADITIONS **30** EVALUATION **63**
DUNDAI
FOLLOW THE DRINKIN' GOURD

UNIT 2 Music of Many Cultures...65

Sound Prints............ 66

CULTURE 1 TIME AND PLACE 66
Dance Song (LISTENING)
Azuma Jishi (LISTENING)
Anduve (LISTENING)

CULTURE 2 TIMBRE............. 68
Vocal Sound Prints (ACTIVITY)
THE MIRACLE

CULTURE 3 TIMBRE, TIME AND
PLACE 70
The Whole Earth Sings (ACTIVITY)
La Huichola (LISTENING)
Saeta (LISTENING)
Rabbit Dance (LISTENING)

CULTURE 4 TIME AND PLACE 72
Zenizenabo (LISTENING)

CULTURE 5 TIME AND PLACE 73
"Ketjak" Chorus from the Ramayana
(LISTENING)

CULTURE 6 TIME AND PLACE 74
THE WRECK OF THE EDMUND
FITZGERALD

CULTURE 7 TIME AND PLACE 76
GOIN' UP YONDER

CULTURE 8 TIME AND PLACE 79
LAKOTA NATIONAL ANTHEM

CULTURE 9 TIME AND PLACE 80
ALLA EN EL RANCHO GRANDE

Instrumental Sound
Prints 82

CULTURE 10 TIMBRE 82
Characteristics of Single Sounds
(ACTIVITY)
Characteristics of Combined Sounds
(ACTIVITY)

CULTURE 11 TIMBRE, TIME AND
PLACE 84
Idiophones (ACTIVITY)
Sematimba ne Kikabanga (LISTENING)
Trouble in Mind (LISTENING)

CULTURE 12 TIMBRE, TIME AND
PLACE 86
Membranophones (ACTIVITY)
Oldest Rabbit Song (LISTENING)

CULTURE 13 TIMBRE 88
Atsia (LISTENING)

CULTURE 14 EXPRESSION........ 89
Hudan Mas (LISTENING)

CULTURE 15 TIMBRE, TIME AND
PLACE 90
Chordophones (ACTIVITY)
Kalamtianos (LISTENING)

CULTURE 16 TIMBRE, TIME AND
PLACE 92
Aerophones (ACTIVITY)
Kele'a (LISTENING)
What Makes My Baby Cry? (LISTENING)
Rakish Paddy (LISTENING)

CULTURE 17 TIMBRE 94
Make your Own Aerophones and
Chordophones (ACTIVITY)
SHADY GROVE

CULTURE 18 TIME AND PLACE,
TIMBRE 96
Electrophones (ACTIVITY)
Conversation With Milton Babbitt
(LISTENING)
A Piece for Tape Recorder (LISTENING)
Composition for Synthesizer (LISTENING)
Silver Apples of the Moon (LISTENING)
The Song of the Wandering Aengus (POEM)

Rhythm and Melody 98

CULTURE 19 RHYTHM 98
TEENS

CULTURE 20 MELODY 100
Melodies Around the World (ACTIVITY)
MWATYE

CULTURE 21 MELODY 102
Raga Puriya Dhanashri (LISTENING)

CULTURE 22 FORM 104
Organizing Music in Time and Space
(ACTIVITY)
BANUWA

Musical Texture **106**

CULTURE **23**   HARMONY,
TEXTURE 106
GOOD NEWS

The Symphony Orchestra
.... **109**

CULTURE **24**   TIME AND PLACE ... 109
Attending a Symphony Concert

CULTURE **25**   TIME AND PLACE 110
The Modern Symphony Orchestra
   (ACTIVITY)

Magic Fire Music from Die Walküre
   (LISTENING)
Badinerie from Orchestra Suite in B
   minor (LISTENING)
De Natura Sonoris (LISTENING)

CULTURE **26**   FORM 114
First and Third Movement from
   Symphony No. 40 in G minor
   (LISTENING)

CULTURE **27**   EVALUATION 116
The Music of Today (ACTIVITY)
Monkey Chant (LISTENING)
Kalagala Ebwembe (LISTENING)
Badinerie (LISTENING)

UNIT 3 Playing Folk Instruments ... 117

INSTRUMENTS **1**   TIME AND
   PLACE 118
You, the Record Collector (ACTIVITY)
I Walk the Line (LISTENING)
Wedding March (LISTENING)

INSTRUMENTS **2**   TIMBRE 119
Concerto in G Major (LISTENING)

INSTRUMENTS **3**   TIME AND
   PLACE 120
Stardust (LISTENING)

INSTRUMENTS **4**   EXPRESSION ... 122
Fanfare for the Common Man
   (LISTENING)

INSTRUMENTS **5**   FORM 124
Language and Music of the Wolves
   (ACTIVITY)
Solo and Group Wolf Howls (LISTENING)
Wolf Eyes (LISTENING)
Duet (LISTENING)

INSTRUMENTS **6**   FORM 125
JUNGLE

Performing Folk Music
. . . . **128**

INSTRUMENTS **7** TIME AND PLACE **128**
BILE THEM CABBAGE DOWN

INSTRUMENTS **8** RHYTHM **130**
The Spoons *(ACTIVITY)*
Spoon Demonstration *(LISTENING)*
RED RIVER VALLEY

INSTRUMENTS **9** TIMBRE **132**
The Jug *(ACTIVITY)*
WORRIED MAN BLUES
SHE WORE A YELLOW RIBBON

INSTRUMENTS **10** TIMBRE **134**
More Skiffle Instruments *(ACTIVITY)*
OLD JOE CLARKE

INSTRUMENTS **11** TIMBRE, TIME
AND PLACE **136**
The Mouthbow *(ACTIVITY)*
THE M.T.A. SONG

INSTRUMENTS **12** TIMBRE **138**
The Washtub Bass *(ACTIVITY)*
The Limberjack *(ACTIVITY)*
SIXTEEN TONS

INSTRUMENTS **13** TIMBRE,
MELODY **140**
The Colorado Trail *(LISTENING)*
The Harmonica *(ACTIVITY)*
BABY, PLEASE DON'T GO

INSTRUMENTS **14** TIMBRE **142**
DOWN IN THE VALLEY
ALABAMA BOUND

Playing the Guitar **144**

INSTRUMENTS **15** HARMONY **144**
CLEMENTINE

INSTRUMENTS **16** HARMONY . . . **146**
PUTTING ON THE STYLE
GUANTANAMERA

INSTRUMENTS **17** HARMONY **148**
THE 59th STREET BRIDGE SONG
Spinning Wheel *(LISTENING)*

INSTRUMENTS **18** HARMONY . . . **150**
ROCKA MY SOUL
HE'S GOT THE WHOLE WORLD IN HIS
   HAND
TALKING GUITAR BLUES

INSTRUMENTS **19** HARMONY **152**
PUT YOUR HAND IN THE HAND
Bottleneck Guitar *(ACTIVITY)*
This Train *(LISTENING)*
Reelin' and Rockin' *(LISTENING)*

INSTRUMENTS **20** HARMONY . . .**154**
MAMA DON'T 'LOW
Color Him Folky *(LISTENING)*

INSTRUMENTS **21** HARMONY . . **156**
ON TOP OF OLD SMOKY
I'M GOING DOWN THE ROAD
DEEP FORK RIVER BLUES

INSTRUMENTS **22** EXPRESSION . .**158**
HOLD THE WIND
BO WEEVIL

INSTRUMENTS **23** HARMONY . . **160**
Menuetto II from String Quartet in F
   (LISTENING)
Instrumental Combos *(ACTIVITY)*

INSTRUMENTS **24** EXPRESSION **162**
THE OSCAR MAYER WIENER SONG
THE ARMOUR HOT DOG SONG

INSTRUMENTS **25** EXPRESSION **164**
Donkey Kong Theme *(LISTENING)*
Robot Basketball Theme *(LISTENING)*

INSTRUMENTS **26** EVALUATION
. . . . **166**
OH, LONESOME ME

INSTRUMENTS **27** EVALUATION
. . . . **168**
Bile Them Cabbage Down *(LISTENING)*

UNIT 4 *Choral Singing*...169

CHORAL **1** EXPRESSION **170**
LORD, LORD, I'VE GOT SOME SINGING
   TO DO

CHORAL **2** EXPRESSION **172**
SONG SUNG BLUE
Gotta Gitta *(CHANT)*

CHORAL **3** EXPRESSION **174**
Big Important People *(CHANT)*
GETTING TO KNOW YOU

CHORAL **4** EXPRESSION **177**
THERE'S A MEETIN' HERE TONIGHT
Du-Bee *(CHANT)*

CHORAL **5** HARMONY **178**
ENCOURAGEMENT

CHORAL **6** HARMONY **181**
SUMMER MORNING

CHORAL **7** HARMONY **182**
TIE ME KANGAROO DOWN

CHORAL **8** HARMONY **185**
I Gotta Song *(CHANT)*
I WRITE THE SONGS

CHORAL **9** FORM **186**
EASE ON DOWN THE ROAD

CHORAL **10** TIME AND PLACE **188**
DELTA DAWN

CHORAL **11** TIME AND PLACE **190**
LA BAMBA

CHORAL **12** EXPRESSION **192**
THE HOME ROAD

CHORAL **13** TEXTURE **194**
THE BAGPIPERS' CAROL

CHORAL **14** HARMONY **196**
GO DOWN, MOSES AND JOSHUA
   FOUGHT THE BATTLE OF JERICHO

CHORAL **15** FORM **199**
THE WOODCHUCK

CHORAL **16** EXPRESSION **200**
SCARBOROUGH FAIR

CHORAL **17** FORM **203**
GING GONG GOOLI

CHORAL **18** TEXTURE **206**
FIVE HUNDRED MILES

CHORAL **19** TEXTURE **210**
EVERYTHING IS BEAUTIFUL

CHORAL **20** TEXTURE.......... **212**
WHICH IS THE PROPEREST DAY TO
   SING?

CHORAL **21** TIMBRE **214**
Route 66 *(LISTENING)*
BOURRÉE FOR BACH

CHORAL **22** RHYTHM **217**
BELL GLORIA

CHORAL **23** EVALUATION........ **218**
RAIN

Pupil Glossary **220**
Piano Accompaniments **222**
Teacher's Glossary **401**
Suggested Recordings for Student
   Listening **403**
Acknowledgments and Credits...... **405**
Classified Index of Music, Art,
   and Poetry **408**
Classified Index of Activities
   and Skills **411**
Alphabetical Index of Music........ **414**

Meet the Authors

Eunice Boardman Meske is Director of the School of Music and Professor of Music and Education at the University of Wisconsin, Madison. She works with university students in a "lab school" where she and her students teach grades K-8. Meske holds a Ph.D. from the University of Illinois.

EUNICE BOARDMAN MESKE

BARBARA ANDRESS

Barbara Andress is Professor in the School of Music at Arizona State University, Tempe. She received a B.A. and M.A. in education from Arizona State University. Andress has taught general music and instrumental music and for over twenty years was a district music supervisor.

Mary Pautz is Assistant Professor of Music Education at the University of Wisconsin, Milwaukee. In addition to teaching music education methods, she also teaches elementary music classes as part of a practicum for music majors. Pautz is a doctoral candidate at the University of Wisconsin, Madison.

MARY PAUTZ

FRED WILLMAN

Fred Willman is Associate Professor of Music Education at the University of Missouri, St. Louis. Willman holds a Ph.D. from the University of North Dakota, Grand Forks. He has worked extensively in the development of computer software for use in music education.

Consultants

Nancy Archer
Forest Park Elementary School
Fort Wayne, Indiana

Joan Z. Fyfe
Jericho Public Schools
Jericho, New York

Jeanne Hook
Albuquerque Public Schools
Albuquerque, New Mexico

Danette Littleton
University of Tennessee at Chattanooga
Chattanooga, Tennessee

Barbara Reeder Lundquist
University of Washington
Seattle, Washington

Ollie MacFarland
Detroit Public Schools
Detroit, Michigan

Faith Norwood
Harnett County School District
North Carolina

Linda K. Price
Richardson Independent School District
Richardson, Texas

Buryl Red
Composer and Arranger
New York, New York

Dawn L. Reynolds
District of Columbia Public Schools
Washington, D.C.

Morris Stevens
A.N. McCallum High School
Austin, Texas

Jack Noble White
Texas Boys Choir
Fort Worth, Texas

Contributing Writers

Hilary Apfelstadt
University of North Carolina
at Greensboro
Greensboro, North Carolina

Pat and Tom Cuthbertson
Professional Writers
Santa Cruz, California

Louise Huberty
(*Special Kodaly Consultant*)
Milwaukee Public Schools
Milwaukee, Wisconsin

Susan Kenney
Brigham Young University
Salt Lake City, Utah

Janet Montgomery
Ithaca College
Ithaca, New York

Richard O'Hearn
Western Michigan University
Kalamazoo, Michigan

Diane Persellin
Trinity University
San Antonio, Texas

Arvida Steen
(*Special Orff Consultant*)
The Blake School
Minneapolis, Minnesota

Field Test Sites

While HOLT MUSIC was being developed, parts of the program were field tested by 25 teachers in 18 states. These teachers played a crucial role in the program's development. Their comments, suggestions, and classroom experiences helped HOLT MUSIC become the workable, exciting program it is. Our grateful appreciation goes to the following teachers who used our materials in their classrooms.

ARKANSAS
Judy Harkrader
Vilonia Elementary School
Vilonia

COLORADO
Nancylee Summerville
Hutchinson Elementary School
Lakewood

Robert Horsky
Goldrick Elementary School
Denver

Joan Tally
Eiber Elementary School
Lakewood

Germaine Johnson
University of Northern Colorado
  Laboratory School
Greeley

GEORGIA
Angela Tonsmeire
Cartersville Elementary School
Cartersville

Nancy Clayton
Norman Park Elementary School
Norman Park

INDIANA
Nancy Archer
Forest Park Elementary School
Fort Wayne

Elizabeth Staples
School #92
Indianapolis

Pat Gillooly
School #90
Indianapolis

KANSAS
Shelli Kadel
El Paso Elementary School
Derby

KENTUCKY
Patricia Weihe
Wright Elementary School
Shelbyville

MASSACHUSETTS
Marya Rusinak
Kennedy School
Brockton

MISSISSIPPI
Dottie Dudley
Crestwood Elementary School
Meridian

Mira Frances Hays
Forest Seperate School District
Forest

MISSOURI
Elizabeth Hutcherson
Parker Road Elementary School
Florissant

NEW JERSEY
Lorna Milbauer
North Cliff School
Englewood Cliffs

NEW YORK
Ruthetta S. Smikle
Hillary Park Academy
Buffalo

NORTH CAROLINA
Julie Young
Burgaw Elementary School
Burgaw

OKLAHOMA
Cindy Newell
Washington Irving Elementary School
Durent

OREGON
Larry Verdoorn
Hall Elementary School
Gresham

PENNSYLVANIA
Marianne Zimmerman
Steele School
Harrisburg

TENNESSEE
Sarah Davis
Powell Elementary School
Powell

WEST VIRGINIA
Eva Ledbetter
Cross Lanes Elementary School
Cross Lanes

WISCONSIN
Jill Kuespert Anderson
Lannon Elementary School
Lannon

The HOLT MUSIC program can help you provide rich and enjoyable experiences for all of your students. The information given below will help you get acquainted with the Pupil Book, the Teacher's Edition, the Teacher's Resource Binder, and the Recordings.

Organization Of The Program

Levels 7 and 8 of HOLT MUSIC are divided into four self-contained units for maximum flexibility. Each unit contains two tools for tracking the students' musical growth: a **Checkpoint** and an **Evaluation.** The Checkpoint allows the teacher to monitor the students' comprehension of material presented early in the unit. The Evaluation is a final unit test.

Types Of Lessons In The Book

☐ **Song lessons**—Most lessons in the program are song-based. Song lessons are identified by a colored band above and below the title. Usually both the music and the words are in the Pupil Book. However, in certain lessons only the words appear in the Pupil Book, and it is expected that students will learn the song by listening. The lessons are designed so that students will grow in note-reasoning skills as they progress through the grades. For this reason it is strongly recommended that the lessons in each unit be followed in page order.

☐ **Listening lessons**—These lessons are built around a recording of a classical, folk, or contemporary work. Listening lessons featured in the Pupil Book are identified by a logo. Complete titles, composers, and performer credits are listed in the "Materials" section of the Teacher's Edition.

Many of the listening lessons have a chart or an illustration designed to help guide the children through the listening experience. In some lessons the recording includes "call numbers"—spoken numbers recorded over the music. The call numbers correspond to the numbers on the chart and help to focus attention on important features as the music continues.

☐ **Activities**—Many activity-based lessons are included in HOLT MUSIC. The type of activity in the Pupil Book is identified by a special logo: a quill pen and an ink bottle for creative activities, a French horn for performance activities, and a human figure for activities involving movement.

The activity is always structured in some way; for example, a poem, a story, or a picture in the Pupil Book might serve as a focal point for creative exploration, or the students could be invited to explore certain sounds on instruments.

Using The Recordings

The recordings are essential teaching aids for HOLT MUSIC. The song recordings may be used in various ways: to help students learn words and melody if songs are beyond their current reading level; and to provide examples of appropriate tempo, diction, expression, and vocal tone quality. For teaching flexibility, song recordings have voices on one channel and instruments on the other. By turning the balance control completely to the right, you will hear instruments only. The grooves between all selections are locked.

Special Helps For The Teacher

☐ The **Scope and Sequence Chart,** pages xxviii–3, summarizes concepts, terms, and skills covered in each grade level.

☐ The **Teacher's Glossary,** page 401, gives definitions of musical terms used in the text.

☐ A discography, **Suggested Recordings for Student Listening,** lists representative listening selections from each historical era. The recordings may be acquired through local retail outlets or libraries. These recordings may be used to augment the classroom listening program in HOLT MUSIC or they may be suggested to individual students who are interested in pursuing musical study on their own.

☐ Complete **Classified and Alphabetical Indexes,** starting on page 408, provide a convenient way to locate songs, poems, listening lessons, and particular skills and concepts.

☐ Step-by-step **lesson plans** are provided for each page of the Pupil Book. The **Lesson Focus** indicates the concept to be studied and gives, in abbreviated form, an indication of the primary behavior and mode stressed. *P–I,* for example, means "perform" in the "ikonic mode." (See "The Generative Approach to Music Learning," page xxvi.)

☐ The **Teacher's Resource Binder** includes Activity Sheets, Biographies, Evaluations, and suggestions for Instrumental Accompanimentss, Enrichment, Kodaly, Mainstreaming, and Orff. All binder materials are cross-referenced to lessons in the Teacher's Edition. This enables you to adapt or expand individual lessons to fit your special needs.

☐ **Instrumental accompaniments**—Most songs contain chord names for autoharp or guitar accompaniment, and many lesson plans include accompaniments for students to perform on classroom instruments. Piano accompaniments, provided in the back of the Teacher's Edition, are cross-referenced to each lesson plan. The piano score includes markers showing where a new line begins in the Pupil Book. The symbol ⌄ above the score, for example, indicates that the second line of music in the Pupil Book begins at this point.

To the Classroom Teacher

The classroom teacher's role in music education varies from school to school. Whatever the situation in your district, the classroom teacher is vital to the success of the total music program.

Many teachers approach music with mixed feelings: enthusiasm, apprehension, curiosity, or insecurity. These attitudes are influenced by the musical knowledge the teacher possesses, the memory of music in his or her own school experience, and by heavy demands on the teacher's time.

HOLT MUSIC welcomes the classroom teacher's participation. The suggestions that follow are provided with the hope that they will alleviate fears and encourage the teacher to enjoy and learn music with the students.

1 "I Don't Know How To Teach Music!"

Every classroom teacher can teach music with HOLT MUSIC—if he or she is willing to learn with the students and read through the lessons in the Teacher's Edition. The "generative" approach used in HOLT MUSIC can help the teacher learn along with the students.

Music presents a special challenge because of the need to occasionally demonstrate by singing, moving, or playing. HOLT MUSIC helps the teacher as much as possible with

- comprehensive, easily understood lesson plans
- quality demonstration recordings
- a teaching sequence that works
- appealing songs, listening lessons, and poetry
- activities that are fun for students to do

2 "There Isn't Time To Teach Music!"

The pressure for students to achieve in all curricular areas is intense. However, music can be interspersed throughout the school day. Sing a song to begin or end the day; create an instrumental accompaniment to enrich a story; share the music from the culture being highlighted in social studies.

The Curriculum Correlation section in the Teacher's Resource Binder provides many suggestions for integrating music into your day. To expand class time for music, set up music centers where small groups may work on their own.

However, a scheduled time devoted to music is just as important as time scheduled for other subjects. Just as reading throughout the day does not take the place of reading class, neither should the use of music throughout the day be considered sufficient. To achieve an understanding of music there must be a sequential course of study.

3 "I Don't Have Time To Hunt For Materials!"

The authors of HOLT MUSIC have gathered and organized all materials for you. You will find

- Complete lesson plans that include a lesson focus, an introduction, a development and a conclusion. Usually a lesson can be completed in 20 to 30 minutes.
- Integration of all types of activities—listening lessons, dances, creative experiences, and songs—within a lesson.
- Boldfaced dialogue in the lesson plans that may help you in presenting the lesson, especially if you are not familiar with musical concepts and terms.

4 "The Kids Will Laugh If I Sing!"

Students may need encouragement at first. However, young people will eventually sing if a positive atmosphere is created. Common teaching errors that hinder singing include

- expecting students to sing before they are ready (A new song must be heard several times before the students sing it.)
- expecting students to sing too loud

The students may laugh the first time they hear you sing. You are not alone: They are even more likely to laugh at a music specialist who has a trained voice! If you can laugh with the class and proceed with the song, the laughter is soon forgotten and the music enjoyed. Or if you prefer, you can rely on the recordings. By adjusting the balance on the stereo, the voice only may be heard; this is especially helpful in teaching a new song.

5 "What Will I Do With the Boys?"

There is nothing inherent in the genes of boys that causes them to have an aversion to music! Often they will be the most enthusiastic supporters. Expect all students to enjoy music; expect everyone to learn. You will find that an activity-based, hands-on experience in music will spark enthusiasm in both boys and girls. They will never tire of opportunities to play bells and autoharps, to use props such as streamers, wands, and balloons, or to work with the activity sheets provided in the Teacher's Resource Binder.

6 "I Can't Play the Piano!"

While playing the piano is helpful, it is not essential for teaching music. Instead, you can play the recordings or use autoharp accompaniments.

7 "I Remember How I Hated Music When I Was In School!"

Teachers who have had pleasant experiences with music are likely to approach music teaching with enthusiasm. Others, unfortunately, may have less pleasant memories. What was it in the experience that caused the bad feelings? You can prevent another generation from having unpleasant experiences by avoiding those stressful practices you recall.

The Generative Approach To Music Learning

HOLT MUSIC'S generative approach is based on the recognition that

Learning begins with a "need to know." Real learning occurs only to the extent that the student willingly makes a commitment to the act of learning. Learning based on intrinsic "need to know" goals, which the learner personally indentifies, is more permanent than learning based on extrinsic goals such as rewards or adult approval.

Learning leads to more learning. Once the student is personally committed to learning, each achievement is "generative"; it provides the foundation and the impetus for further learning.

Learning is future-oriented. The student who becomes enthralled with the learning process continues to seek opportunities to learn as long as each experience leads toward personal independence and self-actualization. Music learning thus approached allows the learner to become

☐ more deeply involved in the aesthetic experience

☐ aware of music as an avenue of one's own personal expression

☐ musically independent

The Generative Instructional Theory

The Generative Instructional Theory recognizes that music learning, whether formal or informal, involves four components. These components include

1. The musical concept to be learned. Musical understanding emerges gradually as the learner develops musical concepts, that is, principles or ways of categorizing musical sounds.

Concepts stressed in the generative approach include

☐ those related to musical elements
  ■ pitch (melody and harmony)
  ■ duration (rhythm and tempo) ■ dynamics
  ■ articulation ■ timbre (qualities of sound)

☐ those that reflect the way musical elements are organized into a complete musical statement that has ■ form ■ texture ■ an expressive nature ■ a cultural context (time and place)

The Scope and Sequence chart beginning on page xxviii gives the concepts covered in HOLT MUSIC.

2. A musical example that embodies the concept to be learned. Examples are selected for their musical value reflecting

  ■ diverse musical heritages
  ■ diverse times and places
  ■ many forms of human emotion
  ■ many different combinations of voices and instruments

3. A musical behavior through which the learner interacts with music, gradually developing essential musical concepts by
  ■ performing music through singing and playing

  ■ describing music through moving, visualizing, and verbalizing
  ■ creating music through improvisation or composition

4. A conceptual mode that enables the learner to communicate understanding and move through three stages of conceptualization:

☐ **The enactive mode:** The learner begins to associate concept with example through observation, manipulation, and experimentation. Understanding is "acted-out" as the student interacts directly and nonverbally with the musical sound.

☐ **The ikonic mode:** The learner internalizes musical sound images that can be recalled even when the musical sound is absent. The learner demonstrates understanding through pictorial representations that "look like" the music sounds or with simple verbal imagery such as up-down, longer-shorter, or smooth-jerky.

☐ **The symbolic mode:** The learner builds on previous enactive and ikonic experiences until verbal and musical symbols gradually become associated with the sound.

The Lesson Focus

Lesson plans in HOLT MUSIC are built on the recognition that these four components must be present in order for learning to take place. The **Lesson Focus** for each plan identifies the concept, the behavior, and the conceptual mode. An example follows.

> **Lesson Focus**
> **Melody:** A series of pitches may move
> up, down, or remain the same. *(P–I)*

  ■ The **behavior** is identified at the end of the concept statement by the first letter.
  P Perform (singing/playing)
  D Describe (move/verbalize/visualize)
  C Create (improvise/compose)
  ■ The **conceptual mode** at which it is expected that most students will be functioning in this lesson is identified by the second capital letter.
  E Enactive   *I* Ikonic   *S* Symbolic

Thus in the example given above, the designation *(P–I)* at the end of the concept statement indicates that the behavior stressed in the lesson is **Perform** and that the students will be primarily using the **Ikonic** mode in that lesson.

The Generative Approach To Music Reading

Lessons that help develop music-reading skills are an integral part of any learning sequence that leads toward musical independence. The generative approach to music reading used in HOLT MUSIC

☐ is based on a cyclic process that takes the learner through three stages corresponding to the three modes of conceptualization (See chart.)

- provides a lesson sequence that recognizes that a learner may be functioning at different stages of the cycle simultaneously—for example, a student might be reading simple rhythms from notation (symbolic stage) while associating melodies with ikons (ikonic stage) and learning harmonies aurally (enactive stage).
- presents each new skill in relation to the musical whole, rather than through pattern drill alone.
- distinguishes between sight-reading (playing an instrument from notation) and sight-singing.

Reading Rhythm

The generative approach to reading rhythm

- recognizes that reading of rhythm depends on the perception of durational relationships
- is based on a two-dimensional approach
  - sensing durations within the melodic rhythm in relation to the underlying beat, and
  - sensing durations in the melodic rhythm in relation to the shortest sound within that rhythm

The **additive approach** described in Step 2 is used because

- it is the rhythmic relationship to which the young person seems to respond most readily
- it allows the student to solve rhythmic problems by using addition rather than division
- it is the basis for rhythmic organization used in the music of many non-Western cultures, as well as in much of the popular music of today.

Reading Melody

The generative approach to reading melody

- begins with melodies based on major or minor modes because these are most familiar to the contemporary American child
- uses the body scale (see below) to help the beginning student internalize pitch relationships
- stresses the hearing and performing of melodies in relation to the underlying harmony
- makes use of scale numbers to describe tonal relationships because numbers

  - provide the learner with a way of internalizing and recalling melodic pitches in relation to a tonal center
  - build on a numerical concept that most children have when this stage is introduced
  - allow for meaningful transfer to the reading of staff notation
  - are commonly used to describe chord structure, thus helping the student to understand the relation of melody to harmony

---

Lessons that develop reading skills take the student through the three conceptual modes.

ENACTIVE MODE The student performs the rhythm of a melody and metric grouping by imitating what is heard.

IKONIC MODE The student associates rhythms with ikons that represent duration in relation to

- the shortest sound
- the beat and accent

As the student associates these ikons with sound patterns, vocabulary is introduced to describe

- sounds that make up the melodic rhythm (short, long, lo-ong)

short short long   short short long   lo-ong

- sounds in relation to the beat (shorter than, longer than)

shorter same longer   lo-ong

- the accent (moves in twos, moves in threes)

moves in twos   moves in threes

SYMBOLIC MODE The process is completed as the child transfers the ability to read ikons to reading traditional music notation.

ENACTIVE MODE The student performs in response to melodies heard. During this stage the body scale is introduced, providing the child with another means of sensing and responding to pitch relationships.

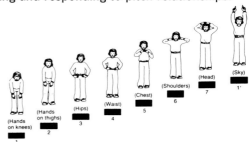

(Hands on knees)   (Hands on thighs) 2   (Hips) 3   (Waist) 4   (Chest) 5   (Shoulders) 6   (Head) 7   (Sky) 1'

IKONIC MODE The child first associates melodies with ikons that represent the up-down, step-skip relationship of pitches. Later, pitches are labeled with scale numbers to show their relationship to the tonal center.

SYMBOLIC MODE The student transfers the ability to read a new melody from scale numbers to staff notation.

Scope and Sequence

As students grow in their understanding of musical concepts, they acquire skills for manipulating their own musical environments. Page numbers following each concept statement guide the teacher to lessons in HOLT MUSIC, Level 7, that focus on that concept. Boldfaced numbers represent lessons where that concept is dealt with as a primary focus of the lesson. Other numbers indicate

Concepts	Ikon	Musical Symbol

RHYTHM

- Music may be comparatively fast or slow, depending on the speed of the underlying pulse. *Pages:* 18–19, 32–33, 34–35, 44–45, 98–99
- Music may become faster or slower by changing the speed of the underlying pulse. *Pages:* 6–7, 98–99, 178–179
- Music may move in relation to the underlying steady beat or shortest pulse. *Pages:* 6–7, 32–33, 34–35, **38–39, 98–99, 130–131,** 217
- A series of beats may be organized into regular or irregular groupings by stressing certain beats. *Pages:* **32–33,** 36–37, **40–41, 42–43, 44–45, 50–51, 56–57,** 76–78, **98–99,** 130–131, 188–189, 194–195
- Individual sounds and silences within a rhythmic line may be longer than, shorter than, or the same as other sounds within the line. *Pages:* 49, 98–99, 130–131
- Individual sounds and silences within a rhythmic line may be longer than, shorter than, or the same as the underlying steady beat or shortest pulse. *Pages:* 20–21, **34–35,** 36–37, 76–78, 98–99, 173–174
- Accented sounds within a rhythmic line may sound with, before, or after the accented underlying beat. *Pages:* 16, 18–19, 23, 34–35, 44–45, 49, 76–78, 98–99

MELODY

- A series of pitches may move up, down, or remain the same. *Pages:* 48–49, **100–101, 102–103,** 106–108
- A series of pitches may move up or down by steps or skips. *Pages:* 6–7, **16–17,** 52–53, **100–101, 102–103, 140–141,** 194–195
- Each pitch within a melody moves in relation to a home tone. *Pages:* **32–33, 34–35, 38–39, 50–51,** 89, 94–95, 106–108
- A series of pitches bounded by the octave "belong together," forming a tonal set. *Pages:* **46–47, 48–49,** 54–55, 94–95, 96–97, 100–101, 118, 119, 172–173
- A melody may be relatively high or low. *Pages:* 6–7
- Individual pitches, when compared to each other, may be higher, lower, or the same. *Pages:* **8–9, 10–11,** 100–101

TIMBRE

- The quality of a sound is determined by the sound source. *Pages:* 8–9, 66–67, 82–83, **84–85, 86–87, 90–91, 92–93, 96–97,** 124
- The quality of a sound is affected by the material, shape, and size of the source. *Pages:* 82–83, 88, 89, **94–95,** 130–131, **132–133, 134–135, 138–139**
- The quality of a sound is affected by the way the sound is produced. *Pages:* **60–62, 68–69, 70–71,** 76–78, 79, **82–83,** 88, 91, **94–95, 132–133, 134–135, 136–137, 138–139, 140–141, 142–143,** 160–161
- The total sound is affected by the number and qualities of sounds occurring at the same time. *Pages:* 6–7, 66–67, **82–83, 119,** 120–121, 136–137, **214–216**

lessons where the concept is dealt with, but not as the primary focus.

The skills list gives a sampling of representative behaviors for Level 7. Page numbers listed give only one example of a lesson where that skill is developed. For a comprehensive listing of skills, refer to the Classified Index of Activities and Skills, page 411.

Verbal Symbols (Terms)	Skills/Behaviors	
meter signature tie (musical plus sign) syncopation dotted eighth sixteenth tala	**Perform**	Play skiffle instruments such as spoons, jug, and washboard with rhythmic accuracy. *130–131* Maintain rhythmic independence in which duple and triple subdivisions of the beat occur simultaneously. *98–99* Chant the words of a song in rhythm from notation while tapping the shortest sound. *16–17*
	Describe	Notate a rhythm representing sounds longer than the shortest sound by connecting the shortest sounds with ties. *34–35* Rewrite a rhythm written in traditional notation by connecting short sounds with ties. *32–33* Determine how tempo, melodic rhythm, accompaniment, and overall style affect perception of the meter. *40–41* Discuss rhythmic characteristics of the music heard and associate them with specific styles. *98–99*
	Create	Combine melodic lines in random order, with each part establishing its own underlying beat; that beat may or may not be in exact rhythmic relationship to the beat of the other parts. *217*

scales: chromatic,
   major, minor, whole-
   tone, pentatonic,
   Dorian, Phrygian, Mixolydian
range
register
treble (G) clef
bass (F) clef
contours: undulating,
   arched, terraced,
   irregular
raga
	Perform	Sing melody and harmony parts by ear. *6–7*
		Play mallet instruments using gamelan tuning from a simplified score. *102–103*
		Play folk songs on the harmonica. *140–141*
		Sing and play songs using the major, minor, Dorian, and pentatonic scales. *46–49*

	Describe	Identify the shape, range, type of motion, and tonal center in music from various cultures. *100–103* Follow music notation in the bass clef. *6–7* Locate pitches in the major, minor, Dorian, and pentatonic scales using the Scale Finder. *46–49*
	Create	Improvise vocally during the measures of rest that follow each melodic fragment of like duration throughout a song. *10–11*

instrument groups:
   membranophones,
   idiophones,
   chordophones,
   aerophones,
   electrophones
traditional instruments of many cultures, such as the calabash (Africa), koto (Japan), gamelan (Java), sitar (India), and harmonica (U.S.)
vibrato
	Perform	Sing a melody in different keys to discover vocal range. *8–9*
		Sing a melody, experimenting with varying the pronunciation of vowel sounds, articulation, tonal quality, register, and amount of vibrato. *68–69*
		Play percussion instruments such as spoons, jug, washboard, mouthbow, kazoo/comb, limberjack, washtub bass, and harmonica in a skiffle band. *130–143*

	Describe	Identify and categorize instruments. *84–97* Compare the effects of performances by different instrument groups of the same composition. *120–121*
	Create	Compose and notate a percussion piece that uses as sound sources only the cymbals or gong and a variety of mallets. *60–61*

	Concepts	Ikon	Musical Symbol	
DYNAM-ICS	■ Music may be comparatively loud or soft. *Pages:* 41–42, 60–61, 73, 76–78, 84–85, 170–171, 200–202 ■ Music may become louder or softer. *Pages:* 6–7, 41–42, 58–59, 60–61, 68–69, 73, 76–78, 200–202		*f* *p*	
ARTICULA-TION	■ A series of sounds may move from one to the next in either a smoothly connected or a detached manner. *Pages:* 10–11, 18–19, 22–23, 40–41, 68–69, 172–173 ■ The quality of a sound is affected by the way the sound begins, continues, and ends. *Pages:* 40–41, 52–53, 58–59, 60–61, 68–69			
HARMONY	■ Chords and melody may move simultaneously in relation to each other. *Pages:* **14–15, 26–27, 54–55, 56–57,** 76–78, **144–145, 146–147, 148–149, 150–151, 152–153, 154–155, 182–184** ■ A series of simultaneous sounds may alternate between activity and rest. *Pages:* 6–7, 10–11, 16–17, 18–19, 22–23, 41, 54–55 ■ Two or more pitches may be sounded simultaneously. *Pages:* 30–31, 76–78, **160–161, 178–180** ■ Two or more musical lines may occur simultaneously. *Pages:* **6–7, 18–19,** 20–21, **52–53,** 76–78, **106–108, 181, 185, 196–198**			
TEXTURE	■ Musical quality is affected by the distance between the musical lines. *Pages:* **106–108, 194–195, 210–211** ■ Musical quality is affected by the number of or degree of contrast between musical lines occuring simultaneously. *Pages:* 59, 76–78, **106–108,** 194–195, **206–209, 212–213**			
FORM	■ A musical whole begins, continues, and ends. ■ A musical whole is a combination of smaller segments. *Pages:* 6–7, 30–31, 40–41, 74–75, **104–105, 114–115, 186–187, 199** ■ A musical whole may be made up of same, varied, or contrasting segments. *Pages:* **30–31,** 59, 60–61, 74–75, **104–105, 114–115, 124, 203–205** ■ A series of sounds may form a distinct musical idea within the musical whole. *Pages:* 74–75, 122–123, **125–127** ■ A musical whole may include an introduction, interludes, and an ending segement. *Page:* 41			
EXPRES-SION	■ Musical elements are combined into a whole to express a musical or extramusical idea. *Pages:* **12–13, 20–21, 22–23, 24–25,** 58, 59, 70–71, **158–159, 162–163, 164–165, 170–171, 192–193,** 206–209 ■ The expressiveness of music is affected by the way timbre, dynamics, articulation, rhythm, melody, harmony, form, tempo, and texture contribute to the musical whole. *Pages:* **36–37,** 68–69, 76–78, **89,** 96–97, **122–123, 172–173, 174–176, 177, 200–202,** 218–219			
TIME & PLACE	■ The way musical elements are combined into a whole reflects the origin of the music. *Pages:* 24–25, **66–67,** 68–69, **74–75, 76–78, 80–81, 84–85, 86–87, 90–91, 92–93, 109, 118,** 119, **156–157, 188–189, 190–191** ■ A particular use of timbre, dynamics, articulation, rhythm, melody, harmony, and form reflects the origin of the musical whole. *Pages:* **28–29, 66–67, 70–71, 72, 73, 79,** 89, **96–97, 110–113, 118, 120–121, 128–129, 136–137,** 138–139, 188–189, 190–191			

Verbal Symbols (Terms)	Skills/Behaviors		
pianissimo piano mezzopiano mezzoforte forte	**Perform**	Sing a song using several dynamic levels from *ppp* to *f*. *200–202*	
	Describe	Identify dynamic levels produced by several unfamiliar instruments. *84–85*	
	Create	Devise a composition that explores the dynamic range of a single percussion instrument. *60–61*	
legato staccato marcato pizzicato envelope	**Perform**	Sing a song, experimenting with *legato, staccato,* and *marcato* articulations. *68–69*	
	Describe	Discuss how the way a sound begins and ends helps express the lyrics of a composition. *172–173*	
	Create	Compose a choral setting of a poem, using a variety of articulations. *59*	
key singnature tonal center chord root major triad minor triad dominant seventh chord sequence	**Perform**	Sing by ear a harmony part consisting of tonic, dominant, and subdominant chord roots. *20–21*	
		Accompany songs on the guitar, using tonic and dominant chords in C, F, and G major. *144–157*	
	Describe	Discuss the unique sound qualities of major, minor, and dominant seventh chords. *54–55*	
	Create	Compose talking blues to a predetermined blues-style chord sequence. *150–151*	
monophonic homophonic polyphonic density drone unison sixth	**Perform**	Sing the musical lines of a song in various combinations and ranges to experience different textures. *106–108*	
	Describe	Identify portions of a chordal composition as homophonic or polyphonic. *206–209*	
		Discuss textural characteristics of music heard and associated with specific styles. *210–211*	
	Create	Devise a musical setting of a poem using various combinations of voices, bells, and xylophones. *59*	

motive
minuet
sonata allegro:
   exposition,
   development,
   recapitulation
movement
solo–tutti
	Perform	Sing a musical idea that recurs repeatedly in a song and identify it where it occurs in notation. *125–127*	

	Describe	Devise a circle or line dance that reflects the form of a piece of music. *30–31*	
		Identify imitation and variation in call-response sound patterns. *124*	
	Create	Organize a series of related musical fragments into a whole in an original sequence. *104–105*	
oral tradition written tradition lyrics word painting	**Perform**	Sing a choral composition using dynamics indicated in the score to support expressive intent. *200–201*	
	Describe	Discuss the extramusical purposes of a composition. *70–71*	
		Identify the ways in which music supports word meaning. *206–207*	
	Create	Compose a tune for an imaginary video game. *164–165*	

Eras: Baroque,   conductor's score
   Classical,   neume
   Romantic,
   Twentieth Century
Styles: country,
   rock, gospel,
   jazz, pop,
   talking blues,
   ballad, classical
Groups: skiffle band,
   mariachi band,
   symphony orchestra
	Perform	Sing an American Indian song in its original language. *79*	

		Sing a contemporary ballad whose style is rooted in a seventeenth-century English ballad form. *74–75*	
	Describe	Identify a song as being in traditional folk-song style by the nature of its melody, rhythm, and harmony. *136–137*	
		Develop a profile of vocal sound produced by various cultures. *70–71*	
		Compare different ways of notating a melody. *28–29*	
	Create	Improvise phrases to interpolate in a gospel song. *76–78*	

TRB Page Identification Key

AS8 = Activity Sheet, p. 8

B1 = Biographies, p. 1

E4 = Enrichments, p. 4

EV2 = Evaluations, p. 2

I2 = Instrumentals, p. 2

K3 = Kodaly, p. 3

M4 = Mainstreaming, p. 4

O2 = Orff, p. 2

Texas Essential Elements for Unit 1:

1A: PE (pages 14–19; 22–24; 26; 29–31; 33–39; 41–43; 47–57; 63)

TE (pages 6; 11; 14–17; 26; 28–29; 32; 42; 48–52; 54; 56–57; 59)

TRB (pages E2; E5; K2; K5; M8; I2–3; O2; O7; O14; EV3; EV5)

1B: PE (pages 14–19; 21; 23; 26; 28–29; 32–43; 46–51; 56–58)

TE (pages 6; 11; 13–18; 20–21; 23; 26; 28–30; 32–35; 38–40; 42; 48–52; 54–61; 63)

TRB (pages O2; O7; O10; O14; O18; O22; E2; E5; E8; K2; K5; K8; K11; M8; M10 M12; M14; M17; I2; I4–8; I9–13; AS10; AS11; AS15; AS16; AS18; AS19; AS20; AS21; AS22; EV3; EV5–6)

1C: PE (pages 8–9; 13–24; 28–29; 32–33; 36–40; 42; 46; 48–51; 54–55)

TE (pages 6; 8; 11; 13–18; 20–23; 26; 28–29; 32–42; 48–52; 55–56; 59)

TRB (pages O2; O7; O14; O18; O22; E5; E8; K2; K5; K8; B3; AS4; M6; EV3; EV5)

1D: PE (pages 13; 16–19; 22–24; 36–43; 46–50; 56–57)

TE (pages 11; 13; 25; 36–42; 46–50; 56–57; 59)

TRB (pages O7; O10; O22; E5; E8; K2; K5; K11; AS18–22; M15; I2; I4–8; I9–13; EV3; EV5–6)

1E: PE (pages 14–16; 26–27; 33–34; 37; 39; 50; 54–55)

1F: TE (page 59)

TRB (page E5)

2: PE (pages 8–9; 12–19; 33–34; 37; 39; 46; 48; 50–51; 55–57; 59)

TE (pages 6; 8–11; 12–15; 17; 19; 21–23; 26; 30; 32; 34–35; 37; 42; 46; 50; 52; 54–56; 58–59; 63)

TRB (pages E2; M8; O2; O7; O10; O14; O18; O22; K2; K5; K8; K11; I9–13; AS11)

3B: PE (pages 7; 39; 45; 53; 62)

TE (pages 6; 13; 25; 30; 34–35; 39; 60)

TRB (pages E2; E5; AS4; AS13; I2; O2; O10; O14; O18; O22; K5; EV2)

4A: PE (pages 12; 40–41; 59)

TE (pages 10; 12; 40–41; 56; 59–61)

TRB (pages E5; AS8; AS12; AS14; B1; B3)

4B: PE (pages 40–41; 59)

TE (pages 41; 59–61)

TRB (pages B1; B3)

5A: PE (pages 8–9; 12–19; 33–34; 37; 39; 46; 48; 50–51; 55–57; 58)

TE (pages 6; 9–11; 12–15; 17; 19; 21–23; 26; 30; 32; 34–35; 37; 39; 42; 44; 46; 50; 52; 54–56; 58–61; 63)

TRB (pages O2; O7; O10; O14; O18; O22; E5; E8; I2; I4–8; I9–13; K2; K5; K8; K11; AS11; M10; M15; M17)

5B: PE (pages 12; 41; 60–61)

TE (pages 10; 12; 34)

TRB (pages AS6)

To the Student

Music is the language of feelings and has the power to touch us. Today we have the opportunity to listen to all kinds of music. The more we know about what we hear, the more fully we will enjoy it. Performing and composing add still other dimensions to our musical experience.

This book will give you the tools to listen to, play, and create music. You will learn about the building blocks of music, such as rhythm and melody, and how to read and write the notation for them. Your musical vocabulary will increase, and you will be more at home with music no matter when or where it was created.

Not all music has been written down, yet today we can hear music created hundreds of years ago. How can this be? Read all about the written and oral traditions of our music in Unit 1.

Each culture has its own special form of musical expression, the subject of Unit 2. Traditional music from Africa and Asia was often intertwined with daily life and was an essential part of the rituals surrounding birth, survival, and death. Discover more about this music as you listen to the recordings and read the text. In the United States and many other countries, much music has been composed for the symphony orchestra. You will find out how the orchestra developed, hear many different kinds of music composed for it, and learn what to expect at a concert.

Before records and mass-produced instruments were widely available in the United States, many people created their own music using everyday objects such as jugs, washboards, and spoons. Played together, along with the guitar and the harmonica, these instruments formed a skiffle band. Unit 3 contains many skiffle songs for you to perform and shows you how to play the guitar and harmonica.

No exploration of music would be complete without choral singing. Unit 4 provides you with a rich variety of music from all over the world.

The study of music can be a lifelong adventure. Whether you participate as a listener, performer, composer, or all three, we hope you will use this book to make your musical experience a memorable one.

4

Unit 1

Exploring Musical Traditions

Unit Overview

Unit 1 presents musical concepts through such activities as singing, creating compositions and accompaniments, playing instruments, listening to a variety of recorded selections, and determining the students' vocal ranges.

In this unit, two important musical traditions are explored: the oral tradition and the written tradition. The study of the oral tradition demonstrates to the students not only how songs have been passed from one generation to the next, but also how the tradition remains alive today through the modern media. The study of the written tradition traces the history of written notation, shows its advantages, and reviews its principles.

☆ Texas Essential Elements, Exploring Musical Traditions, pp. 5–11: 1A, 1B, 1C, 1D, 2, 3B, 4A, 5A, 5B (Please see Unit 1 Opener, page 4, for component and page references.)

5

Lesson Focus

Harmony: Two or more musical lines may occur simultaneously. *(P–I)*

Materials

o **Piano Accompaniments:** pages 222, 224
o **Record Information:**
  • I Write the Songs
    Record 1 Side A Band 1
    Voices: mixed chorus
    Accompaniment: electric bass, piano, electric guitar, percussion
  • Ring, Ring the Banjo
    Record 1 Side A Band 2
    Voices: mixed chorus
    Accompaniment: ocarina, banjo, double bass, piano, percussion
  • *Duelin' Banjos*
    by Eric Weissberg
    Record 1 Side A Band 3
o **Teacher's Resource Binder:**
  ┌─────────┐
  │Activity │ • **Activity Sheet 1**, page A4
  │Sheets   │ • Optional—
  └─────────┘   **Mainstreaming Activity 1,** page M6

In this unit you will have an opportunity to participate in the oral and written tradition of communicating music.

You can learn how to

• sing melodies by hearing songs
• hear and describe musical ideas
• sing harmony by listening
• maximize your own vocal capabilities
• use written clues for increased musical independence
• create and share your own song

Which of these can you already do?

Ring, Ring the Banjo

Traditional

1. The time is nev-er drear-y if a fel-low nev-er groans.
2. Oh nev-er count the bub-bles while there's wa-ter in the spring.

The la-dies nev-er wear-y with the rat-tle of the bones.
A fel-low has no trou-bles when he's got this song to sing.

Ring, ring the ban-jo. I like that good old song.

Ring, ring ban-jo, I like that good old song. So won't you

The Lesson

1. Introduce this unit by informing the students of their potential learning commitment. Draw attention to the list of musical goals on pupil page 6. Discuss each statement. To help the students decide which of the skills they already have, engage in the activities described in Steps 2 through 6. Ask the students to think about their abilities as they participate and to be prepared to make a commitment to improve at least one skill they are unsure of or do not have at this time.

2. Begin by having the students learn a melody by listening, without the aid of written words or music. Play the recording of "I Write the Songs" as often as needed.

3. Challenge the class to learn a harmony part. Play the recording of "Ring, Ring the Banjo." Divide the class into two groups; assign one group to each part and have them try to sing the song after listening a second time.

4. **Will using written clues help you learn the music more easily?** Draw attention to the score on pages 6 and 7. Some students may notice that the harmony part is in an unfamiliar clef. At this point merely acknowledge it as the bass clef, used for music in a lower range. It is enough for now that the students realize that notes written in bass clef move by steps or skips or by remaining the same, just as notes do in the treble clef. Practice "Ring, Ring the Banjo" again, now following the notation.

5. **Listen! What specific musical ideas can you hear in this music?** Play the recorded selection, "Duelin' Banjos." **What instruments do you hear?** The students may be surprised to discover that they are listening to a banjo and a guitar, not two banjos.

Come a-gain my true love. Oh where you been so long?

come a-gain my true love? Where you been so long?

LISTENING

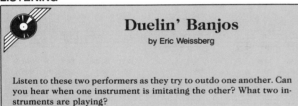

Duelin' Banjos

by Eric Weissberg

Listen to these two performers as they try to outdo one another. Can you hear when one instrument is imitating the other? What two instruments are playing?

7

For Your Information

This unit is to help the students

- grasp the importance of the oral tradition as a legitimate means of communicating musical ideas
- discover that written clues can provide greater independence in communicating musical ideas
- gain experience in reading a variety of musical styles at both the ikonic and symbolic levels
- grow in an understanding of personal development, especially with regard to changing vocal range
- continue the development of performance skills

I Write the Songs

Words and Music by Bruce Johnston

I've been alive forever,
And I wrote the very first song.
I put the words and melodies together;
I am music, and I write the songs.
I write the songs that make the whole
   world sing.
I write the songs of love and special things.
I write the songs that make the young girls
   cry.
I write the songs; I write the songs . . .

6. Distribute Activity Sheet 1 *(Listening Guide Sheet).* Use this as a listening guide as the recording is played again. The selection begins with an introduction of broken chords; full chords rhythmically strummed and echoed follow. The imitative play begins with the guitar playing eight brief melodic ideas that are echoed exactly or with slight variations by the banjo player. (Segments 1–2–4–5–6–7 are the same. In Segment 3, fewer pitches are echoed; in Segment 8 the banjo accompanies the guitar. The music continues with a lively tune played by both instruments and the return of the imitation game. The piece ends with a banjo solo followed by both instruments playing a final strum.

Play the selection, inviting the students to follow the guide sheet. They are to mark whether the first imitative-play ideas are the

same or varied. The students are to decide if the imitation is exactly the same or varied for each segment and mark their answers in Column 2. (Segments 1–2–4–5–6–7 are the same. In Segment 3 fewer pitches are echoed; in Segment 8 the instruments divided into two parts and clear, unaccompanied imitation ceases.)

7. Explain that during this unit the students will be involved in many activities leading to the improvement of the skills they have engaged in today as well as the other skills listed on page 6. At this time you may wish to ask them to make a commitment toward improving one or two of those skills.

Lesson Focus

Melody: Individual pitches, when compared to each other, may be higher, lower, or the same. *(P–S)*

Materials

o **Piano Accompaniments:** pages 224, 226
o **Record Information:**
  • Ring, Ring the Banjo
    (Record 1 Side A Band 2)
  • Lonesome Traveler
    Record 1 Side A Band 4a (Verses 1 and 2)
    Band 4b: Verses 3 and 4
    Band 4c: complete song
    Voices: mixed chorus
    Accompaniment: harmonica, acoustic guitar, electric guitar, double bass, percussion
o **Teacher's Resource Binder:**
  | Activity Sheets | • **Activity Sheet 2,** page A5 |

  • Optional—
    Enrichment Activity 1, page E2
    Instrumental Arrangements 1–3, pages 11–14
    Kodaly Activity 1, page K2
    Mainstreaming Activity 2, page M2
    Orff Activity 1, page O2

Your Singing Voice

To enjoy singing, it will be helpful if you know more about your voice and how it changes from time to time. Begin by finding your singing range. Sing "Lonesome Traveler."

Girls: Most of you will find this a comfortable singing range. You can sing melody or harmony parts. These parts will be called **Treble I** and **Treble II.** Each of you will want to learn Treble I on some songs and Treble II on others.

Lonesome Traveler

Words and Music by Lee Hays

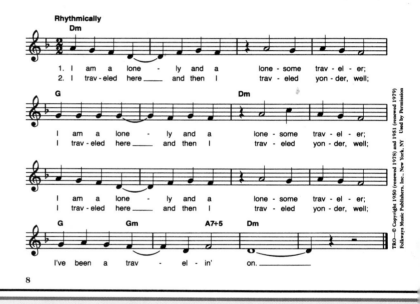

1. I am a lone - ly and a lone - some trav - el - er;
2. I trav - eled here and then I trav - eled yon - der, well;

I am a lone - ly and a lone - some trav - el - er;
I trav - eled here and then I trav - eled yon - der, well;

I am a lone - ly and a lone - some trav - el - er;
I trav - eled here and then I trav - eled yon - der, well;

I've been a trav - el - in' on.

TRO—© Copyright 1950 (renewed 1978) and 1951 (renewed 1979) Folkways Music Publishers, Inc., New York, NY. Used by Permission

8

The Lesson

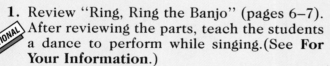

1. Review "Ring, Ring the Banjo" (pages 6–7). After reviewing the parts, teach the students a dance to perform while singing.(See **For Your Information.**)

2. Help the students check their singing voices. Follow the instructions on pupil pages 8–9. Ask the girls to sing the song as written. Explain that their vocal range will be identified as Treble I or II. Their range is such that they may perform either part.

3. Next ask the boys to sing, explaining that while they are singing you will tap some of them on the shoulder. This means they are to drop out and not sing for the moment. Begin the song in the key as written. As they continue to sing, move among the group listening for those who are singing an octave lower than the others. Tap these singers on the

shoulder. Upon completion of this sorting, tell the students who were tapped that they are Baritones as they were singing very low. They will sing a special part of the melody an octave lower than written.

4. Ask the remaining boys to sing the melody again. Change the key of the song to A minor. (Start the melody on E.) Repeat the procedure. This time move among the group and listen for voices that can easily sing in this range. (Some will sing an octave lower.) Tap the students who sing at pitch and later identify them as the Treble I or II voices. These are the boys whose voices are unchanged. Avoid identifying these students as boy sopranos. Rather, place them in either the Treble I or II group.

5. The remaining boys will be those singers whose voices are in the process of changing.

Boys: Now it's your turn to sing. Male voices will fall into different ranges. Some of your voices may be changing. Your teacher may indicate to some of you to stop singing. If so, you are **Baritones.**

I am a lone - ly and a lone - some trav - el - er . . .

If your teacher does not tell you to stop singing, sing the song again in this key:

I am a lone - ly and a lone - some trav - el - er . . .

Your teacher may again indicate that some of you should stop singing. If so, you are Treble I or II singers.

Those of you who are still singing are **Changing-Voice** singers. Your voices are in the process of changing. Form groups and sing the entire song with the record. Baritones and Changing Voices sing Verses 1 and 2; Treble I and II's sing Verses 3 and 4. Notice how the arrangement changes to accommodate the range of your voices.

3. One of these days I'm gonna stop all my travelin';
   One of these days I'm gonna stop all my travelin';
   One of these days I'm gonna stop all my travelin';
   I've been a-travelin' on.

4. Gonna keep on a-trav'lin' on the road to freedom;
   Gonna keep on a-trav'lin' on the road to freedom;
   Gonna keep on a-trav'lin' on the road to freedom;
   Gonna keep right on a-travelin' home.

9

For Your Information

It is important for both boys and girls of this age to understand that their voices are going through changes. An objective approach to this natural phenomenon will help the students become less self-conscious about overt signs such as cracking voices.

Dance instruction for "Ring, Ring the Banjo": Couples form a double circle, facing their partners.

VERSE I   **Phrase I:** Do-si-do right side of partner.
               Phrase II: Do-si-do left side of partner.

REFRAIN   **Phrase I:** Hold partner's hands; skip in a circle.
               Phrase II: Right hand swing; end with girl making a fancy twirl under partner's arm.

VERSE II   **Phrase I:** Hand-clapping patterns with partner, in time with beat—own hands, partner's right, own, partner's left, own, partner's both (three claps).
               Phrase II: Repeat as in Phrase I.

REFRAIN   (Repeat as before)

Place them into a third group—Changing Voices.

6. Change the seating arrangement in the room to accommodate the groupings you have just formed: Treble I and II, Changing Voices, and Baritones. Record the results on Activity Sheet 2 *(Ranges)*.

7. "Lonesome Traveler" has been specially recorded to accommodate the voice ranges of these three groups. Perform the four verses with the record, featuring the groups as follows: Verses 1 and 2 (key of D minor)—Baritones and Changing Voices singing an octave apart; Verses 3 and 4 (key of A minor)—Treble I's and II's. Draw attention to the instrumental interlude between Verses 2 and 3. This interlude "takes the melody" to a new key that accommodates the vocal range of the treble voices. The song may be performed with the recorded accompaniment alone by adjusting the balance on the record player.

Lesson Focus

Melody: Individual pitches, when compared to each other, may be higher, lower, or the same. *(P–S)*

Materials

o **Piano Accompaniments:** pages 226, 227
o **Record Information:**
  • *No Reaction Recording*
    Record 1 Side A Band 5
  • Lonesome Traveler
    (Record 1 Side A Band 4C)
  • Bo Diddley
    Record 1 Side A Band 6
    Voices: mixed chorus
    Accompaniment: synthesizer, electric guitar, electric bass, electric percussion
o **Teacher's Resource Binder:**
  • **Activity Sheet 3,** page A6
  • Optional—
    Mainstreaming Activity 3, page M9

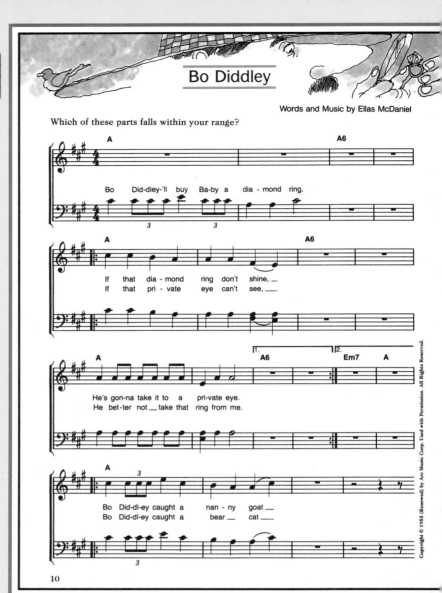

The Lesson

1. Introduce the first listening warm-up. (See **For Your Information.**) This is a "no-reaction challenge." Ask the class to listen to a recording of short excerpts from a variety of music. The students must keep their faces from showing any emotion as the tape is played. They should not squirm, smile, frown, or beat or wave their pencils. This recording includes excerpts from pop tunes, slow and fast orchestral music, operatic music, and "corny" music from the past. After playing the complete recording, discuss the frustration individuals may have felt when having to sit still during certain sections of the recording.

   Distribute Activity Sheet 3 *(Music Reaction Profile).* Read the instructions and again play the recording as the students check their responses to each musical example. Ask the students to share their ideas; conclude that

the appeal of music of various styles is a very individual thing.

2. Introduce a second listening warm-up. **In music it is sometimes important that things be done together, at the same time with everyone in the group. Let's practice doing this.** Ask the students to look at something in the room. They must all look together at the same time. **First we will look at the clock, but not until I tell you. Everyone must look at tne same time. Continue to look until I ask you to look back at my hand. Look at the clock!** (pause) **Look back!** Commend the students and strive for precision. Repeat the command, then surprise them by changing to: **Look at the flag! Look back!**

3. Proceed with the lesson by reviewing the song "Lonesome Traveler" (page 8). Sing in appropriate groups with the recording.

To make his pret-ty ba-by a   Sun-day coat.___
To make his pret-ty ba-by a   Sun-day hat. ___

Won't you come to my house and   rack that   bone?___
Look   at   that   Bo - do.   Oh where's he   been?___

Take my ba - by   all   the way from home.
Up   to   your___ house and gone a - gain.

Bo Did-dl-ey, Bo   Did-dl-ey have you heard?___

My ___   pret-ty ba - by said   she was   a bird.

Repeat and fade

11

For Your Information

Initiate experiences designed to enhance the students' ability to hear and respond appropriately. Provide this practice over a series of several lessons, progressing from responding to environmental sounds to reacting to verbal instructions. This series involves both musical and nonmusical goals leading to the ability to discriminate among specific sounds within a musical performance.

Use these activities as warm-ups prior to the lesson of the day.

No Reaction Recording
Excerpts from:
1. *El Capitan*
2. *Talkin' Guitar Blues*
3. *Let the Sunshine In*
4. *Prelude to Act III from* Lohengrin
5. *Bwana, Ibariki Afrika*
6. *Siam Giunte*
7. *Duelin' Banjos*
8. *Old Hundred*
9. *Ogi No Mat-o*
10. *Farandole*

4. Ask the students to look at pages 10–11. Write the following ranges on the board:

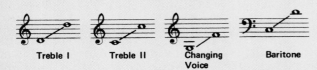

Treble I   Treble II   Changing Voice   Baritone

Discuss the ranges as indicated for each of the voice parts.

5. Play the recording of "Bo Diddley." Ask the students to follow the score as they listen. They are to check their ranges as shown on the chalkboard, then decide which staff (treble or bass) shows their part for this song. Pitches on the first, fourth, and eighth bass-clef staff fall only in Changing-Voices range. All other bass-clef staffs may be sung by both Changing Voices and Baritones. When two notes appear on the same staff, Changing Voices should sing the higher note and Baritones should sing the lower. All treble-clef parts are within the range of the Treble I's and II's. Help the students learn the song by following the appropriate staff.

6. The students will have noticed that, following each two measures of vocal melody, there are two measures of rest. On the recording these measures are filled with an accompaniment. Invite the students to create an echoing statement to fill these measures. The echo can be identical to or a variation of the vocal idea that they have just sung. Some ideas for variations might include: rhythmically chanting the words, echoing on one or two pitches; embroidering the melodic line using many extra pitches; or vocalizing melodic ideas using only neutral syllables, no words. Repeat the song several times, choosing different soloists to improvise each time.

Lesson Focus

Expression: Musical elements are combined into a whole to express a musical or extra-musical idea. *(P–I)*

Materials

○ **Piano Accompaniments:** pages 232, 236
○ **Record Information**
  • I Walk the Line
    Record 1 Side A Band 7
    Johnny Cash
  • Ease on Down the Road
    from *The Wiz*
    Record 1 Side B Band 1
    Voices: mixed chorus
    Accompaniment: electric guitar, piano, electric bass, percussion

---

The Oral Tradition

You hear the songs of today played repeatedly on your radio, TV, or stereo. The ones that are particularly meaningful to you are quickly learned.

When you learn music by hearing it, you are sharing in an old tradition. People have always learned and passed on their most important ideas and feelings from one generation to the next in this way.

Through conversation, poetry, songs, myths, and tales, people have orally communicated what was important to them. Passing on information in this way is called learning through the **oral tradition.**

Continue the oral tradition. Listen to the feelings and ideas expressed in the song "I Walk the Line." Repeat them and pass them on.

I Walk the Line

Words and Music by Johnny Cash

I keep a close watch on this heart of mine.
I keep my eyes wide open all the time.
I keep the ends out for the tie that binds.
Because you're mine, I walk the line.

I find it very, very easy to be true.
I find myself alone when each day is through.
Yes, I'll admit that I'm a fool for you.
Because you're mine, I walk the line.

12

The Lesson

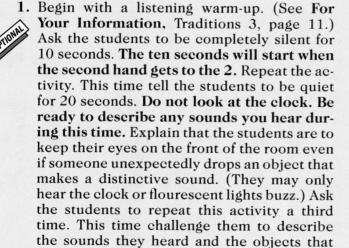

1. Begin with a listening warm-up. (See **For Your Information,** Traditions 3, page 11.) Ask the students to be completely silent for 10 seconds. **The ten seconds will start when the second hand gets to the 2.** Repeat the activity. This time tell the students to be quiet for 20 seconds. **Do not look at the clock. Be ready to describe any sounds you hear during this time.** Explain that the students are to keep their eyes on the front of the room even if someone unexpectedly drops an object that makes a distinctive sound. (They may only hear the clock or flourescent lights buzz.) Ask the students to repeat this activity a third time. This time challenge them to describe the sounds they heard and the objects that made the sounds.

2. Discuss the importance of listening when learning a new pop or rock tune. **Where are you likely to first encounter a new pop tune?** (usually on the radio) **How do you learn the words and melody?** (usually by repeated listening)

3. Tell the students to turn to pages 12–13, read about the oral tradition, and then learn the song "I Walk the Line." Explain that this is a country-western tune sung by many people who probably learned it through the oral tradition, that is, by just hearing it on a recording or the radio or sung by a friend. Play the recording as often as necessary until the students have learned the song. The students may follow the words in their books if they wish.

4. After the students have demonstrated their ability to participate in the oral tradition by singing "I Walk the Line," challenge them to learn a more complicated song, "Ease on

Texas Essential Elements, The Oral Tradition, pp. 12–27: 1A, 1B, 1C, 1D, 1E, 2, 3B, 4A, 5A, 5B
(Please see Unit 1 Opener, page 4, for component and page references.)

Ease on Down the Road

from *The Wiz*   Words and Music by Charlie Smalls

Follow the oral tradition by learning this song. The only clues to the
melody and rhythm will be what you hear.

This song is performed in unison and in two different keys. Which
range is appropriate for your voice?

Come on, ease on down, ease on down the road.
Come on, ease on down, ease on down the road.
Don't you carry nothin' that might be a load.
Come on, ease on down, ease on down the road.

Come on, ease on down, ease on down the road.
Come on, ease on down, ease on down the road.
Don't you carry nothin' that might be a load.
Come on, ease on down, ease on down the road.

'Cause there may be times
when you think you've lost your mind,
And the steps you've taken
leave you three, four steps behind.

Just you keep on keepin'
on the road that you choose,
And don't give up walkin'
'cause you gave up shoes.

Pick your left foot up
when your right one's down.
Come on legs keep movin',
don't you lose no ground.

'Cause the road you're walkin'
might be long sometime,
But just keep on steppin'
and you'll be just fine.

Come on, ease on down, ease on down the road.
Come on, ease on down, ease on down the road.
Don't you carry nothin' that might be a load.
Come on, ease on down, ease on down the road.
(repeat and fade)

13

Down the Road," still using the oral tradition.
Play the complete recording. Guide the students to note that the refrain and the verse
are performed in two different keys to fit the
students' different vocal ranges. (See the
score on pages 186–187.) **As you listen, decide which range is best for you.** Play the
recording several times until the students feel
they are ready to sing it. Ask those who feel
they should sing in the higher range to sing
the first verse. Next, ask those who are more
comfortable in the lower range to sing the refrain.

5. Return to "I Walk the Line." Play the recording and draw the students' attention to the
musical setting for this song. A simple, open
accompaniment is used, including

• almost unnoticeable chordal afterbeats
• a predominant electric bass guitar playing
either a "walking" bass or chord roots

• percussion patterns such as:

In what way does the instrumental accompaniment affect the message of the words?
(gives a sense of walking) Listen to the
recording once more to verify the students'
observations.

Lesson Focus

Harmony: Chords and melody may move simultaneously in relation to each other. *(P–I)*

Materials

o **Piano Accompaniments:** pages 236, 240
o **Record information:**
  • Ease on Down the Road
    (Record 1 Side B Band 1)
  • Mama Don't 'Low
    Record 1 Side B Band 2
    Voices: mixed chorus
    Accompaniment: banjo, acoustic guitar, autoharps, Jew's harp, jug, kazoo, double bass, percussion
o **Teacher's Resource Binder:**
  • Optional—
    Mainstreaming Activity 4, page M4

Mama Don't 'Low

Traditional

Learn this song by following the visual clues. Do these clues help you determine when to sing the words higher or lower?

Ma-ma don't 'low no gui-tar pick-in' 'round here.

Ma-ma don't 'low no gui-tar pick-in' 'round here.

I don't care what Ma-ma don't 'low;

Gon-na pick my gui-tar an-y-how.

Ma-ma don't 'low no gui-tar pick-in' 'round here.

2. ban-jo play-in'
3. mid-night ram-blin'

14

The Lesson

1. Introduce another listening warm-up. Ask the students to close their eyes. Drop something, such as a plastic bracelet, on a table or piano lid. Pick up the object and hide it, then ask the students to open their eyes. They are to tell you everything they can about the sound, but not what the object was (i.e., the thing was plastic, it was wood, it was metal . . .). **Are you referring to the object or the surface it was dropped on? What can you tell me about its shape? How heavy is it? Is it hollow? Now can you name the object?** Repeat this activity using different objects.

2. Invite the class to sing "Ease on Down the Road." Ask them to recall how they learned the melody of this song during the previous class session (by hearing it on the recording —in the oral tradition).

3. Focus attention on the song on page 14. **What clues for learning this song, other than the words, do you find on the page?** (indication of the direction of the melodic line) Ask one student to try to follow this clue and sing a melody on a neutral syllable. She or he does not need to try to sing a specific melody, just perform the up-down ideas. After several students have experimented, play the recording. Ask the students to determine if the song did indeed go up and down as they had interpreted the contour shown in their books.

4. Play the recording again as the students continue to follow the melodic contour. Repeat it until the students feel they can sing the entire song independently. Compare this approach to learning a song with that of the oral tradition, which was used in learning "Ease on Down the Road." **Is it helpful to know when**

14

Sing this song in four parts by adding vocal chording. Choose the part that best fits your vocal range.

1

Ma-ma don't 'low no gui-tar pick-in' 'round here.

Ma-ma don't 'low no gui-tar pick-in' 'round here.

I don't care what Ma-ma don't 'low;

Gon-na pick my gui-tar an-y-how.

Ma-ma don't 'low no gui-tar pick-in' 'round here.

3

Ma-ma don't 'low no gui-tar pick-in' 'round here.

Ma-ma don't 'low no gui-tar pick-in' 'round here.

I don't care what Ma'ma don't 'low;

Gon-na pick my gui-tar an-y-how.

Ma-ma don't 'low no gui-tar pick-in' 'round here.

5

Ma-ma don't 'low no gui-tar pick-in' 'round here.

Ma-ma don't 'low no gui-tar pick-in' 'round here.

I don't care what Ma'ma don't ' 'low;

pick my gui-tar an-y-how.

Gon-na

Ma-ma don't 'low no gui-tar pick-in' 'round here.

15

the words should be sung higher or lower? Does it make learning the song easier? quicker? (Encourage the students' responses; there may be disagreement.)

5. Guide the students to learn the vocal chording parts by following the chart on page 15. Divide the class into four groups:

Baritones: Melody—begin on 1, the tonal center.
Treble I's: Harmony I—use only pitches 1 and 7; begin on 1, the tonal center.
Changing Voices: Harmony II—use only pitches 3 and 4; begin on 3.
Treble II's: Harmony III—use only pitches 5 and 6; begin on 5.

Baritones and Treble I's may exchange parts. Invite the students to experiment with other arrangements.

Practice the parts separately until the students are comfortable following their individual parts. When all groups sing at the same time, vocal chording based on the I, V7, and IV chords will result. These chords will provide appropriate harmony when the melody is added.

Lesson Focus

Melody: A series of pitches may move up or down by steps or skips. *(P–S)*

Materials

○ **Piano Accompaniments:** pages 258, 241, 242
○ **Record Information:**
  • Fiddler on the Roof
    Record 1 Side B Band 3
    Voices: treble chorus
    Accompaniment: small show orchestra
  • Know Where I'm Goin'
    Record 1 Side B Band 4
    Voices: female soloist
    Accompaniment: mountain dulcimer, hammered dulcimer, psaltery, lute, rubbed glasses
  • Memphis, Tennessee
    Record 1 Side B Band 5
    Voices: mixed chorus
    Accompaniment: acoustic guitar, electric guitar, piano, electric piano, electric organ, percussion, sound effects
○ **Other:** pencils
○ **Teacher's Resource Binder:**
  [Activity Sheets] • **Activity Sheet 4**, page A7
  • Optional—
    Kodaly Activity 2, page K2
    Orff Activity 2, page O2

Know Where I'm Goin'

Irish Folk Song

Learn Verse 1 of this song by following the up-and-down visual clues. How will you learn the rhythm of the melody?

1. I know where I'm go-in', and I know who'll go with me.
2. I have stock-ings of silk and shoes of fine green leath-er,

I know who I love, but who knows who I'll mar-ry.
Combs to buck-le my hair, a ring for ev-ery fin-ger.

3. Feather beds are soft,
   And painted rooms are bonny;
   But I would trade them all
   For handsome, winsome Johnny.

4. Some say he's dark,
   But I say he's bonny;
   Fairest of them all
   Is handsome, winsome Johnny.

16

The Lesson

1. Begin the lesson with another listening warm-up. Challenge the students to hear familiar words made less familiar by varying speech patterns in a musical setting. Distribute Activity Sheet 4 (*Fiddler on the Roof*) and pencils to each student. Play "Fiddler on the Roof" and ask the students to write in the words that have been omitted as they listen to the recording. Check for accuracy; then ask the class to sing the song. **Was it helpful or distracting to listen carefully to the words before attempting to sing the song?** (Answers may vary.)

2. Ask the students to look at the words of "Know Where I'm Goin' " at the top of page 16. Draw their attention to the pitch letters in parentheses occasionally appearing under the lines. Tell the students you will play only

these pitches. The students are to first read the words as you play the pitches and then sing only the words marked with pitches and "think" the melodic direction of the other words.

3. Repeat the activity; this time invite a few individuals to sing the melody, moving stepwise up or down from the pitches you provide along the way. Reassure the students that they are not expected to sing the rhythm of the melody and probably will not achieve a precise performance of the stepwise motion of the song. They should be commended if they move in the right direction without large skips in the melodic flow.

4. Explain to the class that they have come close to the melody, but that the information given is not accurate enough to communicate how the song is to be sung. **What musical in-**

Memphis, Tennessee

Words and Music by Chuck Berry

Use clues in the music notation to learn this song. Notice that the melody has only six different pitches:

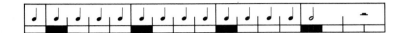

Are you still participating in the oral tradition when you learn this song?

Long dis-tance in-for-ma-tion, give me Mem-phis, Ten-nes-see;
Help me, in-for-ma-tion, get in touch with my Ma-rie;

Help me find the par-ty trying to get in touch with me.
She's the on-ly one who'd phone me here from Mem-phis, Ten-nes-see.

She could not leave her num-ber, but I know who placed the call
Her home is on the south side, high up on a ridge,

'cause my un-cle took the mes-sage, and he wrote it on the wall.
just a half a mile from the Mis-sis-sip-pi Bridge.

17

For Your Information

Notation for "Fiddler on the Roof" found on pages 30–31.

formation is missing? (how beats are grouped—meter; length of individual words; exact distance between pitches)

5. **How can we learn the rhythm of this melody?** Guide the students to conclude that unless someone sings it for us, we must be able to read the precise rhythmic information provided in the score at the bottom of the page. Review the length of notes in relation to the shortest sound. Help the students interpret the rhythm ruler. (An eighth note is the shortest sound; the quarter note equals two short sounds; the dotted quarter note equals three short sounds.) Ask the class to tap the shortest sound as they figure out the rhythm of the melody and chant the words.

6. Challenge the students to see how well they can learn a new song simply by using the clues provided by the music notation. Look at the song "Memphis, Tennessee" on page 17. **What will help you learn the rhythm?** (interpreting the rhythm ruler shown at the top of the page) Help the students determine that in this song, the quarter note is the underlying shortest sound; the half note equals two short sounds; the dotted half note equals three short sounds; two eighth notes equal one short sound.

Will the melody be difficult to learn? (No, it has only six different pitches and moves mostly by steps.) Play these six pitches on the piano. Encourage the students to sing the entire song independently, following the written score as you add a simple chordal accompaniment. **Did you use the oral or written tradition to learn this song?** (written) **Which tradition allows the individual to learn independently with no direct help from others?** (the written)

Lesson Focus

Harmony: Two or more musical lines may occur simultaneously. *(P–S)*

Materials

o **Piano Accompaniments:** pages 243, 244
o **Record Information**
  • *You Are My Sunshine*
    Record 1   Side B   Band 6a
    Aretha Franklin
  • You Are My Sunshine
    Band 6b
    Voices: mixed chorus
    Accompaniment: acoustic guitar, electric guitar, double bass, percussion
  • As Tears Go By
    Record 1   Side B   Band 7
    Voices: mixed chorus
    Accompaniment: English horn, strings, harpsichord, electric piano, synthesizer, electric bass, percussion
o **Teacher's Resource Binder:**
  • **Activity Sheets 5a–c,** pages A8–A10
  • Optional—
    Kodaly Activity 3, page K5

The Lesson

1. Challenge the students to listen to a selection and see if they can filter out certain parts of the music, concentrating on the main melody. Play the recording of "You Are My Sunshine" by Aretha Franklin, without identifying it. Ask the students to identify the familiar song. This may at first be difficult for most of the students to do. If they cannot identify the song, suggest that they listen for the words and write down only those that they immediately recognize. They should not attempt to write down all the words. Key words such as "sunshine" should enable them to guess the title.

2. Play the recorded refrain of the original version of "You Are My Sunshine" (Band 6b) to remind students of the way we usually hear the song.

3. Use Activity Sheet 5a (*Aretha Franklin Sings*) to guide the students as they again listen to the Aretha Franklin version of the song. Ask the students to be prepared to discuss how musical elements such as the melody, rhythm, style, and words were changed. (melody totally different, often freely improvised; rhythm has driving rock-style beat; style changed from country to gospel-rock; new words interjected, often repeated)

4. Have the students open their books to page 18. Play the harmony part of "As Tears Go By" as students listen. When they are familiar with the sound, play the recording, asking them to listen specifically for the harmony part. They may softly sing along with the recording.

5. Divide into groups; Treble Voices are to perform the melody while Changing Voices and

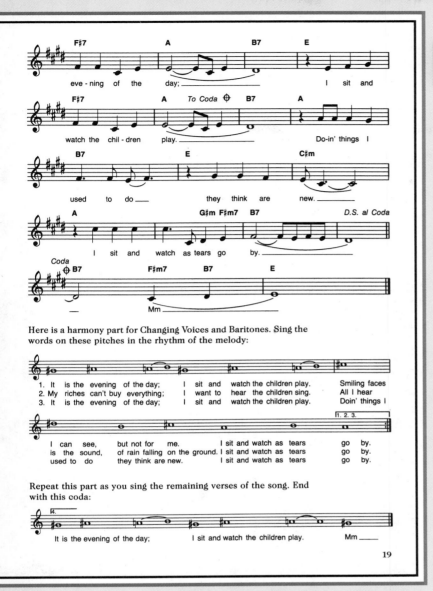

Here is a harmony part for Changing Voices and Baritones. Sing the words on these pitches in the rhythm of the melody:

1. It is the evening of the day; I sit and watch the children play. Smiling faces
2. My riches can't buy everything; I want to hear the children sing. All I hear
3. It is the evening of the day; I sit and watch the children play. Doin' things I

I can see, but not for me. I sit and watch as tears go by.
is the sound, of rain falling on the ground. I sit and watch as tears go by.
used to do they think are new. I sit and watch as tears go by.

Repeat this part as you sing the remaining verses of the song. End with this coda:

It is the evening of the day; I sit and watch the children play. Mm _____

19

Baritones sing the harmony part. Perform the song in two-part harmony.

6. The students may wish to sing the original version of "You Are My Sunshine" in four-part harmony. Use Activity Sheets 5b *(You Are My Sunshine)* and 5c *(The Song in Harmony)* and help the students learn the vocal harmonies. Remind the students that when singing in a group they will need to listen carefully in order to hear how their part helps create the harmony.

Lesson Focus

Expression: Musical elements are combined into a whole to express a musical or extra-musical idea. *(P–S)*

Materials

o **Piano Accompaniments:** pages 247, 250
o **Record Information:**
  • A Place in the Sun
  Record 1 Side B Band 8
  Voices: mixed chorus
  Accompaniment: flute, guitar, double bass, percussion
  • Ramblin' Boy
  Record 2 Side A Band 1
  Voices: mixed chorus, male soloist
  Accompaniment: acoustic guitar, electric guitar, pedal steel guitar, piano, electric bass, percussion
o **Instruments:** autoharp; guitar(s) (optional)
o **Other:** overhead projector
o **Teacher's Resource Binder:**
  Activity Sheets • **Activity Sheet 6,** page A11 (Prepare as a transparency.)

The Message: Words

When a poet or lyricist writes words for a song, the words are carefully chosen to convey feelings and to draw the listener into those feelings. The lyricist may achieve this by deliberate use of

• personal pronouns (such as "you" and "I")
• repetition of words and word patterns
• similes, metaphors, and word pictures
• current slang expressions
• traditional expressions passed on from song to song

A Place in the Sun

Lyrics by Ronald Miller   Music by Bryan Wells

Like a long, lonely stream I keep running towards a dream,
moving on, moving on.
Like a branch on a tree I keep reaching to be free,
moving on, moving on.

'Cause there's a place in the sun
where there's hope for everyone
where my poor restless heart's gotta run.

There's a place in the sun
and before my life is done
got to find me a place in the sun.

20

The Lesson

1. Read the information on page 20 and listen to "A Place in the Sun." **Of the ways lyricists may convey feelings, which are used by Ronald Miller?** (personal pronouns: "I," "my," "me"; repetition: "movin' on," "place in the sun"; simile: "like a branch"; metaphor: "heart's gotta run"; traditional expression: "there's hope for everyone," "a place in the sun")

2. Listen to the recording several times as the students focus on the form of the song (**A A B B**). Turn off the vocal track using the balance knob on the record player. Challenge the class to perform the song while hearing only the instrumental accompaniment.

3. Play the song "Ramblin' Boy." **What message do you think folk singer Tom Paxton was trying to convey about his ramblin' friend?** (loneliness, loss, tribute to a friend, loyalty, happiness in knowing that he's still "ramblin' ")**Did he use any of the means listed on page 20 to convey these feelings?** (repetition of "ramblin'," frequent personal pronouns—"he," "you," "we"; slang expressions—"had no dough," "we'd rather bum")

4. Ask the students to read page 21. Play the recording again. **Besides using expressive lyrics, what did the composer do musically to convey his feelings and draw the listener into them?** Various answers may be offered: The repetitious rhythmic and melodic pattern with minimal change throughout seems to support the feeling of loneliness and loss (see example at end of step); important words such as "cared" or "you" are placed on the highest and longest pitches; the walking-bass accompaniment helps convey the idea of "ramblin' on."

The Message: Music

When a composer creates music for a song, the musical ideas are carefully chosen to convey feelings and to draw the listener into the music.

The composer may achieve this in various ways, including

- stretching a word out over several pitches
- repeating a melodic idea
- repeating rhythmic patterns
- creating a melody over a harmonic sequence
- creating a melody with wide skips

Ramblin' Boy

Words and Music by Tom Paxton

He was a man and a friend always.
He stuck with me in the hard old days.
He never cared if I had no dough.
We rambled 'round in the rain and snow.

Refrain:
    And here's to you my ramblin' boy;
    May all your ramblin' bring you joy.
    And here's to you my ramblin' boy;
    May all your ramblin' bring you joy.

In Tulsa town we chanced to stray.
We thought we'd try to work one day.
The boss said he had room for one.
Says my old pal, "We'd rather bum."
    Refrain
Late one night in a jungle camp,
The weather it was cold and damp.
He got the chills, and he got 'em bad.
They took the only friend I had.
    Refrain
He left me here to ramble on.
My ramblin' pal is dead and gone.
If when we die we go somewhere,
I'll bet you a dollar he's a ramblin' there.
    Refrain

21

For Your Information
Notation for the songs in the lesson may be found on pages 247 and 250.

lems arise, work on the two parts separately, then combine them again.

5. As the students listen to the song again, ask them to determine which voice group could sing the melody. (Treble I's or Baritones).

6. Treble II's and Changing Voices may add harmony by singing the chord roots. Encourage the students to focus on the harmony as they listen to the recording. Display the transparency of Activity Sheet 6 *(Ramblin' Boy)*. **How many pitches will be needed for the harmony?** (three: C, F, G) Experiment by singing the chord roots as the song is played with an autoharp or guitar accompaniment.

7. Challenge the students to practice the two parts at the same time with Baritones and Treble I's singing the melody and Changing Voices and Treble II's harmonizing. If prob-

21

Leaving of Liverpool

Words and Music by Will Schmid

Oh the sun is set-ting on the har-bor,

love, And I wish I could re - main.

For I think it will be ____ some long, long time

be - fore I ____ see you a - gain. ____

Refrain

So ____ fare thee well, my ____ own true love,

And when I re - turn, u - ni - ted we will be. ____

It's not the leav - ing of Liv - er - pool that's griev - ing me,

But my dar - ling, when I think of thee. ____

22

Lesson Focus

Expression: Musical elements are combined into a whole to express a musical or extra-musical idea. *(P–S)*

Materials

o **Piano Accompaniment:** page 252
o **Record Information:**
  • Leaving of Liverpool
  Record 2 Side A Band 2
  Voice: male soloist
  Accompaniment: oboe, French horn, cello, harp, percussion
o **Instruments:** tambourine; drums; wood-blocks with mallets; all available pitched instruments
o **Other:** paper and pencils for each student
o **Teacher's Resource Binder:**

  Activity Sheets
  • **Activity Sheet 7,** page A12
  • Optional—
    Kodaly Activity 22, page K5

The Lesson

1. Review songs from the previous lessons including "Ramblin' Boy" on page 21 and "A Place in the Sun" on page 20.

2. Apply what the students have learned about music and words to "Leaving of Liverpool" on page 22. Ask the students to follow the lyrics as they listen to the song. **What can be learned about the singer?** (He is a British sailor about to leave for America on a clipper ship; and he is sad, not about leaving Liverpool but about leaving his love.) Review the discussions on pages 20 and 21 and ask the students to list on the chalkboard the musical and textual ideas used in this song. (Musical: wide skips, repetition of melodic ideas—most phrases begin 1–2–3–5, stretching syllables across two pitches; textual: personal pronouns "I," "my," "we" and the traditional

expression "sun is setting") Play the recording as often as necessary.

3. After the students have learned the melody, invite some to perform the accompaniment on autoharps or guitars as others sing.

4. Focus attention on page 23 and discuss ideas about how songwriters compose. Perform each pattern as the discussion proceeds to help the students sense how a song is "put together."

5. Give the students the option of adding an accompaniment to "Life Is Like a Teddy Bear" or creating their own song. Organize the class into small groups based on their preference.

6. Provide the groups choosing to add an accompaniment with Activity Sheet 7 *(Your Own Song)*. They may experiment with the

22

Your Own Message

Songs may be created in a variety of ways. We could begin with the words, or the music, or both at the same time. When the same person creates both the words and the music, the songmaker might begin

- by strumming a guitar (or playing the piano) to find an appealing sequence of chords: **G F C C G**
- by discovering an interesting rhythm pattern:

- by creating lyrics:
"Life is like a teddy bear that's lost its stuffing."
- by finding a "hook" that combines key words and musical ideas:

When you're gone, gone, oh ___ so gone.

A song composed in these stages might result as follows:

Life is like a ted-dy bear ___ that's lost its stuf-fing. ___

___ When you're gone, gone, oh ___ so gone. ___

23

different approaches as suggested. Provide volunteers with tambourines, woodblocks, and drums to play the rock accompaniment as the song is sung. Play the blues chord sequence on the piano or guitar while a volunteer (or small group) sings a solo. Be sure the students understand how to create the meter and rhythm changes in the third option.

7. The groups wishing to create their own songs may make use of one or all of the suggestions on page 23. Make pitched and unpitched instruments available to the groups for their compositions. Circulate among the groups offering assistance as requested. Make paper and pencils available to those groups who may prefer to write down their ideas.

8. Tape-record their completed songs. If there is time, invite each group to present its arrangement or new composition to the class.

Lesson Focus

Expression: Musical elements are combined into a whole to express a musical or extra-musical idea. *(D–S)*

Materials

o **Record Information:**
• *Just a Closer Walk With Thee*
   Record 2 Side B Band 1a
   Mahalia Jackson
   Band 1b: Oak Ridge Boys
   Band 1c: Preservation Hall Jazz Band (slow)
   Band 1d: Preservation Hall Jazz Band (fast)

o **Other:** pencils

o **Teacher's Resource Binder:**
   [Activity Sheets] • **Activity Sheets 8 and 9**, pages A13, A14 (Prepare one copy for each group.)

The Message Transmitted: The Performer

This song is well known among gospel, country, folk, and jazz musicians.

Just a Closer Walk with Thee

Traditional

Each soloist or group makes musical decisions that affect the performance and the message.

Mahalia Jackson

24

The Lesson

1. Begin class by reviewing songs from pages 6 through 22 as chosen by the students. Review the two components that have been studied thus far in relating the message to a listener —musical ideas and textual ideas.

2. **Who can think of a third, very essential part of transmitting a message?** (the performance—how the performer communicates the musical and textual ideas) Take time to discuss how songs were created, preserved, and transmitted before the advent of published and recorded music. Point out that numerous songs were probably lost or transformed when passed from person to person. Some changes were due to a faulty memory; some were deliberate as singers contributed their own interpretations of the song.

3. Call attention to page 24. Help the students become familiar with the melody of *Just a Closer Walk With Thee* by playing the opening of the Preservation Hall (slow version).

4. This famous song has been performed by countless gospel, country, and jazz performers for years. Divide the class into small groups and distribute Activity Sheet 9 *(Performers)*. Listen to all four versions of "Just a Closer Walk With Thee." All of the performers began with the same simple song. **How did they change the music? What musical decisions did they make in order to transmit their message?** (See **For Your Information.**) Instruct the students to fill in the activity sheet as they listen to each version. Those students working together may share their ideas, with one person serving as their scribe.

The Oak Ridge Boys

The Preservation Hall Jazz Band

For Your Information

The four arrangements of *Just a Closer Walk With Thee* to be compared in the lesson:

1. Mahalia Jackson (black gospel singer)—embroidered melody, typical of the gospel style
2. Oak Ridge Boys (country group singing in the gospel style)—various soloists with backup singers
3. Preservation Hall Jazz Band (Dixieland band)—traditional, slow New Orleans funeral tempo (excerpt)
4. Preservation Hall Jazz Band—"up-tempo" version.

Answers to Activity Sheet 8 *(Soloists):*

1. solo: clarinet; accompaniment: tuba, banjo, piano; 2. solo: trombone; accompaniment: tuba, banjo; 3. solo: trumpet; accompaniment: tuba, banjo, piano; 4. solo: banjo; accompaniment: tuba, piano; 5. solo: piano; accompaniment: tuba, banjo

25

5. Was one way right and the others wrong? (no) Conclude that each performer or band created a unique piece of music; it is all right to like one version better than the other as preference in musical styles are a matter of personal taste. Share answers that the student groups recorded.

6. OPTIONAL Explain that Dixieland bands will frequently play a song in a slow funeral tempo and then swing into an exciting, faster tempo. At other times they will play an entire song at a slow tempo and improvise in a quiet manner rather than in the more usual "up-tempo" Dixieland style. That is what happens in this version of "Just a Closer Walk With Thee" performed by the Preservation Hall Jazz Band. Distribute Activity Sheet 8 *(Soloists).* Ask the student teams to complete the sheets as they listen. They must determine which

instrument has the solo, which instruments are providing accompaniment, and which instruments are not playing. Play the recording as often as needed until the students have completed the activity sheet to their satisfaction. Then help them check their answers. (See **For Your Information**.)

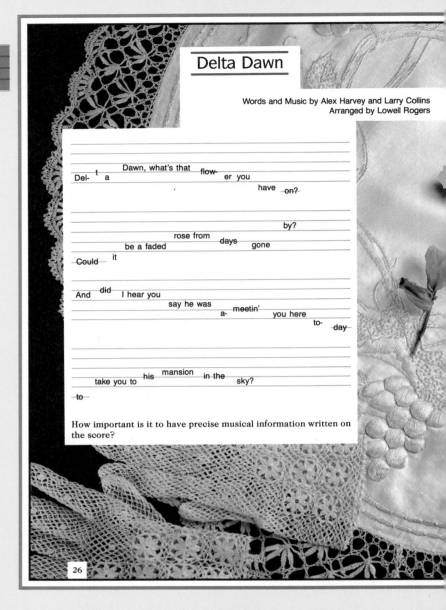

Delta Dawn

Words and Music by Alex Harvey and Larry Collins
Arranged by Lowell Rogers

Del- t a Dawn, what's that flow- er you
have on?

by?
rose from
be a faded days gone
Could it

And did I hear you
say he was a- meetin' you here
to- day

take you to his mansion in the sky?
to

How important is it to have precise musical information written on the score?

26

TRADITIONS 11

Lesson Focus

Harmony: Chords and melody may move simultaneously in relation to each other. *(P–I)*

Materials

o **Piano Accompaniment:** page 254
o **Record Information:**
  • Delta Dawn (unison version)
    Record 2 Side A Band 3a
    Voices: mixed chorus
    Accompaniment: electric bass, piano, electric guitar, percussion
  • **Band 3b:** vocal harmony version
    Voices: mixed chorus
    Accompaniment: electric bass, piano, electric guitar, percussion
o **Instruments:** piano, autoharp, or guitar

The Lesson

1. Play the version of "Delta Dawn" performed in unison (Band 3a). Ask the students to follow the visual description of the melody on page 26 as they listen. Replay the recording several times until the students can sing the melody. (Some students may have a slight problem with range; reassure them that they may drop out when the range becomes too high or too low.) Keep track of the number of repetitions required to learn the song. **Did the visual representation speed up the learning process?**

2. Play the recorded vocal harmony version of "Delta Dawn" (Band 3b). Choose Treble I's and II's and Baritones who have the extended range C to D' to sing the melody. Various assignments can be made for the harmony parts. Here is one possible arrangement:

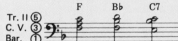

3. Help each group realize that their part has only two or three pitches. They must simply move stepwise up or down to the nearest chord tone as indicated by the line that traces their part. Help the students hear the chord changes by accompanying their singing on guitar, piano, or autoharp. After the harmonizing sections have mastered their parts, add the melody.

4. Invite the students to perform "Down in the Valley," using this same style of vocal harmonization. Treble I's sing the melody while other parts provide the vocal harmony:

26

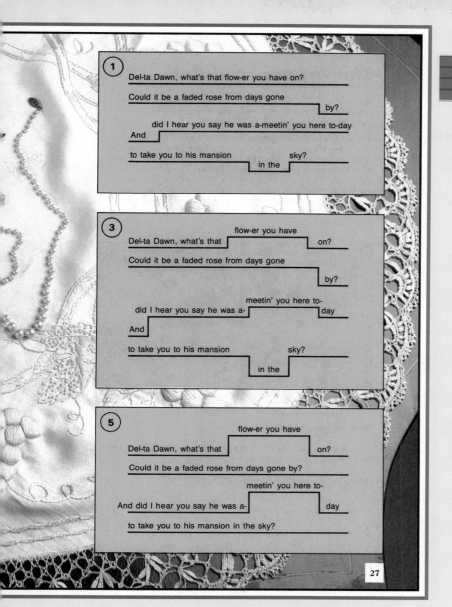

1

Del-ta Dawn, what's that flow-er you have on?

Could it be a faded rose from days gone by?

And did I hear you say he was a-meetin' you here to-day

to take you to his mansion in the sky?

3

Del-ta Dawn, what's that flow-er you have on?

Could it be a faded rose from days gone by?

And did I hear you say he was a-meetin' you here to-day

to take you to his mansion in the sky?

5

Del-ta Dawn, what's that flow-er you have on?

Could it be a faded rose from days gone by?

And did I hear you say he was a-meetin' you here to-day

to take you to his mansion in the sky?

27

Lesson Focus

Time and Place: A particular use of rhythm and melody reflects the origin of the musical whole. *(D–S)*

Materials

o **Teacher's Resource Binder:**
  • Optional —
    Enrichment Activity 12, page E5

The Written Tradition

The oral tradition began with the origin of music. This tradition continues today as an important way of sharing songs and passing them on from one generation to the next.

The written tradition began as musicians realized that they needed a way of representing musical sounds so that a great number of songs could be learned quickly. The earliest notation devised would not have helped you learn a new song. It would, however, have helped you recall a song you already knew. This early notation consisted mostly of signs that stood for individual sounds and groups of sounds. These signs did not represent an exact pitch, nor did they indicate the relative length of individual sounds. The signs for notes were called *neumes*.

Music Notation: 800 A.D. to the Present

Here is a familiar song as it might have looked had it been written about 800 A.D. Can you recognize it?

A hundred years later it might have looked like this.

28

The Lesson

1. Ask the students to read the first half of page 28 silently. Challenge them to follow the neumes and guess the song. ("Are You Sleeping?") Do not identify the song at this point if the students do not guess it. They will have repeated opportunities to determine the name of the song as the lesson proceeds.

2. Comment that more information is probably needed to accurately perform from these written symbols. The performers of a thousand years ago came to the same conclusion and looked for more precise ways to notate musical ideas. Draw the students attention to the progression of notation illustrated on pages 28 and 29. Have them look at the second example on page 28. **What added information is provided?** (lines and letter names) Around the ninth century, lines were added

(as shown at the bottom of page 28) to give more precise pitch information.

3. As the students look at the third example (top of page 29), draw their attention to the additional changes. The symbols were now written on a four-line staff with a clef sign to indicate the beginning pitch. The notes that are hooked together are not to be sung at the same time (as in our present-day system). The connection, in this example, indicates a two-note pattern rising one step. Explain that the shape of the note, along with its stem (if it had one) and the way it was grouped with other notes, provided information about its duration.

4. The fourth example shows what happened within two hundred years. Fewer notes (none in this example) were hooked together. The

The beginning of the same song would have been written like this in the thirteenth century.

In the fourteenth century, you might have been expected to read this.

By the sixteenth century, the same melody probably looked something like this.

Here is the first part of the melody written in the notation system used today. What information is given in this system that you found hard to determine in other examples?

In the nineteenth century, singers in the United States sometimes learned songs from shape notation.

29

For Your Information

The information provided in this lesson is related to the development of notation in western Europe. To help the students put this survey into historical perspective, you may wish to assign research projects on life during the various periods discussed.

different shapes gave precise information as to how the notes related to one another rhythmically.

5. The fifth example shows how the melody would have looked in the sixteenth century. Duration was affected by the stems in about the same way it is in our present-day system. "White note" notation became prevalent.

6. The sixth example shows the same tune in the notation we use today. Notation had developed to its present form by the end of the sixteenth century.

7. The final example shows a special system of notation that developed in this country in the early nineteenth century. Many types of shape-note notation evolved during this period. The type of notation shown here was very popular in rural areas of the South. The

pitches of the notes are indicated by their shape as well as by their position on the staff. Rhythmic notation was similar to that of our present-day system.

8. Encourage the students to compare the notation of today with that of the thirteenth, fifteenth, and sixteenth centuries. Conclude that though we have come a long way in notating music, notation is still changing. There is continued experimentation in notating the unique sounds of today's music.

TRADITIONS 13

Lesson Focus

Form: A musical whole may be made up of same, varied, or contrasting segments. *(D–S)*

Materials

o **Piano Accompaniment:** page 258

o **Record Information:**
  • Fiddler on the Roof
    (Record 1 Side B Band 3)

o **Instruments:** bass xylophone (F#, G, B, and C); resonator bells (D, E, F#, B, and C); glockenspiels (B, C, and E) with mallets; tambourines

Fiddler on the Roof

Words and Music by Jerry Bock
and Sheldon Harnick

You have seen that the written tradition is a more accurate way of transmitting music than the oral tradition. There are many clues in the score that easily communicate how the melody will sound. What do you see that would help you share this song with someone else?

Are any parts of the music the same?

How are the melodies for the verse and the refrain different?

Are the chords for the verse and refrain the same or different?

Listen to the recording. How accurate are your findings?

The Lesson

1. Ask the students to open their books to page 30 and again sing "Fiddler on the Roof." Remind the students that they first heard this song when they were challenged to identify certain words in the lyrics.

2. Use the introductory comments on page 30 as a point of departure for comparison of the merits of written and oral traditions. After the discussion challenge the students to scan the notation for "Fiddler on the Roof" and discern which musical ideas are the same and which are different. The students will find that several patterns are repeated. (The pattern in the first two measures is found six times.) Phrases 1 and 2 are repeated twice in their entirety. During the refrain, patterns are frequently repeated at different pitch levels. Help the students recognize that the harmony in the verse and in the refrain is the same. Because of this, the chord symbols are not repeated for the refrain. Listen to the recording to check their findings.

3. Experiment singing this song in two different ways: (1) Treble Voices: verse; Changing Voices and Baritones: refrain (2) Verse and refrain as partner songs.

4. Use the bass xylophone, resonator bells, glockenspiels, and tambourine to add the accompaniment. Teach the instrumental parts to several individuals in the class. Sing the song with the accompaniment.

5. Provide opportunities for others to play the instruments. A student who has learned a specific part is responsible for teaching it to the next student. Repeat this process several times to enable more students to play.

OPTIONAL

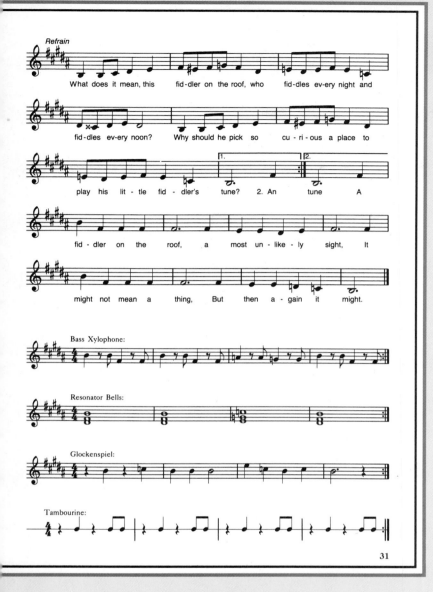

Refrain

What does it mean, this fid-dler on the roof, who fid-dles ev-ery night and

fid-dles ev-ery noon? Why should he pick so cu-ri-ous a place to

1.
play his lit-tle fid-dler's tune? 2. An tune A

2.

fid-dler on the roof, a most un-like-ly sight, It

might not mean a thing, But then a-gain it might.

Bass Xylophone:

Resonator Bells:

Glockenspiel:

Tambourine:

31

For Your Information

Many of your students may have been using the written tradition throughout their school music experience. Traditions 13 through 18 are designed to increase the students' awareness of the value of reading music and to reaffirm that the written score is an important tool for musical independence. When the student can rely on the written page, he or she does not need to rely on others to learn unfamiliar music.

6. Provide an opportunity for volunteers to create a circle or line dance to perform with this music. Use steps such as a traditional grapevine, side-steps, and hops. The dance should reflect the form of the music:

A A B B A A B B A

Perform the dance with the recording or while the other members of the class sing and play the accompaniment.

Lesson Focus

Rhythm: A series of beats may be organized into regular or irregular groupings by stressing certain beats.
Melody: Each pitch within a melody moves in relation to a home tone. **(D–S)**

Materials

o **Piano Accompaniment:** page 257
o **Record Information:**
   • You Just Can't Make It by Yourself
   Record 2 Side A Band 4
   Voices: mixed chorus
   Accompaniment: acoustic guitar, piano, electric bass, percussion
o **Instruments:** various unpitched percussion instruments with appropriate beaters or mallets
o **Other:** pencils
o **Teacher's Resource Binder:**

   [Activity Sheets] • **Activity Sheet 10,** page A15
   • Optional—
      Mainstreaming Activity 5, page M10

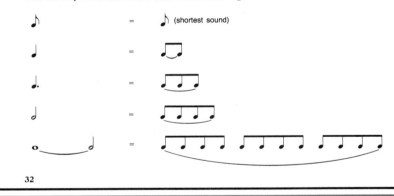

Learn to Read Rhythm

Learn the rhythm of this song by adding short sounds together. Follow the musical "plus" sign: ⌒

Tap all the short sounds while you chant the words in rhythm. Can you decide how long each word should last?

No, — you — just_____ can't _____ make it_____ by — your-

Fine

self._____

Fa - ther, — moth-er,_____ sis - ter, _____ broth-er, _____ you know you're

D.C. al Fine

go - in' to _____ need _____ each _____ oth - er.

Compare the rhythmic notation of the song, as written on page 33, with the way the short sounds have been added together.

♪ = ♪ (shortest sound)

32

The Lesson

1. Have the class open their books to page 32. Read the discussion with the students. Help the students realize that when the "musical plus sign" (the tie) appears, they must sustain that word for the number of short sounds that are added (tied) together. Establish a quick tempo by tapping a series of short sounds; ask the students to say the words as they continue to tap short sounds. Discuss the chart at the bottom of pupil page 32. Use the following terminology:

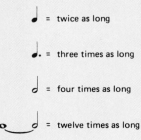

♩ = twice as long

♩. = three times as long

𝅗𝅥 = four times as long

𝅝⌒𝅗𝅥 = twelve times as long

2. Explore the melodic ideas presented on page 33. Students will discover that the song's melody mostly uses scale steps 1, 3, or 5. Ask them to practice singing these pitches. **When will you sing other pitches?** (second and fifth notes of Phrase 2, first beat of last measure) Draw attention to the natural sign preceding the G in the last measure. Explain that while this is the third step of the scale, it will now be lowered. Play and sing B, G♯, E (5 3 1); then B, G, E.

3. So that the students may sing in their own range, perform the song as a dialogue as indicated in the pupil book. The Baritone part will be:

Fine

D. C. al Fine

Learn to Read Melody

Where do you find patterns using these pitches?

You Just Can't Make It by Yourself

Words and Music by Barbara Dane

Tr. II

No, you just can't make it by your - self. _____

Tr. I,II
C.V.

No, you just can't make it by your - self. _____

Tr. I,II

Fa - ther, moth - er, sis - ter, broth - er, you know you're

go - in' to need each oth - er.

Baritones may add a bass part by singing the root of the chords shown above the melodic notation.

33

For Your Information
The additive approach to rhythmic reading is based on recognizing that the concept of addition is easier to grasp than the concept of division. (See page xxvi, for additional information.)

4. Provide additional practice for the students to recognize and relate to the tonal center. Play a game to help them become skilled in singing in relation to a tonal center and to improve their tonal memory.

   • Establish a tonal center and play the scale upon which it is based.
   • Play or sing a pattern using any pitch in the scale except the tonal center.
   • Upon a signal, the class (or an individual) must sing the tonal center.

5. Extend the lesson by giving each student Activity Sheet 10 (*Tying Notes Together*) and a pencil. Each student is to devise an interesting rhythm by tying notes together. Have students trade with other students. Each performs the other's rhythm on a percussion instrument, then writes the tied rhythm in traditional notation. Several of the rhythm patterns may be combined to create a percussion ensemble.

OPTIONAL

Lesson Focus

Melody: Each pitch within a melody moves in relation to a home tone.
Rhythm: Individual sounds and silences within a rhythmic line may be longer than, shorter than, or the same as the underlying shortest pulse. *(D–I)*

Materials

o **Piano Accompaniment:** page 260
o **Record Information:**
  • Bamboo
  Record 2 Side A Band 5
  Voices: mixed chorus, soloists
  Accompaniment: tin whistle, steel drums, electric organ, electric bass, percussion
o **Instruments:** maracas; bongos; conga drum; claves; piano
o **Other:** adhesive tape in two different colors
o **Teacher's Resource Binder:**

Activity Sheets
  • **Activity Sheet 11,** page A16
  • Optional—
  Mainstreaming Activity 6, page M14

Bamboo

Words and Music by David Van Ronk

Figure out the rhythm of the melody.

• Start with the shortest sound.
• Determine the length of the other notes by adding short sounds together.

Figure out the melody.

• Start with the tonal center: 1
• Sing pitches of the I chord: 1–3–5
• Determine the sound of other pitches in relation to these chordal pitches.

1. You take a stick of bam-boo, you take a stick of bam-boo,
2. trav-el on the riv-er, you trav-el on the riv-er,
3. home's a-cross the riv-er, my home's a-cross the riv-er,

You take a stick of bam-boo, you throw it in the wa-ter.
You trav-el on the riv-er, you trav-el on the wa-ter.
My home's a-cross the riv-er, my home's a-cross the wa-ter.

Oh ___ Oh ___ Han-nah!

34

The Lesson

1. Invite the students to look at the song "Bamboo" on page 34. Tap the shortest sound while chanting the rhythm of the verse. Engage the students in an activity to help them grasp how notes of different lengths relate to the shortest sound. Distribute copies of Activity Sheet 11 *(Notate Rhythm).* Explain that the students are to show the rhythm of the verse they just tapped. To do this they are to use the "musical plus sign" to add short notes together to show the length of tones longer than the shortest sound. Proceed phrase by phrase. Chant each phrase while tapping the shortest sound; then give students time to put the musical plus signs in place.

2. Next, invite the students to figure out the melody by following the instructions on pupil page 34. Practice singing the two patterns shown in the tune-up and help the students realize that the entire melody is based on the tones of these two chords.

3. After practicing the two patterns, challenge the students to sing this song using the information they have just acquired. Help them by playing the chords on the piano.

4. After the students have learned the song, play the recording. Instruct the students to listen to the accompaniment. The rhythm of the accompaniment gives this music a calypso style.

5. Show the students how to add their own accompaniment. Ask one student to play the two chords found in the song on the piano. If the performer is unfamiliar with the piano, mark the keys to be played with two colors of tape: one color for the F chord (F A C) and a

You take a stick of bam-boo, you take a stick of bam-boo,
You trav-el on the riv-er, you trav-el on the riv-er,
My home's a-cross the riv-er, my home's a-cross the riv-er,

You take a stick of bam-boo, you throw it in the wa-ter.
You trav-el on the riv-er, you trav-el on the wa-ter.
My home's a-cross the riv-er, my home's a-cross the wa-ter.

Oh _____ Oh _____ Han - nah!

Riv - er _____ she come down. _____

Riv - er _____ she come down. _____ 2. You down. _____
3. My

You take a stick of bam-boo, you take a stick of bam-boo,

You take a stick of bam-boo, you throw it in the wa - ter. _____

When you have learned the rhythm and the melody, listen to the ar-rangement on the recording. What do you notice about the harmony?

35

second color for the Eb Chord (Eb G Bb). The keyboard novice then uses the color clues to play the correct pitches. Establish the ca-lypso rhythm to be played by chanting and clapping.

throw it in____ the wa - ter

Ask the students to think the words while they clap the rhythmic pattern. **Now play the rhythm on the piano, alternating the chords each time you repeat the pattern.** The chord sequence for the verse is: F Eb F Eb F Eb F F; the refrain: F Eb F F F Eb F F.

6. Distribute Latin rhythm instruments. Ask some of the students to create their own rhythmic accompaniment while others sing the song.

throw it in____ the wa - ter

TRADITIONS 16

Lesson Focus

Expression: The expressiveness of music is affected by the way rhythm and melody contribute to the musical whole. **(D–S)**

Materials

o **Piano Accompaniment:** page 263
o **Record Information:**
  • Brethren in Peace Together
  Record 2 Side A Band 6
  Voices: mixed chorus
  Accompaniment: clarinet, trumpet, violin, accordion, double bass
o **Instruments:** autoharp, guitar, or piano; bass xylophone with mallets
o **Teacher's Resource Binder:**
  • Optional—
  Kodaly Activity 5, page K8
  Mainstreaming Activity 7, page M14
  Orff Activity 4, page O7

Sounds Exist in Time

We sense the passing of time by the ticking of the clock. We sense the passing of musical time by the movement of musical sounds.

Listen to the music. Count the passage of time. Look at written music for information about counting musical time.

The meter signature gives one way to count:

  • Look at the upper number.
    It tells you to count in groups.

  • Look at the lower number.
    It identifies the note that lasts for one count.

Look beyond the meter signature for other information:
Bar lines group notes into measures.

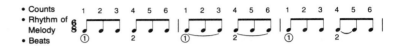

Within each measure, notes may again be grouped to show their relation to the underlying beat.

Brethren in Peace Together

Paraphrase of Psalm 133:1   Jewish Folk Song

36

The Lesson

1. Have the class open their books to page 36 and discuss the first paragraph. Play the recording of "Brethren in Peace Together." Compare the ways different students counted the beats. Some may have counted in groups of two, others in groups of six, or some may have counted continuously throughout the recording. Any method is right. Discuss reasons for the differences. Those counting in twos were sensing the groupings of the underlying beat; those counting in sixes were sensing groupings of the shortest sound.

2. **Which way of counting does the meter signature represent?** (Answers will vary.) Tell the students to study the diagram of counts and beats. Discuss the fact that a meter signature may sometimes direct you to count in groups that are the same as the shortest unit

of sound (as the $\frac{6}{8}$ does in this instance). At other times, the meter signature may direct you to count in groups that are the same as the beat. In $\frac{6}{8}$ meter, counts and beats are frequently different. **We often feel the music in groups of two beats. Why not use a meter signature for "Brethren in Peace Together" that directs us to count with the beat?** Show how the pattern would look in $\frac{2}{4}$ meter:

Agree that the constant triplet sign becomes confusing. It is easier to read the melodic rhythm when written in $\frac{6}{8}$ meter.

3. Continue discovering musical information about this song by discussing the information on pupil page 37. The students may show the melodic movement by drawing the contour

36

Sounds Exist in Space

We sense the rhythmic movement of music through time. We sense its melodic movement through space. Listen to "Brethren in Peace Together."

Draw its melodic movement.

We use numbers to measure rhythmic time. We also use numbers to measure the distance of pitches from the tonal center. In written music the placement of notes on a staff helps us measure the distance between pitches.

To begin measuring melodic movement, first locate the tonal center. Look at the key signature and beyond to the melody. Determine the pitches around which the melody moves.

A song with this key signature might center around these pitches: or   these pitches:

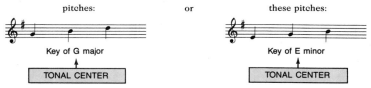

Key of G major — TONAL CENTER   Key of E minor — TONAL CENTER

Look at "Brethren in Peace Together." Which pitch is the tonal center?

Practice singing each pitch in the E minor scale as shown below.

1 — 2   1 — 3   1 — 4   1 — 5   1 — 6   1 — 7   1 — 1'

Add a drone accompaniment on a bass instrument:

B
E

37

---

on paper, or they may simply follow the contour shown in their books.

4. Play and sing the G major and E minor 1–3–5 tonal patterns. Discuss the differences in sound quality. Examine the notation of the song and determine that the melody centers around E, G, and B at the beginning and end of phrases. It is, therefore, in E minor. Practice the scale pattern and determine the pitches used in the song. Sing with scale numbers, then with words.

5. Extend the lesson by examining other songs. Write and sing 1–3–5 for the key of the selected song in both major and relative minor. Guide the students to examine the notation and determine the set of pitches around which the melody seems to move (for example, "Lonesome Traveler": major—FAC; minor—DFA).

OPTIONAL

Test out the chord the students select. Give the beginning pitch; then ask the students to sing the song. End by playing the chosen chord on autoharp, guitar, or piano. **Does the sound of the chord seem to fit with the central pitches of the melody?**

Lesson Focus

Rhythm: Music may move in relation to the underlying steady beat.
Melody: Each pitch within a melody moves in relation to a home tone. **(D–S)**

Materials

o **Piano Accompaniment:** page 264
o **Record Information**
  • Goin' Down to Town
    Record 2 Side A Band 7
    Voice: male soloist
    Accompaniment: bass harmonica, banjo, double bass, percussion
o **Instruments:** skiffle band instruments (see page 128); guitar or autoharp
o **Teacher's Resource Binder:**
  • Optional—
    Kodaly Activity 7, page K11

Look at the meter signature of this song. How will the rhythm be counted? In this song, are beats and counts the same or different?

We could change the meter signature and count this rhythm in a different way. What has changed? What remains the same?

Use one of these ways of counting to learn the rhythm of the melody.

1. I used to have an old gray horse; He weighed ten thou - sand pounds.
2. That horse he had a hol - ler tooth; He could eat ten bush-els of corn.

Ev - ery tooth in his head was eigh - teen in - ches a - round.
Ev - ery time he o-pened his mouth, Two bush-els and a half were gone.

Refrain
I'm go - in' down to town; I'm go - in' down to town; I'm

go - in' down to Lynch-burg town, To car - ry my to - bac - co down.

38

The Lesson

1. To help the students answer the questions at the top of page 38, draw attention to the first diagram. Agree that in this case, beats and counts are the same. **How does the rhythm of the melody move in relation to the beat?** (shorter; usually in a relationship of 2 to 1— two short sounds to one beat) Before practicing the rhythm, draw attention to the next discussion and its diagram. **Has the rhythm of the melody changed?** (no) **Has the beat grouping changed?** (no) **Has the method of counting changed?** (Yes, we are now counting in relation to the shortest unit of sound— the eighth note—instead of the beat—the quarter note.)

2. Count and clap the rhythmic patterns shown in the two diagrams. Ask the students if it is easier to count beats or the shortest unit of sound. (There is no right answer.) Since the

rhythm of the melody moves most consistently with the shortest unit of sound, counting in fours may be easier. Stress the fact that even though they are counting in fours, the beat remains in two. If students have problems with the dotted eighth-sixteenth pattern, practice using the sixteenth note as the shortest sound. **What is the relationship of the dotted eighth note to the sixteenth note?** (three times as long). Suggest that the students lightly tap the sixteenth notes while chanting the dotted pattern on "doo." Then return to tapping eighth notes. **Can you still sense the uneven pattern when it occurs?**

3. Compare the melodies of "Brethren in Peace Together" and "Goin' Down to Town." In "Goin' Down to Town," the pitches at the beginning and end of sections use G, D, and B, as do the important skips. This is in contrast to "Brethren in Peace Together," where the

38

"Goin' Down to Town" has the same key signature as "Brethren in Peace Together."

Review the discussion on page 36; then look at the notation of "Goin' Down to Town." What is its tonal center?

Prepare for reading the melody of the song. Practice singing pitches of the G major scale in relation to the tonal center.

Improvise a skiffle band accompaniment for this song.

Learn to play these instruments by turning to page 128.

39

For Your Information
Changing Voices and Baritones should read this song from the treble clef, sounding an octave lower than the notated pitch.

important pitches are E, G, and B. Therefore, the song is in G major.

4. The students may wish to add skiffle-band sounds to this American folk song. Provide independent study time for the students to work on the instrument of their choice. Refer individuals to the skiffle-band unit on page 117 for ideas on the use of these folk instruments.

Lesson Focus

Rhythm: A series of beats may be organized into regular or irregular groupings by stressing certain beats. *(D–S)*

Materials

o **Record Information:**
- *Gymnopédie No. 3*
  by Erik Satie (sah–**tee**), 1866–1925
  Record 2 Side A Band 8
  Utah Symphony Orchestra
  Maurice Abravanel, Conductor
- Waltz from *Les Patineurs*
  by Giacomo Meyerbeer (**mie**–er–beer),
  1791–1864
  Record 2 Side A Band 9
  Cincinnati Pops Orchestra
  Erich Kunzel, Conductor
- Wedding March
  from *A Midsummer Night's Dream*
  by Felix Mendelssohn (**men**–duhl–son),
  1809–1847
  Record 3 Side A Band 1
  Philharmonic Orchestra
  Otto Klemperer, Conductor

o **Other:** overhead projector

o **Teacher's Resource Binder:**

| Activity Sheets | • **Activity Sheet 12**, page A17 (Prepare as a transparency.) |

(continued on next page)

Interpreting Notation

Erik Satie (1866–1925), a French composer known for his dry sense of humor, influenced many other composers of his time. Giacomo Meyerbeer (1791–1864) was one of the most popular opera composers of the 19th century. Listen to *"Gymnopédie No. 3"* by Satie and "Waltz" from *Les Patineurs* by Meyerbeer.

- How do you sense the rhythmic movement of each example?
- Count softly to yourself as you listen to each piece of music.
- Call each heavy beat "1."

Which of these patterns matches the way you counted the rhythmic movement?

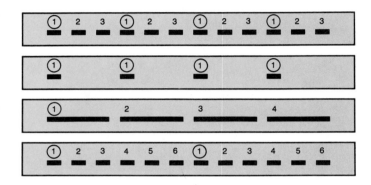

You may have counted the two musical examples in different ways because of differences in the performance style of the two compositions. Elements that affect ways of counting are

- **tempo**
- **the nature of the accompaniment**
- **the rhythm of the melody**
- **the relationship between heavy and light beats**

40

The Lesson

1. Examine the rhythm ikons shown on page 40. Help the students understand that the meter signature may not always tell us all we need to know about how to count, feel, or play a piece of music. Illustrate this by having them count in the four different ways shown, as they tap the patterns. (Be sure to keep the shortest sound moving at the same tempo as each of the patterns is counted.)

2. Listen to *Gymnopédie No. 3* by Erik Satie. Have the students try each of the four patterns to determine which one best fits the music. (Because of the slow tempo, melodic rhythm, and accompaniment, most students will probably count this in threes—Pattern 1.)

3. Repeat the process as the students listen to "Waltz" from *Les Patineurs* by Giacomo Meyerbeer. (This time, because of the faster tempo, melodic rhythm, accompaniment, and overall style, students may count in fours or ones, sensing the rhythm of the phrase rather than the individual measures.)

4. Compare the two scores on page 41. Help the students determine that the **meter signatures** are the same but that the performer needs to look beyond the meter signature to accurately interpret the music.

5. Show students the transparency of Activity Sheet 12 (*A Midsummer Night's Dream*). Listen to the "Wedding March." Have the students count softly to themselves as they listen. **Which of the patterns shown on the transparency best fits the music.** Discuss the students' answers. Some may have counted the music in twos while other's may have counted in sets of four. The tempo, melody, accompaniment, and style may cause most students to feel the music in twos.

Gymnopédie No. 3 (excerpt)
by Erik Satie

Waltz
from *Les Patineurs* (excerpt)
by Giacomo Meyerbeer

Notice that the scores above have the same meter signatures. The players must look beyond the meter signatures to perform them correctly.

41

Materials *(continued)*
- Optional—
- Evaluation • **Checkpoint 1**, page Ev2
  Biography 1, page B1
  Enrichment Activity 3, page E5
  Kodaly Activity 6, page K8
  Mainstreaming Activity 8, page M15

For Your Information
Originally written for the piano, the form of *Gymnopédie No. 3* reflects the tendency of Satie to write with great economy. The piece utilizes two melodies that, because of their modal sounds, are reminiscent of a ceremonial dance.

The simple structure of this composition lends itself to different treatments. This recording features an orchestration by Debussy. The "Waltz" from *Les Patineurs* is composed in the form of a rondo. The main theme is shown on page 41. Although the "Waltz" is in a fast, jaunty three, the ending changes to a driving four as the piece builds to a rousing climax. The structure of the piece is: **A B A C A′ D A D′ A Coda**

"Wedding March" by Felix Mendelssohn is played at a very fast tempo. It contains three main sections (**A, B,** and **C**), a development section (**D**), and a coda. The structure of the composition is as follows: **A B A C C′ A D B Coda**

Lesson Focus

Rhythm: A series of beats may be organized into regular or irregular groupings by stressing certain beats. *(P–S)*

Materials

○ **Piano Accompaniment:** page 265

○ **Record Information:**
   • Sixty-Six Highway Blues
      Record 3 Side A Band 2
      Voice: male soloist
      Accompaniment: baritone saxophone, acoustic guitar, electric guitar, electric organ, electric bass, percussion

○ **Instruments:** bass xylophone with C, E, and B♭ bars and mallet, or double bass or guitar tuned to F, B♭, and C (If using bass: tune fourth string to F, third string to B♭, and second string to C. If using guitar: tune sixth string to F, fifth string to B♭, and fourth string to C. Play only on these strings.)

More Help From the Meter Signature

Perform the following three rhythms. Apply the information supplied by the meter signature.

The upper number helps you know
   • how to count the rhythmic movement of a song.

The lower number helps you determine
   • the note that lasts one count;
   • the relationship of other notes to one beat.

In what ways does the notation for these three patterns look the same? different? Did the rhythms sound the same? different? Why?

Sixty-Six Highway Blues

Words and Music by Pete Seeger, Woody Guthrie, and Jerry Silverman

There is a road from the coast to the coast,

New York to Los An‐gel‐es. _____

42

The Lesson

1. Review the function of the meter signature by focusing the students' attention to the top of page 42.

2. Ask the students to examine the three different rhythm patterns shown. **In what ways does the notation for these three patterns look the same?** (Each one has the same relationship of long and short sounds within the pattern.)

   Have the students perform each pattern by lightly tapping it on their books or desk tops. **Did the rhythms sound the same? different? Why?** (They should all sound the same since the lower number is all that is different. Only the symbol for the beat changes; the relationship of the sounds in the pattern to the beat is the same in each of the three patterns.)

3. Learn to sing "Sixty-Six Highway Blues" by reading the treble clef notation. (Baritones will need to sing an octave lower.)

4. When the song is learned well enough for the students to sing it independently, add the pattern found at the bottom of page 43. Pluck the notes of the bass part on the guitar or double bass or play it on a bass xylophone using a soft (yarn-covered) mallet. Choose as many different students as possible to play the pattern. Each line of notation is written in both treble and bass clefs. Encourage the students to read the pattern in both treble and bass clef.

5. Sing with the recording, adding the pattern on bass, guitar, or bass xylophone.

OPTIONAL

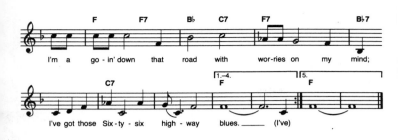

I'm a go - in' down that road with wor - ries on my mind;

I've got those Six - ty - six high - way blues. _____ (I've)

2. I've been to the East and I've been to the West . . . .

3. I've been lookin' for the woman that'd love me the best . . . .

4. Been tryin' to make an honest dollar a day . . . .

5. I ain't got no home in this world anymore . . . .

Add this pattern to your song. Can you read it from both treble and bass clef notation?

Lesson Focus

Rhythm: A series of beats may be organized into regular or irregular groupings by stressing certain beats. **(P–S)**

Materials

o **Piano Accompaniment:** page 266

o **Record Information:**
   • America from *West Side Story*
     Record 3 Side A Band 3
     Voices: male soloist, female soloist
     Accompaniment: small show orchestra

o **Instruments:** maracas; drums; an assortment of South American instruments with appropriate beaters or mallets

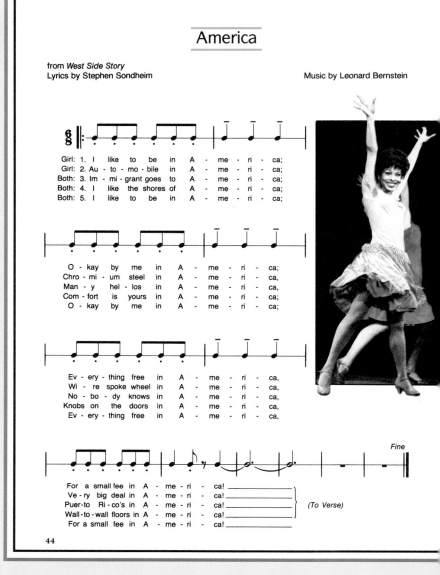

America

from *West Side Story*
Lyrics by Stephen Sondheim

Music by Leonard Bernstein

Girl: 1. I like to be in A - me - ri - ca;
Girl: 2. Au - to - mo - bile in A - me - ri - ca;
Both: 3. Im - mi - grant goes to A - me - ri - ca;
Both: 4. I like the shores of A - me - ri - ca;
Both: 5. I like to be in A - me - ri - ca;

O - kay by me in A - me - ri - ca;
Chro - mi - um steel in A - me - ri - ca;
Man - y hel - los in A - me - ri - ca,
Com - fort is yours in A - me - ri - ca;
O - kay by me in A - me - ri - ca;

Ev - ery - thing free in A - me - ri - ca,
Wi - re spoke wheel in A - me - ri - ca,
No - bo - dy knows in A - me - ri - ca,
Knobs on the doors in A - me - ri - ca,
Ev - ery - thing free in A - me - ri - ca,

Fine

For a small fee in A - me - ri - ca!
Ve - ry big deal in A - me - ri - ca!
Puer - to Ri - co's in A - me - ri - ca!
Wall - to - wall floors in A - me - ri - ca!
For a small fee in A - me - ri - ca!

(To Verse)

44

The Lesson

1. As the students listen to the recording of "America," have them tap the first maraca pattern (page 45) on their knees. **Does it fit throughout the whole song?** (No, the accents do not always seem to fall in the right places.) **Listen a second time and tap the second pattern. Does it fit throughout the song?** (No, the accents do not always fall in the right places with this pattern either.) Lead the students to discover that a combination of the two patterns will fit. (The first pattern will fit the measures of the song that contain six eighth notes. The second pattern will fit all other measures.)

2. Challenge the students to play both the maraca and drum rhythms on their knees. (The maraca part should be played with right hand on right knee and the drum part with left hand on left knee.) Practice Pattern 1 first,

then Pattern 2. When the students appear to be comfortable with the two-handed playing, choose two students to play maracas and drums while the rest of the class continues to play the patterns on their knees to accompany the recording.

3. Help all the students learn to accurately clap the rhythm of the words for Verse 1 while carefully observing each accent and rest shown on the pupil pages.

4. Have the two students chosen in Step 2 add the drum and maraca patterns to the clapping to create a three-part percussion piece.

5. **OPTIONAL** Invite the students to choose three different Latin-American instruments with which each of the three parts could be appropriately played. Add these percussion parts to the recording while the class listens again.

Verse

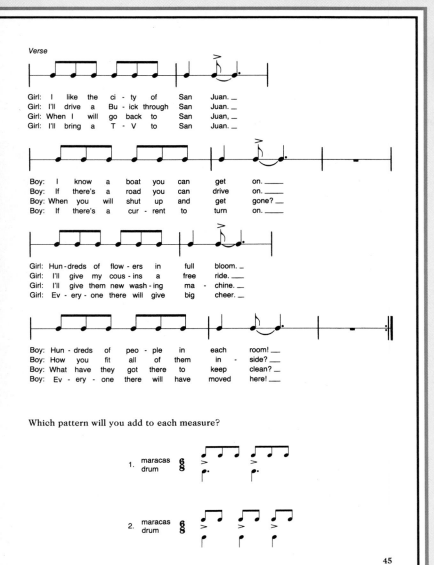

Girl: I like the ci - ty of San Juan. __
Girl: I'll drive a Bu - ick through San Juan. __
Girl: When I will go back to San Juan, __
Girl: I'll bring a T - V to San Juan. __

Boy: I know a boat you can get on. ____
Boy: If there's a road you can drive on. ____
Boy: When you will shut up and get gone? ____
Boy: If there's a cur - rent to turn on. ____

Girl: Hun - dreds of flow - ers in full bloom. __
Girl: I'll give my cous - ins a free ride. ____
Girl: I'll give them new wash - ing ma - chine. __
Girl: Ev - ery - one there will give big cheer. ____

Boy: Hun - dreds of peo - ple in each room! __
Boy: How you fit all of them in - side? __
Boy: What have they got there to keep clean? __
Boy: Ev - ery - one there will have moved here! __

Which pattern will you add to each measure?

1. maracas
   drum

2. maracas
   drum

45

Lesson Focus

Melody: A series of pitches bounded by the octave "belong together," forming a tonal set. *(D–S)*

Materials

o **Piano Accompaniment:** page 268
o **Record Information:**
  • Jacob's Ladder
    Record 3 Side A Band 4a (D major)
    Band 4b: A♭ major
    Band 4c: E major
    Band 4d: C major
    Voices: mixed chorus
    Accompaniment: recorder, harp, celesta
o **Instruments:** keyboards or several sets of chromatic resonator bells with bell mallets
o **Teacher's Resource Binder:**

Activity Sheets | • **Activity Sheets 13a–c,** pages A18–A20

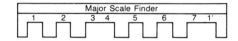

Read Melody in a Major Key

Music is easier to read and sing if you can sense the relationship of the pitches to the tonal center. To do this you need to know where the tonal center of the melody is placed on the staff so that you can determine the **scale** on which the song is based.

Look at page 47. Identify the tonal center and the scale on which each version of "Jacob's Ladder" is based. Follow these steps:

1. Locate the tonal center. This is usually the note around which the song seems to center. It is often the last note of the song.
2. Locate each pitch with a different letter name.
3. Starting with the tonal center, circle all the pitches you have located on a **Chromatic Scale Ruler.** Mark them in order from low to high.

		Chromatic	Scale	Ruler																	
C	C♯/D♭	D	D♯/E♭	E	F	F♯/G♭	G	G♯/A♭	A	A♯/B♭	B	C	C♯/D♭	D	D♯/E♭	E	F	F♯/G♭	G	G♯/A♭	A	A♯/B♭	B	C

4. Place a copy of the **Major Scale Finder** over your Chromatic Scale Ruler so that the tonal center appears below the numeral 1. All of the pitches you circled should appear in the cutouts.

Major Scale Finder							
1	2	3 4	5	6	7	1'	

5. Look at the key signature at the beginning of the song. Apply one of the following rules:

   Sharps—the last sharp to the right is the seventh step of the scale. Count down lines and spaces to locate l.
   Flats—the last flat to the right is the fourth step of the scale. Count down lines and spaces to locate l.

When you count down, you should end on the line or space with the letter name you identified as the tonal center in Step 1.
Learn the melody of "Jacob's Ladder" in the key that is best for your vocal range.

46

The Lesson

1. As the students look at the notated versions of "Jacob's Ladder" on page 47, help them sense the relationship of the pitches (in the melody) to each other. Follow the instructions on page 46, using the Chromatic Scale Ruler and Major Scale Finder to determine the tonal center and the scale for each example of "Jacob's Ladder." Guide students to read and follow the procedures as outlined on page 46. Make available several sets of reso-

nator bells or keyboard instruments for students to check the sound of the scales.

2. After establishing the key of each example, the students are to select the examples that best fit their vocal ranges:

   Key of A♭—Changing Voice
   Key of E—Baritone
   Key of C—Treble I or II
   Key of D—Treble I

   Ask each group to sing the song in the appropriate key.

3. Compare the four versions, discussing what is the same (melody, rhythm, words) and what is different about them (beginning pitches, scale, key signatures).

4. Encourage the students to work independently or in small groups, looking back

Voice	Tonal Center	Scale							
Changing Voice	A♭	A♭	B♭	C	D♭	E♭	F	G	A♭
Baritone	E	E	F♯	G♯	A	B	C♯	D♯	E
Treble II	C	C	D	E	F	G	A	B	C
Treble I	D	D	E	F♯	G	A	B	C♯	D

OPTIONAL

Jacob's Ladder

American Folk Song

Have you identified the tonal center and the major scale pitches for each version of this song by following the steps on page 46? Play the scales on resonator bells or xylophone. Do they sound right?

Compare the four versions of "Jacob's Ladder." What is the same? What is different?

We are climbing Jacob's ladder;
We are climbing Jacob's ladder;
We are climbing Jacob's ladder;
Brothers in our land.

47

For Your Information

The Chromatic Scale Ruler and Major Scale Finder should be reproduced from Activity Sheets 13a–c. Make rulers of oaktag and laminate them or wrap them in translucent plastic so that any marks made with felt-tipped pens can be wiped off. If the rulers are not permanently wrapped or laminated, simply make enough copies so that the students can use a new ruler for each song.

through songs they have previously learned such as "Know Where I'm Goin" (page 16) and "You Just Can't Make It by Yourself" (page 33). They are to use the Chromatic Scale Ruler and Major Scale Finder to determine the tonal center and scale used for each song.

Lesson Focus

Melody: A series of pitches bounded by the octave "belong together," forming a tonal set. *(D–S)*

Materials

○ **Piano Accompaniments:** pages 269, 270

○ **Record Information:**
 • Get Thy Bearings
 Record 3 Side A Band 5
 Voices: mixed chorus
 Accompaniment: 12-string guitar, electric piano, double bass, percussion
 • The Cruel War
 Record 3 Side A Band 6
 Voices: mixed voices
 Accompaniment: recorder, acoustic guitar, double bass, percussion

○ **Instruments:** chromatic resonator bells with bell mallets; keyboard instruments

○ **Other:** Chromatic Scale Rulers and Scale Finders prepared for Traditions 21 (pages 46–47, Activity Sheets 13a–c, pages A18–A20)

The Cruel War

Words and Music by Paul Stookey and Peter Yarrow

1. The cruel war is rag-ing, and John-ny has to
2. I'll go to your cap-tain, get down ____ on my
3. Ten thou-sand gold gui-neas, it grieves ____ my heart

fight; I want to be with him from morn-ing till night.
knees; Ten thou-sand gold gui-neas I'd give for your re-lease.
so; Won't you let me go with you? Oh, no, my love, no.

4. Tomorrow is Sunday, and Monday is the day
 Your captain calls for you, and you must obey.

5. Your captain calls for you, it grieves my heart so;
 Won't you let me go with you? — Oh, no, my love, no.

6. I'll pull back my hair, men's clothes I'll put on;
 I'll pass for your comrade as we march along.

7. I'll pass for your comrade, and none will ever guess;
 Won't you let me go with you? — Yes, my love, yes.

The melody of "The Cruel War" uses only five pitches and can be described as being based on a pentatonic scale. However, it can be accompanied using the pitches of the major scale. Add a vocal chording accompaniment to the song by following this chord sequence. Treble I's and Baritones may take turns singing the melody.

Tr. I
Tr. II

C.V.
Bar.

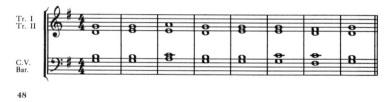

48

The Lesson

1. Introduce this new Scale Finder challenge by reminding the students that in the previous lesson (pages 46–47) they discovered that the song "Jacob's Ladder" could be written in many different keys but remain in the same major tonality. The new challenge will be to look at songs that have the same key signature but are in different tonalities. The students are to study the notation of the two songs in this lesson and determine the actual tonality of each song. They will need to use the Chromatic Scale Ruler and make choices from among the Scale Finders.

2. Have the students determine the scale used in "Get Thy Bearings" by following Steps 1 through 3 on page 46. When naming the pitches, remind them that they must add the appropriate sharp or flat sign after the letter name if a sharp or flat appears either in the key signature or directly before the note on the staff. Review the meaning of these two symbols: A sharp sign indicates that the pitch is to be raised a half step; a flat sign indicates that the pitch must be lowered a half step.

3. After Step 3 on page 46 is completed, the students must undertake one more challenge: **Place the Scale Finders, one at a time, over the Chromatic Scale Ruler until you find the scale that matches the pitches you circled.** The students will find that the scale of this song is Dorian: E F♯ G A B C♯ D E. The Dorian Scale Finder will have shown the circled pitches.

4. Guide the students to play the Dorian Scale on resonator bells or keyboard. Help them understand the effect of the scale on the melody by playing the song first in E major (change G, C, and D to G♯, C♯, and D♯), then

Read Melodies Based on Different Scales

in the Dorian Scale. Discuss the change in the character of the melody. Learn to sing the song as it is written on the page.

5. Repeat the process used to discover the key for "Get Thy Bearings" on "The Cruel War." The students will find this song is in G major pentatonic: G A B D E. Compare patterns of the circled pitches found in this pentatonic song with those of the major scale. Note the differences and similarities. Conclude that the reason it is identified as a different scale is because the whole-step/half-step sequence is altered. It is called pentatonic because only five different pitches are used.

6. After the students are familiar with the melody, introduce the vocal harmony shown on the bottom of page 48. Choose a few voices to sing the melody; others may sing chords as shown, in four parts. Examine the notation to determine which voices move and which remain stationary as each new chord is sung.

OPTIONAL

Lesson Focus

Melody: Each pitch within a melody moves in relation to a home tone.

Rhythm: A series of beats may be organized into regular or irregular groupings by stressing certain beats. *(P–S)*

Materials

o **Piano Accompaniment:** page 271

o **Record Information:**
  • *Gymnopédie No. 3*
    (Record 2 Side A Band 8)
  • Waltz from *Les Patineurs*
    (Record 2 Side A Band 9)
  • Wedding March
    (Record 3 Side A Band 1)
  • Oh Be Joyful from *Gaudeamus Hodie*
    Record 3 Side A Band 7
    Voices: mixed chorus
    Accompaniment: pipe organ

o **Teacher's Resource Binder:**
  • Optional—
    Enrichment Activity 4, page E8
    Instrumental Arrangement 4, page 19

Oh Be Joyful

from *Gaudeamus Hodie (Let Us Rejoice Today)*   Words and Music by Natalie Sleeth

To learn the rhythm of this song:

• Examine the meter signature and the notation for the Treble II part.
• Determine the note that moves with the beat.

• Decide how to count the rhythm. Will you count with the beats or with the shortest sound? Will you count in 2s, 4s, or 8s?

To learn the **syncopated** rhythm in Measures 2, 4, and 6 of the Treble II part, try counting in eights.

The tonal center of this song is C. Tune up with the C major scale:

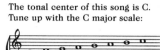

Learn your part by singing it with scale numbers. Measure each pitch in relation to its distance from the tonal center 1.

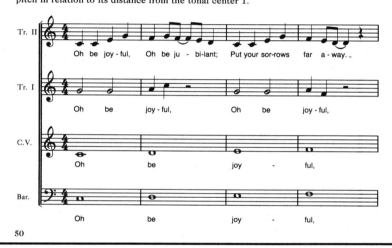

50

The Lesson

1. Listen again to the recorded examples included in Traditions 18, page 40. Review the reasons for sensing and counting rhythmic groupings in different ways even though the meter signature remains the same.

2. Ask the students to follow the instructions at the top of page 50 to learn the rhythm of "Oh Be Joyful." Agree that the song probably should be felt and counted in fours because the rhythm of the melody usually moves with the beat. However, it may be easier while learning it to count in eights until the students can easily perform the syncopated rhythms in Measures 2, 4, and 6. Syncopation in these measures results when the accent in the melodic rhythm occurs before the accent of the underlying beat.

3. After the rhythm has been carefully examined, follow the instructions on pupil page 50 to learn the melody. Establish the tonality; then challenge Treble I's and Treble II's to use scale numbers to sight-sing their parts, at the same time. When they can perform their parts readily, ask Changing Voices and Baritones to simultaneously sing *their* parts using scale numbers.

4. After the Changing Voices and Baritones have finished, ask them what they noticed about their two parts. (Both have the same melody and use the same scale numbers.) Read the discussion on page 51 and discuss

Tr. II	Come re - joice and sing to - geth - er this hap - py day.
Tr. I	Oh be joy - ful; Put your sor - rows a - way.
C.V.	Oh be joy - ful on this day.
Bar.	Oh be joy - ful on this day.

When learning your parts for this song, did you discover that the Changing-Voice and Baritone parts have the same melody? They do not look the same on the staff because . . .

one is written in the treble, or G clef

and the other is in the bass, or F clef

Both parts sing the same scale steps one octave (eight steps) apart. To determine letter names for the pitches of these two clefs, remember that the note between the clefs is middle C.

The Grand Staff

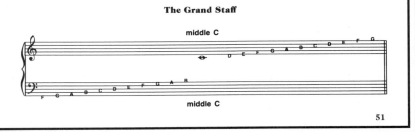

middle C

middle C

51

the explanation. Make sure the students understand the terms used. You may again wish to use the Chromatic Scale Ruler and the Major Scale Finder to demonstrate that the same pitches, that is, pitches with the same letter name, are repeated every seven scale steps and that the distance between this repetition is defined as an octave (*octa-* meaning eight).

at some point that middle C is thus labeled because it is the pitch that occurs in the middle of the Grand Staff.

5. Help the students become comfortable with quickly naming the pitches in the order shown by the lines and spaces of the staff. Practice chanting them in order, both up and down, starting with middle C. Divide the class into teams and have a competition. Put two staffs on the chalkboard; call out letter names and octaves. One member of each team must run to the chalkboard and draw a note on the correct line or space. Add to the challenge by calling out several pitches at a time. Explain

Lesson Focus

Harmony: Two or more musical lines may occur simultaneously. *(P–S)*

Materials

- **Piano Accompaniment:** page 272
- **Record Information:**
  - It's a Long Road to Freedom
    Record 3 Side A Band 8
    Voices: mixed chorus
    Accompaniment: flute, piano, synthesizer, electric bass, percussion
- **Instruments:** snare drum; wire brushes (optional); double bass; guitar

It's a Long Road to Freedom

Words and Music by Sr. Miriam Therese Winter, SCMM

The Lesson

1. Review the terms *D.C.* and *Fine* with the class. **In what order will we sing the staffs of "It's a Long Road to Freedom"?** (Refrain—first four staffs; Verse 1—next three staffs; Refrain; Verse 2; Refrain; Verse 3; Refrain; Verse 4; Refrain) **How will Staffs 5, 6, and 7 of the song be sung?** (in two parts) Help the students discover that the bracket at the left end of each pair of staffs in the verse indicates that the two parts are sung simultaneously.

2. Assign the students to an appropriate part. (All sing the refrain in unison; in the verses, Treble I's and II's should sing Part I, Changing Voices Part II, and Baritones should add the chord roots—see Step 4.) As they listen to the recording, have each group focus attention on their part. **Which group has the melody during the verse?** (Treble I's and II's) **Why**

is the harmony part (II) fairly easy? (It usually stays on the same note or moves by steps. Skips occur only in three places, one of which is in unison with the melody.)

3. Learn the two parts of the song simultaneously by having the students follow the notation one more time as they listen to and then begin singing with the recording. Continue to focus on relating the two parts rather than isolating them from each other.

4. When the students can confidently sing the song, add the percussion and instrumental chord-root parts shown at the bottom of page 53. Baritones sing the chord roots using these pitches:

OPTIONAL

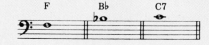

For Your Information

Tune the double bass and guitars as shown at the bottom of page 53. Chord roots are played by plucking the appropriate string at the beginning of each measure.

Accompany Your Song

Tune a double bass or guitar as shown:

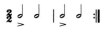

Double Bass	Guitar
F Bb C	F Bb C

Pluck the chord root at the beginning of each measure. The chord symbols above the music will tell you which chord root to use. Continue playing the same chord root until the chord changes.

Play this pattern with brushes or by sliding your hand across a hand drum or snare drum:

53

Lesson Focus

Harmony: Chords and melody may move simultaneously in relation to each other. *(P–I)*

Materials

o **Piano Accompaniment:** page 275
o **Record Information:**
  • Five Hundred Miles
  Record 3 Side B Band 1
  Voices: mixed chorus
  Accompaniment: dobro guitar, rhythm guitar, double bass, percussion
o **Other:** Chromatic Scale Rulers and Scale Finders prepared for Traditions 21 (pages 46–47, from Activity Sheets 13a–c)
o **Teacher's Resource Binder:**
  Activity Sheets • **Activity Sheet 13d,** page A21

Five Hundred Miles

Words and Music by Hedy West

On what type of scale is this melody based?

Verse

If you miss the train I'm on, you will know that I am gone,

You can hear the whis-tle blow_____ a hun-dred miles._____

Refrain

A hun-dred miles, a hun-dred miles, a hun-dred miles, a hun-dred miles,

you can hear the whis-tle blow_____ a hun-dred miles._____

You have been singing songs based on different kinds of scales. Each has a distinctive quality of its own. There are also different types of chords that have distinctive qualities. Listen to the chords shown at the top of the next page. Can you decide which are the same type?

54

The Lesson

1. Ask the students to look at the song on page 54. **Can you determine the scale on which this melody is based?** Distribute a Chromatic Scale Ruler, the five Scale Finders, and a pencil to each pair of students. (See **Other**.) They should name the pitches found in the melody, circle them on the Chromatic Scale Ruler, and determine the appropriate Scale Finder. **Which pitch will you circle as the starting pitch of the scale?** (G) The students should conclude that the song is based on a major pentatonic scale.

2. Ask the class to sing up and down the pentatonic scale several times. They should sing from 5 (D) to 3 (B). Then establish a moderate tempo by tapping the shortest sound (eighth note), and challenge the class to sight-read the melody.

3. When students have learned the melody, have them silently read the discussion following the song. On a piano or autoharp, play the first chord (G major) shown on the staff at the bottom of page 55. **Listen carefully to the quality of the chord. Now listen carefully to the second one.** (Play Em.) **Is it the same as or different from the chord you just heard?** (different) Play the entire sequence as written, pausing after each for the students to make their response. Guide the students to decide that the third and last chords are the same type as the first. Play the second and fourth chords again. **Are they the same?** (No; each has a different quality.)

4. Distribute the three Chord Finders prepared from Activity Sheet 13d *(Chord Finders)* to each pair of students. Give them approximately ten minutes to follow the instructions

You heard three types of chords.

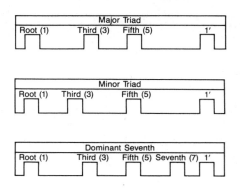

Which type is each of the chords you heard? To decide:

- Circle the letters which make up the chord on the Chromatic Scale Ruler.
- Place a Chord Finder over the Scale Ruler so that the lowest note appears in the cutout marked "root."
- If all other circled pitches appear in the other cutouts, you have located the correct chord type. If not, try a different Chord Finder.

Use these chords to add a vocal chording accompaniment to "Five Hundred Miles."

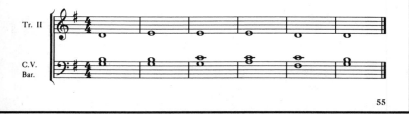

55

at the bottom of the pupil page and identify each type of chord. Remind them that if they are not sure of the letter names of the bass clef, they may look back at page 51. Discover that the chords are as follows: Major Triad; Minor Triad; Major Triad; Minor Triad; Dominant Seventh; Major Triad. Discuss the fact that the difference in quality is a result of the difference in the distance between the pitches that make up the chord. This is shown by the difference in the Chord Finders.

5. Continue the lesson by examining the chord sequence at the top of page 55. Help the students realize that these are the same chords they identified in Step 3. The same pitches are included in each chord; they have been rearranged so that each vocal part moves easily by steps from one pitch to the next. Draw attention to the fact that most of the time

only one voice moves at a time. (The only deviation is when moving from A minor to D7.)

6. Play the chords on a piano or autoharp as the Treble II's, Changing Voices, and Baritones practice singing the chord sequence. When they can move easily from one chord to the next, ask the Treble I's to sing the melody while the lower voices provide the chordal accompaniment.

7. Invite the Baritones and Treble I's to trade parts. The Baritones will sing the melody an octave lower than written, and the Treble I's will sing the Baritone part an octave higher. Ask the students to decide which arrangement of voices they like best. Perform that arrangement again to end the lesson.

Lesson Focus

Harmony: Chords and melody may move simultaneously in relation to each other.
Rhythm: A series of beats may be organized into regular or irregular groupings by stressing certain beats. *(P–S)*

Materials

o **Piano Accompaniments:** pages 280, 282
o **Record Information:**
  • Kid Stuff
    Record 3 Side B Band 2
    Voices: mixed chorus
    Accompaniment: autoharp
  • William Goat
    Record 3 Side B Band 3
    Voices: mixed chorus
    Accompaniment: autoharp
o **Other:** overhead projector
o **Teacher's Resource Binder:**

Activity Sheets
  • **Activity Sheet 14,** page A22
    (Prepare as a transparency.)
  • Optional—
    Mainstreaming Activity 9, page M17

Kid Stuff

Arranged by Emily Bedient   Traditional Song

Learn to perform "Kid Stuff" and "William Goat."

The meter signatures of both songs tell you to count in threes. To decide the appropriate rhythmic style of each song, you will need to "look beyond." Consider

  • the tempo
  • the nature of the accompaniment
  • the rhythm of the melody
  • the beats that should be most strongly stressed

The Lesson

1. Learn to sing the melody and harmony parts for "Kid Stuff." Help the students determine the appropriate rhythmic style of the song by looking beyond the meter signature, which tells them to count in sets of three. Encourage the students to consider the tempo, the accompaniment, the rhythm of the melody, and the location of the beats that should be most strongly stressed. (The rhythmic pattern in the Baritone part stresses the first beat of each set and thereby dictates that the song will probably be felt in three when sung at a moderate tempo.)

2. Project the transparency of Activity Sheet 14 (*Kid Stuff*). Help the students determine that "Kid Stuff" is written in E major. Have the students analyze the notes in the part they are singing. **Which of these pitches fits in**

the I chord? (E, G#, and B) **the V7 chord?** (B, D#, F#, and A)

3. When both the melody and harmony parts are thoroughly learned, try an experiment to stress the relationship between the two. Have the students sing the melody in G major (begin on G) and the accompanying parts in E major (as written). Discuss the sound that results when the melody and accompaniment center around different pitches. This effect is known as bitonality and is sometimes deliberately used in contemporary music.

4. Learn to sing the melody and accompanying parts for "William Goat." Ask the students to examine the song carefully to determine whether the rhythmic style of "William Goat" is the same as that of "Kid Stuff." (The underlying accompaniment rhythms are nearly all the same note value—a dotted half

William Goat

Words Anonymous

American Folk Melody

Will you use the same rhythmic style for "William Goat" that you used for "Kid Stuff"? Will the groupings of threes flow in the same way or in a different way? Look at the meter signature and beyond to make your decision. This song is in the same meter as "Kid Stuff." Follow the same procedures to learn this arrangement.

For Your Information

Some "kids' songs" for use in Step 5:

London Bridge

D
Lon-don Bridge is fall-ing down.

A7   D
Fall-ing down, fall-ing down.

Lon-don Bridge is fall-ing down,

A7   D
My fair la-dy

Sing the song in twos, then in threes. Discuss the change in "style." An accompanying part might consist of words such as "crash," "bang," or "crumble."

Paw-Paw Patch

D
Where, oh where, is pret-ty lit-tle El-lie,

A7
Where, oh where, is pret-ty lit-tle El-lie,

D
Where, oh where, is pret-ty lit-tle El-lie?

A7   D
Way down yon-der in the paw-paw patch.

Accompaniment: Sing the words "come home" with the beat.

57

note. Although the meter signatures for both songs are the same, this song could easily be felt in one rather than three when sung at a moderate tempo.)

Use the same procedure described in Step 2 to help the students determine which of their parts fit in the I and V7 chords.

5. Students may work individually or in small groups to create their own "Kid Stuff" medleys. Begin with one song, continue with a second, then return to the first. Add other "kids' songs." (See **For Your Information** for suggested songs and accompaniments to use.) Explore the accent groupings of these newly created "kids' songs."

Lesson Focus

Expression: Musical elements are combined into a whole to express a musical or extramusical idea. *(P–S)*

Materials

o **Record Information:**
  • I Am Falling Off a Mountain
    Record 3 Side B Band 4
    Voices: mixed chorus

For Your Information

The work of recent composers has given rise to unfamiliar forms of notation. The instructions and principles represented by this notation are very easy to learn. A discussion of all symbols is important for a successful interpretation.

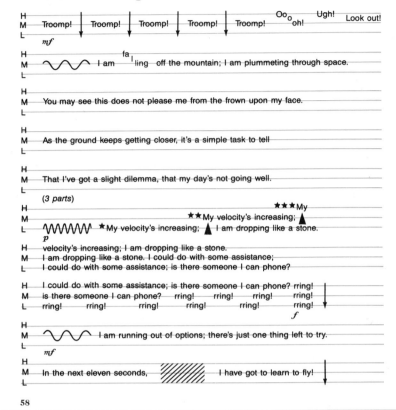

The Lesson

1. Have the students open their books to page 58. Look at the unusual score for "I Am Falling Off a Mountain." Initiate the discussion by stating that some contemporary composers use notation that is not typical of our traditional system. Their lack of precise notation allows the performer to make important decisions regarding how the music will actually sound.

2. Before attempting to perform this choral piece from the score, the students will need to understand what the various symbols indicate. Draw the following symbols on the chalkboard and discuss their meanings.

L — low	★ — Group 1
M — medium	★★ — Group 2
H — high	★★★ — Group 3

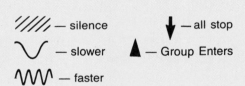

3. Continue discussing the musical markings. The singers are free to choose the specific pitch at which they will sing-speak, while the conductor controls moments of synchronization such as the rhythmic flow of the words.

4. The performance includes voices in unison as well as a middle section where the piece divides into three groups and the text is performed in canon. Assign these group responsibilities before performing the work.

5. Have the students select a conductor. (The teacher may serve in this role at first.) Perform this choral work several times until it is refined to the group's satisfaction.

58

Create a Choral Piece

stinging
gold swarms
upon the spires
silver

  chants the litanies the
great bells are ringing with rose
the lewd fat bells

    and a tall

wind
is dragging
the
sea
with
dream
-s

by e.e. cummings

- Use this poem to create a composition for the chorus.
- Work in small groups to plan the composition. Then use the class as your chorus and perform your work.
- Plan your piece. Will you create a simple melody for the words? Will you add harmony? Will you use unusual vocal sounds?
- How can you most dramatically have the chorus express words such as:

- Write your music plan on a separate sheet of paper.

Luciano Berio (1925–) is a contemporary Italian composer who has done much to promote electronic music in his country. Listen to his 1960 setting (entitled "Circles") of this same poem. Were the ideas of your group and those of Berio similar or very different?

59

Lesson Focus
Expression: Musical elements are combined into a whole to express a musical or extra-musical idea. *(C–I)*

Materials
o **Record Information:**
  - *Circles*
    by Luciano Berio (**beh**-ree-oe), 1925–
    Record 3 Side B Band 5
o **Instruments:** several sets of resonator bells (C, D, E, F♯, G♯, A♯, and C); bell mallets; xylophone or keyboards
o **Other:** large sheet of drawing paper and pencils for each group of five students
o **Teacher's Resource Binder:**
  - Optional—
    Biography 2, page B3

The Lesson

1. Invite two or three students to read the poem. Encourage each of them to find a different way to express the text. Encourage experimentation with different words, especially "stinging," "silver," "ringing," "fat," "wind," "dragging," and "dream." **How many different ways can you say each word?**

2. Choose three students to play the resonator bells. Each student should have two or three of the bells from the whole-tone scale. (If enough bell sets are available, each player may use the entire scale.) The students may experiment with combining various ostinatos or simple melodic ideas that they make up. **What effect does this scale impart to the music?** (When played softly and at the same time, the notes of the scale create a hazy, blurry feeling.)

3. Divide the class into small groups of four or five students. Each group should use the poem and the notes of the whole-tone scale to create a composition for chorus. As the groups plan their pieces, have them record their ideas on paper to create a large written score that shows the sequence of words and sounds to be used. Encourage the students to consider melody, harmony, and unusual vocal sounds as well as dynamics and articulation.

4. Designate (or let the students choose) one student from each group to be the conductor. Each of the groups should share its plan with the entire class, then use the class as a chorus to perform the composition.

5. Listen to Luciano Berio's setting of *Circles.* **Were the ideas of your group and those of Berio similar or very different?**

59

Lesson Focus

Timbre: The quality of a sound is affected by the way the sound is produced. *(C–S)*

Materials

o **Record Information:**
  • *Microtimbre I for Amplified Tam-Tam* by Rich O'Donnell
    Record 3 Side B Band 6

o **Instruments:** cymbals or gongs; mallets (made from various materials, such as wood, felt, rubber, plastic); wire brush; metal triangle beater; contact microphone or microphone on floor stand (optional); record player with microphone input jack may be used as an amplifier; cello or violin bow (optional)

o **Other:** sheets of paper and pencils for each small group

o **Teacher's Resource Binder:**
  • Optional—
    Enrichment Activity 5, page E8

Microtimbre I
for Amplified Tam-Tam
by Rich O'Donnell

ppp

ppp

Muffle mike with palm of right hand

3 seconds

Vibrato

4 seconds

L. H.

R. H.

Flatten BASS on pre-amp

R. H.

L. H.

Blend into brush sound

Muffle tam-tam with left hand

Press mike with right hand

Muffle mike with right palm
Dampen center of tam-tam with right-hand fingers

R. H.

Tam-tam Stand

L. H. scrape tam-tam with metal stick

60

The Lesson

1. Help the students explore a variety of ways of producing different timbres on either a cymbal or a gong. They may tap it with different kinds of mallets or beaters, rub it with their fingertips, flick it with their fingernails, or bow the edge of it with a cello or violin bow. Encourage them to make sounds on different parts of the cymbal or gong, to play with varying degrees of loudness, and to discover as many different timbres as possible.

2. **Rich O'Donnell, a St. Louis composer, used many sounds similar to yours in a piece called *Microtimbre I for Amplified Tam-Tam.* He played his piece on a tam-tam, an instrument that looks and sounds much like a gong.** Ask the students to turn to page 62. **These are some of the printed directions for playing his piece.** Discuss the various playing techniques used. Be sure the students

are aware that a contact microphone has been taped to the tam-tam. (The contact microphone allows many soft sounds and harmonics to be heard that otherwise might be inaudible.)

3. Examine the score for *Microtimbre I* on pages 60 and 61. Refer to the instructions on page 62 to interpret the symbols used.

4. Listen to the recording as the students follow the notation. Replay as needed until the students can follow the score easily.

5. Divide the class into small groups; each group should have a cymbal or a gong and various mallets. If no more than one cymbal or gong is available, the entire class may work together. The small groups (or whole class) should use the sounds explored earlier to create original compositions. Notation should

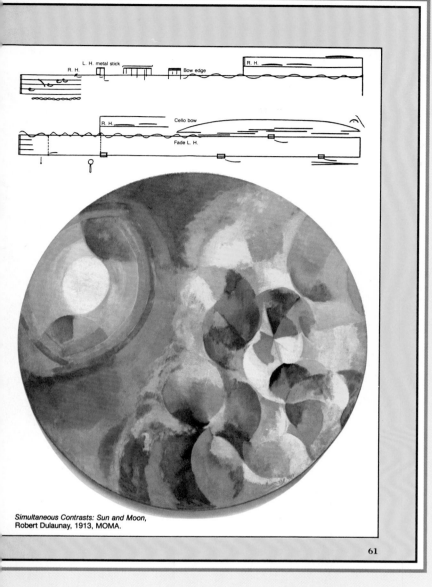

Simultaneous Contrasts: Sun and Moon,
Robert Dulaunay, 1913, MOMA.

61

For Your Information

Rich O'Donnell's works are frequently heard at new-music concerts across the country. O'Donnell is currently principal percussionist of the St. Louis Symphony and Director of the Washington University Electronic Music Studio in St. Louis.

Microtimbre I is a study of the various timbres that can be produced with a single tam-tam. The timbres produced essentially move from dark to light as the piece progresses. The length of performance will vary from performer to performer.

be devised and each composition should be recorded on paper.

6. Share compositions with the entire class. If a contact microphone is available, it may be attached to the cymbal. If not, a floor microphone may be placed near the cymbal or gong to amplify the softer, less obvious sounds.

7. Discuss the similarities and differences between the class compositions and *Microtimbre I.*

Performance Instructions for Microtimbre I

The tam-tam should be from 28–32 inches in diameter.

- - - — Rubber fingertip
(as worn by accountants)
- - - — Finger rub

Rub back of tam-tam like tambourine thumb roll. This will produce a variety of frequencies.

Areas on tam-tam are referred to on five-line staff.
The top must be played from the rear of the tam-tam.

Play with fingertip.

Play with fingernails.

Flick with fingernail.

Soft tam-tam beater

Wire brush

Cello bow—Bow back edge of tam-tam as if bowing string. A series of high-pitched changing frequencies is desired.

Wire stick—bicycle spoke or piece of coat hanger

Xylophone mallet . . . handle only

Where the top line indicates varying pitch with either xylophone mallet or metal stick, this line should be played on the edge of the tam-tam. The pitch is determined by the place on the stick striking the tam-tam:

Low ⟶ **High**

Contact mike: Tape mike onto back of tam-tam. As viewed from the back, placement should be in the second area (see staff diagram above) at about the 10 o'clock position. The vibrato is produced by placing two fingers on each end of the mike and rocking it.

62

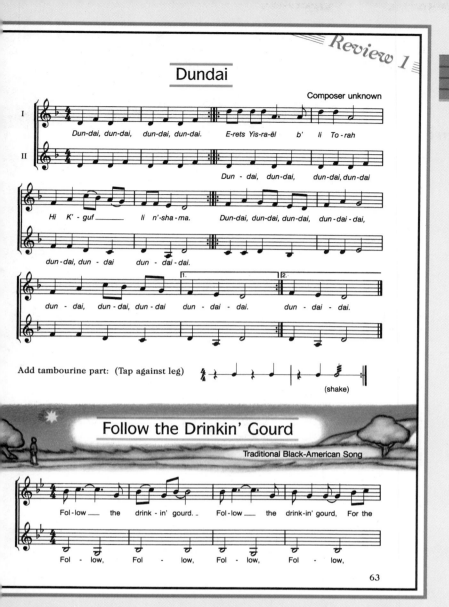

Dundai

Composer unknown

I

Dun-dai, dun-dai, dun-dai, dun-dai. E-rets Yis-ra-ël b' li To-rah

II

Dun - dai, dun-dai, dun-dai, dun-dai

Hi K' - guf _____ li n'-sha-ma. Dun-dai, dun-dai, dun-dai, dun - dai - dai,

dun - dai, dun - dai dun - dai - dai.

1.   2.
dun - dai, dun - dai, dun - dai dun - dai - dai. dun - dai - dai.

Add tambourine part: (Tap against leg)

(shake)

Follow the Drinkin' Gourd

Traditional Black-American Song

Fol-low _____ the drink - in' gourd. _ Fol-low _____ the drink-in' gourd, For the

Fol - low, Fol - low, Fol - low, Fol - low,

63

The Lesson

1. Learn "Dundai" in unison. Distribute tambourines and have the students play the rhythmic pattern on page 63 with the recording.

2. Focus the students' attention on the two parts. Help them select the part most appropriate for their vocal range. (Remind the students of the information gathered in Lesson 2.) Sing the song in two parts. Help the students with either part as needed. When they can perform the song accurately, add the tambourine part.

3. Examine the song again to determine the shortest sound (the eighth note). Distribute copies of Review 1, Chromatic Scale Rulers, Scale Finders, and pencils. The students should complete all questions or portions of

questions that relate to "Dundai." Play the recording as many times as is needed to help the students answer the questions.

4. **Here's another song in two parts that uses the eighth note as its shortest sound.** The students should listen to the recording as they follow the notation for "Follow the Drinkin' Gourd" on pages 63 and 64.

5. Have the students complete the remaining questions and portions of questions that are related to "Follow the Drinkin' Gourd." Play the recording as often as necessary to complete the evaluation.

6. Use the information gained from this evaluation and observations made throughout the unit to complete Musical Progress Report 1.

Lesson Focus

Evaluation: Review concepts and skills studied in the first unit.

Materials

o **Piano Accompaniments:** pages 284, 286
o **Record Information:**
  • Dundai
    Record 3 Side B Band 7
    Voices: mixed chorus
    Accompaniment: clarinet, trumpet, trombone, tuba, violin, mandolin, cimbalom, accordion, double bass, percussion
  • Follow the Drinkin' Gourd
    Record 3 Side B Band 8
    Voices: mixed chorus
    Accompaniment: percussion
o **Instruments:** tambourines
o **Other:** Chromatic Scale Rulers and Scale Finders prepared for Traditions 21 (pages 46–47, from Activity Sheets 13a–c), pencils
o **Teacher's Resource Binder:**
  Evaluation • **Review 1,** page Ev5
  • **Musical Progress Report 1,** page Ev7
  • **Orff Activity 6,** page O10

For Your Information

These are the answers for the Review:

1. As determined by voice testing (See Lesson 2.)
2. Dundai: Treble I, Treble II, Baritone should choose I; Changing Voice should choose II.
   Follow the Drinkin' Gourd: Treble I, Treble II, Baritone should choose I; Changing Voice should choose II.
3. Notes should be tied as shown below. (See example.)

4. Bar lines should be placed as shown above. (See example.)
5. Dundai: 1 2 1 2
   Follow the Drinkin' Gourd: 1 2 3   4
6. Dundai: introduction **A A B B**
   Follow the Drinkin' Gourd: **A B A' B'**
7. Dundai: minor
   Follow the Drinkin' Gourd: minor
8. b, c, f, d, h, a

Unit 2

Music of Many Cultures

TE   (pages 68–69; 72–74; 76–78; 80–81; 89; 94; 98–101; 106–107; 114–115)

TRB   (pages K11; K14; K19; I14; O10; O14; O18; E13; E16; AS24)

1C: PE   (pages 66; 68; 74; 76–78; 82–87; 90–93; 96; 98–105; 106–108; 114–116)

TE   (pages 66; 68–69; 74–81; 82–87; 90–93; 96; 98–105; 106–109; 114–115)

TRB   (pages K14; AS23; AS24; AS29; AS30; I14; O14; O18; E13; E16; EV9–11)

1D: PE   (pages 74; 95; 99; 101; 104–105; 106–108; 114)

TE   (pages 68–69; 72; 76–78; 80–81; 99–101; 107; 114–115)

TRB   (pages K14; I14; O10; O14; O18; E13; E16; AS24)

1F: PE   (pages 68; 105)

TE   (pages 69; 73; 78)

TRB   (pages AS23; AS29; AS30; O18)

2: PE   (pages 68–69; 72–73; 99; 104–105; 106–108)

TE   (pages 68–69; 72–81; 95; 101; 105; 106–108)

TRB   (pages K11; K14; K19; I14; O10; O14; O18)

3A: PE   (pages 96–97; 110–111; 116)

TE   (pages 110–113)

TRB   (page E13)

3B: PE   (pages 82–87; 90–93; 96; 102; 109–114; 116)

TE   (pages 79; 82–87; 90–93; 96; 102; 110–113; 115)

TRB   (pages E13; E16; O10; O14; O18; K19; AS24; AS25–28; M18; EV9–11)

Unit Overview

In Unit 2, the students explore the music of many cultures by singing songs, playing and classifying musical instruments, and analyzing recorded examples in regard to their melody, rhythm, timbre, texture, instrumentation, and form. The students discover characteristics that are common to all music. The recorded examples reveal to the students the wide influence of music of other cultures on the music of the United States.

Texas Essential Elements for Unit 2:

1A: PE   (pages 74; 95; 99; 101; 103–105; 106–108; 113–114)

TE   (pages 68; 72; 74; 76–78; 80–81; 101)

TRB   (pages K11; K14; I14; O10; O14; O18; E13; E16)

1B: PE   (pages 68; 73–74; 88–89; 94–97; 98–105; 106–108; 113–114)

(continued on top of page)

4A: PE   (pages 72–73; 88–89; 96–97; 99; 101–105; 114–116)

TE   (pages 72; 74; 76; 88–89; 96–97; 102–103; 110–113; 115; 116)

TRB   (pages E13; B5; M17; EV11)

4B: PE   (pages 96–97; 102–103; 114; 116)

TE   (pages 96–97; 110–113; 115)

TRB   (pages E13; B7)

5A: PE   (pages 68–69; 72–73; 88–89; 94–95; 99; 101; 104–105; 106–108)

TE   (pages 68–69; 72–81; 88–89; 94–95; 101; 105; 106–108)

TRB   (pages I14; O10; O14; O18; E13; E16; K11; K19; AS25–28; M18)

5B: PE   (pages 67; 72; 84–93; 99; 101–103; 105; 109; 114; 116)

TE   (pages 66–67; 84–87; 99; 101–103; 105; 109; 114–115)

TRB   (page M17)

Lesson Focus

Time and Place: The way musical elements are combined into a whole reflects the origin of the music. *(D–I)*

Materials

o **Piano Accompaniments:** pages 292, 296, 288

o **Record Information:**
- *Dance Song*
  Record 4 Side A Band 1
- *Azuma Jishi*
  Record 4 Side A Band 2
- *Anduve*
  Record 4 Side A Band 3
- *Goin' Up Yonder*
  by Walter Hawkins
  Record 4 Side A Band 4
- *Alla en el Rancho Grande*
  Record 4 Side A Band 5
- *The Wreck of the Edmund Fitzgerald*
  by Gordon Lightfoot
  Record 4 Side B Band 1

o **Teacher's Resource Binder:**
- Optional—
  Mainstreaming Activity 10, page M17

Sound Prints

Music is a people's "sound print." Wherever people have settled, they leave behind a living music that says,

"This is how we think.
This is how we love.
This is what we believe in.
This is how we express who we are!"

66

The Lesson

1. Begin the lesson by asking the students to define the title on page 66, "Sound Prints." **What is a sound print?** Some students may be aware that it is now possible to analyze vocal characteristics electronically and identify the unique quality of an individual's voice with the same degree of exactness that can be done with thumbprints. Just as with thumbprints, no two people have exactly the same combination of vocal characteristics.

   To illustrate, have the students close their eyes. Tap someone on the shoulder. That person is to say, "This is my sound print." Ask the class to identify the person who spoke.

2. Read the opening paragraphs on page 66. Suggest that, just as an individual's voice is unique, so is the music of a particular culture. **Listen to some examples of vocal music from different parts of the world. What does each tell you about the people who first sang these songs?**

   Play excerpts from *Dance Song, Azuma Jishi,* and *Anduve* without discussion between examples. When all of the examples have been played, invite the students to share their reactions. Their initial response to the sounds of the singers may be negative. Encourage the students to be as specific as possible about what they found displeasing and why. **Has anyone ever reacted negatively to the vocal sounds you prefer?** (Many students will undoubtedly admit that their parents or, perhaps, even older brothers and sisters, express their dislike for the recorded popular music they like to hear.) Explain that vocal style and quality, like other aspects of a culture, change from one part of the world to another, and from year to year.

Listen to singers from various parts of the world. Can you sense the thoughts and feelings they are expressing? Can you imagine the setting in which they might be performing?

The music of the United States is a collage of many "sound prints." Listen to these singers who live in the United States today. Can you identify the origin of the music by the quality of their voice? the choice of instruments? the style of the music?

67

Help the students realize that they are most likely to prefer the sounds they are accustomed to hearing.

3. Ask the students to listen to the recordings again. After listening to each one, invite them to speculate about the origin and purpose of the music.

Dance Song is an Eskimo dance song from Point Barrow, Alaska. Traditionally, certain members of the tribe are identified as singers; there are usually five or six, led by an older man. He begins; others may then join in the singing, and the rest dance.

Azuma Jishi, from Japan, is also a dance, but it is performed by professional dancers (translation is "Lion Dance"). Traditionally, it had religious significance and was performed as part of hunting rituals.

Anduve is a masked dance of the Kiwkuru Indians of Brazil. There are two dancers and two musicians who sing in unison most of the time. The music is punctuated by shouts of excitement from the audience.

4. After reading the final paragraph on page 67, continue the lesson by playing recordings by American performers. Listen to each recording listed below; then invite the students to identify the type of music and offer their ideas as from what part of the world the example seems to have drawn some of its characteristics. Reassure the students that this is not a test; you are simply interested in finding out if they can recognize the clues provided in musical sound prints.

Goin' Up Yonder: Afro-American

Alla en el Rancho Grande: Mexican

The Wreck of the Edmund Fitzgerald: British, northern European.

Lesson Focus

Timbre: The quality of a sound is affected by the way the sound is produced. *(P–I)*

Materials

o **Piano Accompaniment:** page 298
o **Record Information:**
  • The Miracle
    Record 4 Side B Band 2
    Voices: mixed chorus
    Accompaniment: handbells, pipe organ, percussion
  • *Dance Song*
    (Record 4 Side A Band 1)
  • *Azuma Jishi*
    (Record 4 Side A Band 2)
  • *Anduve*
    (Record 4 Side A Band 3)
o **Teacher's Resource Binder:**
  Activity Sheets
  • **Activity Sheet 15,** page A23
  • Optional—
    Enrichment Activity 6, page E13

Vocal Sound Prints

The way you sing is affected by your experience. You are likely to sing in a style similar to that of your family and friends. Through careful listening and practice, that style can be changed.

Learn the song on the next page. Then experiment singing it in different ways by paying attention to five vocal characteristics:

Quality: Sing "ah" with relaxed facial and neck muscles. Make the sound as rich and open as you can. Then switch to the vowel "ee," tightening your facial and neck muscles. Make the sound as tense and thin as you can. Try singing through your nose! What happens to the quality? Try imitating your favorite rock singer, an opera singer, a country-blues singer.

Register: Sing a major scale, beginning with the lowest pitch you can sing. Move up step by step to the highest pitch you can sing. Sustain each pitch. Listen! Does a change of register affect the quality of your voice?

Vibrato: Sing a long, steady "ah" on a comfortable pitch in your middle register. Try fluctuating the sound slightly above and below the initial steady pitch; first fluctuate a little, then a great deal.

Articulation: Sing "The Miracle" in a smoothly flowing legato style. Repeat, this time singing in a disconnected, choppy, or staccato manner. Try slightly stressing each note to produce a *marcato*, or marked, style.

Expression: Sing "The Miracle" in a flat, colorless way, with no changes in the characteristics of quality, register, vibrato, or articulation. Repeat the song, this time varying the characteristics already mentioned, as well as the dynamics, to express the ideas of the lyrics.

68

The Lesson

1. Discuss the first paragraph on page 68 with the students. Ask them to recall incidents that support the statement in their books. **For example, has anyone ever told you that you sound just like your mother (or father)? Have you ever heard a stranger speak and immediately guessed what part of the United States (or the world) he or she came from?**

2. Before proceeding with the rest of the discussion on page 68, help the students learn "The Miracle," on page 69. Challenge them to use their music reading skills to learn the song. Then return to page 68 and guide the students as they attempt to change their personal "vocal sound print" by experimenting as suggested in the text.

3. Experiment with changes in quality. Suggest that the students should let their head droop slightly and drop their mouth into an "egg" shape as though yawning, then sing up and down a D minor scale on "ah." To change the quality, tell the students to stretch their neck upward and outward and widen their mouth as though smiling to create a tense tone. Sing the scale again. Create a nasal quality by singing "into" the nose on "eh." Sing "The Miracle," changing the quality on each phrase.

4. Explain that most people have three vocal registers—high, middle, and low. Begin on G below middle C and guide the students to slowly sing a G major scale. Move upward for two octaves. **Can you hear a change in register? For many of us a register change occurs when we have to shift into what is**

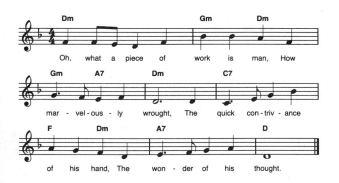

The Miracle

Words by William Shakespeare

Music by Malvina Reynolds

Oh, what a piece of work is man, How
mar-vel-ous-ly wrought, The quick con-triv-ance
of his hand, The won-der of his thought.

69

For Your Information

The following are possible decisions the students may make when completing Activity Sheet 15 (*Vocal Sound Prints*).

Dance Song
Quality: toward tense
Register: toward low
Vibrato: middle amount
Articulation: toward smooth
Expression: limited

Azuma Jishi
Quality: tense
Register: medium low
Vibrato: toward little
Articulation: quite smooth
Expression: toward much

Anduve
Quality: toward open
Register: low (singers)
Vibrato: toward much
Articulation: quite choppy
Expression: toward much

called a *head* register to sing the higher pitches or a *chest* register to sing very low pitches.

5. Demonstrate a vibrato for the students by showing how to make the tone waver slightly above and below the initial pitch. (Sing on G above middle C.) At first make the waver very slow so that the students can hear the differences; then speed up to make it move very quickly, resulting in a vibrato.

6. Demonstrate the different articulations for the students. Then invite them to perform the song, changing articulation on each phrase.

7. Finally, discuss ways of combining the characteristics to create an expressive performance. Include changes in dynamics in the plan.

OPTIONAL

8. Distribute three copies of Activity Sheet 15 (*Vocal Sound Prints*) to each student. Draw attention to the fact that, for each characteristic on the activity sheet, two extremes are listed. Tell the students that they are to listen to three selections (*Dance Song, Azuma Jishi,* and *Anduve*). For each selection they are to mark their sheets to describe its sound print. (See **For Your Information**.)

CULTURE 3

Lesson Focus

Timbre: The quality of a sound is affected by the way the sound is produced.

Time and Place: A particular use of timbre reflects the origin of the musical whole. (*D–I*)

Materials

o **Piano Accompaniments:** pages 288, 292, 296

o **Record Information:**
  • *La Huichola*
    Record 4 Side B Band 3
  • *Saeta*
    (Record 4 Side B Band 4)
  • *Ketjak*
    Record 4 Side B Band 5
  • *Anduve*
    (Record 4 Side A Band 3)
  • *Rabbit Dance*
    Record 4 Side B Band 6
  • *Azuma Jishi*
    (Record 4 Side A Band 2)
  • *Zenizenabo*
    Record 4 Side B Band 7
  • *The Wreck of the Edmund Fitzgerald*
    (Record 4 Side B Band 1)
  • *Goin' Up Yonder*
    (Record 4 Side A Band 4)
  • *Alla en el Rancho Grande*
    (Record 4 Side A Band 5)

(continued on next page)

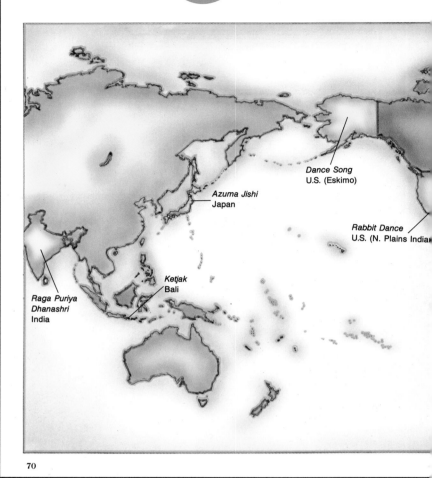

The Whole Earth Sings

Dance Song
U.S. (Eskimo)

Azuma Jishi
Japan

Rabbit Dance
U.S. (N. Plains India

Ketjak
Bali

Raga Puriya Dhanashri
India

70

The Lesson

1. To each student, distribute a pencil and one copy of Activity Sheet 15 (*Vocal Sound Prints*) for each musical example you intend to use. There are 12 examples listed on the students' pages. Depending on the time available, you may wish to select a smaller sampling from those listed. You may want to base your selection, at least in part, on the ethnic backgrounds of the students in your class.

2. Play the examples as the students mark their activity sheets. Reassure them that there are no absolute answers. They are simply to react as they feel is most appropriate. Play each example more than once if the students feel they need additional time to make decisions.

3. After all examples have been heard, display a transparency of the activity sheet. Discuss each example and draw a composite profile

for each by getting a general consensus from the students on each characteristic for each example. Place a dot in the appropriate place on the sheet, then connect the dots with a line. Use a different transparency or different colored overhead pens to mark each example heard.

4. After all examples have been heard, overlay the transparencies. **Are the profiles similar? different?** Discuss reasons. Suggest that voices of different cultures have distinctive characteristics or sound prints just as each individual has a distinctive thumbprint.

5. Discuss the purpose for which each song was originally performed. Make a list of the purposes on the chalkboard. **Do we use music in the same ways? Are there other purposes for which we use music that are not listed here?**

OPTIONAL

Materials *(continued)*
- Mwatye
  Record 4 Side B Band 8
- **Other:** Activity Sheet 15 (*Vocal Sound Prints*) from Culture 2 (copies for each example used); overhead projector

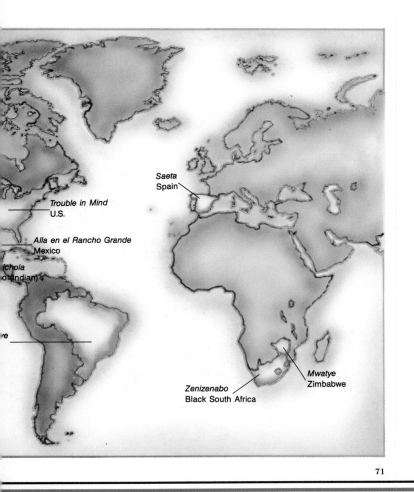

Saeta
Spain

Trouble in Mind
U.S.

Alla en el Rancho Grande
Mexico

Ichola
(Indian)

Mwatye
Zimbabwe

Zenizenabo
Black South Africa

71

Examples included in this lesson are:

La Huichola (Mexico)—ballad
Saeta (Spain)—religious ceremony
Ketjak (Bali)—music drama
Anduve (Brazil)—ritual dance
Rabbit Dance (American Indian)—social
  dance
Azuma Jishi (Japan)—ritual dance
Zenizenabo (Africa)—war chant
The Wreck of the Edmund Fitzgerald
  (American)—ballad
Goin' Up Yonder (Black American)—
  religious
Alla en el Rancho Grande (Mexico)—ballad
Mwatye (Africa)—work song

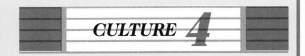

CULTURE 4

Lesson Focus

Time and Place: A particular use of timbre reflects the origin of the musical whole. *(D-I)*

Materials

o **Record Information:**
  • *Zenizenabo*
    (Record 4 Side B Band 7)
  • **Teacher's Resource Binder:**
  • Optional—
    Biography 3, page B5

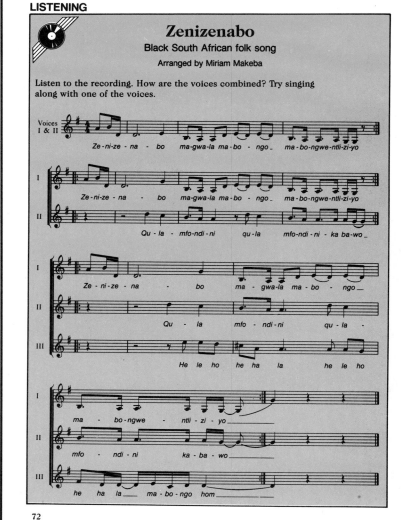

LISTENING

Zenizenabo
Black South African folk song

Arranged by Miriam Makeba

Listen to the recording. How are the voices combined? Try singing along with one of the voices.

72

The Lesson

1. Play the recording of *"Zenizenabo"* as performed by Miriam Makeba and others. Makeba is a Black South African musician who has done much to bring the music of Africa to the attention of people in the United States. Invite the students to offer their views on the sound prints of these singers. Base your discussion on the characteristics discussed on page 68.

2. Ask the students to turn to page 72 and follow the notation as they listen to the recording. Warn them that they will hear slight variations from the melody as it is sung, for it is nearly impossible to notate folk songs exactly as performed.

3. Invite the students to sing along with the recording, attempting to match the quality of the voices heard.

OPTIONAL

4. Play the complete recording. Help the students realize that the voices combine three patterns to make up the song. Some patterns are varied as they are repeated. Divide the class into three groups. Each group should sing one pattern. Experiment with combining the patterns in ways similar to those heard on the recording.

"Ketjak" Chorus
from the *Ramayana*

In Bali, as darkness falls, the Monkey Chorus enters the temple gate chanting *"ketjak, ketjak"* as they surround the stage. The dancers and singers dramatize an ancient story about Rama, the hero, and Rawana, King of the Underworld. The chorus represents the army of monkeys who, led by Sugriwa their king, help Rama rescue his wife, Sita. While some singers continue chanting, others add a repetitive melodic accompaniment:

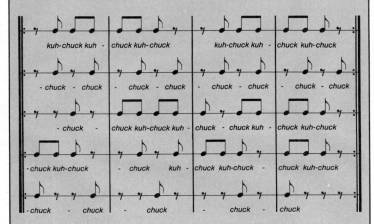

Plan your own performance:

- Choose several actors to dramatize the story.
- Choose some people to perform a repetitive refrain. They should make up a short melody and words.
- Everyone else takes the part of the chorus. Listen to the recording again. Try to imitate the vocal characteristics.
- After performing your own story of Rama, listen again to the recording and compare your performance.

73

Lesson Focus
Time and Place: A particular use of timbre reflects the origin of the musical whole. *(P–I)*

Materials
o **Record Information:**
  - *Ketjak,* from the *Ramayana* (Record 4 Side B Band 5)
o **Instruments:** assorted drums and sticks
o **Other:** transparency of Activity Sheet 15 (*Vocal Sound Prints*) from Culture 2; overhead projector

For Your Information
Ramayana means "Story of Rama" in Sanskrit. The third century epic is the story of Rama, a prince who is the seventh incarnation of the god Vishnu. The tale (narrated in seven books) begins with Rama's birth. It relates how he wins Sita, the daughter of the king, through acts of prowess. Sita is kidnapped by the evil king, Ravana. With the aid of armies of monkeys and bears, Rama slays Ravana and rescues Sita. The part of the epic told through the musical excerpt here is a segment about the battle between the monkey army and the evil king's forces.

The Lesson

1. After reading the discussion at the top of page 73, play the recording in its entirety. As the students share their reactions to the performance, provide additional information about the many *Ramayana* legends (see **For Your Information**). Liken it to some American legends which have many parts and numerous versions, such as those of Paul Bunyan.

2. Play the recording again, this time asking the students to concentrate on the "voice prints." Prepare a profile for these voices using a transparency prepared from Activity Sheet 15 (*Vocal Sound Prints*).

3. Try performing the rhythmic fragments drawn from the chorus parts which are shown on pupil page 73. Perform each line separately. Repeat it several times, varying the tempo and dynamics. Divide the class into groups and try combining the lines while still varying the tempo and dynamics. A student conductor may indicate when changes are to occur.

4. Follow the suggestions on the bottom of the pupil page and plan a performance. The students may prefer to work in small groups, each planning their own presentation. They might also add a drum accompaniment as heard on the recording. Stress the importance of role playing. **If you lived in Bali, how would you feel participating in the dramatization of an epic that has been repeated in the same way for generations?**

5. End the lesson by having each group present their interpretation, and then listen once again to the recording.

OPTIONAL

CULTURE 6

Lesson Focus

Time and Place: The way musical elements are combined into a whole reflects the origin of the music. (**D–I**)

Materials

o **Piano Accompaniment:** page 288
o **Record Information:**
  • The Wreck of the Edmund Fitzgerald
    (Record 4 Side B Band 1)
o **Instruments:** autoharp or guitar
o **Teacher's Resource Binder:**
  • Optional—
    Instrumental Accompaniment 5,
    page 114

The Wreck of the Edmund Fitzgerald

Words and Music by Gordon Lightfoot

Ballads are one of the oldest of song traditions. Many tell the tale of actual events that were important to the people in the community. It was often the only way such events were recorded and kept alive in people's memory.

The musical form of the ballad frequently consisted of a single melody of from two to four phrases. This melody was repeated as many times as needed to tell the complete story. The original melody was varied as needed to adjust to word and meaning changes.

The tradition of ballads continues. "The Wreck of the Edmund Fitzgerald" was written to commemorate an event that occurred on Lake Superior in 1975. The basic melody is given below. This melody is repeated, with slight variations, four times for every verse. Learn to read it from the notation. Then listen to the recording to see how the melody and rhythm are adjusted for each two lines of text.

1. The legend lives on from the Chippewa on down
   of the big lake they called "Gitche Gumee."
   The lake, it is said, never gives up her dead
   when the skies of November turn gloomy.
   With a load of iron ore twenty-six thousand tons more
   than the Edmund Fitzgerald weighed empty,
   that good ship and true was a bone to be chewed
   when the Gales of November came early.

2. The ship was the pride of the American side
   coming back from some mill in Wisconsin.
   As the big freighters go it was bigger than most
   with a crew and good captain well seasoned,
   concluding some terms with a couple of steel firms
   when they left fully loaded for Cleveland.
   And later that night when the ship's bell rang,
   could it be the north wind they'd been feelin'?

74

The Lesson

1. Read the explanation at the top of page 74. Engage the students in a discussion of the history and evolution of the ballad (see **For Your Information**). Ask the students if they can think of other ballads they have learned either in school or at home.

2. **Does this song meet the criteria of a ballad? Does it tell a story that is true, gripping, and of great importance at the time the event took place?** (Agree that this is so.) **For people who make their living on the water, the sinking of a ship is a terrible event, the memory of which does not soon die.**

3. **What about the music? Is it a simple melody? What makes a melody simple?** To help the students answer the questions, ask them to scan the rhythm. Agree that the melody has a simple rhythm that usually moves with the beat. The melody is considered simple because it moves mostly by steps.

This twentieth century song is tied to the older ballad tradition because it is based on the Mixolydian mode. The Mixolydian mode is similar to the major scale, except that there is a half step between steps 6 and 7 and a whole step between 7 and 1′.

The form of this song is also very simple. There are only two different phrases. These are repeated four times to complete the verse. Challenge the students to sight-read the first two phrases. You may wish to accompany them softly on the autoharp or guitar. Then ask them to sing the entire first verse.

4. Follow the suggestion at the top of page 74 and listen to the ballad. Tell the students to watch the words carefully and listen to see how the melody and the rhythm are altered to

3. The wind in the wires made a tattletale sound,
   and a wave broke over the railing.
   And every man knew as the captain did too
   'twas the witch of November come stealin'.
   The dawn came late, and the breakfast had to wait
   when the Gales of November came slashin'.
   When afternoon came, it was freezin' rain
   in the face of a hurricane west wind.

4. When suppertime came, the old cook came on deck
   sayin', "Fellas, it's too rough t' feed ya."
   At seven P.M. a main hatchway caved in;
   he said, "Fellas, it's been good t' know ya!"
   The captain wired in he had water comin' in,
   and the good ship and crew was in peril.
   And later that night when 'is lights went outta sight
   came the wreck of the Edmund Fitzgerald.

5. Does anyone know where the love of God goes
   when the waves turn the minutes to hours?
   The searchers all say they'd have made Whitefish Bay
   if they'd put fifteen more miles behind 'er.
   They might have split up or they might have capsized;
   they may have broke deep and took water.
   And all that remains is the faces and the names
   of the wives and the sons and the daughters.

6. When Lake Huron rolls, Superior sings
   in the rooms of her ice-water mansion.
   Old Michigan steams like a young man's dreams;
   the islands and bays are for sportsmen.
   And farther below Lake Ontario
   takes in what Lake Erie can send her,
   and the iron boats go as the mariners all know
   with the Gales of November remembered.

7. In a musty old hall in Detroit they prayed,
   in the Maritime Sailors' Cathedral.
   The church bell chimed 'til it rang twenty-nine times
   for each man on the Edmund Fitzgerald.
   The legend lives on from the Chippewa on down
   of the big lake they called "Gitche Gumee."
   "Superior," they said, "never gives up her dead
   when the Gales of November come early!"

75

CULTURE 6

For Your Information

The ballad began as a dance song, but by the 1700s it came to mean a tale told in simple verse. Most ballads are narrative tales dealing with gruesome, miraculous, or fabulous events, some true, some not. They were often embellished with political and social commentary aimed at the various institutions of the day. Ballad singers would sing their compositions in the streets, at fairs, or for private audiences. Settlers coming to the New World brought the English ballad form with them. In the Appalachian Mountains many of the old English ballads may still be heard sung much as they were in England three hundred years ago.

In addition to keeping the old songs alive, Americans of British descent have continued to add to the tradition by commemorating important events in the ballad. "The Wreck of the Edmund Fitzgerald" is a contemporary version of this ancient form.

fit the words and phrases of the remaining verses. The structure of the recording is as follows, with some changes listed. (Note that occasionally the melody goes up on the last note in Measure 7, instead of down as in this notated version.)

Introduction—16 measures (Notice the sound of the acoustic guitar; the synthesizer provides high-pitched, sustained sounds near the end of the introduction; steel guitar is prominent.)

Verse 1—as written except for three measures of rests at end of second and fourth statements

Verse 2—same rests at the end of second statement; the verse is followed by a 12-measure instrumental interlude.

Verse 3—three measures of rests at end of the first, second, and third statements followed by a 16-measure interlude

Verse 4—three measures of rests after first and second statements followed by a 16-measure interlude

Verse 5—three measures of rests after second statement followed by a 36-measure interlude

Verse 6—three-measure rest after the first and third statements; the 30-measure coda gradually diminuendos.

5. Invite the students to sing the complete song.

CULTURE 7

Lesson Focus

Time and Place: The way musical elements are combined into a whole reflects the origin of the music. (*P–I*)

Materials

○ **Piano Accompaniment:** page 292
○ **Record Information:**
  • Goin' Up Yonder
    (Record 4 Side A Band 4)
○ **Instruments:** suspended cymbal and drumstick
○ **Other:** Activity Sheet 15 (*Vocal Sound Prints*) from Culture 2

The Lesson

1. Play the recording for the class. Ask them if they can identify the origin of the music. Many students will recognize it as gospel music. Discuss the fact that gospel music is a truly American genre, heard in many communities throughout our country. The spirited, full, rich sound, driven by powerful rhythms, is an important part of America's folk sound. Explain that many of the rhythms heard in popular music of various types, from rhythm and blues to rock, had their origin in the nineteenth century gospel music of freed slaves.

2. Distribute a copy of Activity Sheet 15 (*Vocal Sound Prints*) and a pencil to each student. Play the recording again as the students mark their decisions as to the vocal qualities. Ask the students to share their decisions to see if there is unanimity in describing the sounds.

Reassure the students that there are no wrong answers.

3. Ask the students to open their books to page 76 and examine the arrangement that has been prepared for them. This is not the complete arrangement they heard on the recording, but a simplified, shortened version. The verse may be sung by a soloist, or by a small vocal group in harmony, or in unison. These might be students who are familiar with the gospel style or who choose to listen carefully to try to imitate the style and vocal quality.

4. Examine the melody of the verse. It is made up of two-measure motives that are somewhat terraced (the second motive ends higher than the first; motive 3 begins a step higher than motives 1 and 2). The last eight measures are an almost identical restatement

of the first eight. **What is one musical characteristic that you can observe just by looking at the notation?** (Guide the students to identify the many examples of syncopation.) This is anticipatory syncopation in that the stress usually occurs before the normal first beat of the measure.

Guide the students to read the words of the verse expressively, in the correct rhythm, as someone lightly maintains the shortest sound on a suspended cymbal (tap with a drumstick). Then play a simple chordal accompaniment as they learn the melody.

5. Ask the students to scan the three vocal parts of the chorus and decide which they should learn. Treble I and Changing Voices may sing the top part (Changing Voices sing an octave lower than written). Treble II may sing the middle part; Baritones should sing the lower part, written in the bass clef. Guide the students to observe that the refrain, like the verse, is based on two-measure motives, many of which are the same or similar.

6. To help the students learn their parts, draw attention to the fact that most pitches (in all voices) are drawn from the chords written above the staff. Play the following chord sequence and ask the students to improvise vocal patterns using the pitches they hear within each chord. Play each chord several times, sustaining the sound until the students have had ample time to play with a variety of

CULTURE 7

patterns; then proceed to the next chord in the sequence.

After the students have improvised in response to the chord sequence, ask them to study their parts as written in the book while you play each chord again. **I will play two chords to a measure. As I play, try to think the pitches that are written on the staff for you to sing.**

After hearing and thinking the chord sequence several times, challenge the students to sing the refrain. Remind them that the rhythm is similar in nature to that sung for the verse, with the accent in the voices regu-

larly anticipating the accent in the underlying accompaniment.

7. When the students can sing their parts readily, work on developing a gospel style. Discuss appropriate tempi, dynamic changes, and vocal quality. Some students may wish to add their own improvisations at points where the written arrangement indicates that voices be sustained or rest (as on Measures 5, 8, 11, 13, and 16 of the Refrain).

Lakota National Anthem

Transcribed by Lynn Hueneman

1. E - ya   le - he   he - ha   ya - he   la - he   le - hoi
2. Tun - ka - si - la - ya - pi   ta - wa - pa - ha   kin ha

hi - yo   yo - hi   yo ho - yo hi   ye yo   he ye   he ye   he ye
o - i - han-ke   sni he   na-jin   kte - lo   he ye   he ye   he ye

hi - ya   yo - he   o - yoi   ye - ha   o - he   le - ha
i - yoh - la - te   ha - ya   o - ya - te kin   o - yoi

ye - ha   yo - he   yo - ho   he - o   yo - he   ye - lo
wi - ci - ca - gin   kta - ca   le - ca - mon we - lo - yo

(2nd time only)

he ye   he ye   he ye   yo!

Lesson Focus

Time and Place: A particular use of timbre reflects the origin of the musical whole. *(P–I)*

Materials

o **Record Information:**
  • *Lakota National Anthem*
    Record 5   Side A   Band 1
o **Instruments:** tom-tom and stick

For Your Information

A number of American Indian tribes have flag songs. Among those tribes are the Sioux, the Kiowa, and the Winnebago. Many of these songs are national anthems which express loyalty to this, their homeland, as well as to the government of the United States. Flag songs are usually dance songs.

The Lesson

1. Play the recording of the *Lakota National Anthem* with the books closed. Ask the students to be ready to identify the origin of the song. Most of the students will recognize it as American Indian.

2. Play the recording as the students listen and follow the notation on page 79. Read the following translation to the class: "The flag of the United States will fly forever. Under it the people will grow and prosper. Therefore have I [fought for my country]."

   Discuss the way the old (the music and performing style) has been combined with the new (the recognition by the American Indians that they are citizens of the United States).

3. Explain that the words in the first verse are simply vocables; they have no specific meaning (somewhat like the "la la" refrains in many English songs). Listen again to the recording. Pay careful attention to the enunciation of each word and the quality of the singer's voice. Urge the students to imitate the quality and the expressiveness of the recorded performance as they sing.

4. One student may add the drum accompaniment as the class sings the flag song.

OPTIONAL

Lesson Focus

Time and Place: The way musical elements are combined into a whole reflects the origin of the music. *(P–I)*

Materials

o **Piano Accompaniment:** page 296
o **Record Information:**
  • *Alla en el Rancho Grande*
    (Record 4   Side A   Band 5)

Alla en el Rancho Grande

Translated by Bartley Costello   Music by Silvano R. Ramos

> I love to roam out yon-der, Out where the buf-f'lo
> A-llá en el ran-cho gran-de, A-llá don-de vi-
>
> wan-der, _____ Free as the eag-le fly-ing, I'm
> ví - a, _____ Ha-bía u-na ran-che-ri - ta, Que a-
>
> rop-ing and a-ty-ing, I'm rop-ing and a-ty-ing. _____
> le-gre me de-ci - a, Que a-le-gre me de-ci - a. _____

The Lesson

1. Help the students learn the song from the notation, using the information they have gained in Unit I. To account for ranges you may want to have the students learn the parts as follows:

   Treble I's—always the highest pitch (Sometimes this is the melody, sometimes not.)
   Treble II's—lower (or middle) pitch whenever voices divide, otherwise the melody line
   Changing Voices—Refrain: Phrase I—highest pitches, an octave lower; Phrase 2—melody or lower pitches, as written. Verse: melody or lowest pitch when the voices divide, as written
   Baritones—Verse: Same harmonizing part as Treble II's, an octave lower, or they should sing the chord roots throughout, following the chord symbols above the staff.

2. As the students learn to perform the song, discuss characteristics which reflect its Mexican origin: the melody which frequently outlines the I or V7 chords, the harmonization in thirds and sixths (especially typical is the harmonization above the melody), and the use of syncopation.

3. After the students have learned the song, play the recording. Discuss ways that they can adjust their vocal quality and performance style to more accurately reflect a traditional Mexican performance.

Verse

Give me my ranch and my cat - tle, _____
Te voy ha - cer tus cal - zo - nes, _____

_____ Far from the great cit - y's rat - tle; _____
_____ Co - mo los u - sa/el ran - che - ro; _____

_____ Give me a big herd to bat - tle, _____ For I just
_____ Te los co - mien - zo de la - na, _____ Te los a -

love herd - ing cat - tle. _____
ca - bo de cue - ro. _____

81

Lesson Focus

Timbre: The total sound is affected by the number and qualities of sounds occurring at the same time.
Timbre: The quality of a sound is affected by the way the sound is produced. *(C–I)*

Materials

o **Instruments:** orchestral instruments belonging to students; glockenspiels (or any xylophone-type instruments); recorders; bongo drums; autoharp

o **Other:** environmental sound sources as described in **For Your Information;** different colored overhead pens; overhead projector

o **Teacher's Resource Binder:**

> Activity
> Sheets

  • **Activity Sheet 16,** page A23 (Make one transparency and three copies for each student.)

Instrumental Sound Prints

Just as with the sounds of voices, instrumental sounds may seem pleasing or displeasing to you because of your past experience. The quality of the instrumental sound, how the sounds are organized, and the style of performance are also influenced by the performers' own background.

Experiment with different sound sources. As you explore ways of producing sounds on each, think about some of the same characteristics you considered when you explored ways of changing the quality of your voice.

82

The Lesson

1. Read the first two paragraphs on page 82 with the students. Divide the class into four small groups. Give each group one of the sound sources listed (see **For Your Information**). Provide several examples of each so that each pair of students may have a sound source to explore.

   Explain that they are to read the explanation of sound characteristics given in their book, then experiment with producing sound on the sources they have been given. **After you have experimented, be ready to share your answers to the questions in your book with the rest of the class.**

2. Give the students ample time to explore, then reassemble everyone. Distribute three copies of Activity Sheet 16 (*Instrumental Sound Prints*) to each student. Call on members of

each group to demonstrate ways of producing sound on their instruments and discuss its quality in terms of the characteristics listed. After each group plays, ask the class to suggest where they would place a mark to describe each characteristic listed on the activity sheet. Display the transparency. As the students offer ideas, place a mark in the appropriate position. Use a different colored overhead pen for each type of instrument.

3. Follow the final suggestion given on pupil page 83. Reorganize the groups so that there are some instruments of each type (as originally distributed) in each of the new groups. Suggest that they improvise a short piece of music by starting with an idea or motive developed by one class member. Others should then join in, responding to that original idea. **Explore ways of combining your sounds until you are satisfied with the results.**

Texas Essential Elements, Instrumental Sound Prints, pp. 82–97: 1A, 1B, 1C, 1D, 2, 3A, 3B, 4A, 4B, 5A, 5B (Please see Unit 2 Opener, page 65, for component sound page references.)

Characteristics of Single Sounds

Some of the characteristics that affect the quality of the sound, making the quality seem thin or rich, include:

Loudness

Does the sound, when produced without effort, seem to be loud; easily carrying; or soft, with little carrying power?

Character

Does the sound seem to have a brilliant and penetrating character or a subdued and mellow character?

Energy

Does the sound seem to be intense, with a high degree of energy, or "comfortable," with low energy?

Range and Register

Can you produce sounds of varying pitch? Are they mostly high, low, or extended over a wide range from high to low? Does the quality of the sound seem to change as you move up and down over the range of the instrument?

Vibrato

Can you produce a vibrato on your instrument? If so, is it wide or narrow?

Envelope

Envelope describes the way the sound begins and ends, somewhat like articulation. Is the initiation of the sound, the attack, sudden or gradual? How does the sound end—suddenly or gradually?

Contrast

As you experiment with producing sounds on a single instrument, consider the possibilities. Can you create a variety of qualities of sound with a great deal of contrast? Or do most of the sounds you produce seem to have a similar quality?

Characteristics of Combined Sounds

Now work with your classmates and try combining some sounds by playing two or more instruments at once. As you play, think about:

Balance

Are all the sounds heard equally? Does one seem to overwhelm the others?

Blend

Do all the sounds seem to "melt together" to create a unified sound, or does each retain its individual character?

83

For Your Information

For this lesson the students should explore sound production with both traditional instruments and environmental sound sources. For environmental sound sources obtain the following materials: several lengths (and widths, if possible) of metal pipe; soft drink bottles or jugs into which students may blow; at least two sizes of plastic ice cream cartons; rubber bands of various lengths and thicknesses; and a small hardwood board (breadboards work well), preferably with a handle.

To explore changes in string sound, insert three nails into the board. Stretch a rubber band around the three nails to form a triangle. To produce a sound, the student should pluck each segment of the rubber band. The sound is delicate; the student should hold it so that part of the board is pressed against their ear. Experiment with changes in quality resulting from the use of different sizes of rubber bands.

Think about the two characteristics described in your book.

4. As in Step 2, call the class together and have each group present their improvisation while others decide how to describe the blend and balance as listed on the activity sheet.

5. End the lesson by inviting the students who play wind or string instruments to perform for the class. Depending on the number of instruments available, instruct some members of the class to complete their activity sheet for each instrument heard. When all have been heard, draw a profile of each instrument sound on the transparency, using a different colored pen for each instrument.

Lesson Focus

Timbre: The quality of a sound is determined by the sound source.
Time and Place: The way musical elements are combined into a whole reflects the origin of the music. *(D–I)*

Materials

o **Record Information:**
- *Sematimba ne Kikwabanga*
  (Record 5   Side A   Band 2)
- *Hudan Mas*
  Record 5   Side A   Band 3
- *Trouble in Mind*
  (Record 5   Side A   Band 4)
- *Anduve*
  (Record 4   Side A   Band 3)

o **Other:** Activity Sheet 16 (*Instrumental Sound Prints*) from Culture 10, four copies for each student and one transparency; overhead projector

For Your Information

Answers for Activity Sheet 16:

Sematimba ne Kikwabanga
Loudness: medium to loud
Character: medium brilliant
Energy: toward high
Vibrato: slight

(continued on next page)

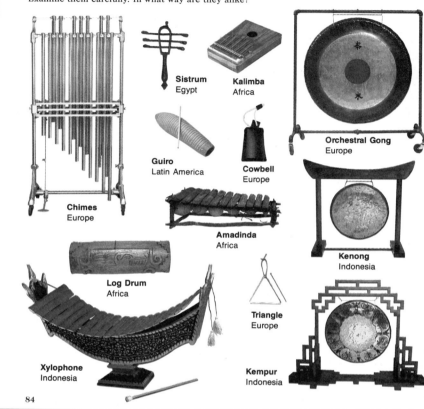

Idiophones

All the ancient and modern instruments shown on these two pages belong to the same category. Although you see many different types of sound-makers, all are **idiophones** because they have something in common.

Examine them carefully. In what way are they alike?

Sistrum
Egypt

Kalimba
Africa

Guiro
Latin America

Cowbell
Europe

Orchestral Gong
Europe

Chimes
Europe

Amadinda
Africa

Kenong
Indonesia

Log Drum
Africa

Triangle
Europe

Xylophone
Indonesia

Kempur
Indonesia

84

The Lesson

1. Ask the students to follow the instructions on pupil pages 84–85, and answer the question. Conclude that instruments can be alike in the material they are made of, the size, shape, and color, or the way the sound is produced. Guide the students to realize that the only thing these instruments have in common is the way the sound is produced, that is, through the vibration of a solid material. The material might be metal or wood; it may be initiated in any of a variety of ways such as striking, rattling, or scraping.

2. Clarify the word *idiophone.* The first syllable, *idio-,* comes from the Greek word meaning individual or unique. *Phone* means sound. Each of these instruments has a unique characteristic sound. Ask the students if they can recall another name that might be used to describe instruments of the type shown here.

Some students may suggest the term *percussion.* Discuss the fact that, in the past, they may have learned to organize instruments into orchestral families. The categories they will be learning about in this unit, starting with the idiophones, are groupings devised by *ethnomusicologists* (people who study the music of the whole earth) to create categories broad enough so that all instruments can be assigned to a group.

3. Distribute four copies of Activity Sheet 16 to each student. Play the following excerpts, giving students time after each to complete the activity sheet. Answers may be found in **For Your Information**.

Sematimba ne Kikwabanga
This excerpt, from Uganda, is performed on an *amadina,* a free-key xylophone with twelve bars. The *amadina* is tuned to a five-tone scale for two octaves, with two addi-

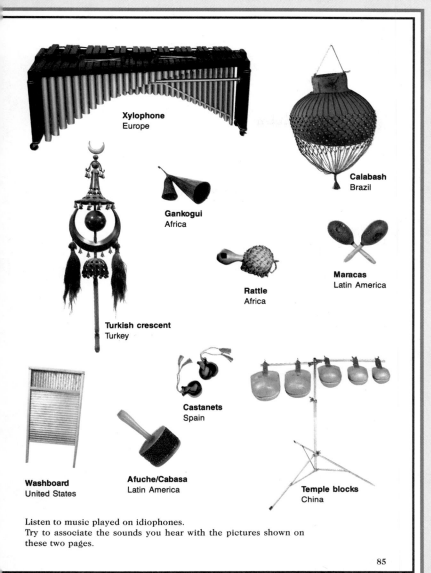

Xylophone
Europe

Gankogui
Africa

Calabash
Brazil

Maracas
Latin America

Rattle
Africa

Turkish crescent
Turkey

Castanets
Spain

Washboard
United States

Afuche/Cabasa
Latin America

Temple blocks
China

Listen to music played on idiophones.
Try to associate the sounds you hear with the pictures shown on
these two pages.

85

For Your Information *(continued)*

Envelope: sudden attack, fairly sudden
decay
Contrast: similar
Balance: even
Blend: unified

Hudan Mas
Loudness: quite loud
Character: toward brilliant
Energy: toward intense
Vibrato: toward little
Envelope: sudden attack, gradual decay
Contrast: similar
Balance: uneven
Blend: individual

Trouble in Mind
Loudness: toward loud
Character: toward dull
Energy: toward intense
Vibrato: none
Envelope: sudden attack, sudden decay
Contrast: similar
Balance: middle
Blend: individual

Anduve
Loudness: toward soft
Character: toward dull
Energy: medium
Vibrato: none
Envelope: sudden attack, fairly sudden
decay
Contrast: similar
Balance: even
Blend: toward unified

tional pitches in a third octave. The xylophone is played by three musicians. The melody results from the interlocking pitches of two of the players. The third player plays the two pitches in the highest octave. In this excerpt the two melody players first demonstrate their parts. The music then begins with player one, followed by player two, then player three.

Hudan Mas
This music is performed by a Javanese gamelan (orchestra) that includes metal-keyed xylophones, gongs, drums, a flute, two-stringed bowed lute, wooden-keyed xylophone, plucked zither, and male and female vocalists. Focus the students' attention on the two idiophones, the xylophones and gongs, as they complete their activity sheet.

Trouble in Mind
This performance demonstrates the use of the washboard, another idiophone. Other in-

struments are heard which belong to other families. The students should describe the sound of the washboard on the activity sheet.

Anduve
The final example is from Brazil. It features two dancers and two musicians who sing and play two idiophones. The first musician sits on a wooden seat against which he or she strikes an empty half-calabash (a gourd); the other musician plays a traditional calabash filled with seeds and strung on a wooden handle. The students may describe either or both sounds.

4. After the students have completed the activity sheets, display a transparency of the sheet and compile a group profile for each instrument heard. As the students share their ideas, locate the instrument(s) pictured in their book. Turn back to the map on pages 70–71 and locate where each sound originated.

OPTIONAL

85

Lesson Focus

Timbre: The quality of a sound is determined by the sound source.
Time and Place: The way musical elements are combined into a whole reflects the origin of the music. *(D–I)*

Materials

o **Record Information:**
  • *Dance Song*
    (Record 4 Side A Band 1)
  • *Oldest Rabbit Song*
    (Record 5 Side A Band 5)
  • *Saeta*
    (Record 4 Side B Band 4)
o **Other:** Activity Sheet 16 (*Instrumental Sound Prints*) from Culture 10, three copies for each student and one transparency; overhead projector

Membranophones

The instruments shown on these two pages are all **membranophones.** All belong to this category because they have something in common. In what way are they alike?

Tambourine
Europe

Timpani
Europe

Bongos
Latin America

Conga Drum
Latin America

Tabla drums
India

86

The Lesson

1. As with Culture 11, pages 84–85, begin by asking the students to speculate about the characteristics which make the instruments on pages 86–87 belong together. After they have offered ideas, suggest that they analyze the word that defines this category, "**membranophone.**" **What does the last syllable, *-phone* mean?** (sound) **What about the first two syllables, *mem-bran*?** The students may know the word *membrane,* a thin, pliable layer of tissue.

Conclude that membranophones must be instruments which include a membrane. The sound results from the vibration of a stretched skin of some type (including plastic). This is in contrast to idiophones where the vibrating body is a solid substance. Most membranophones are drums of some type.

The sound is initiated by striking, either with the hand or a mallet of some type.

2. Distribute three copies of Activity Sheet 16 (*Instrumental Sound Prints*) and a pencil to each student. Play the following excerpts, pausing after each selection to give the students time to complete the activity sheet.

Dance Song
Four drummers are heard on this recording. The drum is the only ancient Eskimo instrument. The drums are made by stretching skins on frames made of wood or animal bones; two of the membranes for these drums are made from reindeer skin; another is made from a walrus stomach and the fourth from a seal liver.

Oldest Rabbit Song
This Sioux Indian song features a tom-tom, played with a beater.

Tenor drum
Europe

Snare drum
Europe

Bass drum
Europe

Tom tom
North America

Kaganu
Africa

Sogo
Africa

Kidi
Africa

Listen to music played on membranophones. Try to associate the sounds you hear with the pictures shown on these two pages.

87

For Your Information

Dance Song
Loudness: quite loud
Character: medium brilliant
Energy: toward intense
Vibrato: toward little
Envelope: sudden attack, some decay
Contrast: similar
Balance: even
Blend: individual

Oldest Rabbit Song
Loudness: quite loud
Character: medium brilliant
Energy: toward intense
Vibrato: toward little
Envelope: sudden attack, some decay
Contrast: similar
Balance: even
Blend: individual

Saeta (Field Drum)
Loudness: quite loud
Character: toward brilliant
Energy: toward intense
Vibrato: toward little
Envelope: sudden attack, some decay
Contrast: similar
Balance: uneven
Blend: individual

Saeta
This Spanish processional song features field drums (such as those found in marching bands or drum and bugle corps) during the introduction. The students will also recognize the trumpets.

3. Display a transparency of the activity sheet and help the students come to a group decision about the characteristics of each instrument. Create a profile for each instrument and compare the profiles to one another.

Lesson Focus

Timbre: The quality of a sound is affected by the material, shape, and size of the source.
Timbre: The quality of a sound is affected by the way the sound is produced. *(P–I)*

Materials

o **Record Information:**
  • *Atsia*
    Record 5 Side A Band 6
o **Other:** environmental sound sources: plastic containers of three different sizes to serve as high, middle, and low range membranophones; plastic or wooden containers filled with dried beans to serve as rattles; several lengths of metal pipe to serve as double bells
o **Teacher's Resource Binder:**
  Activity Sheets
  • **Activity Sheet 17,** page A24
  • Optional—
    Enrichment Activity 7, page E13

For Your Information

"*Atsia*" is a dance based on a two-pulse pattern played by the *gankoqui;* other instruments move in relation to its pattern. Each has its own rhythm, relating freely to the others.

LISTENING

Atsia

African Ewe Dance

Listen to an African Ewe Dance performed on membranophones and idiophones. The musicians are led by a master drummer who plays complex rhythms. Here is an example of some of the patterns played:

Transcribed by James Koetting

Gankogui	H		H		H	H		H		H		H
Sogo	o		o	/	/	/	o		o	/	/	/
Kaganu		o	o		o	o		o	o		o	o
Kidi	o			o			o			o		
Axhatsi	D			D			D			D		

O = Stick strikes drumhead and rebounds.   D = Strike rattle downward against your thigh.
/ = Stick strikes drumhead and remains.   H = Play a high tone.

Search for materials that would make good idiophones and membranophones. Make your own instruments. Then perform your own version of "*Atsia.*"

You will need:

Three membranophones: Two idiophones:
Sogo—low drum   *Axhatsi*—gourd rattle
Kaganu—middle drum   *Gankogui*—double bell
Kidi—high drum

After playing the brief excerpt of "*Atsia*" shown on this page, plan your own sound score. Compose parts for these or other membranophones and idiophones. Use symbols such as those used in the score on this page, or devise new ones. Combine several individual scores to make an extended composition.

88

The Lesson

1 Play the recording of "*Atsia*" as the students observe the sample score shown on pupil page 88. Be sure the students realize that this score would not have been used by the performers. Patterns have been transcribed by western musicians who have studied the music of various African tribes. The musicians playing the music learned their parts through the oral tradition. (Review the concepts of the oral tradition discussed in the opening lessons of Unit 1.)

2. After listening to the dance, follow the remaining suggestions in the pupil book. You may either provide materials for students to use in devising their own instruments, or postpone this part of the lesson and ask the students to bring environmental sound sources to school. Drums might be devised from plastic containers of three different sizes. Rattles can be developed by putting dried beans or peas in small plastic or wood containers. Lengths of metal pipe can be struck to suggest the sound of the double bell.

3. Distribute a copy of Activity Sheet 17 (*Sound Score*) to each student. The students should follow the instructions on the activity sheet. After all the students have completed their scores, they may work in small groups of four or five and develop their performance.

Hudan Mas

(excerpt)

Javanese Gamelan Music

Listen to *"Hudan Mas."* Develop your own Javanese gamelan. What instruments can you find or make to suggest the sound of the instruments you hear?

On the right is a simplified score of the first melody in *"Hudan Mas."* To play it, you will need:

Sarons—metal-keyed xylophones in several sizes. The smallest is the *Peking.* Find instruments that can play E♭, F, A, B♭, and C.

Three Drums—low, middle, and high

Gongs (four kinds):

Kempul—suspended gongs; you need two with the pitches A and F.
Kenong—pitched gongs set in racks. You need E♭ and F.
Ketuk—small gong with a deadened sound.
Gong—largest, nonpitched gong with a deep sound.

The pitches in the score are written with numbers. You can approximate the gamelan tuning with these pitches:
2 = E♭   3 = F   5 = A   6 = B♭   7 = C

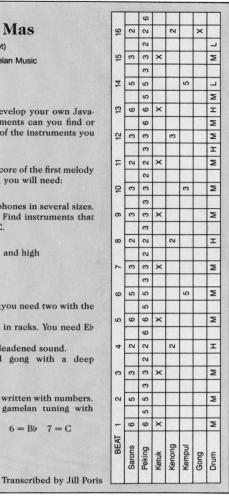

Transcribed by Jill Poris

89

Lesson Focus

Expression: The expressiveness of music is affected by the way timbre contributes to the musical whole. *(P–I)*

Materials

o **Record Information:**
   • *Hudan Mas*
     (Record 5   Side A   Band 3)
o **Instruments:** several sets of resonator bells; soprano glockenspiel; bass metallophone; cymbal; large gong; three sizes of drums and beaters (If no gong is available, use a metal garbage can lid or a large resonant pot lid.)
o **Other:** Activity Sheet 17 (*Sound Score*), page A24, from Culture 13, page 88
o **Teacher's Resource Binder:**
   • Optional—
     Mainstreaming Activity 11, page M18

The Lesson

1. Play the recording of *Hudan Mas*. This type of piece is known as a *burbaran*. It is usually played at the end of a performance while the audience leaves, but it may also be played to accompany dancers or scenes in a puppet play involving marching soldiers.

2. **OPTIONAL** Focus the students' attention on the layers of sound that can be heard. Instruments of the Javanese *gamelan* (orchestra) may be grouped according to function. One group features barred percussion instruments that carry the melody or theme. Another pitched group provides a second layer with variations on the melody. A third group, consisting of different-sized gongs, marks equal musical segments. This group plays a repeated pattern.

3. Suggest to the students that they follow the instructions in their book to develop their own Javanese *gamelan*. To suggest the sounds of the *gamelan* instrumentation, the following classroom instruments might be used:

Sarons—resonator bells E♭, F, A, B♭, and C
Peking—soprano glockenspiel (same pitches as resonator bells)
Kempul—bass metallophone, pitches F and A
Kenong—bass metallophone, pitches E♭ and F
Ketuk—cymbal, lightly dampened with fingers
Gong—heavy metal lid with deep, resonant pitch if a large gong is not available
Drums—Obtain three different sizes to produce low, middle, and high pitches.

4. The students may work in small groups to perform *Hudan Mas*. They may wish to use Activity Sheet 17 and develop additional patterns to play on their instruments.

Lesson Focus

Timbre: The quality of a sound is determined by the sound source.
Time and Place: The way musical elements are combined into a whole reflects the origin of the music. *(D–I)*

Materials

o **Record Information:**
  • *Azumi Jishi*
    (Record 4   Side A   Band 2)
  • *Kalamtianos*
    Record 5   Side A   Band 7
  • *Color Him Folky*
    (Record 5   Side B   Band 1)
o **Other:** Activity Sheet 16 (*Instrumental Sound Prints*) from Culture 10, three copies for each student

Chordophones

The instruments pictured here are **chordophones**. What characteristics do they have in common?

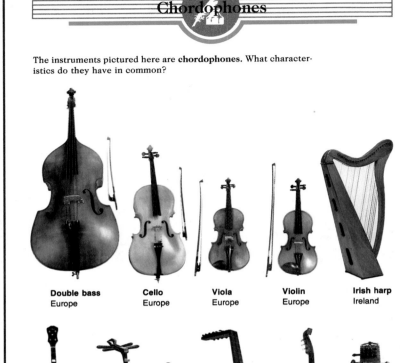

| Double bass | Cello | Viola | Violin | Irish harp |
| Europe | Europe | Europe | Europe | Ireland |

| Banjo | Biwa | Mandolin | Lauto | Lute | Sarangi |
| United States | Japan | Italy | Greece | Europe | India |

90

The Lesson

1. Remind the students of the process they used to determine the defining characteristics of the two categories of instruments they have already studied (Culture 11 and Culture 12). **Can you follow the same procedure to decide what these instruments have in common?** By examining the pictures and analyzing the word *chordophone*, conclude that this category includes instruments where sound is produced by the vibration of a stretched string.

2. Provide each student with three copies of Activity Sheet 16 (see **Materials**). Play the excerpts listed below while students make decisions about the characteristics of each instrument and appropriately mark their activity sheet.

Azumi Jishi
Performed by voice, *koto*, *samisen*, and *shakuhachi*; the first two instruments are chordophones. The *koto* is a large zither, about six feet long with thirteen strings. Each string is supported by a movable bridge which makes it easy to adjust tuning; it is played with plectra (or picks) which are placed over the fingers of the right hand; the left hand produces vibrato and special effects. The *samisen* is a three-stringed instrument somewhat similar to the banjo. It is played by plucking with a plectrum.

Kalamtianos
This is a Greek dance played by the violin and accompanied by the *lauto*, a lutelike instrument. In this lesson, focus on the violin.

Color Him Folky
This is from the United States. It is performed

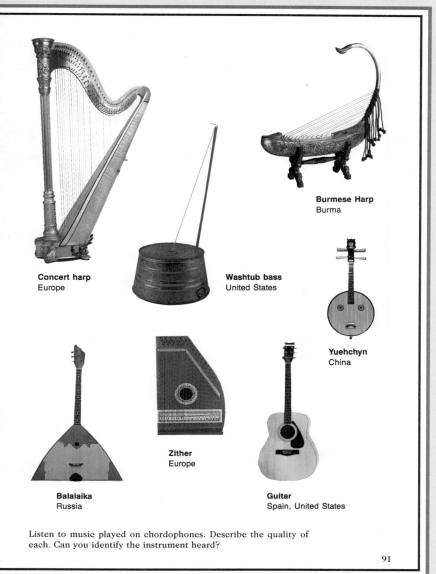

Concert harp
Europe

Burmese Harp
Burma

Washtub bass
United States

Yuehchyn
China

Balalaika
Russia

Zither
Europe

Guitar
Spain, United States

Listen to music played on chordophones. Describe the quality of each. Can you identify the instrument heard?

91

For Your Information

Azumi Jishi (describe *samisen*)
Loudness: medium
Character: medium
Energy: toward comfortable
Vibrato: toward considerable
Envelope: gradual attack, gradual decay
Contrast: toward similar
Balance: toward even
Blend: unified

Kalamtianos (violin and *lauto*; describe only violin)
Loudness: loud
Character: brilliant
Energy: intense
Vibrato: toward much
Envelope: toward sudden attack
Contrast: toward similar
Balance: toward uneven
Blend: individual

Color Him Folky (twelve-string guitar)
Loudness: medium
Character: medium
Energy: toward comfortable
Vibrato: some
Envelope: gradual attack, gradual decay
Contrast: different
Balance: not relevant
Blend: not relevant

on a twelve-string guitar. Draw attention to the fact that both melody and accompaniment are played on the same instrument.

3. Compare the students' decisions regarding the quality of each instrument. Discuss the differences in the way the sound is initiated. In the case of the guitar, the strings are plucked with the fingers. The *koto* is plucked with a plectrum. The violin's sound is initiated by drawing a bow across the string.

Lesson Focus

Timbre: The quality of a sound is determined by the sound source.
Time and Place: The way musical elements are combined into a whole reflects the origin of the music. *(D–I)*

Materials

o **Record Information:**
  • *La Huichola*
    (Record 4   Side B   Band 3)
  • *Kele'a*
    Record 5   Side B   Band 2
  • *What Makes My Baby Cry?*
    Record 5   Side B   Band 3
    Rakish Paddy
    Record 5   Side B   Band 4

o **Other:** Activity Sheet 16 (*Instrumental Sound Prints*) from Culture 10, four copies for each student and one transparency; overhead projector

For Your Information

La Huichola (chirimia)
Loudness: toward loud
Character: toward brilliant
Energy: toward intense
Vibrato: medium
Envelope: toward gradual attack
              toward sudden decay

(continued on next page)

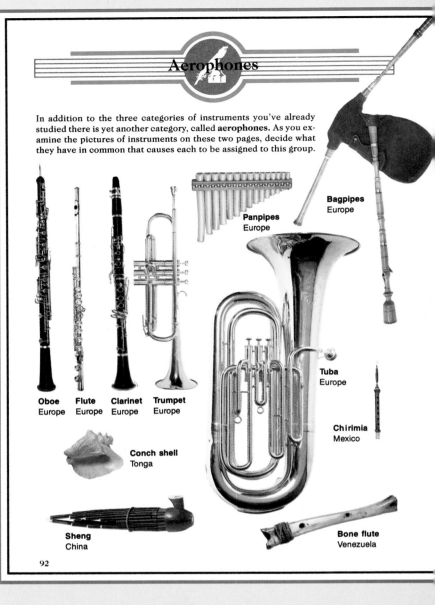

Aerophones

In addition to the three categories of instruments you've already studied there is yet another category, called **aerophones.** As you examine the pictures of instruments on these two pages, decide what they have in common that causes each to be assigned to this group.

Panpipes Europe

Bagpipes Europe

Oboe Europe   **Flute** Europe   **Clarinet** Europe   **Trumpet** Europe

Tuba Europe

Chirimia Mexico

Conch shell Tonga

Sheng China

Bone flute Venezuela

92

The Lesson

1. Tell students to open their books to page 92. **This is the last of the instrumental categories. What do aerophones have in common? What clue does the title of this category give you?** The students should quickly conclude that *aero* suggests *air* and that these instruments belong together because the sound is caused by a vibrating column of air. This vibration may be initiated by blowing into or across a mouthpiece.

Additional subgroups might be identified according to the instrument's vibrating agent or the material from which it is made. Instruments such as the oboe, clarinet, harmonica, *chirimia,* and *sheng* are reed instruments because a reed is the vibrating agent that initiates the sound. There are instruments where the vibrating agent is the lips of the performer. Examples of these are European brass instruments and Polynesian conch shells. Another grouping might be identified as those where the sound results from air moving across the mouthpiece, such as the jug, the panpipes, and the flute.

2. After distributing four copies of Activity Sheet 16 (see **Materials**) to each student, play the following examples of aerophones. In each case the student should complete the activity sheet, then locate the picture of the instrument producing the sound.

La Huichola is performed on a *chirimia,* a reed instrument similar in size and shape to the recorder. It is related to the oboe and it has a reedy, nasal sound. This religious song from the Terascan region of Mexico is also accompanied by a drum.

Kele'a, from Tonga, is performed on conch shells. Shells of different sizes are blown into

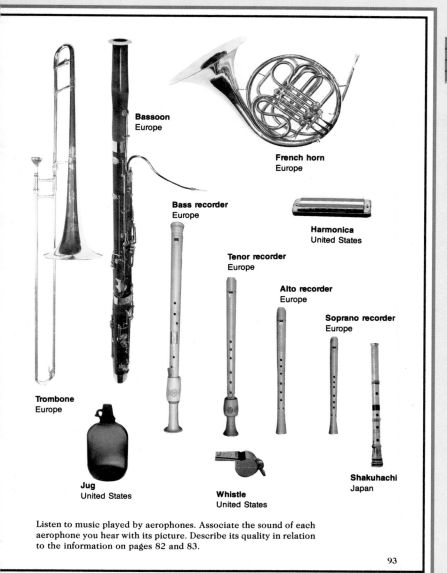

Bassoon
Europe

French horn
Europe

Trombone
Europe

Bass recorder
Europe

Harmonica
United States

Tenor recorder
Europe

Alto recorder
Europe

Soprano recorder
Europe

Jug
United States

Whistle
United States

Shakuhachi
Japan

Listen to music played by aerophones. Associate the sound of each aerophone you hear with its picture. Describe its quality in relation to the information on pages 82 and 83.

93

For Your Information (continued)

Contrast: similar
Balance: toward different
Blend: individual

Kele'a (conch shells)
Loudness: toward soft
Character: toward dull
Energy: toward comfortable
Vibrato: toward little
Envelope: gradual attack
      toward sudden decay
Contrast: similar
Balance: even
Blend: unified

What Makes My Baby Cry? (jug and harmonica)
Loudness: soft; medium
Character: dull toward brilliant
Energy: comfortable medium
Vibrato: little toward considerable
Envelope: toward gradual attack
      toward sudden decay
Contrast: both toward similar
Balance: toward different
Blend: toward individual

Rakish Paddy
Loudness: loud
Character: brilliant
Energy: intense
Vibrato: toward considerable
Envelope: toward gradual attack
      toward gradual decay
Contrast: toward similar
Balance: not relevant
Blend: not relevant

to produce different pitches. Tuning is varied by putting the hand inside the shell.

What Makes My Baby Cry? utilizes, in addition to the chordophones identified during Culture 15, two aerophones: the harmonica and the jug. After a short banjo introduction the harmonica plays the melody. Later in the arrangement the jug can be heard playing a bass accompaniment.

Rakish Paddy is played on bagpipes that produce three pitches. The melody is played on a pipe called a chanter, which is somewhat like a clarinet. Three drones in octaves play a pedal tone D. Regulators, which are part drone and part chanter, provide simple harmony. The piper holds the pipes with bellows under the right elbow and a bag under the left upper arm; he or she plays the chanter with both hands while chording the regulators with the edge of the right hand.

3. End the discussion of aerophones in the same way as the previous lessons, by building a composite profile of each instrument. Display a transparency prepared from Activity Sheet 16. Discuss the differences and similarities in the sound and possible reasons for those similarities or differences.

Lesson Focus

Timbre: The quality of a sound is affected by the material, shape, and size of the source.
Timbre: The quality of a sound is affected by the way the sound is produced. *(P–I)*

Materials

o **Piano Accompaniment:** page 299
o **Record Information:**
  • Shady Grove
  Record 5   Side B   Band 5
  Voices: mixed chorus
  Accompaniment: mandolin, hammered dulcimer, banjo, harmonium, psaltery, whistle, double bass
o **Teacher's Resource Binder:**

  Activity Sheets
  • **Activity Sheet 18,** page A25
  Activity Sheet 19, page A26
  Activity Sheet 20, page A27
  Activity Sheet 21, page A28
  • Optional—
  Orff Activity 7, page O14

Make Your Own Aerophones and Chordophones

From the time people began inventing musical instruments, they have used materials from their environment. What objects could you find to make an aerophone or a membranophone?

Collect the following items and then follow the instructions on your activity sheets to make chordophones and aerophones.

  • bottles of different sizes, shapes, and materials
  • various lengths of bamboo or pipe not more than 1/2″ interior diameter
  • pine board 1″ × 2″ × 33″
  • ice-cream stick, small nail, screw eye
  • guitar or banjo string

Music for Aerophones

Form an ensemble of four aerophone players. Try "hocketing." Tune your instruments as close as possible to steps 1, 2, 3, and 5 of a major scale.

Play this tune by hocketing. Each performer plays just one of the pitches in the tune. You must think the rhythm of the piece as it is played, entering with your pitch at exactly the right time. If you play correctly, you will recognize a famous tune!

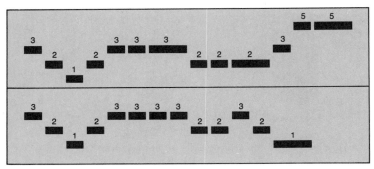

94

The Lesson

1. Give the students the opportunity to choose an instrument they would like to devise: pan-pipes from bamboo, bottle flute, or a one-string dulcimer. Distribute appropriate activity sheets as the students work in small groups in class, or give them an assignment to complete at home to be brought to a subsequent class period.

2. Invite the students who have prepared aerophones to follow the suggestions at the bottom of page 94 and perform the tune by "hocketing." The four-member ensembles need to be able to produce pitches 1, 2, 3, and 5 of a major scale. Each performer is assigned one pitch and must be prepared to play that pitch at the correct time without interrupting the rhythmic flow. The students should quickly recognize the tune as "Mary Had a Little Lamb."

3. Students who have chosen to make a one-string dulcimer should learn to play the song on page 95. **Before trying to play the melody on the dulcimer, learn to sing this traditional Appalachian ballad.** Invite dulcimer players to play the melody while bottle-flute players add an accompaniment.

4. OPTIONAL Give the students time to look through their books to locate other melodies they can perform on their instruments. A number of the songs in Unit 3 will be appropriate.

Music for Chordophones

Try performing this traditional song from the Appalachian mountains on your aerophones and chordophones.

Can you play the melody on the aerophone? Tune your chordophones to D, C, and A. Play an accompaniment by following the chord markings.

Shady Grove

American Folk Song

Refrain: Shad - y Grove, my lit - tle love,
1. Wish I was in Shad - y Grove,
2. Had a ban-jo made of gold,
3. When I was in Shad - y Grove,

Shad - y Grove, I say, Shad - y Grove,
Sit-tin' in a rock - in' chair, And if those blues would
Ev - ery string would shine; The on - ly song that
Heard them pret-ty birds sing; The next time I go to

my lit - tle love, Bound for Shad - y Grove.
both - er me, I'd rock a - way from there. *(to Refrain)*
it would play was Wish that gal was mine. *(to Refrain)*
Shad - y Grove, take a - long a dia - mond ring. *(to Refrain)*

95

Lesson Focus

Time and Place: A particular use of timbre reflects the origin of the musical whole.
Timbre: The quality of a sound is determined by the sound source. *(D–I)*

Materials

o **Record Information:**
  • *Conversation with Milton Babbitt*
    Record 6 Side A Band 1
  • *A Piece for Tape Recorder* by Vladimir Ussachevsky (oo-sah-**chev**-skee), 1911–
    Record 6 Side A Band 2
  • *Composition for Synthesizer* by Milton Babbitt, 1916–
    Record 6 Side A Band 3
  • *Silver Apples of the Moon* by Morton Subotnick, 1933–
    Record 6 Side A Band 4
o **Teacher's Resource Binder:**
  • Optional—
    Biography 4, page B7

Electrophones

The Newest Instrument Category

Electronic instruments and conventional instruments that can be modified electronically have changed the sounds of our music. By these new means, our ears have been stretched to new capacities and fresh forms of musical communication have created possibilities for new journeys through musical time and space.

Electrophones are a product of the twentieth century. One of the first ways composers experimented with electronic composition was through the use of the tape recorder. Listen to Milton Babbitt, a contemporary American composer, explain some of the ways sounds were transformed through the manipulation of audio tape and tape recorders.

96

The Lesson

1. Read the opening discussion on pupil page 96 with the students. Help the students realize that electronic music is the result of sounds produced in an entirely different manner. Instead of by vibration of a physical body, as with traditional instruments, sounds are produced by electrical impulses. Electronic music and processes for creating electronic music have been evolving since the 1940's. Begin this study by listening to Milton Babbitt, one of the pioneers in electronic music composition. Explain some of the early ways that electronic music was composed, by the manipulation of audio tape through reel-to-reel tape recorders.

2. The composition, *A Piece for Tape Recorder* by Vladimir Ussachevsky, was composed on tape, using some of the techniques described by Babbitt. Three different sound sources are used: musical instruments (a gong, piano, cymbal, kettledrum, and an organ); natural sounds (the noise of a jet plane); and electronic sounds (four pure tones produced by an oscillator and a vibrato resulting from the reverberation of the sound of a click of the tape recorder switch). At the beginning, the original sound sources can be identified. Gradually, these sounds are submitted to transformation until the source is no longer evident. The piano and jet plane sounds provide points of interest and contrast; the other sounds provide a background of constantly changing textures.

3. Babbitt composed most of his electronic music on the first synthesizer, built by RCA. The students will be familiar with portable synthesizers which have become a standard instrument in many rock groups. This synthesizer fills an entire room; it is the grandfather of the minisynthesizers that are regularly

A Piece for Tape Recorder
by Vladimir Ussachevsky

This composition was one of the earliest electronic compositions created using the tape recorder. Ussachevsky began with a combination of real and electronic sounds as his sound source. These sounds were then subjected to a series of transformations to create the completed composition. At the beginning, you may be able to identify the origin of some of the sounds. As the music progresses, it becomes almost impossible to identify the original sound source.

Composition for Synthesizer
by Milton Babbitt

This composition was created on one of the first synthesizers constructed by RCA. A synthesizer allows the composer to create the original sounds as well as their transformations directly on the machine. The composer may experiment on the synthesizer until sound patterns are found that he or she likes. The patterns are then organized into a composition. A composer using the synthesizer must make several decisions for each sound included in the composition. Information regarding the frequency (pitch), tone color, duration, and envelope must be given to the synthesizer before the final composition can be developed.

Silver Apples of the Moon
by Morton Subotnick

This composition was also composed on a synthesizer. However, in contrast to the RCA Electronic Sound Synthesizer, which filled an entire room, this synthesizer is compact enough to be housed in the composer's studio. The system generates time and sound configurations. It is possible to produce a specific sound where everything is predetermined; or one can tell the machine the kind of sound wanted, without deciding the specific details. The composer can then listen and make final decisions as to the details.

97

For Your Information

THE SONG OF THE WANDERING AENGUS
by William Butler Yeats

I went out by the hazel wood,
Because a fire was in my head,
And cut and peeled a hazel wand,
And hooked a berry to a thread;
And when white moths were on the wing,
And moth-like stars were flickering out,
I dropped a berry in a stream
And caught a silver trout.

When I laid it on the floor
I went to blow the fire aflame,
But something rustled on the floor,
And someone called me by my name;
It had become a glimmering girl
With apple blossom in her hair
Who called me by my name and ran
And faded through the brightening air.

Though I am old with wandering
Through hollowlands and hilly lands,
I will find out where she has gone,
And kiss her lips and take her hands;
And walk among long dappled grass,
And pluck till time and times are done,
The silver apples of the moon,
The golden apples of the sun.

used today. The purpose of the synthesizer is to do exactly that—synthesize (combine) all basic ingredients of sound: frequency, timbre, intensity, and so on. This process makes it possible for the composer to create sounds in ways no human performer could. As the students listen to Babbitt's *Composition for Synthesizer*, ask them to find musical devices observed in traditional music. **Is there form? repetition? contrast? Can you hear melody? rhythm?**

4. The next composition, *Silver Apples of the Moon,* was created on a special electronic instrument developed by several individuals interested in electronic composition, including the composer, Morton Subotnick. The composer developed a store of sound patterns and then manipulated them. In some sections he programmed the electronic instrument to produce the general outlines of the desired musical event. He then listened to the sounds and altered them until the effect was achieved. The title and the overall mood of the composition was based on a poem by Yeats. (See **For Your Information**.) Ask the students to think about the ideas of the poem and try to decide if Subotnick was trying to communicate literally the ideas of the poem or simply suggest its feeling.

5. End the class by reminding the students of the earlier discussions regarding the way music reflects the society which produced it. Ask the students to suggest ways they feel this music reflects contemporary American society. One obvious way is the actual production of the sounds—no electronic music could be composed until engineers had invented devices that could produce electronic sounds. Encourage the students to offer ideas.

Lesson Focus

Rhythm: Music may move in relation to the underlying steady beat.
Rhythm: A series of beats may be organized into regular or irregular groupings stressing certain beats. *(D–I)*

Materials

o **Record Information:**
  • *Silver Apples of the Moon*
    (Record 6 Side A Band 4)
  • *Rabbit Dance*
    (Record 4 Side B Band 6)
  • *Kalamtianos*
    (Record 5 Side A Band 7)
  • *Teens*
    (Record 6 Side A Band 5)
    Voices: mixed chorus
    Accompaniment: synthesizer, sound effects

o **Other:** overhead projector

o **Teacher's Resource Binder:**
  | Activity Sheets | • **Activity Sheet 22**, page A24 (Make three copies for each student and one transparency.) |
  • Optional—
    Kodaly Activity 12, page K19

Rhythm and Melody

Rhythms of the Whole Earth

Music begins with a single sound. As other sounds follow and flow through time, we become aware of rhythm.

Compare ways that sounds may be combined to create musical rhythm. Try to turn each illustration of rhythm into sound.

Beat

Most of the world's music moves in relation to an underlying beat or pulse that may be regular

• • • • • • • • • •

or irregular.

• • • • • • • • • • • • • • •

Tempo

Music may move at varying speeds, depending on the length of each underlying beat or pulse.

• • • • • • • •••••••• • • • • •

Accents

Sometimes these beats are grouped through the use of accents that may result in regular groupings

> • • • > • • •

or in groupings that are irregular.

> • • • > • > • >

The beat and the accent may be strongly sounded or almost absent.

Rhythmic Line

A single rhythmic line may move with an irregular flow

▬ ▬ ▬ ▬ ▬▬ ▬ ▬▬▬ ▬ ▬ ▬▬ ▬ ▬▬ ▬

or with a more regular flow that is controlled by an underlying beat (even though the beat is not sounded).

▬▬ ▬▬ ▬▬ ▬▬ ▬▬ ▬▬ ▬▬ ▬▬

98

The Lesson

1. Begin the lesson, with books closed, by asking the students to define *rhythm*. Encourage the students to provide verbal definitions as well as to illustrate what they mean through sound. Invite other students to challenge the definitions offered. **Does (student's name)'s definition clearly define rhythm, or is it mixed up with other musical elements? Did (student's name) include all aspects of rhythm in his (or her) definition?**

2. After the students have shared ideas, ask them to open their books to pages 98 and 99 to examine the headings. **Did we include each of these aspects of rhythm in our definition?** Read the discussion about each rhythmic characteristic. Invite one or more students to turn the pictured representation into sound.

3. After reading the discussion of rhythmic texture, divide the class into two groups to perform the two lines simultaneously.

4. Continue the lesson by examining the notation for "Teens." **Can you describe the rhythmic characteristics of this song by studying the notation? What about the beat, the accents, the tempo?** (The beat will move regularly, with each beat the same length, grouped in twos.) This information can be ascertained by studying the meter signature. The tempo is quite slow, as indicated by the tempo marking at the beginning of the song. The rhythmic flow is somewhat irregular, although it always moves in relation to the underlying steady beat. The relationship of the sounds within the line to the beat changes as the song progresses. It begins as a 1-1 relationship, changes to 2-1, 3-1, and 6-1. **Will there be a rhythmic texture resulting**

  Texas Essential Elements, Rhythm and Melody, pp. 98–105: 1A, 1B, 1C, 1D, 1F, 2, 3B, 4A, 4B, 5A, 5B (Please see Unit 2 Opener, page 65, for component and page references.)

Rhythmic Texture

Two or more rhythmic lines may be sounded simultaneously. They might:

- move with an irregular flow and be unrelated to each other

- move with a regular pattern and be closely related to each other

- move irregularly, as when one line moves against one or more regular patterns

Learn "Teens" in unison, then perform it as a canon. Describe its rhythm in relation to the characteristics presented on these pages.

Listen to performances by musicians from other parts of the world. Are the rhythmic characteristics the same?

Teens

Traditional Round

Adagio

1. One teen talk-ing, "Gab-ble, gab-ble." Now we hear two

teens con-vers-ing, "Gib-ble, gab-ble, gib-ble, gab-ble." Lis-ten to three of them

chat-ter-ing end-less-ly, "Gib-ble-dy, gab-ble-dy, gib-ble, gab-ble, gib-ble, gab-ble-dy!"

99

CULTURE 19

For Your Information

Characteristics of songs heard during Step 7.

Silver Apples of the Moon
The beat is almost nonexistent; if sensed at all, it is irregular. The tempo frequently changes; accents do occur, but irregularly. Line and texture are irregular.

Rabbit Dance
The beat is strong and steady throughout. The accents are few in number and irregular. The tempo is medium with little change throughout. The rhythmic line for the drum often moves in a triplet figure, with the softer note sometimes unsounded. The voices have a freer rhythmic line; its relationship to the drum line is not strong (sometimes its accents follow the drum line; sometimes it moves in opposition).

Kalamtianos
The underlying pulse is continuous but, as a result of accents moving in groups of 7 (3 + 2 + 2), it seems irregular to us, although the recurrence is regular. The tempo is fairly fast with little change. The rhythmic line might be described as irregular, with many changes in the durations of individual sounds. The violin line and the *lauto* ostinato move in regular relationships with each other. The grouping of 7 is easiest to hear in the repeated *lauto* pattern.

---

from the combination of lines? (yes, when it is performed as a canon)

5. Challenge the students to chant the rhythm on the word "ten." Students may have trouble shifting from two sounds to a beat to three sounds to a beat. Suggest that they find the smallest common denominator, which is six sounds to a beat. Divide the class into two groups. Group 1 should tap the underlying short pulse in groups of six. (Slow the tempo if need be, but keep it moving as quickly as possible.) Group 2 will tap the rhythmic line. **As you tap, think 1–2–3–4–5–6.** Group 2 should begin by clapping on 1 and 4. **On my signal, shift to clapping on beats 1–3–5.**

Next, divide the class into three groups. While Group 1 taps underlying short sounds, Group 2 should clap on 1–3–5 and Group 3 should snap their fingers on beats 1 and 4.

6. Ask the students to observe the melody. Note that it uses only tones of the I chord. (C–F–A–C′) Establish the key and ask the students to sing in unison, then as a two-part canon.

7. Distribute three copies of Activity Sheet 21 (*Rhythmic Characteristics*) to each student. Review the definitions. Be sure the students understand that there are no absolutely correct answers and that they may mark any place along the continuum from one extreme to the other. Play *Rabbit Dance, Kalamtianos,* and *Silver Apples of the Moon.* (See **For Your Information** for descriptions of the rhythmic characteristics of each.)

8. After the students have completed their activity sheets, display the transparency and develop a composite of each example. Discuss reasons for differences of opinions.

OPTIONAL

Lesson Focus

Melody: A series of pitches may move up, down, or remain the same.
Melody: A series of pitches may move up or down by steps or skips. *(D–I)*

Materials

o **Record Information:**
  • *Mwatye*
    (Record 4 Side B Band 8)
  • *Dance Song*
    (Record 4 Side A Band 1)
  • *Rabbit Dance*
    (Record 4 Side B Band 6)
  • *Saeta*
    (Record 4 Side B Band 4)

o **Instruments:** keyboard or mallet instruments (soprano, alto, bass xylophones)

o **Other:** overhead projector

o **Teacher's Resource Binder:**

| Activity Sheets | • **Activity Sheet 23,** page A29 (Make four copies for each student and one transparency.) |

  • Optional—
    Enrichment Activity 8, page E16

Melodies Around the World

The music of the world moves rhythmically through time. It also moves through space, creating contours called melody. Just as each culture organizes rhythm in distinctive ways, each may combine melodic elements to develop unique melodies.

Melodies are created by combining pitched sounds in various ways. One may define melody by describing its special characteristics:

Shape: The up-down contour of a melody may be described as

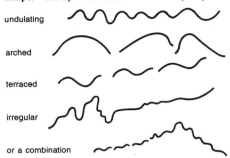

Range: The distance between the highest and lowest pitches of a melody may be

narrow or wide

or in between.

Motion: The distance between individual pitches within the melody may be described as moving by

steps   skips   repeated tones

or a combination of the three.

100

The Lesson

1. Remind the students of their attempts during the previous lesson (pages 98–99) to define rhythm. **Today, let's consider another musical element: melody.** Invite the students to offer definitions either through example or verbal description. Guide the students' thinking with questions as the discussion proceeds. **What characteristic of sound must be present for there to be melody?** (pitch) **We can describe the relationship of individual sounds in a rhythmic line as longer or shorter; what terms might be used to describe the relationship of pitches within a melody?** (higher or lower, moving up or down)

2. Ask the students to open their books to page 100 and read the introductory discussion about characteristics of melodies. Ask student volunteers to vocally improvise a melody to illustrate each contour, or call on a student to improvise a short melody on a mallet instrument or keyboard.

3. Draw attention to the song *Mwatye.* Ask the students if they can describe its melodic characteristics by studying the notation. Choose some students to go to the chalkboard and draw the shape. Reassure them that they should not attempt to be exact with the contour but to draw its overall shape. The class may conclude that different sections illustrate contrasting shapes. (Measures 1–4: undulating; Measures 5–8 and 9–12: terraced) The range is somewhat wide (a tenth) and it moves (motion) with a combination of steps, repeated tones, and skips. There does not seem to be a strong sense of a tonal center.

4. The song is to be sung in three parts. Ask the students to examine the range of the song and

Tonal Center: Some melodies are grouped around a central pitch; all other tones move in relation to that pitch.

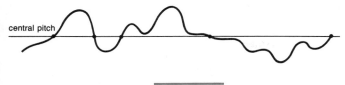

central pitch

Mwatye

Shona People of Zimbabwe

Describe the melodic characteristics of this Zimbabwean song. Then learn to perform it.

A. Mwa-tye ru-pun-ga saun-ya-ma.__ Mwa-tye ru-pan-ga saun-ya-ma.__

B. Heh-ya, heh-ya va saun-ya-ma.__ Heh-ya, heh-ya va saun-ya-ma.__

C. I-ye wo-ye i-ye.____ I-ye wo-ye i-ye.____

Listen to performances by musicians from various parts of the world. Use the activity sheet *Melodic Characteristics* to describe the melodies you hear. Compare profiles of the different melodies.

101

For Your Information

Dance Song
This song could be described as terraced, with similar patterns at different pitch levels. The range is narrow (based on five pitches); it moves primarily by steps with some repeated tones and occasional skips. To our ears, the tonal center seems to shift.

Rabbit Dance
The shape of the melody may be described as terraced-descending. Each pattern starts high and moves downward with the next starting at a slightly lower level. The motion is primarily by steps over a fairly wide range (in contrast to the other examples). Each sequence of descending patterns moves toward a "tonal center," although this shifts during the performance.

Saeta
This religious composition has a melody (focus on the singer) best described as undulating. Note how each section revolves around a central pitch (although this changes from one section to another). The motion is primarily by steps and the overall range is fairly narrow. Notice how the melody becomes increasingly ornamented as it progresses.

choose the part that seems best fitted for their voice range. Some possibilities are:

Part A—Changing Voices and Treble II's
Part B—Trebles I and II and Baritones (an octave lower than written)
Part C—Treble Voices and Changing Voices (an octave lower than written)

5. Guide the students to discover that the rhythm for Part A is the same as Part B. Practice chanting the melody on "du." The groups should work independently to learn the melody, singing it on a neutral syllable. One student in each group may assist by playing the part on an instrument. (Part A: soprano xylophone; Part B: bass xylophone; Part C: alto xylophone)

6. When the three melodies have been learned, listen to the recording to learn the pronuncia-

tion and to observe how the three parts are combined. Play the recording a second time; the students may sing along.

7. Distribute four copies of Activity Sheet 23 (*Melodic Characteristics*) to each student. Play the first melodic idea of each of the recordings. (See **For Your Information**.) The students should first draw the shape in the blank space below the words that describe shape. After completing that, they should circle the word that best describes that shape. They should then mark each category to describe the other characteristics.

8. End the class by discussing the students' conclusions. You may wish to develop a class profile of each melody on a transparency of the activity sheet.

OPTIONAL

Lesson Focus
Melody: A series of pitches may move up, down, or remain the same.
Melody: A series of pitches may move up or down by steps or skips. *(D–I)*

Materials
○ **Record Information**
• *Raga Puriya Dhanashri*
Record 5   Side B   Band 6
Performed by Ravi Shankar
○ **Instruments:** resonator bells and mallet

LISTENING

Raga Puriya Dhanashri
Performed by Ravi Shankar

Most traditional music of the western world is based on a scale. Indian music is usually based on a *raga*, the series of pitches that are used as a basis for the creation of melodic shapes by Indian performers. The term *raga* is also used in the same way we might use the term *composition*—to mean a complete piece of music.

Listen to an evening raga, *Raga Puriya Dhanashri*, performed by Ravi Shankar on the *sitar*. It is important to remember as you listen that the music is entirely improvised. It is not notated to be studied and memorized. Each raga is formed of a unique combination of pitches that must be memorized. The performer then uses those pitch sequences when improvising the raga. Here is the raga that forms the basis for the music you will hear. Notice that the ascending and descending forms are different.

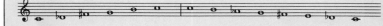

102

The Lesson

1. Review the characteristics of melody discussed during the previous lesson. Explain that you are going to play a short musical example. Ask the students to be ready to describe it in terms of the five melodic characteristics identified during that lesson. Play approximately 20 seconds of *Raga Puriya Dhanashri*. Then invite the students' comments. They may feel that the melody is either undulating or irregular with a medium to wide range. The motion seems to be primarily steps with some repeated tones. Some students may sense the drone pitch that frequently recurs as a central tone.

2. Ask the students to open their books to page 102. Read the opening discussion of Indian music, pausing to discuss the various ideas presented. Invite a student to determine the correct resonator bells needed for the raga

pitches given in their book and play the raga for the class. **What is one important difference you notice between a raga and the scales you are accustomed to singing and playing?** (The descending form of the raga is different from the ascending form.) Play the raga several times. Invite the students to sing with the bell player until they are comfortable with the sound of the raga.

3. Read paragraph two. Play approximately two minutes of the raga. Encourage the students to listen carefully to try to sense the mood of the raga, what Indians call the *rasa* — the "taste" of the raga. Explain that each raga has its own particular "flavor," much as different types of scales have their own characteristics.

4. Read paragraph three. Students will undoubtedly agree that they found the short

Usually the performance of a raga takes a very long time, perhaps all night. This performance is quite short, only 11 1/2 minutes long! At first it may seem monotonous because you are not accustomed to Indian ways of organizing musical sounds. If you continue to listen, you will begin to sense this different way of combining musical elements to create an expressive piece of music.

Raga Puriya Dhanashri has two large sections; the first is called the *Alap*; the second is called the *Gat*.

Alap: This section is organized into three shorter parts. Part 1 is also called the *alap*. It begins with an exploration of the pitches of the raga. This section is played freely, with no strong rhythmic feeling. Try to sense the mood.

Listen for the *mohra*. This is a brief melodic phrase that is played as a separation, or resting point, between musical ideas. Here is the *mohra* heard in this performance. If you listen carefully, you will hear the performer return to this idea several times throughout this section.

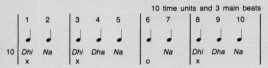

Part 2 is called the *jor*. It can be identified by the clearly heard steady pulse, which distinguishes this part from the opening part. You should still be able to hear the performer occasionally return to the *mohra*.

Part 3 is the *jhala*, which begins without warning. You can identify this part because there is added ornamentation, higher pitches, and faster rhythmic figures that create an intense feeling. This section ends with a strum across all the strings of the sitar.

Gat: The opening of the second large section is easy to recognize because it is accompanied by the *tabla*, a type of drum. The rhythmic cycle performed by the *tabla* is called a *tala*. This *tala* is ten beats long. Try to count the beats. Each *tala* has its own name. This one is called *Jhaptal*.

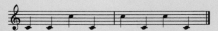

			10 time units and 3 main beats						
1	2	3	4	5	6	7	8	9	10
♩	♩	♩	♩	♩	♩	♩	♩	♩	♩
10									
Dhi	Na	Dhi	Dha	Na		Na	Dhi	Dha	Na
x		x			o		x		

For Your Information

Instruments heard on this recording include the sitar, a stringed instrument common in northern India. It has a long neck with seven strings stretched across curved frets and attached to pegs at the top. To produce a pitch, the performer presses the strings against these curved frets at various points, using the fingers of the left hand, while strumming with a wire plectrum placed on the right-hand index finger. Semitones and slides in pitch are produced by pulling the strings to one side with the fingers of the left hand. There is a large gourd that forms the body of the instrument and a smaller one near the top of the neck. Both of these help amplify the sound.

The other instrument is the tabla, which is a pair of drums. These can be heard in the *Gat* section of the piece. Famous performers on the tabla can produce an astounding variety of sounds on these drums as they provide the rhythmic framework of the *Gat*.

portion they have heard to be monotonous. Continue by reading the description of the structure. Play the *mohra* on the bells. **Listen to the *alap*. See if you can find the *mohra*.** Play the *alap* portion of the recording (approximately 2 minutes and 20 seconds).

5. Before beginning the *Gat*, read the description of the *jhaptal tala* — the rhythmic cycle that is the basis for this section. *Tala* refers to certain recurring metric patterns in the music. It also refers to the palm of the hand, or clapping of hands to keep time.

Guide the students to practice speaking and tapping the tala. Begin at a moderate tempo and increase the tempo until they are whispering the syllables or numbers as fast as possible. Play this section of the raga. Invite the students to either whisper or tap along with the music.

6. Before playing the complete evening raga, discuss the fact that music in India is an integral part of life. It is rarely performed in a concert hall as in music in the western world. As the performer plays a raga, listeners might sit quietly or wander around the area, listening and responding to the music and its mood. Encourage the students to get in a comfortable position and listen again, letting the music add to a relaxed mood.

CULTURE 22

Lesson Focus

Form: A musical whole is a combination of smaller segments.
Form: A musical whole may be made up of same, varied, or contrasting segments. *(D–S)*

Materials

○ **Record Information:**
  • *Banuwa*
    Record 6 Side B Band 1
  • *La Huichola*
    (Record 4 Side B Band 3)
  • *Sematimba ne Kikwabanga*
    (Record 5 Side A Band 2)
  • *Azumi Jishi*
    (Record 4 Side A Band 2)

○ **Teacher's Resource Binder:**

[Activity Sheets] • **Activity Sheet 25,** page A30 (Make three copies for each student.)
  • Optional—
    Orff Activity 9, page O18

For Your Information

La Huichola
Repetition is considerable, both within and between sections (instrumental, vocal, instrumental). Instrumental consists of a two-

(continued on next page)

Composers must make many decisions when they compose a piece of music. The composer may begin with a single small idea, or **motive.**

1. *Ba - nu - wa, ba - nu - wa, ba - nu - wa yo.*

The idea might be repeated exactly,

2. *Ba - nu - wa, ba - nu - wa, ba - nu - wa yo.*

with a small change,

3. *Ba - nu - wa, ba - nu - wa, ba - nu - wa yo.*

or with a variation.

4. *Ba - nu - wa, ba - nu - wa, ba - nu - wa yo.*

A new idea may be introduced to provide contrast

5. *A - la - no, neh - ni - o la - no.*

or there may be a return to the original idea to provide unity

6. *Ba - nu - wa, ba - nu - wa, ba - nu - wa yo.*

104

The Lesson

1. Review the previous discussion regarding characteristics of melody (Culture 20, page 100) and rhythm (Culture 19, page 98). Discuss the fact that, although we can examine either independently, most music combines these two elements into a musical whole which possesses form. Tell the students to turn to page 104 and guide them through a discussion of the ways musical form is derived. Help the students sing each example before proceeding to the next. (The words mean, "Don't cry, pretty girl, don't cry.") As each new example is learned, go back to the beginning and sing all the examples in sequence, without interruption.

2. Invite the students to develop their own organization of these fragments into a musical whole. Remind the students that any segment can be repeated and sung by one, a few, or all

singers. One possible sequence might be: Treble II's and Changing Voices begin by repeating motive 1 over and over. Treble I's and Baritones (Baritones sounding an octave lower) join in singing motive 2. Soloists or small groups of voices then add motive 4 over the continued repetition of motives 1 and 2. Gradually *crescendo* and *diminuendo*, then fade out.

Begin a new section with Treble II's and Baritones performing Motive 5, followed by Treble I's and Changing Voices on Motive 6. Invite the soloists to add Motive 7 and create additional variations. Build this section to a climax, stop abruptly and begin the opening section again, very softly. Gradually build to a *forte* climax and end the composition.

3. Encourage the students to work together in small groups to plan a performance which they may then teach to the entire class.

OPTIONAL

or other new ideas may be introduced or combined with the original idea.

Use ideas on these two pages to organize your own arrangement of this song.

- Begin with a few voices singing the first motive.
- Continue while others add variations.
- Other singers might introduce contrast while the original motive is continued.
- Repeat the motive many times, change the dynamics, and end softly.
- Begin a new musical idea as you began the first, with some singers performing the motive, then other voices entering. How will you end?

Listen to the music from different parts of the world. Describe what you notice about the form of each example. Can you hear motives? contrast? What provides unity?

105

For Your Information *(continued)*

motive phrase repeated and followed by a contrasting phrase which is also repeated; voice performs the two basic ideas in reverse order, interrupted by improvisatory sections. Variation seldom occurs, although no two repetitions are exactly the same. Contrast is provided by the alternation of instruments and vocal sections.

Sematimba ne Kikwabanga
It begins with performance by a single player outlining the theme which is used as a basis for this composition. A second player then plays a part which might be described as a countermelody; then three performers play together. This music has both considerable repetition and considerable variation, for while the basic melodic idea is repeated throughout, the variations are highly complex and continuous. Contrast is minimal.

Azumi Jishi
This is an excerpt from a late eighteenth century composition originally for voice and *koto;* in this version one also hears the *samisen* (could be likened to our banjo) and *shakuhachi* (a bamboo vertical flute). The composition unfolds with little exact repetition as each new idea introduced is then elaborated on, providing a great deal of variation. Sections do provide contrast through different combinations of sounds and changes in tempo, as well as through the introduction of new ideas.

4. Play the recording of *Banuwa.* Ask the students to identify how these performers organized the motives. It begins with motive 1, is joined by motive 2, then motive 5. This section continues for some time, then ends abruptly. A brief section combining patterns from motive 7 occurs; the arrangement ends with unison singing of motive 4.

5. Distribute three copies of Activity Sheet 25 (*Musical Form*) to each member of the class. Discuss the terms listed on the activity sheet to be sure that the students understand each. Play the recordings as the students complete one sheet for each musical example. (See **For Your Information.**) End the lesson by comparing the completed sheets and discussing reasons for different answers.

Lesson Focus

Harmony: Two or more musical lines may occur simultaneously.
Texture: Musical quality is affected by the distance between the musical lines.
Texture: Musical quality is affected by the number of and degree of contrast between musical lines occurring simultaneously. *(P–I)*

Materials

o **Piano Accompaniment:** page 300
o **Record Information:**
  • Good News
    Record 6   Side B   Band 2
    Voices: mixed chorus
    Accompaniment: banjo, acoustic guitar, double bass, percussion
  • *Rakish Paddy*
    (Record 5   Side B   Band 4)
  • *Kalamtianos*
    (Record 5   Side A   Band 7)
  • *Kele'a*
    (Record 5   Side B   Band 2)
  • *Rabbit Dance*
    (Record 4   Side B   Band 6)
o **Teacher's Resource Binder:**

Activity Sheets
  • **Activity Sheet 24,** page A29 (Make four copies for each student.)
  • Optional—
    Kodaly Activity 8, page K11
    Orff Activity 5, page O10

Musical Texture

Texture is the way musical lines are put together:

• one line or many lines at the same time
• lines moving together or independently
• lines that are close together or far apart

Texture may be described as

monophonic—single musical line
homophonic—main melody with other lines providing harmonic support
polyphonic—each line having its own melody and rhythm

Perform each of the examples shown on these pages. Then decide whether it may be described as monophonic, homophonic, or polyphonic.

Refrain

Good news, Char-i-ot's a-com-in', Good news,
Char-i-ot's a-com-in', Good news, Char-i-ot's a-com-in' and I
don't want it to leave a-me be-hind.

106

The Lesson

1. Ask the students to recall the components of music that they have studied during this unit: timbre, rhythm, melody, form. **As we have examined each of these, we have usually been concentrating on a single musical line; but music is frequently made up of several lines.** Follow pages 106–108 to help students gain an understanding of a fifth musical component, texture.

2. Say the word "monophony" for the students. **Can you figure out its meaning by analyzing the syllables? What does the last part of the word, -phony, mean?** (phonesound) **What about mono-?** (one, single) **Monophony is a single musical line. This is the simplest of musical textures. Look at "Good News." What can you observe about the form of this short tune? What is the first motive?** ("Good news, Chariot's a comin'")

What happens after the first motive? (It is repeated with a slight change, then repeated and extended to end the phrase.) Establish the key. The students should be able to quickly learn the three-pitch melody. (Baritones should sing an octave below the notated pitch.)

3. Combine the musical lines given in the pupil book to create the various textures that are illustrated. Begin by asking the Baritones and Changing Voices to sing to the drone on A while the Treble Voices sing the melody.

4. Continue by discussing the meaning of texture created through **parallel motion.** (All voices move together, remaining the same distance apart.) Treble II's and Baritones may sing the melody (Baritones an octave lower) while the Treble I's and Changing Voices sing the melody a third higher, starting on A.

★ Texas Essential Elements, Musical Texture, pp. 106–108: 1A, 1B, 1C, 1D, 1F, 2, 3A, 3B, 4A, 4B, 5A, 5B (Please see Unit 2 Opener, page 65, for component and page references.)

Some may play or sing a drone while others sing "Good News."

You will need to divide into three groups to sing this texture. Describe what happens.

Good news! Char - i - ot's a - com - in'! Good news!...

This time, Trebles I and II should sing the melody while Changing Voices and Baritones begin a sixth lower and sing the melody in parallel motion.

Good news! Char - i - ot's a - com - in'!...

Divide into four groups. Who is singing the melody? What are the other voices doing?

Good news! Char - i - ot's a - com - in'! Good news!

Good news!_____ Good news!_____

Good news!_____ Good news!_____

107

For Your Information

Kele'a
One might describe the texture as a combination of drones. Each conch shell plays a single tone so the result is a single chord that remains consistent throughout. The texture remains fairly thick throughout most of this excerpt.

Kalamtianos
The texture is made up of two lines played by the violin and the *lauto*. Note that the *lauto* provides a recurring drone plus an ostinato (repeated pattern). The density is fairly thin.

Rakish Paddy
While the chanter plays the melody, harmony is created by the consistent drone of the drone pipes and chordlike accompaniment provided by the regulator pipes.

Rabbit Dance
This performance is monophonic. Voices sing in unison throughout.

5. Examine the example of homophony. Agree that, in this example, the highest voice (to be sung by Treble I's) sings the melodies, and the other voices provide harmonic support. In homophony, supporting voices usually move with a rhythm that is nearly the same as the rhythm of the melody.

6. Guide all of the students to learn the verse of "Good News" at the top of page 108. Experiment with different combinations of voices to decide which is most pleasing.

7. To create a thin texture, choose the Treble I's who have a particularly high tessitura to sing the chorus an octave higher than notated. If there are Baritones who can reach a low A, they might sing the verse an octave lower than notated.

8. Invite the students to develop a thick texture. For example, some Treble I's could sing the chorus while others provide a drone on A. Some Treble II's might then sing the verse with the Changing Voices and Baritones.

9. End the class by distributing Activity Sheet 24 (*Musical Texture*). You may wish to play each excerpt several times so that the students may decide which type of texture is heard in each example. Warn them that more than one texture might be heard in a single example. After the students have heard all of the examples and marked their activity sheets, discuss their conclusions.

OPTIONAL

107

Perform "Good News" in two parts. Some sing the chorus while others sing the verse at the same time.

There'll be peace and free - dom in this world, I know;

Peace and free-dom in this world, I know; Peace and free-dom in this

world, I know, and I don't want it to leave a - me be - hind.

Textural density can be described as "thin" or "thick" depending on the number of musical lines heard at the same time and the distance between them.

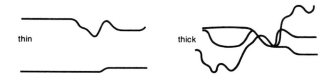

thin   thick

Experiment with thin texture. Sing or play two lines as far apart in range as possible. Now try a thick texture. Divide into five or six small groups. Each group should perform a different part. Combine several of the types of textures given, such as polyphony, homophony, and drone.

Listen to the music of different people. For each example, mark the terms on your activity sheet, Musical Texture, that describe the texture you hear.

108

The Symphony Orchestra

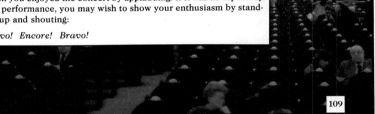

Attending a Symphony Concert

Get Ready

Find out what compositions will be presented in the concert you have chosen to attend. Do some research to find out something about the composers whose music you will be hearing, the period in which they lived, and the compositions you will hear in this concert. If possible, listen to a recording. It is always more fun to hear music that you know something about.

At the Concert

Give your ticket to an usher. He or she will guide you to your seat and give you a program. Spend time before the concert begins

- reading the program notes
- visiting quietly with your neighbors
- watching the orchestra members file on stage and warm up

You will know the concert is about to begin when

- the concertmaster enters and the orchestra has a final tune-up
- the lights dim
- the conductor strides on stage   *Applaud!*

During the concert

Listen quietly and attentively. Try to identify important themes; listen for them to return. Are they repeated exactly or are they varied? Listen for different instruments.

At Intermission

Go into the lobby and visit with friends. When the bell sounds to signal the end of intermission, return promptly to your seat.

At the End of the Concert

Let the orchestra players, the soloists, and the conductor know how much you enjoyed the concert by applauding. If it was an especially fine performance, you may wish to show your enthusiasm by standing up and shouting:

Bravo! Encore! Bravo!

109

Lesson Focus
Time and Place: The way musical elements are combined into a whole reflects the origin of the music. *(D–E)*

Materials
o **Teacher's Resource Binder:**
  • Optional
    Checkpoint 2, page Ev8

The Lesson

1. If appropriate, use this lesson to help the students prepare to attend a youth concert. If such concerts are not available, students might plan their own concert (with recordings) using the selections discussed in the following lesson as the program. Assign the students to the roles of orchestral performers, conductor, ushers, and audience. Others might prepare program notes.

2. If the students are to attend a live concert, try to take a field trip to the hall to purchase the tickets so that the students understand this is something they can do — they do not have to depend on someone to get the tickets for them. Another option would be to have the students order the tickets by mail.

3. Read the discussion on the pupil page. Help the class realize that the concertmaster is the first violinist who sits in the first chair directly to the left of the conductor. In the Baroque and early Classical periods, the conductor and concertmaster were usually the same person.

4. Make sure the students understand the word *movement.* Help them understand that a movement is a section of a long work such as a symphony, a suite, or a concerto, which also has a complete form in and of itself. Explain that most symphonies have four movements; the audience is expected to not interrupt the flow of the music and should applaud only after the final movement is completed.

5. Explain that *bravo* and *encore* are words of Italian and French origin, respectively. *Bravo* is an expression connoting approval. *Encore* is used to demand that the performers play another piece.

Lesson Focus

Time and Place: A particular use of timbre reflects the origin of the musical whole. *(D–I)*

Materials

○ Record Information:
- Magic Fire Music from *Die Walküre* by Richard Wagner (**vahg**-nuhr), 1813–1881
  Record 6   Side B   Band 3
  New York Philharmonic
  Leonard Bernstein, Conductor
- Badinerie from *Orchestra Suite in B Minor*
  by Johann Sebastian Bach (**bahk**), 1685–1750
  Record 6   Side B   Band 4
  English Chamber Orchestra
  Raymond Leppard, Conductor
- *De Natura Sonoris*
  by Krzysztof Penderecki (pen-duh-**rhess**-skee), 1933–
  Record 6   Side B   Band 5
  Buffalo Philharmonic
  Lukas Foss, Conductor
  Minuet from *Symphony No. 40 in G Minor*
  by Wolfgang Amadeus Mozart (**moet**-sahrt), 1756–1791
  Record 6   Side B   Band 6
  Cleveland Orchestra
  George Szell, Conductor

The Modern Symphony Orchestra

Cymbals Triangle Gong French Horns Bass Drum Snare Drum Celesta Chimes Bass Clarinet Clarinets Piccolo Flutes Timpani Second Violins Harp First Violins Podium (center stage)

Baroque (1600–1750)

Orchestra not standardized
● **Strings:** 20–25 (violins 1, 2; violas; cellos; basses)
●●● **Woodwinds, Brass, and Percussion:** various types used as needed
Misc.: harpsichord; orchestra led by first violinist or harpsichordist from their respective positions

Classical (1750–1825)

Orchestra standardized
● **Strings:** 35–40
● **Woodwinds:** 2 each (flute, oboe, clarinet, bassoon)
● **Brass:** 2 each (French horn, trumpet)
● **Percussion:** 2 timpani
Misc.: harpsichord no longer used; orchestra led by conductor with score and baton from the podium

110

The Lesson

1. Begin the class by asking the students to open their books to pages 110–111. Examine the seating chart, which shows a typical modern symphony orchestra. Discuss the fact that when describing orchestral instruments, we frequently discuss them in relation to families, such as woodwind, brass, percussion, and string, rather than as aerophones, membranophones, and so on.

2. Read the discussion at the bottom of each page, which describes the typical make-up of the orchestra during different historical periods. **What is the most important difference you notice as you compare the orchestras of the different periods?** (number and variety of instruments) Tell the students that you are going to play examples of orchestral music from different periods.

Challenge them to use their listening skills and identify the period of each example. Play excerpts (two to three minutes) of the following compositions. Pause after each to ask the students to offer ideas as to period and to give reasons for their choices.

"Magic Fire Music" from *Die Walküre* by Richard Wagner
"Badinerie" from *Orchestra Suite in B Minor* by Johann Sebastian Bach
De Natura Sonoris by Krzysztof Penderecki (twentieth century)
"Minuet" from *Symphony No. 40 in G Minor* by Wolfgang Amadeus Mozart

3. After the students have given their ideas and the reasons for them, play each excerpt again and discuss it in greater detail. Help the students realize that it is not only the numbers and types of instruments that provide clues to

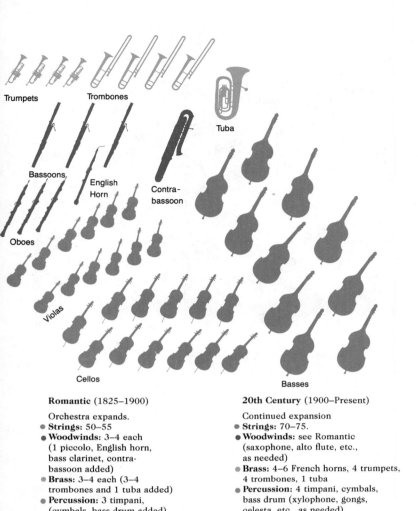

Trumpets

Trombones

Tuba

Bassoons

English Horn

Contra-bassoon

Oboes

Violas

Cellos

Basses

Romantic (1825–1900)

Orchestra expands.
- **Strings:** 50–55
- **Woodwinds:** 3–4 each (1 piccolo, English horn, bass clarinet, contra-bassoon added)
- **Brass:** 3–4 each (3–4 trombones and 1 tuba added)
- **Percussion:** 3 timpani, (cymbals, bass drum added)
- **Misc.:** harp added

20th Century (1900–Present)

Continued expansion
- **Strings:** 70–75.
- **Woodwinds:** see Romantic (saxophone, alto flute, etc., as needed)
- **Brass:** 4–6 French horns, 4 trumpets, 4 trombones, 1 tuba
- **Percussion:** 4 timpani, cymbals, bass drum (xylophone, gongs, celesta, etc., as needed)
- **Misc.:** electronic instruments

111

period, but the manner in which the instruments are used and the kind of music that they play. Some of the information that might be included in the discussion is as follows:

"Magic Fire Music." Wagner uses many extremes in his music, including wide variations in dynamics, articulation, and tempo. He often uses the extreme ranges of instruments from the highest to the lowest pitches they can play. The melodies and harmonies are often highly chromatic (moving by half steps, using pitches not in the key).

"Badinerie." The orchestra in Bach's time did not yet have a set instrumentation. Strings were always present, but in far fewer numbers than later (usually no more than two or three on a part). The harpsichord often reinforced the string parts. Wind and brass instruments were used occasionally in various combinations, but usually not more than two or three in any single composition. The music moves in a steady rhythm. Often several instruments will have independent melodies, creating a polyphonic texture. Dynamics are either loud or soft, with no gradual changes through *crescendos* or *decrescendos*.

De Natura Sonoris. Penderecki uses a similar instrumentation to that of the Romantic period, but treats the instruments in very different ways. The performers produce sounds and patterns not traditionally performed on these instruments. The music is very free, with little melodic or rhythmic structure as would be heard in music of earlier periods.

"Minuet." By Mozart's time the orchestra instrumentation was becoming more stable. The entire family of strings was always

The men and women who play in professional symphony orchestras are highly skilled artists. Continual study and practice is needed to maintain the superior performance skills required for this occupation.

During a performance, the conductor guides the orchestra by signaling changes in tempo and dynamics, cueing entrances, and controlling the overall balance. The greater part of the conductor's job, however, is preparing the orchestra for performances. Many hours are spent rehearsing for each performance.

Look at page 113. This is a page from a conductor's score. It shows the parts for all the instruments in the orchestra. The conductor must be aware of what each instrument is playing at any given time.

112

present, as were most of the wind and brass families. Instead of using brass and wind instruments individually in contrasting ways, the instruments in Mozart's orchestra are more likely to play in families, with an occasional solo by one of them.

4. Listen again to "Magic Fire Music." (You may wish to do this on another day.) Prepare the students by providing them with the following information. The composition is from the opera *Die Walküre,* by Richard Wagner. It is the second of four operas known collectively as *The Ring.* In this work, Wotan, the God of War, punishes his daughter, Brünnhilde, because she has not followed his commands. He decrees that she is to lie in a charmed sleep with leaping flames protecting her until a hero, who fears nothing, summons her to life with a kiss. As Wotan bids his child farewell, we hear "Magic Fire Music." This orchestral interlude opens with a theme depicting Wotan extending his spear to summon the fire god, Loge. On a mountaintop, the fire god surrounds Brünnhilde with a barrier of crackling flames. High woodwinds sound the motive of the fire. The slumber theme of Brünnhilde is heard repeatedly in the strings. Under this theme the brasses prophesy the arrival of the hero. These themes continue, intertwined, as Wotan turns his back on Brünnhilde and disappears slowly down the mountainside.

Examine the score on page 113. This shows the last two measures of this composition. Focus the students' attention on the number of staffs. In some cases, one staff represents more than one instrument. This helps the students visualize the size and variety of instruments found in a Wagnerian orchestra. Observe how the pitches stretch from ex-

113

tremely low to very high. Wagner makes use of the entire range of the various instruments available to him.

Draw particular attention to Wagner's interesting use of orchestral colors as he develops his various motives. This rich variation of timbral color is one of the characteristics of all Wagnerian music and was true of many composers of the Romantic period.

5. Play the complete excerpt of *De Natura Sonoris* by Penderecki for the students. Ask them to note the differences between the way Wagner, of the Romantic period, and Penderecki, of the late twentieth century, use musical ideas and instruments.

CULTURE 26

Lesson Focus

Form: A musical whole is a combination of smaller segments.
Form: A musical whole may be made up of same, varied, or contrasting segments.
(D–S)

Materials

o **Record Information:**
  Minuet from *Symphony No. 40 in G Minor*
  (Record 6 Side B Band 6)
  • First Movement from *Symphony No. 40 in G Minor*
    by Wolfgang Amadeus Mozart
    Record 7 Side A Band 1
  • Cleveland Orchestra
    George Szell, Conductor

LISTENING

Symphony No. 40 in G Minor

First and Third Movements

by Wolfgang Amadeus Mozart

What do you know about a symphony? Do you know how many large sections or movements there are?

Two Austrian composers, Joseph Haydn (1732–1809) and Wolfgang Amadeus Mozart (1756–1791), developed a special design for the first movement of the symphony, called "sonata allegro." The design has frequently been used by composers of symphonies ever since that time.

Listen to the first and third movements of Mozart's *Symphony No. 40 in G Minor*. Begin by listening to the third movement, which is a minuet.

Theme One (strings)

Theme Two (woodwinds)

When do you hear repetition? Do you hear any variations? When does theme two begin? How many large sections are in the movement? Describe the design of the sections with letters.

Now listen to the first movement. Here are the themes:

Theme One

Theme Two

When do you hear repetition and variations? When do you hear new musical material? How many large sections do you find in this movement? Describe the design with letters.

114

The Lesson

1. Discuss the questions in the opening paragraph of the students' book. The students may be able to recall from previous study that a symphony is a composition usually written for orchestra. Most symphonies have four movements: fast, slow, dance, fast.

2. Read paragraph two; notice the dates of when these composers were born and died. **What was happening in this country at that time?** (Country was settled; Revolutionary War; Washington became President, etc.)

3. Continue the lesson by studying the third movement. Play the themes on piano or bells. Help the students notice that the first theme is in G minor and that the rhythm has a feeling of syncopation in Measures 1 and 4. The second theme is in the *parallel major* (both scales start on same pitch but use different

tones for third and sixth steps), G, with a steady, even rhythm.

4. Play the complete movement as the students follow the design on page 115. Help the students conclude that there are three large sections: A (minuet) B (trio) A (minuet). Each of these sections has its own smaller design of contrasting sections, which are repeated.

5. Draw attention to the instrumentation. The full orchestra plays the minuet. Woodwinds and strings are predominant in the trio as the theme is passed from one to another. The movement closes with a return to the minuet, this time without repetition.

6. Continue the lesson by proceeding to study the first movement's form, which is known as "sonata allegro." Play the themes. Notice that these also contrast. The first theme is in G minor and the second theme is in B♭ major,

114

When you have studied the two movements, listen to them again and compare their designs. Discuss ways that they are similar and ways that they are different. This chart may help you in your discussion.

Third Movement (Minuet)	First Movement (Sonata Allegro)
A SECTION	
(Minuet)	(Exposition)
Theme One (G minor)	Theme One (G minor)
a	Bridge
a	Theme Two (B♭ major)
b	Closing section (material from theme one)
b	
B SECTION	
(Trio)	(Development)
Theme Two (G major)	Theme One restated (new key)
a	Fragments of theme are played in many different ways, that is, "developed."
a	
b	
b	
A SECTION	
(Minuet)	(Recapitulation)
Theme One	Theme One (G minor)
a	Bridge (longer than in Exposition)
b	Theme Two (G minor)
	Closing section (Coda—material from theme one)

For Your Information

Form of First Movement:

Exposition: Theme 1 is stated by strings and repeated with a slight change at the end, leading into a vigorous bridge. Theme 2 is quiet and is stated by clarinets and bassoons, answered by strings. Echoes of the opening theme are heard as the first three notes are played again and again. The coda is announced by the full orchestra.

Development: The entire section is based on ideas drawn from Theme 1. The section begins with an almost exact repetition of the first theme as it is sounded at the beginning of the exposition. It is passed from instrument to instrument and played at many different pitch levels. Listen for it in the bass against a high countermelody. A three-note fragment from the theme is the subject of a dialogue between violins and woodwinds. It is next heard upside down. Flutes and oboes prepare for the recapitulation with soft chords under which the violins softly repeat the opening tones of the first theme.

Recapitulation: The last section is similar to the first. The main difference is that the second theme is also in minor instead of major. The bridge between the themes has been extended, as has the coda.

which is the *relative major.* (Same pitches are used, but in the minor scale the scale begins on G; in the major scale it begins on B♭.)

7. Play the complete movement as the students follow the map on page 115. Help them recognize that this movement can also be described as having three large sections — a big A B A. Help them hear repetitions and variations of the themes. See **For Your Information** for guidance during this discussion.

8. Discuss the appropriateness of the terms *exposition, development,* and *recapitulation.* In the first section the themes are exposed. In the second section the ideas are manipulated, expanded, or developed. The final section restates, or recaps, the first section.

9. Read the discussion at the top of page 115. Listen again to both movements. Discuss important similarities and differences. Similarities include the fact that both movements are made up of three large sections with the last section the same as (or similar to) the first. Both use contrasting themes.

An important difference is the way the themes are introduced and treated. In the minuet one theme is introduced during A, another during B. When these themes are repeated, they are either repeated exactly or with minor changes. In the *sonata allegro* movement, both themes are introduced during A. B does not introduce new material but develops ideas already presented in A. When A returns, it is entirely in the key of G minor. Help the students realize that this form is representative of Mozart, Haydn, and other composers of the Classical period. Mozart's music is especially characterized by the lyric quality of the melodies and the imaginative treatment of themes.

Lesson Focus

Evaluation: Review concepts studied during this unit. *(D–S)*

Materials

o **Record Information:**
  • *Monkey Chant* by Joe Field and Tony Duhig
    Record 7 Side A Band 2
  • *Kalagala Ebwembe* arranged by Paul Winter
    Record 7 Side A Band 3
  • *Badinerie* by Wendy Carlos
    Record 7 Side A Band 4
o **Teacher's Resource Binder:**
  • **Review 2,** page Ev11 (Make three copies for each student.)

For Your Information

The answers to questions 1, 4, and 5 of Review 2 may be discerned from the text on pupil page 116. Questions 2 and 3 will not have exact answers.

Review 2

The Music of Today

The music of today is the music of people in all our yesterdays. There is no completely new music. What we call *new* grows out of our ability to use and adapt the same ideas in different shapes, in different forms, and with different sound sources.

Monkey Chant

by Jon Field and Tony Duhig

This is a modern composition based on the original *"Ketjak"* you heard on page 73. Listen again to *"Ketjak,"* then listen to this new performance. Can you hear the performers on this recording imitate the vocal qualities as well as the melodic and rhythmic patterns? The electric guitar and bass make it definitely a sound of today.

Kalagala Ebwembe

from *Africanus Brasilerias Americanus*

(excerpt)

arranged by Paul Winter

The origin of this composition is *Sematima ne Kikwahanga.* Listen again to that composition from Uganda; then listen to *"Kalagala Ebwembe."* Can you hear that the melodies are similar in contour and feeling? The saxophone and English horn performers use the same hocketing technique in their performance. Later the *amadinda,* the same instrument used in the original performance, is heard. The bass and saxophone timbres and the percussion improvisations tell us this is not traditional Ugandan music.

Badinerie

by Wendy Carlos

How quickly did you recognize the melody on which this contemporary composition is based? It is the same composition you heard during Culture 25. Composers frequently borrow themes from composers of other times. This practice has gone on since music began. The electronic instruments clearly make this a composition for today.

116

The Lesson

1. **During this unit we have looked at similarities and differences in music from many places around the world.** Discuss with the students the idea that, as communication increases, and people move from place to place, the music of one part of the world affects the music of other parts. **Today we are going to hear examples of contemporary music that clearly have their roots in music of other times and places. Try to apply the information you have gained about music of different cultures to discover the origin of this music.**

2. Distribute a pencil and three copies of Review 2 to each student. Go through the questions to be sure the students understand each question. Then play each example. You may wish to provide quiet time between the examples and play each at least twice in order to give the students ample time to make their response.

3. After the students have completed the evaluations for the three examples, have them open their books to page 116. Read the discussion about each music example and listen again to the three compositions.

4. Use the information gained through this evaluation as well as observations made throughout the unit to complete the *Student Progress Report* for each class member.

Unit 3

Playing Folk Instruments

UNIT 3

1B: PE (pages 119–123; 125–127; 129–143; 144–146; 150; 152; 160; 162–163)

TE (pages 119–123; 125–126; 129; 130; 132; 136–138; 146; 148; 154; 158–160; 162–165)

TRB (pages K17; AS35–37; AS46; AS51–53; AS54; AS55–65; M18; M21; M23; E16; E17; EV14–16)

1C: PE (pages 119–127; 128–143; 144; 152; 160; 163)

TE (pages 118–126; 128; 134; 136–138; 140; 142; 150; 152; 154; 158; 160; 162–165)

TRB (pages K17; AS32–34; AS43; AS51–53; AS54; AS65; M18; E17; EV14; EV16)

1D: PE (pages 119–123; 129–143; 144–146; 160; 162–163)

TE (pages 125–126; 129; 130; 132; 136–137; 140; 146; 148; 154; 160; 162; 165)

TRB (pages K17; AS35–37; AS51–53; AS54; AS65; M21; M23; E17; EV14; EV16)

1F: PE (pages 119; 163)

TE (pages 120; 163)

TRB (pages AS54; EV16)

2: PE (pages 131; 134; 144–146; 153; 155)

TE (pages 125–129; 131; 133–135; 137; 139; 141; 145–146; 150–152; 154; 158)

TRB (pages K17; E17; EV15)

3A: PE (pages 137–138)

TE (pages 132; 138; 141)

3B: PE (pages 119; 120; 124; 128; 130; 132; 134; 137–142; 144–146; 149–150; 152–155; 160–161; 166)

TE (pages 119–126; 128–142; 144–146; 154; 160–161; 162; 165)

TRB (pages AS37; AS39–42; AS45; AS49; AS54; M21; M23; E16; E17)

4A: PE (pages 119–123; 125–127; 162–163)

TE (pages 119–124; 137)

TRB (pages K17; AS31; AS32–34; B13; EV16)

4B: PE (pages 119–123; 125–127)

TE (pages 121–124)

TRB (pages K17; AS32–34; B9; B11; B13)

5A: PE (pages 131; 134; 142; 144–146; 150; 153–155)

TE (pages 125–126; 129; 131; 133–135; 137; 139; 141; 142; 145–146; 148; 150–154; 156; 159–161; 162–163; 165)

TRB (pages K17; AS35–36; AS38; AS43–44; AS45–49; AS54; M18; M21; M23; E16; E17; I15–19; EV15)

5B: PE (pages 119; 128; 130; 149; 151–153; 160)

TE (pages 118–124; 128–142)

Unit Overview

Unit 3 opens with a discussion of record collecting, the various types of music available on recordings, and how that music should be stylistically classified. Students are then given the opportunity to perform American folk music on skiffle instruments such as the guitar, harmonica, limberjack, spoons, jug, kazoo, mouthbow, and washtub bass. The unit concludes with a section on commercial music in which the students compose their own video-game music.

Texas Essential Elements for Unit 3:

1A: PE (pages 119–123; 125–127; 129–143; 160; 162–63)

TE (pages 120–123; 125–126; 129; 132; 136–7; 142; 146; 148; 154; 158; 160; 162–165)

TRB (pages K17; AS35–37; AS51–53; AS54; M21; E17; EV14–16)

(continued on top of page)

☆ **Texas Essential Elements, Playing Folk Instruments, pp. 117–127: 1A, 1B, 1C, 1D, 1E, 1F, 2, 3B, 4A, 4B, 5A, 5B** (Please see Unit 3 Opener, page 117, for component and page references.)

117

Lesson Focus

Time and Place: The way musical elements are combined into a whole reflects the origin of the music. *(D–S)*

Materials

o **Record Information:**
  - *Jungle*
    Record 8   Side A   Band 1
    Performed by The Electric Light Orchestra
  - *Just a Closer Walk With Thee* (Jackson)
    (Record 2   Side B   Band 1a)
  - *Stardust*
    by Hoagy Carmichael, 1899–1981
    Record 7   Side B   Band 1b
    Performed by Wynton Marsalis
  - *I Walk the Line*
    (Record 1   Side A   Band 7)
  - *Wedding March*
    (Record 3   Side A   Band 1)
  - *Concerto in G Major for Two Mandolins*
    by Antonio Vivaldi, 1678–1741
    Record 7   Side A   Band 5
    New York Sinfonietta
    Max Goberman, Conductor

o **Teacher's Resource Binder:**
  Activity Sheets   • **Activity Sheet 26,** page A31

You, the Record Collector

Where do you hear recorded music?

On what type of equipment?

What do you think will be the next step in recording technology?

Do you have a record or tape collection?

What kind of player do you have?

What kinds of music do you have in your collection?

118

The Lesson

1. Discuss the three ways of interacting with music (listening, performing, and creating). Explain that the class will engage in all three ways of interacting in this unit. Discuss the ideas presented on page 118. Ask the students to share their reactions regarding the types of music shown.

2. The students may make negative comments about some types of music. Compare taste in music to taste in food. As infants we are limited to one kind of food—milk. As we grow, we are introduced to new foods. Some become our favorites; others are eaten only if someone insists! We like some foods immediately; others we must try several times before we like them. Preferences in music develop the same way. Some we like immediately; some we grow to enjoy after many hearings.

The important thing is for us to be willing to try new kinds of music.

3. Organize the class into teams. Explain that all will be hearing the same recordings but will each have a different task. Distribute Activity Sheet 26(*The Record Store*). Read and discuss the instructions and give each group an assignment.

4. Play excerpts from the compositions listed in **Record Information**. Give the students time after each to complete their assignment.

5. OPTIONAL Ask one member from each team to write key ideas from their assignment on the chalkboard. Since each task focused on a different aspect of listening, there will be different responses to the same music. Share ideas. Ask for input from the teams that did not have the assignment being discussed.

LISTENING

Concerto in G Major
for Two Mandolins, Strings, and Organ
by Antonio Vivaldi

What does the term *classical* mean to you? Can you define the term *concerto*?

Follow the opening theme as you listen to this concerto.

Do you hear
- dynamic or tempo changes?
- other instruments in addition to the mandolins?
- a return of the opening statement?
- solo and tutti sections?
- distinctive rhythmic figures?

119

Lesson Focus
Timbre: The total sound is affected by the number and qualities of sounds occurring at the same time. *(D–S)*

Materials
○ **Record Information:**
Concerto in G Major
(Record 7 Side A Band 5)
○ **Teacher's Resource Binder:**
• Optional—
Biography 5, page B9
○ **Kodaly Activity 11,** page K17

For Your Information
Antonio Vivaldi was a prolific Baroque composer. Best known for his work *The Four Seasons,* he composed operas and church music as well as hundreds of concerti. The *Concerto in G Major* is for two mandolins and a string orchestra. Terraced dynamics (accomplished by adding or subtracting instruments), uninterrupted 16th-note figures, and frequent imitation are all typical of Baroque music. The opening statement is played in unison by the mandolins and violins. It is never repeated exactly. Fragments of the theme, however, are repeated, imitated, and varied. The music unfolds as a continuation of the opening idea.

The Lesson

1. Initiate a discussion regarding the students' impression of classical music. Discuss possible influences on their perceptions, such as, home environment, prior musical education, or pressure from friends. Ask the students to define the term *classical*. Conclude that there are several definitions: symphonic or operatic music in general, music of any style that has stood the test of time, a specific style associated with music written between 1750 and 1820.

2. Play the beginning of the *Concerto in G Major.* **Would you describe this music as classical?** (yes) **Which definition would you use if you knew that the composer, Antonio Vivaldi, lived from 1678–1741?** (the first) **This music is a concerto. What will you expect to hear?** OPTIONAL

3. Remind the students of the listening exercises during Unit 1. Suggest that, as in those exercises, it may be helpful to focus on a specific aspect of the music (the melody, rhythm, or instrumentation) as they listen.

4. After playing the complete recording, ask the students to comment on what aspects of the music they noticed. Comment that the solo instruments were mandolins. **Listen again. Be ready to answer the questions at the bottom of page 119.** Discuss the students' observations. (See **For Your Information**.)

5. Suggest that the students follow the opening theme on page 119 as they listen. **Does it help to have something to watch when hearing unfamiliar music?** Define the concerto as a composition where segments of the music alternate between solo instruments and "tutti" (full ensemble).

119

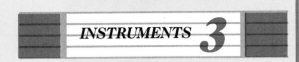

INSTRUMENTS 3

Lesson Focus

Time and Place: A particular use of timbre, dynamics, articulation, rhythm, melody, and harmony reflects the origin of the musical whole. *(D–S)*

Materials

○ **Record Information:**
  • *Stardust*
    by Hoagy Carmichael
    (Record 7 Side B Band 1a)
    Band 1b: Wynton Marsalis
  • *Just a Closer Walk With Thee*
    (Record 2 Side B Band 1d)
    Preservation Hall Jazz Band

○ **Teacher's Resource Binder:**
  • **Activity Sheets 27a–c,** pages A32–A34 (Prepare as transparencies.)
  • Optional—
    Biography 6, page B11

The Lesson

1. Write the words *classical music* and *jazz* on the chalkboard. Review the meaning of classical from the preceding lesson. Ask if anyone has ever heard of cars, clothes, or other objects referred to as classic. (The Model T, the LaSalle, or certain cars of the fifties are often referred to as classics; a tailored suit may be said to have classic lines as opposed to fad styles, etc.) **What about popular music?** (Yes, there are classics sometimes referred to as "golden oldies," such as "Rock Around the Clock.") Ask the students to follow the piano score of *Stardust* as they listen to the recording. It is a classic popular song. Written in the twenties, it has subsequently been published in a variety of arrangements, including voice, organ, accordion, guitar, xylophone, brass, wind instruments, and full orchestra.

2. **If you were to hear a jazz rendition of this classic, what would you expect to hear?** List words the students suggest to describe jazz and the sound they would expect from a jazz rendition. (Answers will vary.)

3. Play the jazz version of *Stardust*. **Was it what you expected?** (Probably not; the students may think of jazz as always fast and loud.) Compare the predictions.

4. Ask the students to follow the piano score as they listen to the jazz version again. **What does the soloist do to the rhythm?** (elongates several notes, shortens others) **to the dynamics?** (uses a great deal of contrast; relies on very soft sounds to create a mood) **to the melody?** (improvises on it; plays enough to keep it recognizable) **What effect does the orchestration have on the composition?** (creates tension; helps to create the

Hoagy Carmichael

For Your Information
You may wish to enlarge Activity Sheets **27a–c** *(Jazz Time Line)* to display on a bulletin board for ready reference during any lessons where jazz is discussed.

121

mood) **Does changing the solo instrument from piano to trumpet change the effect of the music?** (yes)

5. Return to *Just a Closer Walk With Thee* (page 24) to hear another style of jazz, Dixieland. Point out that jazz cannot be neatly defined and stereotyped. It is a music native to America that has evolved over many years.

6. Display a transparency of Activity Sheets 27a–c *(Jazz Time Line)* and identify the important composers and performers who have contributed to the evolution of jazz. If possible obtain recordings to play for the students that demonstrate the various styles.

7. Ask the students to research popular rock stars or arrangers who have been influenced by jazz and report back to the class.

OPTIONAL

Lesson Focus

Expression: The expressiveness of music is affected by the way timbre, dynamics, articulation, rhythm, melody, harmony, and form contribute to the musical whole. *(D–S)*

Materials

o **Record Information:**
- *Fanfare for the Common Man* by Aaron Copland
  Record 7 Side B Band 2
  New York Philharmonic
  Leonard Bernstein, conductor

LISTENING

Fanfare for the Common Man

by Aaron Copland

Follow the percussion section (marked in red) as it dramatically punctuates this fanfare.

1. Introduction

(timpani)

(bass drum)

(tam-tam)

2. Theme I

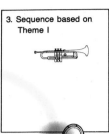

3. Sequence based on Theme I

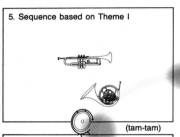

5. Sequence based on Theme I

(tam-tam)

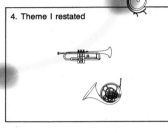

4. Theme I restated

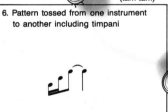

6. Pattern tossed from one instrument to another including timpani

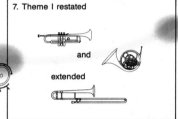

7. Theme I restated

and

extended

122

The Lesson

1. Begin by discussing what a fanfare is and where it might be heard. Students may offer ideas such as: A fanfare announces that something important is about to happen; fanfares are heard at events such as the Olympics, important government functions, or holiday celebrations. Add background information as appropriate. (See For Your Information.) Explain that the piece they will be hearing is written for three trumpets, four French horns, three trombones, a tuba, timpani, bass drum and tam-tam. (The tam-tam is similar to a gong.)

2. Help the students become familiar with **Theme 1** (box 2 on page 122) and **Theme 2** (box 8 on page 123). Play the themes on the piano or on a set of bells as the students follow the notation. When you feel that the students can recognize the two themes, play the recording as they follow the series of numbered boxes. They can easily keep their place on the chart by touching the next red section of the path each time the percussion part is heard.

Ask the students to read ahead, focusing on the theme being played and the instruments playing during each of the series of events in the piece.

3. Discuss the term sequence. Help the students understand that the sequential treatment of **Theme 1** means that the theme is being performed at a higher pitch level each time it is repeated. Play the recording again. Ask the students to focus their attention on the use of the sequence and the way in which a fragment of **Theme 1** is "tossed" from one instrument to another. (See box 6.) As before, they will be guided by the percussion section.

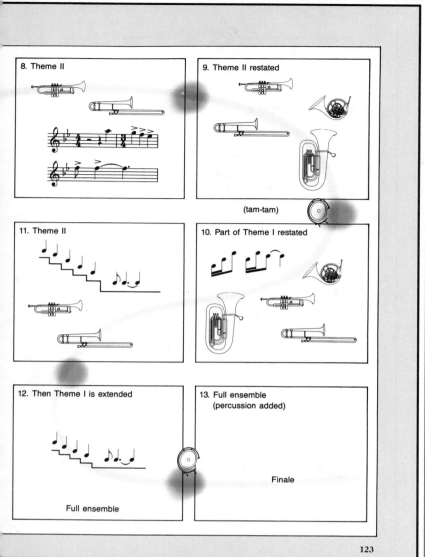

For Your Information

This fanfare is one of ten works written for brass and percussion that were intended to pay tribute to all those involved in the action of World War II. The title *Fanfare for the Common Man* was chosen by Copland to honor the men who performed no deeds of heroism on the battlefield but rather shared the labors, sorrow, and hopes of all those striving for victory.

Lesson Focus

Form: A musical whole may be made up of same, varied, or contrasting segments. *(D–I)*

Materials

o **Record Information:**
  • *Solo and Group Wolf Howls*
    Record 7   Side B   Band 3
  • *Wolf Eyes*
    by Paul Winter
    Record 7   Side B   Band 4a
  • *Duet*
    Record 7   Side B   Band 4b
o **Teacher's Resource Binder:**
  • Optional—
    Biography 7, page B13
    Mainstreaming Activity 12, page M18

For Your Information

Wolves are social creatures. They live in a society with a hierarchy of leaders and followers. Like people, wolves also have distinctive voices. Wolves howl for some of the same reasons we use our voices. They contact other wolves; they identify themselves; they warn each other of danger; and they caution their pups. Sometimes their howls take on an almost musical form.

Language and Music of the Wolves

Wolves howl to identify themselves, to maintain contact with the pack, and to indicate the boundaries of their territory.

LISTENING

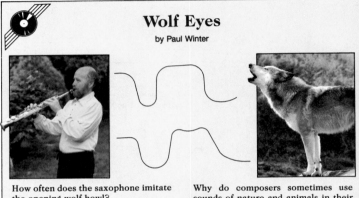

Wolf Eyes
by Paul Winter

How often does the saxophone imitate the opening wolf howl?

How is the opening theme altered throughout the piece?

Why do composers sometimes use sounds of nature and animals in their music?

124

The Lesson

1. Discuss the social ways of wolves presented on the student page. (See **For Your Information** for additional information.) Play the recording of *Solo and Group Wolf Howls* (Band 3). Help the students find musical devices in this "natural music": call-response, melodic contour, and "polyphony."

2. Explain that the contours at the bottom of the page represent a howl produced by a single wolf. **The composer used a howl as the main theme for *Wolf Eyes*. Listen to the recording. Be ready to answer the questions in your book.** (The saxophone imitates the melodic contour of the opening wolf howl. This theme is varied melodically and rhythmically. The sequence is as follows:
   • solo wolf's howl
   • piano plays somber chordal accompaniment with pronounced harmonic changes

   • saxophone plays variations on the wolf's howl
   • saxophone is joined by strings (guitar and cello)
   • cello plays countermelody
   • wolf is accompanied by piano and strings
   • saxophone and cello reenter
   • instruments fade out leaving saxophone
   • *Duet* begins between the saxophone and wolf with wolf responding to saxophone

3. Discuss the *Duet*, at the end of *Wolf Eyes*. Explain that Paul Winter reasoned that since howls are a means of communication for wolves, they would respond to something that sounded like a howl. Play *Duet* again (Finder Band 4b) as the students focus on the call/response aspect of the music. **In what musical ways does the wolf respond?** (imitates some of the patterns; varies others)

Jungle

Words and Music by Jeff Lynne

Moderately

I was stand-in' in the jun-gle, I was feel-in' al-right __ mm __
I was wand-'rin' in the dark-ness in the mid-dle of the night __ mm __

hmm, mm __ hmm, The moon be-gan to shine, I saw a

clear-ing a-head, __ mm __ hmm, mm __ hmm, But

what's that go-in' on, I think I'm out of my head, __ mm __

hmm, mm __ hmm. __ Choo-ka choo-ka hoo la ley.

Look-a look-a koo la ley. __ A hun-dred an-i-mals were gath-ered

'round this night, __ mm __ hmm, mm __ hmm. And they were

sing-in' out __ a love-ly song un-der the pale __ moon-light, mm __

125

Lesson Focus
Form: A series of sounds may form a distinct musical idea within the musical whole. *(D–S)*

Materials
o **Piano Accompaniment:** page 302
o **Record Information:**
  • Jungle
    (Record 8 Side A Band 1)
    Performed by The Electric Light Orchestra
o **Instruments:** 3 soprano or alto glockenspiels: (1) A, A#, and B bars; (2) E, F#, and G bars; (3) C# and D bars; 6 mallets; synthesizer, or bass xylophone with pitches F#, G, A, and D; 2 mallets; vibraslap; claves; hand drum; cowbell; sleigh bells; maracas
o **Other:** pencil for each student
o **Teacher's Resource Binder:**

Activity Sheets
  • **Activity Sheets 28a–c,** pages A35–A37
  • Optional—
    Mainstreaming Activity 13, page M21

The Lesson

1. On the chalkboard write the scale numbers for two of the melodies used in "The Jungle." (Each number indicates a pitched eighth note; a dash indicates to hold the previous pitch for an additional eighth note; a slash indicates an eighth rest.)
   A **(Phrase 1)**
   2 1 3 3 2 1 3 3 2 1 3 2 2 1 — —
   6' 1 1 — — — // 6' 1 1 — — —
   B **(Phrase 5)**
   1 1 1 1 1 — 7' 6 — — — — / / / /
   1 1 1 1 1 3 — 2 1 — — — — / / / /
   Ask the class to read and sing A, first with numbers then on a neutral syllable such as "choo."

2. Ask the students to open their books to page 125 and examine the key signature at the beginning of the song. Help the class determine that the song is in D major with the melody starting on the second scale step. **Can you find the part we just sang?** (yes, Phrase 1) **Does it occur more than once?** (yes, on the repeat) **Can you find any other places where the melody is similar to this one?** (phrases that begin "The moon began . . . ," "What's that goin' on . . . ," "A hundred animals . . . ," "I said now please . . . ,")

3. Ask the students to read and sing B from the chalkboard. **Where is this melody located in the song?** (each time the words "chooka chooka hoo la ley . . ." occur)

4. Help the students review the use of the symbol *D.S.* Discuss the fade-out coda. Play the entire song as the class follows the notation in their books. Adjust the balance controls on the stereo so the call numbers are not heard.

5. Help the students learn to play an instrumental accompaniment with the song. Distribute

125

INSTRUMENTS 6

For Your Information

This piece includes a wide variety of instrument timbres. The unpitched percussion sounds are structured in layers, in the style of an African rhythm complex.

Answers for Activity Sheet 28c (*Jungle Call Chart*):

1) G 2) F 3) D, E, F 4) A, D, E, F
5) B, D, E, F 6) A, C, D, E, F
7) B, D, E, F 8) A, D, E, F
9) B, D, E, F 10) E, F, G
11) C, D, E, F 12) B, D, E, G
13) A, D, E, F

copies of Activity Sheets 28a and 28b (*Jungle*). Divide the class into three groups. Group 1 will work with the chords; Group 2 will work with the bass line; and Group 3 will work with the percussion patterns. Ask each group to read its patterns and practice softly, first with each person working individually, then combined with other members of their group. After a brief practice period, ask each group to play its part for the rest of the class, then combine all three groups to perform the composition together.

6. Distribute copies of Activity Sheet 28c (*Call Chart*) and pencils. Adjust the balance control on the stereo so both channels will be heard. Ask the students to listen to the recording, following instructions to complete the call chart. Provide an answer sheet (see **For Your Information**) to which students may refer when correcting their answers.

OPTIONAL

126

Choo-ka choo-ka hoo la ley. ___ Look-a look-a koo la ley. ___ (Do

you know the an-swer? Have you heard the word?) *Inter-lude*

Pret-ty soon ___ I knew the tune ___ and we

sat and sang un-der the moon ___ and the *D.S. and fade*

jun-gle rang in joy-ful har-mo-ny. ___

127

Lesson Focus

Time and Place: A particular use of timbre reflects the origin of the musical whole. *(P–E)*

Materials

o **Piano Accompaniments:** pages 306, 240
o **Record Information:**
  • Bile Them Cabbage Down
    Record 8 Side A Band 3
    Voices: mixed chorus
    Accompaniment: banjo, harmonica, jug, washtub bass, spoons
  • Mama Don't 'Low
    Record 8 Side A Band 2
  • What Make's My Baby Cry?
    Record 5 Side B Band 3
o **Other:** overhead projector
o **Teacher's Resource Binder:**

  [Activity Sheets]
  • **Activity Sheet 29**, page A38 (Prepare as a transparency.)
  • Optional—
    Orff Activity 2, page O22

Performing Folk Music

Skiffling is informal music making using homemade and store-bought instruments. In a typical skiffle band, the instruments are grouped something like this:

Melody
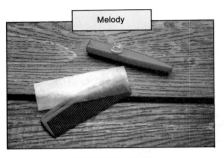

Bass

Melody and Drone
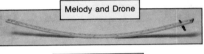

Melody and Harmony

Rhythm

• Listen to a skiffle band.
• Can you identify the instruments that take solo "rides"?

128

The Lesson

1. Begin class by playing the recordings of "Mama Don't 'Low" and "Bile Them Cabbage Down." Ask for the students' reactions to the music. **What kind of music is it? Where did it originate? What type of instruments were playing?**

2. Give the students a few minutes to scan the section titled "Performing Folk Music" (starting on page 128). Discuss the possibilities of learning to make and play a variety of instruments. Display the transparency of Activity Sheet 29 (*Commitment to Learning*) and discuss the options.

3. Read the information about skiffling on page 126. Explain that skiffling is a type of improvisation. When skiffling, someone starts a familiar melody then everyone else joins in, reinforcing the melody by improvising an interesting rhythmic part or harmonic accompaniment. Skiffling requires knowledge of a wide repertoire of "foot-stomping" and "easygoing" folk songs. It also requires a good ear since skiffling is usually performed without written music.

4. **By looking at the lists of songs on page 129, can you decide what the terms *foot-stompers* and *easygoing folk songs* mean?** (Foot-stompers are songs that move at a quick tempo and lend themselves to variety in accompaniment. They will probably be sung *forte!* In contrast, easygoing folk songs are just what they suggest: They are played at a relaxed tempo; their rhythms are not too complex and their dynamic level is *mezzo-piano* or *piano*.) Encourage the students to develop their own lists of songs that they know and like to perform.

Foot-Stompers

She'll be Comin'
  'Round the Mountain
Skip to My Lou
Oh, Susanna
This Land Is Your Land

Easygoing Folk Songs

Home on the Range
On Top of Old Smoky
Down in the Valley
Worried Man Blues

Bile Them Cabbage Down

American Folk Song

D   G   D   A7

Bile them cab-bage down, down, turn them hoe cakes 'round.

D   G   D   A7   G

The on-ly song that I could sing was bile them cab-bage down.

D   A7

Went up on the moun-tain just to give my horn a blow,

D   G   D   A7   D

Thought I heard my true love say, "Yon-der comes my beau."

129

INSTRUMENTS 7

For Your Information

This lesson is an introductory lesson for the section ending on page 143. The way to use these lessons will depend on the number of instruments available for practice. Spend some class time doing large group work in the basic presentation of each instrument. If possible follow this with time for the students to practice individually. Ask the students to select two or three instruments that they wish to specialize in.

5. Play the song "What Makes My Baby Cry?" Ask students to identify the instruments used (jug, banjo, harmonica, kazoo, guitar, and washboard). Help the students identify the instruments that are pictured and to place each in its correct category (Aerophones: pennywhistle, recorder, jug; Membranophone: kazoo (or comb); Chordophone: guitar, banjo, fiddle, mandolin, washtub bass; Idiophone: spoons, washboard, jawharp, limberjack).

6. Listen again to "Bile Them Cabbage Down" and "Mama Don't 'Low" in order to give the students an opportunity to answer the question on page 128 regarding solo "rides" ("Bile": banjo, harmonica, spoons, washtub bass; "Mama": guitar, kazoo, washboard, jug).

7. End the class by inviting the students to follow the notation for "Bile Them Cabbage Down" and softly sing the melody as they listen again to the recording.

OPTIONAL

INSTRUMENTS 8

Lesson Focus
Rhythm: Music may move in relation to the underlying steady beat. *(P–E)*

Materials
o **Piano Accompaniments:** pages 240, 306, 307
o **Record Information:**
  • Soldier's Joy
    Record 8 Side A Band 4
  • Spoon Demonstration
    Record 8 Side A Band 5
  • Mama Don't 'Low
    (Record 8 Side A Band 2)
  • Bile Them Cabbage Down
    (Record 8 Side A Band 3)
  • Red River Valley
    Record 8 Side A Band 6
    Voices: mixed chorus
    Accompaniment: banjo, fiddle, harmonica, bass, jaw harp, guitar
o **Other:** pairs of spoons, preferably metal (Each pair should be of matching size.)

The Spoons

Some American folk instruments are found at home rather than made at home. The spoons are one example of "found sounds." They are a must for skiffling and adding lively rhythmic accompaniments. Listen for their sound in this recording of "Soldier's Joy."

Hold the Spoons

Hold the Bottom Spoon

  • Place one spoon between the index and middle fingers of the hand you write with.
  • Keep the round side up.

Add the Top Spoon

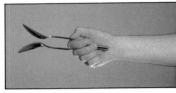

  • Place the second spoon over your index finger.
  • Keep the round side down.
  • Keep the top spoon parallel to the bottom spoon.
  • Be sure the spoon ends are wedged into your palm.

Your thumb should be lying on the top spoon. The index finger keeps the spoons apart while the other three fingers hold the spoons in place.

Play the Spoons

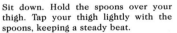

Sit down. Hold the spoons over your thigh. Tap your thigh lightly with the spoons, keeping a steady beat.

Next place your free hand about four inches above the spoons so that the spoons hit your hand just before they hit your thigh.

130

The Lesson

1. Before the students open their books, play the recording of "Soldier's Joy." **Who can identify the instruments?** (guitar, pennywhistle, and spoons) Invite the students to learn to play the spoons.

2. Hand out as many pairs of spoons as are available. Have the students open their books to page 130. Follow the instructions and pictures showing playing positions. Begin by spending time learning to hold the spoons. (The students should use their dominant hands.) Proceed by gently tapping the spoons with a steady beat on the thigh. Sing a familiar folk song, such as "She'll Be Coming 'Round the Mountain" or "Skip To My Lou" while continuing to tap.

3. Read the instructions for each new playing technique. Play the demonstration band.

Give the students an opportunity to practice after listening to each band.

4. Play recordings of "Mama Don't 'Low" and "Bile Them Cabbage Down" while the students practice playing steady beats with their spoons. When they are able to keep a steady beat using several of the techniques such as "thigh tap" and "thigh-palm taps," invite them to play along with the recording of "Soldier's Joy."

5. Challenge the students to combine their playing techniques to produce another rhythmic pattern. Invite them to play thigh–hand–thigh–hand–thigh. Notate the following pattern on the board and point out what the resulting rhythm sounds like:

The Roll

The "roll" presents a bigger challenge. Extend your top hand outward as if you were going to shake hands. Spread the fingers wide apart. Turn the palm slightly upward. Now run the spoons across your fingers, top to bottom. Land on your thigh. The rhythm should sound like this:

"de-de-de-de-DUM, d-d-d-d-D, d-d-d-d- D"

Try accompanying yourself as you sing a familiar folk tune, such as "Skip to My Lou." When you have the techniques mastered, try playing along as you sing "Red River Valley."

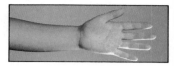

Red River Valley

American Folk Song

1. From this val - ley, they say you are go - ing, _____ We will
Refrain: Come and sit by my side if you love me, _____ Do not
2. Won't you think of the val - ley you're leav - ing? _____ Oh, how

miss your bright eyes and sweet smile, For they say you are tak - ing the
has - ten to bid me a - dieu, But re - mem - ber the Red Riv - er
lone - ly, how sad it will be. Oh, __ think of the fond heart you're

sun - shine That bright - ens our path - way a - while.
Val - ley And the girl that has loved you so true.
break - ing And the grief you are giv - ing to me.

131

Suggest to the students that they try other combinations to produce additional patterns.

6. The most difficult technique to master on the spoons is the "roll." Instructions are given in the pupil book on page 131. Encourage those who are able to hold the spoons, keep the beat, and play rhythms, to move toward mastering the roll. The goal is to use the roll as a part of a rhythm pattern. For example, it might be played on the first beat of the pattern. Practice by singing "Skip to My Lou" and creating an accompaniment pattern that includes the roll.

7. Direct attention to "Red River Valley" on page 131. Help the students learn the song so that they may sing as they play. The students may use one or all of the spoon techniques to improvise a rhythmic accompaniment.

OPTIONAL

Lesson Focus

Timbre: The quality of a sound is affected by the material, shape, and size of the source.
Timbre: The quality of a sound is affected by the way the sound is produced. *(P–E)*

Materials

o **Piano Accompaniments:** pages 308, 306, 310
o **Record Information:**
  • What Makes My Baby Cry?
    (Record 5 Side B Band 3)
  • Jug Demonstration
    Record 8 Side A Band 7a
  • Worried Man Blues
    Record 8 Side A Band 7b
    Voices: mixed chorus
    Accompaniment: harmonica, banjo, guitar, bass
  • Bile Them Cabbage Down
    (Record 8 Side A Band 3)
  • She Wore a Yellow Ribbon
    Record 8 Side A Band 8
    Voices: mixed chorus
    Accompaniment: ocarina, autoharp, tack piano, ukulele, jaw harp, jug, spoons
o **Other:** a variety of jugs (as many as possible); sterilizer and cloths; pairs of spoons
o **Teacher's Resource Binder:**
  • Optional—
    Orff Activity 11, page O22

The Jug

The jug is another found sound that is a very popular American skiffle instrument. It is easy to find, inexpensive to own, and handy to carry around! One thing that makes it so popular is its unique tonal quality. In many traditional groups the jug provided the bass lines that we associate with the sound of the string bass. Listen to its sound in "What Makes My Baby Cry?"

Learn to play by buzzing your lips like a trumpet player. Hold the jug close enough to your lips to "catch" and resonate the sound. To change pitch, tighten or relax your buzzing lips.

You may have to experiment with moving the jug around until you find just the right position to produce the sound.

Worried Man Blues

American Folk Song

G

It takes a wor-ried man to sing a wor-ried song. It

C   G

takes a wor-ried man to sing a wor-ried song. It

132

The Lesson

1. Review knowledge gained about skiffling: the kind of music used (folk music) and the instruments featured (guitar, spoons, pennywhistle, jug, etc.). Ask the students to listen to "What Makes My Baby Cry?" paying particular attention to the sound of the jug. The bass line played by the jug during the third repeat provides a solid foundation under the melody. The jug was not used as a novelty. It was played because it produced a good sound and was readily available.

2. Ask the students to imitate the lip position of the picture on page 132. Divide the class into as many groups as there are jugs. Hand out the jugs and challenge the students to make a sound. Some students will have trouble at first. Encourage them to practice "buzzing" their lips. Then have them bring the jug to their lips, tilting it at different angles until the jug "catches" the sound.

3. After listening to the demonstration bands on the recording, invite the students to make the "oompah" bass sound. Practice will be needed until the students can determine the exact amount of tension needed in their lips or the exact angle to tilt the jug to create the correct pitch. They will need to listen carefully to know when to change pitches to match the changing chords. They can also follow the chord markings above the notation. Usually the jug plays the root of the chord.

4. If the students are not familiar with the songs on pages 132 and 133, guide them to learn the melodies by reading the notation. Listen again to the recordings to check for accuracy.

takes a wor - ried man to sing a wor - ried song. I'm wor - ried

now, _____ but I won't be wor - ried long.

She Wore a Yellow Ribbon

Traditional

'Round her neck she wore a yel - low rib - bon. She wore it in the

spring-time and in the month of May. And if you asked her

why the heck she wore it, she'd say, "It's for my lov - er who is

far, far a - way." Far a - way, _____ far a - way, _____ She wore it for her

lov - er far a - way. _____ 'Round her neck she wore a yel - low

rib - bon. She wore it for her lov - er who is far, far a - way.

133

For Your Information

A variety of jugs including fruit juice bottles, old-fashioned crockery jugs, or plastic milk jugs will make good instruments. A sterilizer such as that used by band teachers should be available; encourage the students to wipe the jugs before and after they finish using them.

5. When they know the melodies, invite some of the students to accompany "Worried Man Blues" and "She Wore a Yellow Ribbon" while others sing. Add the spoons to provide a rhythmic accompaniment.

6. Return to the list of "Foot-stompers" on page 129. Sing and play along with these songs.

OPTIONAL

Lesson Focus

Timbre: The quality of a sound is affected by the material, shape, and size of the source.
Timbre: The quality of a sound is affected by the way the sound is produced. *(P–E)*

Materials

○ **Piano Accompaniments:** pages 224, 309
○ **Record Information:**
  • Ring, Ring the Banjo
    (Record 1 Side A Band 2)
  • Trouble in Mind
    Record 5 Side A Band 4
  • Washboard Demonstration
    Record 8 Side B Band 2
  • Old Joe Clarke
    Record 8 Side B Band 1
    Voices: male soloist
    Accompaniment: guitar, banjo, washtub bass, limberjack
○ **Instruments:** kazoos; combs; washboards
○ **Other:** wax paper
○ **Teacher's Resource Binder:**
  • Optional—
    Instrumental Accompaniment 6,
    page 115
    Orff Activity 8, page O14

More Skiffle Instruments

First play the Comb

• Place a comb wrapped in paper against your lips.
• Hum. Did you get a "buzz" tone?
• Play "Ring, Ring the Banjo" on the comb.
• Now you are ready to join the skiffle group.

Next play the Kazoo

The kazoo consists of a small tube with a tissue membrane disc enclosed in a circular holder. It might be described as a "hum-buzz" instrument: You hum into it, and the tune buzzes back to you with a special nasal quality! If you can hum a tune, you can play the kazoo!

The Washboard

Along with the spoons, one of the most popular found instruments is the washboard. It was first popular in the rural blues bands of the 1920s. You can still hear it in folk- and country-music bands today. Virgil Perkins, a rural blues musician, mounted his washboard on a stand. Listen to the variety of rhythms and tonal qualities he is able to produce on this recording of "Trouble in Mind."

Play the washboard

• Put thimbles on the thumb and first two fingers of your writing hand.
• Hold the washboard with the other hand, cradling it against you.
• Tap and scrape your thimbled fingers on the ridges of the board. You can even tap on the wooden frame. Hum, whistle, or sing "Old Joe Clarke," and accompany yourself.

134

The Lesson

1. Ask the students to open their books to page 134 and read about playing the comb. Distribute combs and wax paper and play the recording of "Ring, Ring the Banjo" (pages 6–7). Invite the students to perform with the recording. Remind them that they will feel a tickling sensation on their lips as they play the wax-paper-covered comb. Licking their lips will alleviate the problem.

2. For those who have never played a comb, demonstrate that simply blowing will produce no sound. They will need to hum or "sing" a song using a "doo" sound. Demonstrate the need for holding the wax paper taut over the comb. Encourage the students to experiment with different sizes and thicknesses of combs. **What does this do to the tone quality?**

3. Distribute as many kazoos as are available. Ask the students to again play "Ring, Ring the Banjo" using the same performance techniques as when playing the comb. **How does this sound differ from that of the comb?** Conclude that the two sounds are essentially the same.

4. Before adding the sound of the washboard to the ensemble, ask the students to look at page 134. Read the text and discuss the use of the washboard as an instrument. **Listen to an excerpt of "Trouble in Mind" to hear what a washboard can sound like in the hands of a rural blues musician.** Play the excerpt of "Trouble in Mind."

5. Explain that the washboard is scraped downward on the accented beats, using one or two fingers. Short scrapes and thumb taps are played on other beats. Thimbles are usually

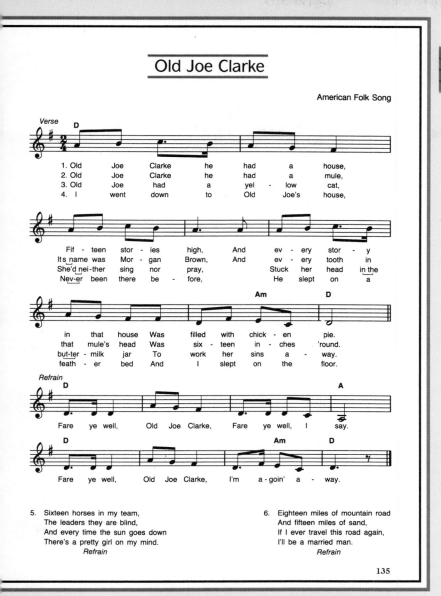

Old Joe Clarke

American Folk Song

Verse

1. Old Joe Clarke he had a house,
2. Old Joe Clarke he had a mule,
3. Old Joe had a yel-low cat,
4. I went down to Old Joe's house,

Fif - teen stor - ies high, And ev - ery stor - y
Its name was Mor - gan Brown, And ev - ery tooth in
She'd nei-ther sing nor pray, Stuck her head in the
Nev-er been there be - fore, He slept on a

in that house Was filled with chick - en pie.
that mule's head Was six - teen in - ches 'round.
but-ter - milk jar To work her sins a - way.
feath - er bed And I slept on the floor.

Refrain

Fare ye well, Old Joe Clarke, Fare ye well, I say.

Fare ye well, Old Joe Clarke, I'm a - goin' a - way.

5. Sixteen horses in my team,
   The leaders they are blind,
   And every time the sun goes down
   There's a pretty girl on my mind.
   Refrain

6. Eighteen miles of mountain road
   And fifteen miles of sand,
   If I ever travel this road again,
   I'll be a married man.
   Refrain

135

worn on the thumb and first two or three fingers of the hand. Play the demonstration band on the recording (Record 8 Side B Band 2). Then invite several students to play the washboard.

6. Listen to the recording to help the students learn to sing "Old Joe Clarke" on page 135. When they are familiar with this song, ask the students to prepare their own skiffle arrangement using the instruments they have learned to play. Suggest that they plan a different instrumentation for each verse. Some students might take solo "rides" similar to those heard in "Bile Them Cabbage Down."

7. Divide the class into groups. Hand out all available kazoos, combs, washboards, jugs, and spoons. Encourage each group to choose a familiar song to practice and perform. Pro-

OPTIONAL

vide time for them to share their performance with their classmates.

Lesson Focus

Timbre: The quality of a sound is affected by the way the sound is produced.
Time and Place: A particular use of melody, rhythm, harmony, and timbre reflects the origin of the musical whole. *(P–S)*

Materials

o **Piano Accompaniment:** page 312
o **Record Information:**
  • The M.T.A. Song
    Record 8 Side B Band 4
    Voices: mixed chorus
    Accompaniment: saxophones, clarinet, synthesizer, electric bass, percussion
  • Groundhog (Mouthbow Demonstration)
    Record 8 Side B Band 3
o **Instruments:** skiffle instruments
o **Other:** overhead projector
o **Teacher's Resource Binder:**
  | Activity Sheets | • **Activity Sheet 30**, page A39 (Prepare as a transparency.) |

The M.T.A. Song

Words and Music by Jacqueline Steiner and Bess Hawes

1. Well let me tell you of the sto-ry of the man named Char-lie, on a trag-ic and fate-ful day. _____ He put ten cents in his pock-et, kissed his wife and fam-'ly, went to ride on the M. T. A. Well, did he ev-er re-turn, _____ No he nev-er re-turned _____ And his

2. hand-ed in his dime _____ at the Ken-dall Square Sta-tion, and he changed for Ja-mai-ca Plain. _____ When he got there the con-duc-tor told him one more nick-el, Char-lie could-n't get off that train. But did he

3. Now _____ all night long _____ Char-lie rides through the tun-nel say-ing, "What will be-come of me? _____ How can I af-ford to see my sis-ter in Chel-sea, or my cous-in in Rox-bur-y?" But did he

4. Char-lie's wife goes down _____ to the Scol-lay Square Sta-tion, ev-ery day _____ at quar-ter past two. _____ And through the o-pen win-dow she hands Char-lie a sand-wich, as the train _____ comes rum-blin' through. Well, did he

Refrain

136

The Lesson

1. After reading page 137, display the transparency of Activity Sheet 30 (*The Mouthbow*). Read the directions with the students. Stress the need for lightweight, flexible wood. The bow should be curved by very gradually applying tension so that the lightweight stick does not snap.

2. Ask the students to listen to the recording of "Groundhog," paying particular attention to the sound of the mouthbow. After listening, ask the students to carefully examine the pictures on the page. Of all the skiffle instruments, they are probably least familiar with the playing position and sound of the mouthbow. Play the demonstration record so that the students will have an idea of the sound that they should try to achieve with the mouthbow.

OPTIONAL

3. If there is a real mouthbow available, permit one or more of the students to experiment until they find the right placement of the bow against the cheek so that the mouth "catches" the sound and acts as a resonating chamber.

4. Challenge the students to use their music-reading skills gained during Unit I to learn "The M.T.A. Song." Examine the rhythm; conclude that it moves in twos, with the half note being the note that moves with the beat. If the students feel it necessary to practice the rhythm before adding the melody, ask one student to establish the tempo of the shortest sound and continue to tap it as the class reads the words of the song in rhythm.

5. Scan the melody, noticing that it is in the key of C. Warm up by singing the scale and pitch sequence 1–3–5; challenge the students to

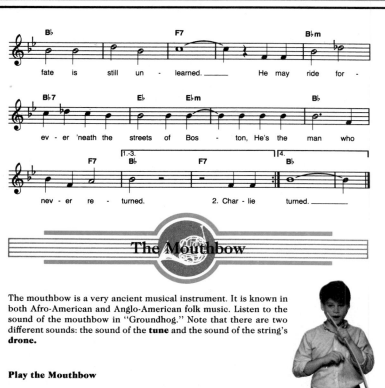

fate is still un - learned. _____ He may ride for -

ev - er 'neath the streets of Bos - ton, He's the man who

nev - er re - turned. 2. Char - lie turned. _____

The Mouthbow

The mouthbow is a very ancient musical instrument. It is known in both Afro-American and Anglo-American folk music. Listen to the sound of the mouthbow in "Groundhog." Note that there are two different sounds: the sound of the **tune** and the sound of the string's **drone**.

Play the Mouthbow

- Tighten the strings as you bend the bow: Place the end with the small hole against the floor. Gently bend the wood with your hand as you tighten the string by turning the peg.
- Hold the bow in your left hand about six inches from the end with the small hole.
- Hold the flat side of the bow against your right cheek. Slightly open your lips and press them against the bow near the upper end of the string. Your mouth is the resonating chamber that will amplify the sound of the bow as well as make the melodic pitches.
- With the pick in your other hand, pluck up and down the string as you open and close your mouth. Do you hear the pitch change? Keep experimenting until you can control the sound and the pitch.

137

For Your Information
Obtain lightweight, flexible yardsticks or use lightweight $\frac{1}{8}$-inch lath cut into 26-inch strips. Ukelele or violin pegs can be purchased at any instrument store. See instructions on Activity Sheet 30 (*The Mouthbow*) for making the mouthbow.

sight-sing with scale numbers while you or a student accompanies them on the autoharp.

6. Discuss the style of the song. Agree that it is in a traditional folk-song style, with a repetitive melody that centers around common chords (1–3–5, 1–4–6, or 2–5–7–4), a rhythm that moves regularly, and a harmony based on the I, IV, and V7 chords. Contemporary country music finds its roots in these traditional patterns. This song is a ballad (song that tells a story through many verses), a popular form brought by settlers from England.

7. When the students can sing the song, divide the class into small groups. Each group is to plan its own skiffling performance of the ballad. One student may play the autoharp to provide a harmonic accompaniment. There must be both melody and rhythm instruments. **Work for balance and interest in** your arrangement. Who will sing? Will you perform each verse in the same way?

8. If time and materials are available, allow some students to build mouthbows, following the instructions on the activity sheet. (See **For Your Information** for materials sources.) Some students might choose to make one at home as a special project for extra credit.

OPTIONAL

Lesson Focus

Timbre: The quality of a sound is affected by the material, shape, and size of the source.
Timbre: The quality of a sound is affected by the way the sound is produced. *(P–E)*

Materials

o **Piano Accompaniments:** pages 330, 314
o **Record Information:**
  • Deep Fork River Blues
    Record 8 Side B Band 5a
    Voice: male soloist
    Accompaniment: guitar, harmonica, washtub bass
  • Limberjack Demonstration
    Record 8 Side B Band 5b
  • Sixteen Tons
    Record 8 Side B Band 6
    Voices: mixed chorus
    Accompaniment: trumpet, bass clarinet, accordion
o **Instruments:** washtub bass; limberjacks
o **Other:** wooden block to prop up washtub; glove for playing washtub bass; overhead projector
o **Teacher's Resource Binder:**
  Activity Sheets • **Activity Sheet 31,** page A40

(continued on next page)

The Washtub Bass

You may decide to make a washtub bass for the same reason that this instrument became popular in the early 1900s—its cost! Although people could order musical instruments from catalogues, at that time a string bass would cost well over $20.00! So people turned to materials at hand and created their own instruments. A well-constructed and well-played washtub bass sounds very much like a string bass.

To produce different bass notes on this washtub bass, you need to change the tension of the string. You can do this by pulling back on the stick with one hand as you pluck with the other to create a "walking-bass" accompaniment or by fretting the string to make an "oompah-bass" accompaniment.

Listen to "Deep Fork River Blues."

Which method is the performer using?

Root bass   Walking bass

There are many "tricks of the trade" that you will pick up as you practice. For example:

  • Put your foot on the tub's edge to keep it from "dancing" away.
  • Wear a glove on your hand to prevent blisters and sore fingers.
  • Prop up one side of the tub with a block of wood to allow more sound to escape.

138

The Lesson

1. Have the students open their books to pages 138–39 and read the introduction to two new folk instruments, the washtub bass and the limberjack. Display the transparencies that show how to make the two instruments. Discuss how folk instruments are often developed from materials at hand, such as an old washtub or kindling that can be easily whittled into shape. Be sure students realize that these are not toys but authentic folk instruments, frequently found in the Appalachian Mountains.

2. Play the recording of "Deep Fork River Blues." Point out that the washtub performer plays a walking bass line. Explain that a walking bass line moves up and down by steps to and from the root of each chord employed. Another way of playing this instrument is to play only the root of each chord. This is known as a root bass.

3. Invite the students to play the washtub bass after reading the material on page 138. Demonstrate the need for tension on the string. The performer must keep plucking the string as it is tightened until a good sound is created with the least amount of tension on the stick. Other pitches can then be produced by pulling further back on the stick. Demonstrate a walking bass and a root bass.

4. Ask the students to look for the chord symbols on the music score for "Bile Them Cabbage Down" on page 129. Remind them that they can determine the root bass part to be played by following the chord symbols (D G A) although they will have to listen to be sure the pitches are in tune. Provide time for sev-

The Limberjack

- Sit on the yardstick so that the platform reaches to about the end of your knees.
- Hold the limberjack by the dowel so that its feet almost touch the platform.
- With the other hand, tap the yardstick so that the platform bounces. You do not need to move the limberjack up and down.

Sixteen Tons

Words and Music by Merle Travis

139

Materials *(continued)*

- **Activity Sheets 32a–b,** pages A41–A42 (Prepare a copy for each student, and prepare as transparencies.)
- Optional— **Mainstreaming Activity 14,** page M21

For Your Information

Kits for making limberjacks are available from various hobby shops and folk-instrument outlets. Consult music education journals or local music stores for sources. Industrial arts teachers might be persuaded to allow the students to make instruments during class time.

To play a limberjack, hold the dowel in one hand and tap a quick, steady pulse with the other hand at the point just beyond the chair seat. The platform will bounce up and down touching the limberjack's feet, causing him to "dance." The limberjack's arm joints will also begin to swing rhythmically. The limberjack imitates a style of dancing called step dancing or clog dancing.

eral students to play the root bass while classmates sing the song.

5. Play the demonstration recording of the limberjack as students silently read about this folk instrument on page 139. Give a limberjack to a student and ask him or her to duplicate the sitting position shown on page 139. Remind the students that if too much of the stick is on the chair, the stick will not bounce freely. The amount of stick extending beyond the chair controls the tempo: The more the stick is extended, the slower the tempo of the limberjack's dance; the less the stick is extended, the faster the tempo.

6. Listen to the recording of "Sixteen Tons." Challenge the students to devise and play rhythms with spoons and limberjacks as they sing the song.

OPTIONAL

7. Hand out copies of Activity Sheets 31 (*Washtub Bass*) and 32a and b (*Limberjack*). Read and answer questions the students may have about the construction of the two instruments, including where kits can be purchased. (See **For Your Information**.) Encourage interested students to make these instruments.

Lesson Focus

Timbre: The quality of sound is affected by the way the sound is produced.
Melody: A series of pitches may move up or down by steps or skips. *(P–I)*

Materials

o **Piano Accompaniment:** page 316
o **Record Information:**
  • The Colorado Trail
    Record 8 Side B Band 7
  • Baby, Please Don't Go
    Record 8 Side B Band 8
    Voices: male choir
    Accompaniment: clarinet, trumpet, piano, double bass, percussion
o **Instruments:** C harmonicas
o **Teacher's Resource Binder:**
  • Optional—
    Enrichment Activity 9, page E16

The Harmonica

Harmonica playing styles are as numerous as the performers who choose the harmonica as their favorite instrument. Listen to the expressive sound of the harmonica accompanying "The Colorado Trail."

Begin by exploring your harmonica.

• Turn it over.
• Pick it up.
• Blow into it. Find the low pitches that are at the left end of the instrument.

Hole Numbers 1 2 3 4 5 6 7 1′   Scale Steps

Play a Tune by Ear

Begin with a tune that you have heard so often you can hear it in your mind.

• Tune up by playing the scale on your harmonica:
  4-4-5-5-6-6-7-7.
  When will you blow into the hole? When will you draw air out of the hole?
• Think and hum the first pitch of the song; then try to match it on your harmonica. It will almost always require a blow, not a draw.
• As you play try to think about the shape and direction of the tune.

  Does it go up or down? Does it move by steps or by skips?

140

The Lesson

1. Introduce the harmonica by asking the students to listen for it when the recording of "The Colorado Trail" is played. Comment on the instrument's plaintive sound. Because of this distinctive quality, it is often associated with country or blues music. Discuss the instrument's popularity. (See **For Your Information.**)

2. Explain how sound is produced on the harmonica. Inside the harmonica there is a row of small metal "tongues" or reeds that are free at one end but attached to a close-fitting metal frame at the other end. As the player blows or draws air across these metal reeds, they vibrate, producing a sound. For this reason the harmonica is classified as a "free-reed aerophone."

3. Help the students realize that the hole numbers and the scale numbers do not match. On the C harmonica, the first step of the C scale is obtained by blowing into Hole 4. All other pitches of that scale are found either by blowing into or drawing air out of Holes 4, 5, 6, and 7 (additional holes provide these same pitches higher or lower).

4. Distribute all available harmonicas to the students. Ask them to follow the instructions on page 140. Encourage them to explore the many sounds of the instrument, to play the C scale (4–4–5–5–6–6–7–7), and to play tunes such as "Mary Had a Little Lamb" (begin by blowing into Hole 5) or "Are you Sleeping?" (begin by blowing into Hole 4) by ear.

5. Explain the "shorthand system" for notating harmonica melodies. Read the information on page 141 together. First sing "On Top of Old Smoky" without accompaniment. Once the melody is again established in their ears,

Remember by Writing It Down

Here is a sort of shorthand notation you might use. It shows the **hole numbers** to play, not the scale steps. Uncircled numbers mean **blow.** Circled numbers mean **draw.**

This is what "On Top of Old Smoky" would look like:

4   4   5   6   7   ⑥   ⑥   ⑤   6   ⑥   6

On top of Old Smok-y, All cov-ered with snow,

4   4   5   6   6   ④   ④   5   ⑤   ④   4

I lost my true lov-er, By court-ing too slow.

Baby, Please Don't Go

Words and Music by Big Bill Broonzy

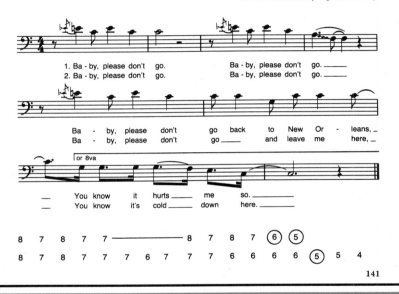

1. Ba - by, please don't go. Ba - by, please don't go. _____
2. Ba - by, please don't go. Ba - by, please don't go. _____

Ba - by, please don't go back to New Or - leans, ___
Ba - by, please don't go and leave me here, ___

— You know it hurts ____ me so. _____
— You know it's cold ____ down here. _____

8   7   8   7   7 ———————— 8   7   8   7   ⑥   ⑤
8   7   8   7   7   7   6   7   7   7   6   6   6   ⑤   5   4

141

For Your Information

Instructions in this lesson are for playing the ten-hole C harmonica. Other models in other keys are available, but the ten-hole, twenty-note diatonic C model is best for beginners.

The harmonica is a well-traveled instrument! Explorers have played the harmonica during expeditions to both poles, to the top of Mt. Everest, and even into outer space. Astronaut Walter Schirra played the harmonica while orbiting the earth in *Gemini VI!*

Before putting harmonicas away for the day, students should gently tap the harmonica to remove all moisture and leave it upside down.

challenge the students to follow the numbers and blow or draw on the holes to play it. The students may work independently or in pairs for this activity. For most students the most difficult part will be finding the starting pitch. Be prepared to assist them.

6. Take time to introduce the blues song "Baby, Please Don't Go." Repeatedly sing this song with Baritone and Changing Voices (C.V. sing last two measures an octave higher) during the next few sessions. When the song is very familiar ask the students to return to this page and follow the number notation to learn this plaintive blues song on the harmonica.

INSTRUMENTS 14

Lesson Focus

Timbre: The quality of a sound is affected by the way the sound is produced. *(P–I)*

Materials

o **Piano Accompaniments:** pages 317, 299
o **Record Information:**
  • Down in the Valley (full-chord version)
  Record 9   Side A   Band 1a
  Band 1b: single-note version
  • Alabama Bound
  Record 9   Side A   Band 2
  Voices: mixed chorus
  Accompaniment: harmonica, electric guitar, acoustic guitar, double bass, percussion
  • Shady Grove
  Record 5   Side B   Band 5
o **Instruments:** C harmonicas; skiffle instruments
o **Teacher's Resource Binder:**
  Activity Sheets
  • **Activity Sheet 33,** page A43
  Activity Sheet 34, page A44
  • Optional—
  Mainstreaming Activity 15, page M23
  Orff Activity 10, page O18

Two Ways to Play the Harmonica

Full-Chord Style

You play one melody and three harmony pitches at the same time. This is the style you have been practicing.

Single-Note Style

Only the melody sounds. This is the style most harmonica players prefer.

Listen to "Down in the Valley." It is recorded in both styles.

Try playing in the single-note style. To do this, place your mouth over the four holes as before. This time let your tongue block the three holes to the left. This cuts off the air to the harmony pitches and allows only the melody pitch to sound. Practice your **C scale** in this manner until it feels comfortable to sound only a single note. Do not get discouraged if it takes a while to learn to position your tongue correctly!

Can you read this harmonica shorthand and play in the single-note style?

3   4   ④   5   4   5   5   6   6   ④

Down in the val - ley, The val - ley so low,

3   ③   4   6   6   ⑤   5   ④   4

Hang your head o - ver, Hear the wind blow.

Play From Notation

This is what all the pitches of the ten-hole C harmonica look like on the music staff:

Follow the shorthand written above the staff on the next page. Learn to play "Alabama Bound." Ask someone to accompany you on guitar or washtub bass.

142

The Lesson

1. Use the song "On Top of Old Smoky" (page 141) to review the shorthand notation for the harmonica; remind the students of the purpose of the circled and uncircled numbers.

2. Have the students open their books to page 142. Read about the two styles of playing harmonica. Some students will already be using the single-note style. Identify these students and reassure everyone that both styles are very acceptable ways of playing this instrument. Ask the students to listen as "Down in the Valley" is performed in both styles.

3. Challenge the students who are proficient at the full-chord style to practice playing single notes. Ask them to follow the harmonica shorthand to play "Down in the Valley."

4. Draw the students' attention to the notation guide on the bottom of the page. Explain that this is a handy reference for their use as they independently learn new melodies on the harmonica.

5. Assign some students to independently learn to play the first, second, and fourth phrases of "Alabama Bound" by following the harmonica notation written over the staves. When they are able to do this, ask the group to decide on an arrangement of this tune. (They might use call-response ideas, train sounds, and so on.) Skiffle-band players may be invited to join and contribute to the arrangement.

6. *OPTIONAL* Make Activity Sheets 33 (*Shady Grove*) and 34 (*Polly Wolly Doodle*) available to those students who wish to continue learning new melodies and to try adding vibrato.

142

Alabama Bound

Traditional

(Leader)
C 4 5 6 ⑥ 6 4 *(Answer)*

I'm Al - a - bam - a bound, ____ I'm Al - a - bam - a bound, ____
Oh don't you leave me here, ____ Oh don't you leave me here, ____
Oh well, your hair don't curl, ____ And your ___ eyes ain't blue, ____

(Leader)
F ⑤ ⑥ 7 ⑧ 7 ⑤ *(Answer)*

I'm Al - a - bam - a bound, ____ I'm Al - a - bam - a bound, ____
Oh don't you leave me here, ____ Oh don't you leave me here, ____
Oh, well your hair don't curl, ____ And your ___ eyes ain't blue.

C

And if the train don't stop and turn a - round, ____
But if you must go ____ an - y - how, ____
Well if you don't want me, sweet Pol - ly Ann, ____

(Leader)
4 5 6 ⑥ 6 4 *(Answer)*

I'm Al - a - bam - a bound, ____ I'm Al - a - bam - a bound. ____
Don't let me see a tear. ____ Don't let me see a tear. ____
Well I ____ don't want you. ____ Well I ____ don't want you.

143

For Your Information

Single-note style harmonica playing is diffi-cult. Do not move the students to this style until they are comfortable with the full-chord style of playing. Depending on time, interest, and motivation, many students may be con-tent with the full-chord style.

Lesson Focus

Harmony: Chords and melody may move simultaneously in relation to each other. *(P–S)*

Materials

○ **Piano Accompaniment:** page 318

○ **Record Information:**
  - Duelin' Banjos
    (Record 1   Side A   Band 3)
  - Clementine
    Record 9   Side A   Band 3
    Voices: treble chorus
    Accompaniment: guitar, tack piano, double bass

○ **Instruments:** guitars (standard tuning) that students may share

○ **Other:** coffee cans or similar objects to rest left foot on; overhead projector

○ **Teacher's Resource Binder:**
  Activity Sheets • **Activity Sheet 35**, page A45 (Prepare as a transparency.)

Playing the Guitar

C Chord (four strings)

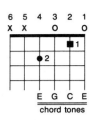

```
6 5 4 3 2 1
X X   O     O
          ■ 1
      ● 2

  E G C E
  chord tones
```

O means "open string."
X means "do not strum."

Press firmly on the strings with your left-hand fingers. Place the thumb behind the middle finger (2) to provide support. Play this "short" C chord. Strum only the four highest strings: 4 3 2 1.

The numbers on the chord chart tell you which fingers to use.

The root of the chord is shown by a ■.

Other pitches are shown by a ●.

Practice strumming the C chord.

Sing these familiar rounds as you strum the C chord.
  • "Row, Row, Row Your Boat" (begin singing on C).
  • "Three Blind Mice" (begin singing on E).

144

The Lesson

1. Review "Duelin' Banjos" (page 7). Display the transparency of Activity Sheet 35 (*The Guitar*). Help the students explore the parts of the guitar shown at the top of the transparency so that they will become familiar with the names and locations of each part of the instrument.

2. Focus the students' attention on the playing position shown on the transparency. The students should hold the guitar as shown; it should feel comfortable and secure. The left foot should be raised by placing it on a coffee can or other small object. The guitar should make contact with the body at four points: 1) underneath the right forearm, 2) against the chest, 3) inside the right thigh, and 4) on the left knee. The body should be aligned vertically with the shoulders level. The guitar should be slanted so that its head is slightly higher than the player's shoulders.

3. Practice the correct left-hand position by touching the thumb to the middle finger. Apply pressure. The thumb should provide a balance point for the fingers. This same position should be maintained while playing— the thumb on the back of the guitar neck for balance and support, the fingertips pressing down on the strings. Be sure the students use their fingertips to avoid touching adjacent strings. The students should refer to the drawing as needed.

4. The right hand should be placed in a relaxed position with the thumb over the sound hole. Chords may be strummed by brushing the thumb from the lowest to the highest string. Have the students try this without forming a left-hand chord. They may also experiment

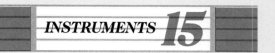
Clementine

G7 Chord (four strings)

Traditional

To find the G7 chord, play the C chord; then roll your index finger back to the first string. All other fingers are off the strings. Strum only the four highest strings.

Practice moving between the C and G7 chords until you can find them easily.

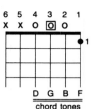

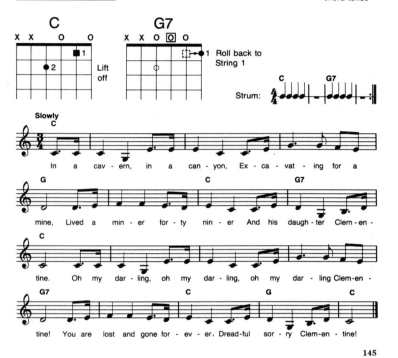

For Your Information
Guitars should be tuned as shown on Activity Sheet 35 (*The Guitar*) before the students begin the lesson.

with plucking by first plucking the lowest string of the top four (4) with the thumb, then the highest three strings (1, 2, 3) with the second, third, and fourth fingers so the following pattern is played.

5. Have the students open their books to page 144. Follow the directions given to play the "short" C chord. Practice strumming the C chord as shown at the bottom of the page. Sing "Row, Row, Row Your Boat" and "Three Blind Mice" while strumming. When the class is comfortable with strumming, the songs may be sung as rounds or they may be sung simultaneously as partner songs.

6. Explore the G7 chord and practice changing from C to G7, then back to C as shown on page 146. When the students are able to make the change easily, strum the chords as an accompaniment for "Clementine."

OPTIONAL

145

Lesson Focus

Harmony: Chords and melody may move simultaneously in relation to each other. **(P–S)**

Materials

o **Piano Accompaniments:** pages 318, 322, 324
o **Record Information:**
  • Clementine
    (Record 9   Side A   Band 3)
  • Putting on the Style
    Record 9   Side A   Band 4
    Voices: mixed chorus
    Accompaniment: guitar, bass clarinet, trumpet, trombone, double bass, percussion
  • *Guantanamera*
    Record 9   Side A   Band 5
    Voices: mixed chorus
    Accompaniment: 12-string guitar, rhythm guitar, bass, percussion
o **Instruments:** guitars (standard tuning) that students may share
o **Other:** coffee cans or other footrests

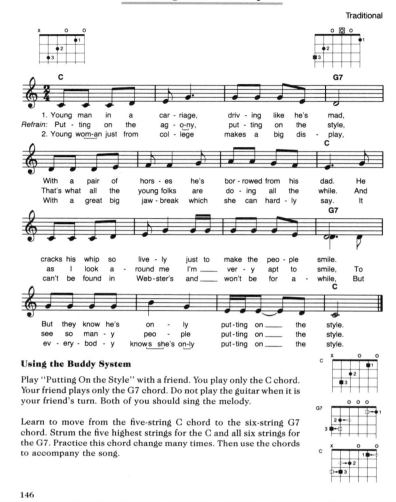

Putting On the Style

Traditional

1. Young man in a car-riage, driv-ing like he's mad,
Refrain: Put-ting on the ag-o-ny, put-ting on the style,
2. Young wom-an just from col-lege makes a big dis-play,

With a pair of hors-es he's bor-rowed from his dad. He
That's what all the young folks are do-ing all the while. And
With a great big jaw-break which she can hard-ly say. It

cracks his whip so live-ly just to make the peo-ple smile.
as I look a-round me I'm ____ ver-y apt to smile, To
can't be found in Web-ster's and ____ won't be for a-while, But

But they know he's on — ly put-ting on ____ the style.
see so man-y peo-ple put-ting on ____ the style.
ev-ery-bod-y knows she's on-ly put-ting on ____ the style.

Using the Buddy System

Play "Putting On the Style" with a friend. You play only the C chord. Your friend plays only the G7 chord. Do not play the guitar when it is your friend's turn. Both of you should sing the melody.

Learn to move from the five-string C chord to the six-string G7 chord. Strum the five highest strings for the C and all six strings for the G7. Practice this chord change many times. Then use the chords to accompany the song.

146

The Lesson

1. Review the "short" C and G7 chords learned in Instruments 15 by playing "Clementine." Have the students open their books to page 146. Play the recording of "Putting on the Style" as the students listen and follow the notation. Learn to sing this song. Then accompany it with the same chords used for "Clementine."

   Practice the new (5-string) C chord shown on page 146. Substitute it for the "short" C chord to play the accompaniment for "Putting on the Style."

2. Learn the 6-string G7 chord. Practice using "the buddy system" as described on page 146 to use the expanded versions of the C and G7 chords. When the students are comfortable with the new chords, practice moving from C to G7 and back, strumming the five highest strings for C and all six strings for G7. When the changes are easily made, the students may accompany all the songs they have learned in this section that use these two chords.

3. Listen to the recording of *"Guantanamera."* When the students are familiar with the melody, add a bass part. The bass part in this song would usually be played on the *guitarron,* a large, round-bottomed bass guitar used in mariachi bands. It is plucked by the performer rather than strummed. This can be done on a regular guitar by playing only the root of each chord on the two lowest strings. (The three-note pattern is shown at the top of page 147.) Make sure the guitars are in tune with the recording, then add the root bass part to the sounds of the mariachi musicians.

4. Learn to sing the song and add the root bass part as the class sings.

OPTIONAL

146

Guantanamera

Words and Music by José Fernandez Dias

For Your Information

The phonetic pronunciation of the Spanish lyrics for *"Guantanamera"*:

gwahn-tah-nah-mehr-ah gwah-hee-rah gwahn-tah-nah-mehr-ah

1. yoh soy oon ohm-breh seen-seh-roh
deh dohn-deh kreh-seh lah pahl-mah
yahn-tehs deh mohr-reer-meh kyeh-roh
eh-chahr mees vehr-sohs dehl ahl-mah
gwahn-tah-nah-mehr-ah gwah-hee-rah
gwahn-tah-nah-mehr-ah

2. mee vehr-soh ehs deh oon vehr-deh
klah-roh
ee deh oon kahr-meen ehn
sehn-dee-doh
mee vehr-soh ehs oon see-ehr-oh
nehr-ee-doh
keh boos-kah ehn el mohn-teh
ahm-pah-roh

3. kohn lohs poh-brehs deh lah
tee-eh-rah
kee-eh-roy-yoh mee swehr-teh
eh-chahr
ehl ah-roy-yoh deh lah see-eh-rah
meh kohm-plah-seh mahs keh ehl mahr

147

Lesson Focus

Harmony: Chords and melody may move simultaneously in relation to each other. *(P–S)*

Materials

o **Piano Accompaniments:** pages 324, 326
o **Record Information:**
  • *Guantanamera*
    (Record 9   Side A   Band 5)
  • The 59th Street Bridge Song
    Record 9   Side A   Band 6
    Voices: male soloist
    Accompaniment: guitar, electric piano,
    electric bass, percussion
  • *Spinning Wheel*
    Record 9   Side A   Band 7
o **Instruments:** guitars (standard tuning)
  that students may share
o **Other:** coffee cans or other footrests;
  overhead projector
o **Teacher's Resource Binder:**

Activity Sheets • **Activity Sheet 36,** page A46
    (Prepare as a transparency.)
    Activity Sheet 37, page A47
    (Prepare as a transparency.)

The 59th Street Bridge Song

Words and Music by Paul Simon

Slow down, — you move too fast, —

You got to make the morn - ing last. — Just

kick - in' down the cob - ble - stones, —

look - in' for fun and feel - in' groov - y. ———

Hel - lo lamp - post, what - cha know - in',

I've come to watch your flow - ers grow - in'.

Ain't 'cha got no rhymes ——— for me?

Doot - in' doo-doo, feel - in' groov - y. ——— Got

148

Copyright © 1966 Paul Simon   Used by permission

The Lesson

1. Review the root bass accompaniment for *"Guantanamera"* from the previous lesson.

2. Listen to the recording of "The 59th Street Bridge Song" as the students follow the notation on pages 148 and 149. Discover which notes will be used for a root bass accompaniment. (G, D, and E) Display Activity Sheet 36 (*Pitch Chart*). Use the Finger-Placement Pitch Chart at the top of the transparency to determine that these chord roots may be played using three open strings. Inform the students that the chords given in the first line repeat over and over to the end. Play the root bass part with the recording.

3. In a similar fashion learn the root bass part for "Spinning Wheel." Distribute Activity Sheet 37 (*Spinning Wheel*). The song con-

tains four sections, three of which are almost the same. The students will discover they can play most of the song on open strings. Only the third section requires that they press down strings to get additional pitches. As a rule the single root bass pitches are played with the following left-hand fingers: first finger on first fret, second finger on second fret, third finger on third fret, and fourth finger on fourth fret. The students should refer to the Finger-Placement Pitch Chart to find the pitches needed to play the roots of each chord.

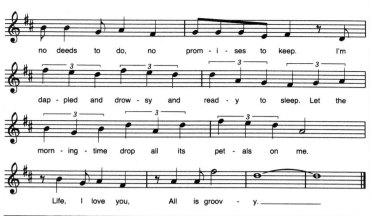

no deeds to do, no prom-i-ses to keep. I'm

dap-pled and drow-sy and read-y to sleep. Let the

morn-ing-time drop all its pet-als on me.

Life, I love you, All is groov-y. _____

LISTENING

Spinning Wheel
by David C. Thomas

Listen to "Spinning Wheel."

Can you play the root bass accompaniment for the song?

Which parts are the same? different?

149

Lesson Focus

Harmony: Chords and melody may move simultaneously in relation to each other. *(P–S)*

Materials

o **Piano Accompaniments:** pages 319, 323
o **Record Information:**
  • *Talkin' Guitar Blues*
    Record 9 Side B Band 3
  • Rocka My Soul
    Record 9 Side B Band 1
    Voices: mixed chorus
    Accompaniment: acoustic guitar, electric guitar, trumpets, trombones, piano, electric bass, percussion
  • He's Got the Whole World in His Hands
    Record 9 Side B Band 2
    Voices: mixed chorus
    Accompaniment: acoustic guitar, electric guitar, trumpets, trombones, piano, electric bass, percussion
o **Instruments:** guitars (standard tuning) that students may share
o **Other:** coffee cans or other footrests
o **Teacher's Resource Binder:**
  [Activity Sheets] • **Activity Sheet 38,** page A48 (Prepare a copy for each student, and prepare as a transparency.)

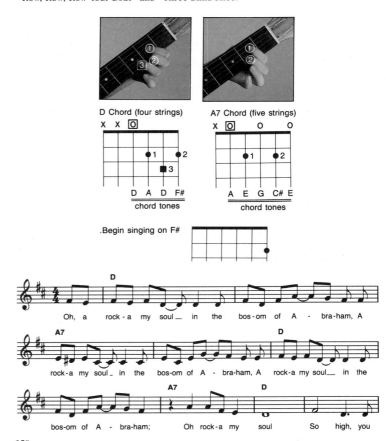

Rocka My Soul

Traditional

Learn the D Chord. Strum it on the first beat of each measure of "Row, Row, Row Your Boat" and "Three Blind Mice."

D Chord (four strings)
X X [O]
1 2
3
D A D F#
chord tones

A7 Chord (five strings)
X [O] O O
1 2
A E G C# E
chord tones

.Begin singing on F#

Oh, a rock-a my soul __ in the bos-om of A - bra-ham, A

rock-a my soul __ in the bos-om of A - bra-ham, A rock-a my soul __ in the

bos-om of A - bra-ham; Oh rock-a my soul So high, you

150

The Lesson

1. Help the students find the correct finger positions for the D major chord as shown on page 150. Strum the chord to accompany "Row, Row, Row Your Boat" then accompany "Three Blind Mice." Combine the two as partner songs. Encourage the students to pluck the root of the chord (fourth string, D) with the thumb alternating strings 1, 2, and 3 to accompany the songs.

2. Practice the A7 chord shown at the middle of page 150. When the students are comfortable with the finger positioning, have them practice changing from D to A7 and back to D as indicated on page 150. Help them analyze the changes that need to occur (first and second fingers each move over one string; third finger is lifted; first and second fingers move back one string each and third finger is

placed on the string between them at the next fret over).

3. Practice accompanying both "Rocka My Soul" and "He's Got the Whole World in His Hands" using only the thumb to brush across the strings. When the chord change is mastered, the students should be encouraged to use the thumb-pluck pattern used in Step 1. The verse and refrain of "Rocka My Soul" may be sung as partner songs; then "He's Got the Whole World in His Hands" may be added as a third partner while the students accompany the three-part texture.

4. Distribute copies of Activity Sheet 38 (*Talking Guitar Blues*). Students may follow the words of *Talkin' Guitar Blues* as they listen to the recording. **What is a *talking blues*?** (lyrics spoken over a blues guitar accompaniment) Listen a second time. Focus on the

can't get o-ver it; So low you can't get un-der it;

So wide, you can't get a-round it, You must go in at the door.

He's Got the Whole World in His Hands

Spiritual

He's got the whole world __ in His hands, He's got the
He's got the wind and rain __ in His hands, He's got the
He's got both you and me __ in His hands, He's got both

whole world __ in His hands, He's got the whole world __
wind and rain __ in His hands, He's got the wind and rain
you and me __ in His hands, He's got both you and me

in His hands, He's got the whole world in His hands. _____
in His hands, He's got the whole world in His hands. _____
in His hands, He's got the whole world in His hands. _____

LISTENING

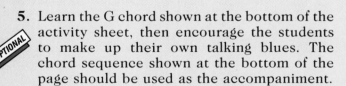

Talking Guitar Blues

by Ernest Tubbs

Listen as the "Talking Guitar Blues" is performed. This piece uses three chords: G, D7, and C. Can you hear when the performer changes from one chord to another?

151

need to make chord changes without losing the rhythmic drive of the song.

5. Learn the G chord shown at the bottom of the activity sheet, then encourage the students to make up their own talking blues. The chord sequence shown at the bottom of the page should be used as the accompaniment.

OPTIONAL

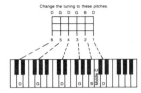

INSTRUMENTS 19

Lesson Focus
Harmony: Chords and melody may move simultaneously in relation to each other. *(P–S)*

Materials
- **Piano Accompaniment:** page 320
- **Record Information:**
  - Put Your Hand in the Hand
    Record 9 Side B Band 4
    Voices: mixed chorus
    Accompaniment: trumpets, trombones, electric guitar, piano, organ, percussion
  - *This Train*
    Record 9 Side B Band 5
  - *Reelin' and Rockin'*
    by Chuck Berry
    Record 9 Side B Band 6
- **Instruments:** guitars
- **Other:** ''bottleneck'' for each guitar (See **For Your Information.**)
- **Teacher's Resource Binder:**
  - Optional—
    Enrichment Activity 10, page E17

Bottleneck Guitar

Change the tuning to these pitches.

Play the I–IV–V chord sequence.

I (G chord)—strum open strings.
IV (C chord)—move the cylinder to the fifth fret.
V (D chord)—move the cylinder to the seventh fret.

LISTENING

This Train
American Folk Song

Listen to the bottleneck guitar in ''This Train.'' As the guitarist slides up and down the fret board, you will hear the bottleneck bend and change the guitar's pitches.

152

The Lesson

1. Introduce the song ''Put Your Hand in the Hand'' by asking the students to open their books to page 153. After listening once, suggest that they again sing along as the recording is played. Repeat the song several times, adding claps or snaps on the afterbeats to reinforce the slow, punctuated rhythmic flow of the music.

2. Ask the students to retune their guitars for bottleneck playing. Direct them to the diagram for bottleneck tuning on page 152.

3. Help the students determine where the fifth and seventh frets are located on the guitar. The students are to use a bottleneck slipped over the finger. They should move it up and down the finger board, exploring the different sounds. Call attention to the ''bending

pitches'' that are heard as the bottleneck slides over each fret. Listen to ''This Train'' to hear how the playing technique is used in that song.

4. Play specific chords using the bottleneck. Ask the students to follow the instructions on page 152 and practice the chord sequence G C G D G.

5. Call attention to the D7 chord shown in ''Put Your Hand in the Hand.'' Help the students understand that a D chord must be substituted for a D7 chord each time it occurs in the song when using bottleneck accompaniment. Allow time for students to learn to play this accompaniment. Then perform it with the entire group singing and playing.

6. Invite the students to play *Reelin' and Rockin'* using the same chords. They are to

OPTIONAL

152

Put Your Hand in the Hand

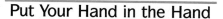

Words and Music by Gene MacLellan

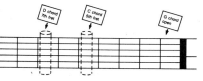

- Tune your guitar to G tuning (page 154).
- Accompany this song using the bottleneck technique.
- Begin singing on D.

G
Put your hand in the hand of the man who stilled _ the

D7
wa - ter. _____ Put your hand in the hand of the

G(C)   G
man who calmed _ the sea. Take a look at your-self and - a

G7   C
you can _ look at oth - ers dif - f'rent - ly _____ By put - tin' your

G   D7   G   C   G
hand in the hand of the man from - a Gal - i - lee. _____

LISTENING

Reelin' and Rockin'
by Chuck Berry

Listen and play along with the recording. Your ear should tell you when to change the chord.

Chord sequence: **G C G D C G**

153

follow the sequence shown at the bottom of page 153 as they play along with the recording. They will need to depend on their ear to tell them the appropriate time to make the chord changes. (The guitars will need to be in tune with the recorded version.)

For Your Information

The "bottleneck" used in this lesson may be made from either plastic or metal. Glass bottlenecks (the original sources) are too dangerous even when the edges have been smoothed out. Harder materials play best.

Finger splints (aluminum or plastic) are sold at most drugstores and work without modification. Small diameter plastic pipes (sold at plumbing or hardware stores) may be cut into short lengths to accommodate finger length and the width of the guitar neck.

Lesson Focus

Harmony: Chords and melody may move simultaneously in relation to each other. *(P–S)*

Materials

o **Piano Accompaniment:** page 240
o **Record Information:**
  • Mama Don't 'Low
    (Record 8   Side A   Band 2)
  • *Color Him Folky*
    Record 5   Side B   Band 1
o **Instruments:** guitars

The Lesson

1. Review the song "Mama Don't 'Low." The students may wish to sing just the melody line as written on page 154 or perform the arrangement learned earlier in the year involving vocal chording.

2. Introduce the students to the fingering position for the 6-string G chord on page 154. Provide time for the students to practice finding this chord and then moving from it to D7 and C. When the changes are performed with some ease, ask the students to use these chords to accompany "Mama Don't 'Low."

3. Sing the new skiffle-band words to the song on page 155. Utilize the many instruments the students have explored throughout this unit. Invite them to select their favorite folk instrument and add it to the skiffle-band performance of this song.

OPTIONAL

4. Ask the students to follow the chart on page 155 as they listen to the recording of "Color Him Folky." **Is this music typical of rock and roll or of folk-rock?** (folk-rock) **What is the form of the piece?** (A B A B A) **The sections of music move within which scales: pentatonic? major? minor? whole tone?** (major and minor) Discuss the sound of the 12-string guitar. Doubling the strings makes a louder, more twangy sound.

Sing new words to "Mama Don't 'Low."

Mama don't 'low no skiffle-band playin' 'round here.
(Repeat)
I don't care what Mama don't 'low,
Gonna play in a skiffle-band anyhow.
Mama don't 'low no skiffle-band playin' 'round here.

Add the sounds of the skiffle band to the guitar accompaniment.

Kazoo, comb: play the melody or improvise a harmony part.
Spoons, washboard, limberjack: improvise rhythms.
Washtub bass, jug: play root bass harmony.
Mouthbow: play the melody or make up a harmony part.

LISTENING

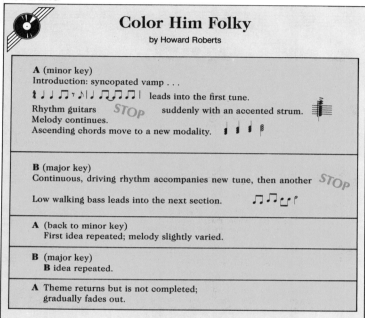

Color Him Folky
by Howard Roberts

A (minor key)
Introduction: syncopated vamp . . .
♪ ♩ ♩ ♫ ⁷ ♪| ♩ ♫♫♫| leads into the first tune.
Rhythm guitars *STOP* suddenly with an accented strum.
Melody continues.
Ascending chords move to a new modality. ♩ ♩ ♩ 𝅝

B (major key)
Continuous, driving rhythm accompanies new tune, then another *STOP*

Low walking bass leads into the next section. ♫ ♫ ♩♩

A (back to minor key)
First idea repeated; melody slightly varied.

B (major key)
B idea repeated.

A Theme returns but is not completed;
gradually fades out.

155

For Your Information
To play each specific chord on a guitar is a relatively simple task. The difficulty for the performers arises when they are required to move from one chord to another, quickly trying to find each new position. This lesson deals with that problem by helping the students learn techniques such as pivoting and sliding. These techniques will make the transition from one chord to another easier.

Lesson Focus

Time and Place: The way musical elements are combined into a whole reflects the origin of the music. *(P–S)*

Materials

o **Piano Accompaniments:** pages 328, 329, 330
o **Record Information:**
  • On Top of Old Smoky
    Record 9 Side B Band 7
    Voices: male soloist
    Accompaniment: fiddle, banjo, harmonica, dobro guitar, harp, bass
  • I'm Going Down the Road
    Record 9 Side B Band 8
    Voices: mixed chorus
    Accompaniment: kazoo, jug, jaw harp, guitar, double bass, washboard, percussion
  • Deep Fork River Blues
    (Record 8 Side B Band 5a)
o **Instruments:** guitars; skiffle instruments; alto metallophone; alto xylophones; piano
o **Teacher's Resource Binder:**
  | Activity Sheets | • **Activity Sheet 39,** page A49 |

The Lesson

1. Suggest to the students that they plan their own performance of the songs presented on these pages. When planning arrangements, remind the students to consider the expressive nature of each song. **Is each a foot-stomper or an easy listening type? How will "On Top of Old Smoky" be different from "I'm Going Down the Road"?** ("Old Smoky" is a plaintive, lyrical ballad, and the accompaniment needs to convey a quiet, reflective mood. Strumming strings, sustained vocal sound, or harmonica might be appropriate.) Make those instruments available and allow time for the students to plan the accompaniment as a class or in small groups.

2. In contrast, "I'm Going Down the Road" is a more raucous foot-stomping type of song. Therefore, instruments appropriate for playing a fast, hard-driving rhythmic accompaniment would be suitable. An arrangement for a full skiffle band would be most effective.

3. **How will you plan to accompany "Deep Fork River Blues"?** The students may devise their own ideas based on the model heard in the recording, or they may wish to use the accompaniment on Activity Sheet 39 (*Instrumental Accompaniment*) as a basis for adding other instrumental sounds.

| | G | | | | | D | D |

I'm   go - ing   down   the   road   feel - in'   bad, _____
Two   dol - lar   shoes   hurt   my   feet, _____
Takes a ten ___ dol - lar   shoe to fit   my   feet, _____
I'm   go - ing   where   the   wa-ter   tastes   so   fine, _____
I'm   go - ing   where   the   cli-mate   suits   my   clothes, _____

A7   D

I   ain't   gon - na be   treat - ed   this - a   way.

Deep Fork River Blues

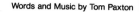

Words and Music by Tom Paxton

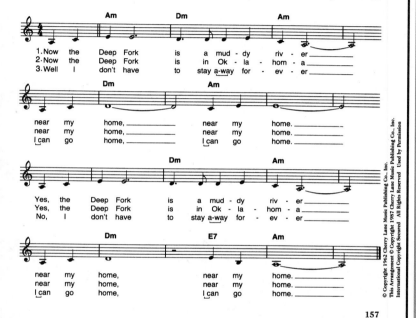

| | Am | | Dm | | Am | |

1. Now   the   Deep Fork   is   a   mud - dy   riv - er _____
2. Now   the   Deep Fork   is   in   Ok - la - hom - a _____
3. Well   I   don't   have   to   stay a-way   for - ev - er _____

Dm   Am

near   my   home, _____   near   my   home. _____
near   my   home, _____   near   my   home. _____
I can   go   home, _____   I can   go   home. _____

                         Dm   Am

Yes, the   Deep Fork   is   a   mud - dy   riv - er _____
Yes, the   Deep Fork   is   in   Ok - la - hom - a _____
No,   I   don't   have   to   stay a-way   for - ev - er _____

Dm   E7   Am

near   my   home,   near   my   home. _____
near   my   home,   near   my   home. _____
I can   go   home,   I can   go   home. _____

157

INSTRUMENTS *21*

For Your Information

The songs on pages 156–157 may serve as an additional resource for skiffle-band arrangements. Two of the songs on this page have already been introduced to the students as a part of this unit: "Deep Fork River Blues" (page 139) and "On Top of Old Smoky" (page 141). The students may need to review these songs before making decisions about arranging them with instrumental accompaniment. The words and music should help the students perform together, as an ensemble, independent of the recorded selection. The new song, "I'm Going Down the Road," will need to be learned by the students before instruments are added. When planning accompaniments, the students will need to consider the sounds of the instrument to be used (timbre), root bass pitches/chords (harmony), readability and playability of the melody, and ideas for percussion instruments (rhythm).

Lesson Focus

Expression: Musical elements are combined into a whole to express a musical idea. *(P–I)*

Materials

o **Piano Accompaniment:** page 332, 334
o **Record Information:**
  - Hold the Wind
    Record 10   Side A   Band 1
    Voices: mixed chorus
    Accompaniment: alto flute, cello, harp, celesta, percussion
  - Bo Weevil
    Record 1O   Side A   Band 2
    Voices: mixed chorus
    Accompaniment: ocarino, banjo, guitar, piano, hammered dulcimer, double bass, percussion
o **Instruments:** piano; resonator bells; xylophone; skiffle instruments

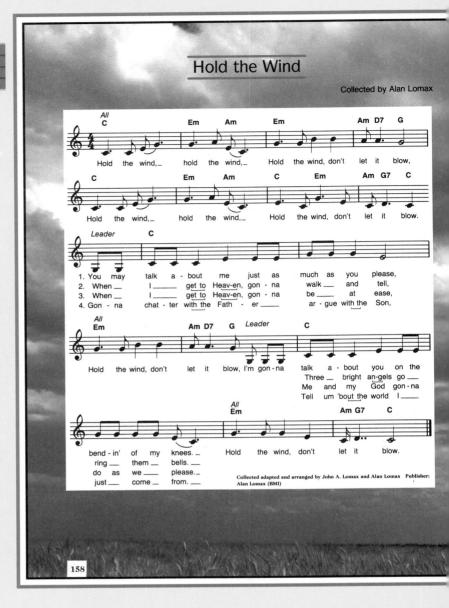

Hold the Wind

Collected by Alan Lomax

1. You may talk a-bout me just as much as you please,
2. When I get to Heav-en, gon-na walk and tell,
3. When I get to Heav-en, gon-na be at ease,
4. Gon-na chat-ter with the Fath-er ar-gue with the Son,

Hold the wind, don't let it blow, I'm gon-na talk a-bout you on the
Three bright an-gels go
Me and my God gon-na
Tell um 'bout the world I

bend-in' of my knees. Hold the wind, don't let it blow.
ring them bells.
do as we please.
just come from.

Collected adapted and arranged by John A. Lomax and Alan Lomax   Publisher: Alan Lomax (BMI)

158

The Lesson

1. Play the pitches C, E, and G on the piano or bells and identify them as a C major triad. Ask the students to echo sing these pitches (on the syllable "loo") as you perform them several times. Sing the triad from the root upward, but occasionally repeat one of the tones. Write the pitches on the chalkboard.

2. Explain that these three pitches are used several times in the song "Hold the Wind." Ask the students to open their books to page 158, look at the notation, and sing the words that appear with the triad pattern each time it is found in the song. They are not to concern themselves with the rhythm at this time. (The triad pattern is found in Measures 1, 5, 7, 9,

10, 13, 14, and 15.) Sing the melody for the students as they check to see if they found all the patterns that used pitches from the C major triad. Invite them all to sing the song as the recording is played.

3. **OPTIONAL** Discuss the expressive performance style of folk singers who sing their music from the heart. Encourage one of the students to be the folk singer who expressively sings the leader part while the other students respond as the chorus. Ask the leader to perform it more than one time in order to refine his or her expressive ideas.

4. Introduce the upbeat song "Bo Weevil" by listening to the recording. The students will quickly recognize the contrast in expression between "Bo Weevil" and "Hold the Wind" when the two songs are compared. After the students are familiar with the melody, divide

Bo Weevil

Words and Music by A. Domino and D. Bartholomew

On Sat-ur-day night, where I was born, _ down on the farm, _

Gui - tar plink-ing and we start-ed sing-ing 'til the break of dawn.

A-bout twelve o' - clock ev-'ry - thing gets hot, _ up steps old Jones. _

We start-ed clap-pin' and he start-ed sing-in' a sweet lit - tle coun - try song.

Bo Wee - vil, Bo Wee - vil,
where've you been all day? _ Your
where did you go and stay? _

mom - ma's been look - in', has-n't stopped look-in' since you went a - way. Bo
You'll _ get a lick-in' as sure as I'm sit-tin' on this bale of hay.

159

the class into smaller groups. Provide time for each group to plan a skiffle-band arrangement of this song. The melody often repeats pitches D, E, F♯, G, and A. Encourage the students to play the tune on keyboard, resonator bells, or xylophones. Ask each group to share its performance with the class, then have all the groups "skiffle" together at the same time.

Lesson Focus

Harmony: Two or more pitches may be sounded simultaneously. *(C–S)*

Materials

o **Record Information:**
  • Menuetto II from *String Quartet in F* Attributed to Benjamin Franklin, 1706–1790
    Record 10 Side A Band 3
    Kohon Quartet
o **Instruments:** Soprano glockenspiel with pitches C, G, C′ and F′; Alto glockenspiel with pitches F, B♭, and E′; Soprano metallophone with pitches A, E and D′; Alto metallophone with pitches F, C, B♭ and G; or resonator bells with pitches A, B♭, C, E, F, G, B♭′,C′, E′, F′ and G′; two mallets for each player; guitars and bass tuned as shown on page 159; various band and orchestra instruments that students are studying, including 3 violins and 1 cello
o **Teacher's Resource Binder:**
  Activity Sheets • **Activity Sheets 40a-c,** pages A50–A52
  • **Activity Sheet 41,** page A53

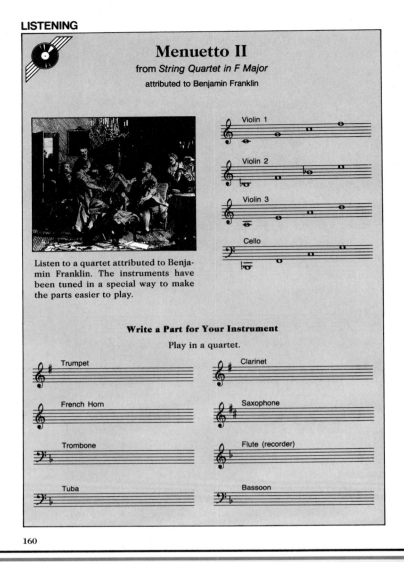

LISTENING

Menuetto II
from *String Quartet in F Major*
attributed to Benjamin Franklin

Listen to a quartet attributed to Benjamin Franklin. The instruments have been tuned in a special way to make the parts easier to play.

Violin 1

Violin 2

Violin 3

Cello

Write a Part for Your Instrument

Play in a quartet.

Trumpet   Clarinet

French Horn   Saxophone

Trombone   Flute (recorder)

Tuba   Bassoon

160

The Lesson

1. Discuss *scordatura* tuning with the class. Help them understand that in this example, the special tuning makes it easy for players with limited technique to perform. Ask each student to choose one part to follow on Activity Sheets 40a–d (*Menuetto Parts*). Play the recording as the students follow their chosen part.

2. Examine the tunings of each instrument in the string quartet (shown on page 160); then examine the ranges of the glockenspiels and metallophones shown on page 161. Help the students realize that by playing all of the pitches that fall below middle C (as used in the second, third, and fourth string instrument parts) an octave higher, the mallet instruments can be used to play each of the string parts.

3. Look at the guitar and bass tunings shown on page 161. These instruments may also be used to play the string parts when tuned as shown. If wind instrument players are in the class, help them decide how to rewrite parts so that they can also play in an ensemble: C instruments—trombone, tuba, flute, recorder, and bassoon can perform the parts as written on Activity Sheets 40a–d; B♭ instruments—trumpet and clarinet will need to transpose the treble clef versions of the parts by writing all pitches one whole step higher (C becomes D, D becomes E, etc.); E♭ instruments—saxophone may transpose any of the parts written on the treble clef by moving all pitches up four scale steps higher on the staff (C becomes F, D becomes G, etc.).

4. Divide the class into quartets. Use as many string, wind, guitar, resonator bell, glocken-

Instrumental Combos

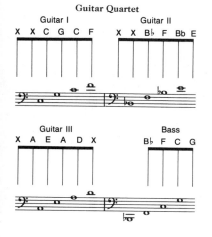

For Your Information

This "Menuetto" is the second menuetto found in an eighteenth-century string quartet attributed to Benjamin Franklin. It is known that Franklin often enjoyed making music with friends and it is thought by some that he may have composed this piece with *scordatura* tuning so that musicians with limited playing technique could play it successfully. Each instrument plays a maximum of four pitches (all on open strings). For *scordatura* tuning, the strings are tuned in a nonstandard fashion. The reason in this case, is to create a technically simple work that does not require that the strings be stopped.

spiel, and metallophone groups as appropriate for your class. The band and orchestral players should determine which part their instrument can best play, choose the appropriate part, and adapt it as described in Step 3. They may use Activity Sheet 41 (*Transcribe Your Part*) to write out the transposed parts. Members of each quartet should work individually until each part is mastered. The quartets should then practice as an ensemble. Invite each quartet to play for the rest of the class.

5. Combine all quartets to perform a large-scale version of the "Menuetto."

OPTIONAL

Lesson Focus

Expression: Musical elements are combined into a whole to express a musical or extra-musical idea. *(C–S)*

Materials

o **Record Information:**
  • The Oscar Mayer Weiner Song
    Record 10   Side A   Band 4
    Voices: mixed chorus
    Accompaniment: piccolo, flute, trumpet, baritone horn, bassoon, bass clarinet, percussion, sound effects
  • The Armour Hot Dog Song
    Record 10   Side A   Band 5
    Voices: mixed chorus
    Accompaniment: violin, clarinet, tuba, synthesizer, piano, celesta, percussion

o **Instruments:** resonator bell sets with mallets or other keyboard type instruments

o **Other:** ads cut from magazines or newspapers (These will be used by the students as a stimulus for writing the music for a commercial. Choose ads that are appropriate, both in terms of interest to seventh-grade students and in terms of classroom suitability.); pencils for each student.

(continued on next page)

Composing Commercial Music

Listen to these commercials.

What made them musically successful?

The Oscar Mayer Wiener Song

Oh I wish I were an Os - car May - er Wie - ner, ____

That is what I'd tru - ly like to be.

'Cause if I were an Os - car May - er Wie - ner, ____

Ev - ery one would be in love with me.

162

The Lesson

1. **Look at the notation for "The Oscar Mayer Weiner Song." What do you see that appears to be especially interesting?** (the use of dotted rhythms, elongated phrase endings, chromaticism [notes not in the key of C], and repetition.) **Why is repetition especially useful in this kind of music?** (It helps the listener quickly learn the tune so that it is easily recognized when heard again.) Listen to the recording to reinforce the discoveries made from the notation and to find others that may have been overlooked.

2. Follow a similar procedure to analyze the characteristics of "The Armour Hot Dog Song." Help students recognize the numerous distinctive features found in this song: the use of the dotted rhythm pattern; repeated tones (especially at the beginning of Line 2 when only two tones are used repeatedly); and rests and scale passages at the end of Lines 2 and 3. Listen to the recording to confirm discoveries made from the notation. Again emphasize the importance of making the tune immediately recognizable and easy to recall.

3. Distribute one ad selected from a magazine or newspaper, a copy of Activity Sheet 42 (*Commercial Music*), and a pencil to each student. The students should also have access to a set of resonator bells or a keyboard instrument so that they may test the effectiveness of their tunes as they work on them. Suggest that the students begin by writing words for their commercial that are concise, yet capable of communicating a strong feature of the product to be advertised. They may then compose the melody to support the words and write it down on the activity sheet.

The Armour Hot Dog Song

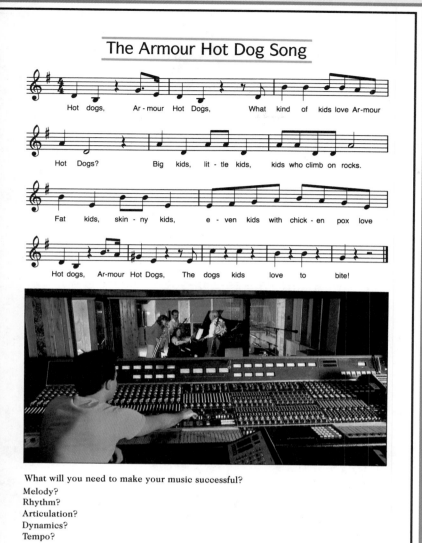

Hot dogs, Ar-mour Hot Dogs, What kind of kids love Ar-mour

Hot Dogs? Big kids, lit - tle kids, kids who climb on rocks.

Fat kids, skin - ny kids, e - ven kids with chick - en pox love

Hot dogs, Ar-mour Hot Dogs, The dogs kids love to bite!

What will you need to make your music successful?
Melody?
Rhythm?
Articulation?
Dynamics?
Tempo?

163

Materials (continued)

o **Teacher's Resource Binder:**
Activity Sheets
• **Activity Sheet 42,** page A54
• Optional—
Enrichment Activity 11, page E17

For Your Information

Commercial music is an interesting career opportunity for people involved in composing. Because most commercials use only a brief segment of music, the music must make an immediate impact on its listeners. Since music plays such an important role in many of today's media-oriented commercials, it is important to help students understand how the composer communicates his or her message in a concise, powerful manner.

Remind them that as they compose, they should consider characteristics discovered in the commercials they previously analyzed. They should consider melody, rhythm, articulation, dynamics, and tempo as they seek ways of creating an effective commercial.

4. Ask the students to share their tunes with the class. After hearing each, engage the class in a discussion of the features that make the tune effective and ways the tune might be altered to make it more effective. (This discussion should be carried out in an atmosphere that promotes constructive criticism and suggestions that are positive and supportive.)

5. Divide the class into small groups to produce commercials using several of their favorites from the tunes just created. Videotape pictures of the ad, the product, or the original artwork that will help sell the product. Use a short script and the composed music as the sound track for the video tape.

OPTIONAL

Lesson Focus

Expression: Musical elements are combined into a whole to express a musical or extra-musical idea. *(C–S)*

Materials

o **Record Information:**
  • *Donkey Kong Theme*
    Record 10 Side A Band 6
  • Sample theme for *Robot Basketball*
    Record 10 Side A Band 7

o **Instruments:** individual resonator bell sets and mallets or keyboard instruments

o **Other:** IBM PC, Apple II, or Commodore 64/128 computers; pencils

o **Teacher's Resource Binder:**

  Activity Sheets
  • **Activity Sheet 43,** page A55
  • **Activity Sheets 44a–c,** pages A56–A58
  • **Activity Sheets 45a–c,** pages A59–A61
  • **Activity Sheets 46a–c,** pages A62–A64
  • **Activity Sheet 47,** page A65

You, the Composer of Video-Game Music

What makes this melody easy to remember?

How long is the melody?

What musical decisions did the composer make about pitch?

rhythm (duration)?

tempo?

form?

Donkey Kong

164

The Lesson

1. Review the two commercials analyzed in the previous lesson (pages 162–63). **Composers are often asked to write short, catchy tunes for video games or other computer applications. You have just been hired by a company that is planning to produce a game called Robot Basketball.** Explain that the students' job is to create an appropriate melody that will help catapult the game to the top of the charts. You have decided it will be helpful to carefully examine the tune of an already successful program before beginning to write their own.

2. Ask the students to listen to and analyze the tune for *Donkey Kong.* After it is heard, list under the title the musical ideas that the students comment upon. Guide the students to be especially cognizant of musical features that are related to the content of the game.

   Donkey Kong begins with a series of long tones followed by a series of short tones that suggest a trill. The "minor" quality of the melody creates a feeling of suspense.

3. The students may work in small groups to create original tunes for the imaginary video game "Robot Basketball." Distribute copies of Activity Sheet 47 (*Robot Basketball*) and a pencil to each student. They should use resonator bell sets or keyboard instruments to try out their musical ideas. When the students are satisfied with their melodies, they should write the tunes on the staff at the bottom of the sheet. Groups may then share their completed melodies, discuss their effectiveness, and suggest possible improvements.

Use the information you have learned about the theme to help you write the music for a game called . . .
Robot Basketball.

For Your Information

The creation of music for a wide variety of computer applications, including video games, has resulted in new opportunities for many composers. The composer of tunes for video games is challenged to create a brief, captivating, yet interesting melody that the listener will easily remember but not become overly tired of when hearing it many times throughout the game. This challenge provides the students with an interesting and valid musical problem to solve.

165

OPTIONAL

4. If computers are available, the students may type the program provided on Activity Sheets 44a–c *(Apple II Version)*, 45a–c *(Commodore 64)*, or 46a–c *(IBM PC)* into the computer and save it on disk or tape. The students should then code their original tunes as shown on Activity Sheet 43 *(Pitch and Duration)* and replace the indicated lines of the program with data that will allow them to substitute their tune for the sample tune in the program.

INSTRUMENTS 26

Lesson Focus

Evaluation: Review concepts and skills learned in the third unit.

Materials

o **Piano Accompaniment:** page 336
o **Record Information:**
  • Oh, Lonesome Me
    Record 10   Side B   Band 1
    Voices: mixed chorus
    Accompaniment: electric guitar, piano, vibraphone, double bass, percussion
o **Instruments:** harmonica, guitar, spoons, washtub bass, mouthbow, limberjack, kazoo/comb, jug
o **Other:** a pencil for each student
o **Teacher's Resource Binder:**
  Evaluation • **Checkpoint 3,** pages Ev13

Oh, Lonesome Me

Words and Music by Don Gibson

How many instruments can you use
to perform this song?

Ev- ery- bod- y's   go- in' out and   hav- in' fun; _____   I'm
bad mis- take I'm   mak- in' by just   hang- in' 'round; _____   I

just a fool for   stay- in' home and   hav- in' none. _____   I
know that I should   have some fun and   paint the town. _____   A

can't get o- ver   how she set me   free, _____
love- sick fool that's   blind and just can't   see, _____

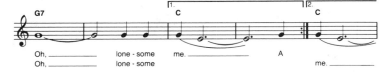

Oh, _____   lone- some   me. _____   A
Oh, _____   lone- some   me. _____

_____ I'll   bet she's not like   me, she's   out and fan- cy   free,

Flirt- ing with the   boys with all her   charms. _____   But I still love her

166

The Lesson

1. Explain to the students that they will have an opportunity to apply the performance skills acquired in Unit 3. Distribute Checkpoint 3, a pencil, and a textbook to each student. Tell the class they will be asked to respond to each numbered direction by writing and/or doing something. Since they will be working on numbers 1–6 at their own pace, it will be necessary for them to play, sing, or chant softly in order to keep the noise level down.

2. Written tasks occur in numbers 1–3, and the answer key for them appears in **For Your Information.** Performance skills are challenged in numbers 4–6, so allow students practice time to satisfactorily complete these tasks. It will be necessary to establish a procedure for the orderly sharing of instruments. You may decide that every student need not play every instrument.

To complete number 7, students may make a check beside the names of the instruments they can play and select one upon which to improvise rhythms or accompaniments. The improvisations may be performed by the entire class as the recording is played. The students may also play their improvisations without the recording, as suggested in number 8.

3. Help the students prepare a summary of the number of songs they have learned to play on each instrument listed in number 9.

You may wish to use more than one session to complete this evaluation process if the interest of the students is still keen.

For Your Information

Answer key for written questions in Checkpoint 3:

''Oh, Lonesome Me'' (Notation):

1. c
2a. 1–2–3–4–5–6–7–1'
2b. 1 and 7 should be circled.
3. The following pitches may be used in any combination:

They should be rhythmicized to produce four measures in $\frac{2}{2}$ meter.

INSTRUMENTS 27

Lesson Focus

Evaluation: Review concepts and skills learned in the third unit.

Materials

o **Record Information:**
   • Bile Them Cabbage Down
     Record 10 Side B Band 2a (Rock)
     Instruments: saxophone, double bass, guitar, electric organ, percussion
     Band 2b: Classical
     Instruments: clavichord
     Band 2c: Gospel
     Instruments: electric organ, piano

o **Other:** a pencil for each student; records 1, 2, 3, and 7 used with Unit 3, pages 118–123

o **Teacher's Resource Binder:**
   | Evaluation | • **Review 3,** page Ev16
     Musical Progress Report 3, page Ev17

For Your Information

Answer key for Review 3:

Box 1:
   1A. gospel B. classical C. rock
   2A–C. student's choice
Box 2:
   1A. rock B. classical C. gospel
   2A–C. student's choice

Categories of Musical Style

Music is composed and performed in many different styles. Can you recall some of the styles of music you have studied during this unit? Which of these styles can you identify by hearing?

A composer has arranged a melody in three different styles. Here is the first part of the score for each style. Can you identify the style by looking at the score? What clues help you make your decision?

168

The Lesson

1. Ask the students to answer the questions in the first paragraph at the top of page 168. List the styles of music on the chalkboard as the students name them (rock, soul, etc.).

2. Play examples of the styles found on pages 118–123. Encourage the students to suggest stylistic clues. List musical elements as the students identify them (melody, harmony, rhythm, timbre, form, etc.).

3. Distribute Review 3, on which the students are to record their answers to the questions in the second paragraph on page 168. Allow about five minutes to answer the questions in Box 1. Then play each example at least twice and ask the class to answer the questions in Box 2. The answer key appears in **For Your Information.**

4. Various aspects of the music offer many different clues. Encourage the students to give reasons for their choices. Timbre may provide the primary clues, especially with regard to sound quality and articulation.

Additional clues to the classical style include melodic ornamentation (arrows show main notes of melody) and a broken-chord accompaniment pattern in the bass. Secondary clues for both rock and gospel styles are the rhythmic accompaniment and the use of characteristic harmonic patterns (gospel: IV–I "Amen" cadence; rock: I–VI–IV–V chord sequence).

5. Use the information acquired from this evaluation as well as other observations made during this unit to prepare Musical Progress Report 3. This may be sent to parents and added to student files.

Unit 4

Choral Singing

Unit Overview

Unit 4 concentrates on choral music and vocal-ensemble technique. A wide variety of choral arrangements reinforce what has been learned in the previous units with an emphasis on texture and expression. All of the songs have from two to five parts and are especially selected and arranged for early teenage voices.

⭐

Texas Essential Elements for Unit 4:

1A: PE (pages 172–173; 185–189; 217)

  TE (pages 170; 172–173; 175; 177; 178; 181–183; 185–186; 188; 192; 194–197; 199–201; 203–204; 206–207; 210–212; 214; 217)

  TRB (pages O7; O22; K19; AS67; M25; I20–21; I22; EV19; EV22)

1B: PE (pages 172–173; 185–189; 206–209; 217)

  TE (pages 170; 172–173; 175; 177–179; 181–183; 185–186; 188; 190; 192; 194–197; 199–201; 203–204; 206–207; 210–212; 214; 217–218)

  TRB (pages O7; O22; E19; K19; AS66; AS67; M25; I20–21; I22; EV19; EV21)

1C: PE (pages 172–173; 185–189; 206–209)

  TE (pages 172–173; 175; 177–179; 181–183; 185–186; 188; 190; 192; 194–197; 199–201; 204; 206–207; 211–213; 214–215; 217)

  TRB (pages O7; O22; E19; K19; AS67; I22; EV19; EV21)

1D: PE (pages 172–173; 186–189)

  TE (pages 170; 175; 177; 178; 181–182; 185–186; 188; 196; 199; 203; 210–211; 214; 217)

  TRB (pages O7; O22; K19; AS67; M25; I20–21; I22; EV19)

1E: TE (page 195)

1F: PE (page 200)

  TE (pages 170; 173; 195; 200–201; 214)

  TRB (pages O22; K14; I22; EV19)

2: PE (pages 170–173; 185; 200–202; 217)

  TE (pages 170; 172–173; 175; 177–179; 181–183; 185–186; 188; 191; 192; 194–197; 199–201; 204; 207; 211–212; 214; 217–218)

  TRB (pages O7; E19; K14; K19; M23; EV19)

3B: TE (pages 173–175; 178; 182–183; 190; 194; 197; 200; 203; 214; 217–218)

  TRB (pages O7; O22; AS67)

4A: TE (pages 211—212; 215)

4B: TRB (page B15)

5A: PE (pages 170–173; 185; 200–202; 217)

  TE (pages 170; 172–173; 175; 177–179; 181–183; 185–186; 188; 191; 192; 194–197; 199–201; 204; 207; 211–212; 214; 217–218)

  TRB (pages O7; O22; K14; K19; AS67; M23; M25; I20–21; I22)

5B: TE (pages 186; 190; 192; 201; 204; 206; 213; 214; 218)

  TRB (page K14)

 Texas Essential Elements, Choral Singing, pp. 169–219: 1A, 1B, 1C, 1D, 1E, 1F, 2, 3B, 4A, 4B, 5A, 5B (Please see Unit 4 Opener, page 169, for component and page references.)

169

Lesson Focus

Expression: Musical elements are combined into a whole to express a musical or extra-musical idea. *(P–S)*

Materials:

o **Piano Accompaniment:** page 340

o **Record Information:**
  • Lord, Lord I've Got Some Singing to Do
  Record 10 Side B Band 3
  Voices: mixed chorus
  Accompaniment: clarinet, saxophone, trumpet, trombone, electric piano, electric guitar, electric bass, percussion

o **Teacher's Resource Binder:**
  • Optional —
  Orff Activity 13, page O22

You now have the opportunity to participate in the choral-singing experience. In this section you will learn to

• interpret and perform various choral styles
• perform using good choral techniques
• sing in tune
• understand how music is arranged for chorus
• express the relationship between lyrics and musical settings

Expressively perform this song:

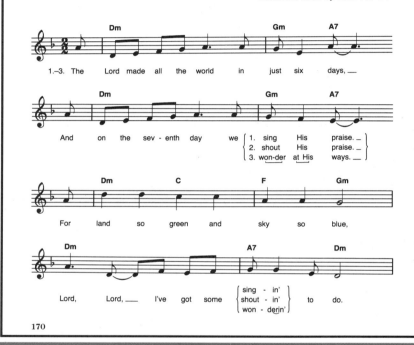

Lord, Lord, I've Got Some Singing to Do

Words and Music by Robert Schertz

170

The Lesson

1. Read the list of learning opportunities available to the students in this unit. (See **For Your Information.**) Help the students evaluate their present ability to do the listed skills. Discuss what they would like to accomplish while completing this unit. Throughout the unit periodically remind the students of this discussion and help them determine their individual musical progress.

2. Introduce the song, "Lord, Lord I've Got Some Singing to Do," on pages 170–171. Help the students determine the scale on which the song is based by examining the key signature and melody. When the students have identified the key as D minor, warm up by singing the D minor scale. Challenge the students to sight-read the verse as you provide a chord accompaniment on the guitar or piano.

Follow a similar procedure to help the Treble I's and Baritones learn the refrain. Then encourage the Treble II's and Changing Voices to read their part as the Treble I's and Baritones continue to softly sing theirs. Play the recording to allow the students to check their performance.

3. Sing the remaining verses of the song. Invite the students to make some performance decisions when expressing such words as "shout" or "sing." **How will you musically express each of these verses?** (by changing dynamics or tempos)

171

For Your Information

Stressed in this unit:

Musical Styles: country, gospel, contemporary, popular, classical, hymn, blues, folk, rock

Choral Techniques: intonation, breath support, phrasing, articulation, dynamics, blend, diction, breath control, vocal color

Choral Arranging: relationship of lyrics to music, texture, structure, harmony

Lesson Focus

Expression: The expressiveness of music is affected by the way dynamics and articulation contribute to the musical whole. *(P–S)*

Materials

○ **Piano Accompaniment:** page 348
○ **Record Information:**
  • Song Sung Blue
  Record 10 Side B Band 4
  Voices: mixed chorus
  Accompaniment: electric piano, acoustic guitar, electric bass, percussion

Song Sung Blue

Words and Music by Neil Diamond

Sing Verse 1 in unison or follow the performance suggestions given in the score. On Verse 2, the Baritones should sing the echoes an octave lower than notated while the others sing the melody.

172

The Lesson

1. Write the following pattern on the board:

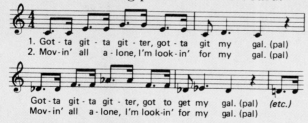

Warm up by repeating the phrase several times, each time transposing it up one step. Help the students develop an understanding of how articulation (the way a sound begins and ends) helps express the ideas in the lyrics. Sing the two verses appearing under the melodic pattern. Discuss how each might be articulated: first, "Gotta gitta gitter, gotta git my gal" (short and crisp); second, "Movin' all alone, I'm lookin' for my gal" (smoothly connected). When performing, you may wish to place staccato dots under the first verse. Then erase and add slurs joining the pitches when performing the second verse.

2. Tell the students to open their books to "Song Sung Blue," on page 172. Ask a student to read the lyrics aloud. Discuss various ways that these words might be expressed. The students may decide that the ideas would be best communicated by using articulation that is smooth and connected *(legato)*.

3. Prepare for learning the song by singing patterns based on chord tones. Write the following patterns on the chalkboard:

Randomly point at the notes in each pattern until the students can accurately sing the pitches within the chords.

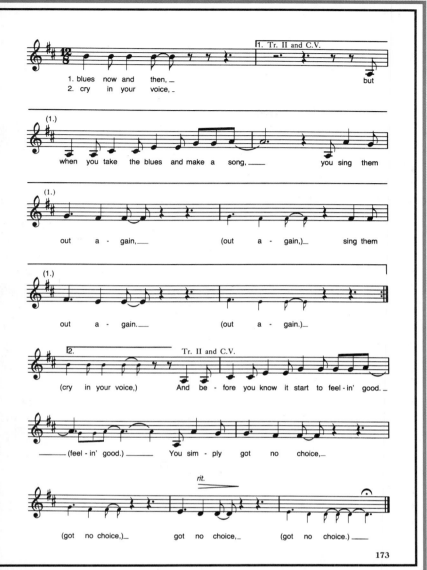

4. Ask the students to examine "Song Sung Blue" and locate patterns based on each of these chords. They should identify the chords as follows:

Measures 1–2:   D(I)
Measures 3–6:   A/A7 (V/V7)
Measures 7–11:   D/D7 (I/I7)
Measures 12–13: G (IV)
Measures 14–15: A7 (V7)
Measures 16–17: D (I)
Measures 18–19: A (V7)

5. Play the chord sequence on the guitar or piano as the students softly hum the melody. Notice when it moves by skips (outlining chords) and when it moves by steps.

6. Play the recording as the students listen to the melody while lightly tapping the underly-ing shortest sound (eighth note) to be sure they have grasped the rhythm.

7. Assign parts to accommodate the ranges of the performers. Baritones may sing an octave below the Treble I's or listen during Verse 1, then sing the echoes during Verse 2.

8. Discuss how the dynamics might affect the expressiveness of the song. **What should be the general dynamic range of the piece?** (probably soft to moderately loud) **What should be the dynamic level of the echoes?** (softer) Expressively sing both verses of the song.

CHORAL 3

Lesson Focus

Expression: The expressiveness of music is affected by the way articulation contributes to the musical whole. *(P–S)*

Materials

○ **Piano Accompaniment:** page 352

○ **Record Information:**
  • Getting to Know You
    Record 10 Side B Band 5
    Voices: mixed chorus
    Accompaniment: small show orchestra

○ **Teacher's Resource Binder:**
  • Optional —
    Kodaly Activity 13, page K19
    Mainstreaming Activity 16, page M23

Getting to Know You

Lyrics by Oscar Hammerstein II

Music by Richard Rodgers

174

The Lesson

1. Begin the class by asking the students to name famous people that they admire. The list might include favorite popular singers, sports figures, and the like. Use the names in a call-response jazz warm-up to provide tone-matching practice. Play the piano accompaniment given below.

Piano Accompaniment

Teach the first two phrases of the warm-up by asking the students to echo you.

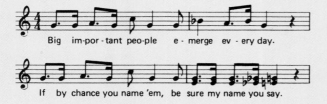

Proceed by inserting three of the famous names that the students listed into an improvised jazz pattern. Indicate to the class that they should continue to echo you. The patterns shown below are suggestions.

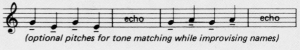

(optional pitches for tone matching while improvising names)

Adjust the suggested patterns to fit the names and your own vocal style. Your final phrase should use the name of a student in the class. Repeat the warm-up several times using different names; encourage the students to add their own improvisations by inserting words such as "yeh" or "alright."

2. Continue the jazzy feeling by asking the students to learn the chant that accompanies the

song, "Getting to Know You," on page 174. Establish a steady beat and challenge the students to sight-read the chant.

3. Prepare the Treble Voices for learning the melody by asking them to scan the song and identify any repeated melodic patterns. Help them realize that many patterns begin with a rising contour. Put the following patterns on the chalkboard and ask the students to sing them as you point from pattern to pattern:

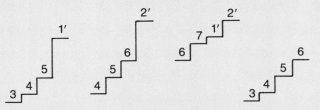

Challenge the Treble Voices to sight-sing their part while you provide a chordal accompaniment. When they can sing the song read-

ily, ask the Changing Voices and Baritones to add the chant.

4. Discuss the idea that making elaborate contrasts will add to the fun of this arrangement. Treble Voices should sing very seriously, in a *legato* style, while the others sing *staccato*, with clearly enunciated words.

5. Play the recording for the students to evaluate their performance and correct their errors. Adjust the balance on the record player so that they may sing with the accompaniment alone.

OPTIONAL

There's a Meetin' Here Tonight

Words and Music by Bob Gibson

TRO—© Copyright 1960 and 1964 Melody Trails, Inc., New York, NY   Used by Permission

177

CHORAL 4

Lesson Focus
Expression: The expressiveness of music is affected by the way timbre and articulation contribute to the musical whole. *(P–S)*

Materials
o **Piano Accompaniment:** page 356
o **Record Information:**
  • There's a Meetin' Here Tonight
    Record 10 Side B Band 6
    Voices: mixed chorus
    Accompaniment: piano, electric organ, electric bass, percussion
o **Teacher's Resource Binder:**
  • **Activity Sheet 48,** page A66
    (Prepare one copy, cut out each strip, and attach.)

The Lesson

1. Examine the notation of "There's a Meetin' Here Tonight" on page 177. The complete song is made up of three sections (refrain–verse–refrain). **Which phrases are alike?** (In the refrain, Phrases 1 and 3 are similar and Phrases 2 and 4 are the same; the verse consists of two similar phrases.)

2. Display the Scale Strip prepared from Activity Sheet 48. Warm up by singing the C major scale. Direct the students (by pointing to the appropriate numbers) to sing melodic patterns drawn from the song, such as

   1–3–5–1'–6–5, 5–6–7–1'–5–6–7–1', 3–1–2–1–3–5–1, and 5–4–3–2–1.

3. Establish the underlying short sound (represented by the quarter note in this song) and challenge the class to sight-read the song. Re-

assure the Baritones and Changing Voices that it is all right to drop out momentarily if some pitches are too high or too low. Listen to the recording so that the students can evaluate their success as sight-readers.

4. Encourage the students to invent scat syllables to be used with this song. Use the syllables "du-bee" on the dotted eighth-sixteenth note pattern found in the song or on other improvised rhythms. Invite the Baritones and Changing Voices to add the scat syllables on the chord roots.

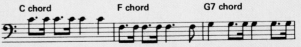

Remind the students that they will need to observe the chord symbols to determine when to change from one pitch to the next.

![Choral 5 banner]

CHORAL 5

Lesson Focus

Harmony: Two or more pitches may be sounded simultaneously. *(P–I)*

Materials

o **Piano Accompaniment:** page 358
o **Record Information:**
  • Encouragement
    Record 11 Side A Band 1
    Voices: mixed chorus
    Accompaniment: piano, electric organ, electric bass, synthesizer, percussion
o **Other:** Scale Strip prepared for Choral 4 (page 177, from Activity Sheet 48)

The Lesson

1. Begin the class by asking the students to read the rhythm patterns shown on the Rhythm Ruler on page 178. Establish the shortest sound at a moderately fast tempo and guide the students to chant each pattern several times. Gradually increase the tempo to a very fast pace. (Quarter note = 112.)

2. Ask the students to locate the two rhythmic patterns they've just practiced in the song. The first corresponds to the lyrics "doot, doot, doot, doot" (Measure 1). The second matches "Encouragement is something everybody needs" (Measures 5–7). Guide the students to realize that much of the song is based on the rhythmic material found in these patterns.

3. Continue preparation for the song by displaying the Scale Strip. (See **Materials**.) Es-

tablish the key of G and ask the students to sing scale steps as you point to pitches. Use patterns drawn from the verse, such as the following:

(1)–5,–3,–5,–1
(1)–5,–6,–3–2–(1)
(1)–3,–5,–7,–3–1
(1)–6,–4–3–2–(1)

Can you think the sounds we've just sung as you sight-read the verse? To help the students sense the harmony, play the chords or the piano accompaniment on page 358 as they work on the verse. Students for whom the range is too wide may lightly tap the rhythm when they are not singing.

4. Divide the class into two groups: Group 1 — Treble I and Baritones (They will sing an octave apart.); Group 2 — Treble II and Changing Voices. Using the Scale Strip, point to two

Tr. I and II

1. When some-thing has ___ you down and out, ___ don't give up hope, just
2. When some-thing seems ___ to be too hard, ___ don't hang it up, just

stand and shout. ___ It can't keep you down ___ 'cause I will be a-
stay on guard. ___ I pro-mise it's true ___ that I will come to

Add C.V. and Bar. (8va lower)

round with some en - cour - age - ment.
you with some en - cour - age - ment.

3.

In ev - ery-thing that we do, In ev - ery-thing that we do,

From those who real - ly love you, En - cour - age - ment

___ is some - thing ev - ery-bod - y needs, en - cour - age - ment

___ from those who love you. You give it to me ___

179

scale numbers a third, sixth, or eighth apart. Group 1 will sing the higher pitch while Group 2 sings the lower one. This exercise will help develop the skill of performing intervals of thirds and sixths in tune. Perform patterns such as:

Group 1: 1′ 1′ 7 5 6 7 1′
Group 2: 1 3 5 5 4 5 1

Group 1: 1 3 5 3 1 4 3 2 1
Group 2: 1 5, 7,5,6,6,5,4,3,

Help the students apply their skills to reading the refrain.

5. Play the recording, inviting the students to join in on the "doot" sections. Discuss how the syncopated rhythms and rising skips give the music a carefree feeling.

6. Discuss the ideas inherent in the lyrics. **How important is encouragement to the individ-**

ual? **Do we function better when encouraged or when faults are pointed out to us?** Continue the discussion by suggesting that the music reflects a light-hearted approach to an important message. **Is this light-hearted musical approach best or should it have been more somber and serious?** (All answers are correct.)

7. When the students can easily sing both parts of the song, invite them to create their own "swing choir" movements for the song. They might use gestures such as arm movements or pivots. They may also change position by kneeling or stretching.

OPTIONAL

OPTIONAL

and I will give it back to you ___ in ev-ery-thing that we do,

En-cour-age-ment ___ in ev-ery-thing that you do, En-cour-age-ment ___

___ from those who real-ly love you. En-cour-age-ment ___

in all that we do! ___

180

Summer Morning

Words by Barbara Young   Music by William S. Haynie

Brightly

Sum - mer morn - ing, bright and ear - ly, Winds are

wak - ing, clouds are curl - y. Ev - ery - thing is ros - y,

pearl - y, Sum - mer morn - ing, bright and ear - ly.

181

CHORAL 6

Lesson Focus

Harmony: Two or more musical lines may occur simultaneously. *(P–I)*

Materials

o **Record Information:**
  • Summer Morning
    Record 11 Side A Band 2
    Voices: mixed chorus
    Accompaniment: piccolo, string ensemble

o **Teacher's Resource Binder:**
  • Optional —
    Enrichment Activity 12, page E19
    Orff Activity 3, page O7

The Lesson

1. Begin the class by reviewing well-known rounds such as "Row, Row, Row Your Boat" and "Are You Sleeping?" Discuss the ways harmony is created through the performance of a round. When each group sings an equally important but different melodic line, the texture is described as being polyphonic; when each group sings the exact same melody at a different time, the form is described as a round or canon.

2. To help the students become aware of the relationship of the parts to each other, ask them to sing "Are You Sleeping?" as a four-part round, with each part singing scale numbers.

3. Ask the students to turn to "Summer Morning" on page 181 and examine this round.

Guide the students to realize that the song consists entirely of a single rhythmic pattern repeated eight times. Sing the song as is, not as a round.

4. Divide the class into two, three, or four groups and perform "Summer Morning" as a round. If boys with changing voices have difficulty singing the melody, they may add the following limited-range part while others continue to sing the round:

C.V.

Sum - mer morn - ing, bright and ear - ly, winds are
Ev - ery - thing is ro - sy, pear - ly, sum - mer

wak - ing, clouds are cur - ly.
morn - ing, bright and ear - ly.

181

Lesson Focus

Harmony: Chords and melody may move simultaneously in relation to each other. *(P–S)*

Materials

o **Piano Accompaniment:** page 363
o **Record Information:**
  • Tie Me Kangaroo Down
    Record 11 Side A Band 3
    Voices: mixed chorus
    Accompaniment: didgerdoo, panpipe, percussion
o **Instruments:** bass xylophone; mallets; piano; double bass
o **Other:** Scale Strip prepared for Choral 4 (page177, from Activity Sheet 48)

Tie Me Kangaroo Down

Words and Music by Rolf Harris
Arranged by Buryl Red

182

The Lesson

1. Begin the class by singing songs in four-part harmony, such as "Mama Don't 'Low," pages 14–15, or "Delta Dawn," pages 26–27. Remind the students to listen carefully to each other so that they can hear the four-part harmony and sense how their parts complement the others.

2. Tell the students to turn to page 182 and examine the notation of "Tie Me Kangaroo Down." Observe that the phrases frequently begin with skips that outline the I, IV, or V7 (F, B♭, or C7) chords. Use the Scale Strip to review singing these chord outlines. (See **Materials**.) Play a chordal accompaniment on the piano as the students sight-read the melody. To help the students sense the syncopated rhythms, suggest that they lightly tap the shortest sound as they sing.

After the students learn the melody, look at the parts available for harmonizing the verse. Explain to the students that any or all of these parts may be used to create a two- to five-part arrangement. Begin by asking Trebles, Changing Voices, and Baritones each to decide which of the harmonizing parts best fits their voice range. Help them discover that during the verse, Trebles I and II may sing any part, Changing Voices may sing Parts IV or V, and Baritones may sing any part an octave lower.

As some voices (Treble Voices or Baritones) take turns singing the melody, help the other groups learn each of the four harmonizing parts. Experiment with different combinations until the class finds one that is satisfying to them.

3. The refrain requires only a melody and one harmony part. Changing Voices and Treble

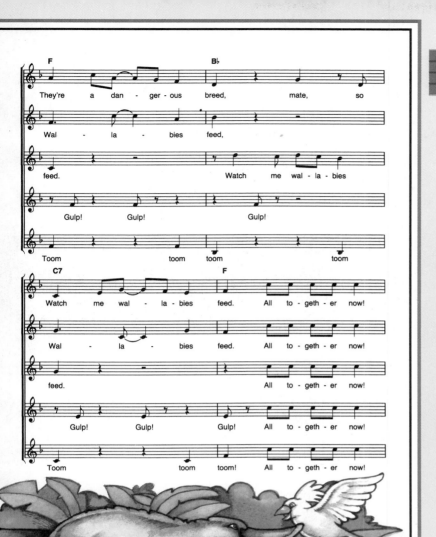

II's will find the harmony part within their range. Treble I's and Baritones should sing the melody. (Baritones should sing an octave below notated pitch.)

4. Learn the additional verses of this song. By looking at words such as kangaroo, cockatoo, and platypus duck, the students should be able to determine the song's place of origin. (Australia) Explain that this is a very popular nonsense song with the Australian people because of the playful use of the animal names.

5. Perform ''Tie Me Kangaroo Down'' again. This time, students may add instruments in place of the vocal harmony parts. Use the bass xylophone, low piano keys, or double bass to play Parts IV or V while continuing to sing the other parts.

Refrain

F   **Gm**

Tie me kang - a - roo down,   sport,

C7   **F**

Tie   me kang - a - roo   down.

F   **Gm** Tie me kang - a - roo,

Tie   me kang - a - roo   down,   sport,

Tie   me kang - a - roo   down.

C7   **F**

Tie   me kang - a - roo   down.

2. Keep me cockatoo cool, Curl,
    Keep me cockatoo cool.
    Don't go acting the fool, Curl,
    Just keep me cockatoo cool. All together now!
    Refrain

3. Take me koala back, Jack,
    Take me koala back.
    He lives somewhere out on the track, Mac,
    So take me koala back. All together now!
    Refrain

4. Mind me platypus duck, Bill,
    Mind me platypus duck.
    Don't let him go running amok, Bill,
    Mind me platypus duck. All together now!
    Refrain

5. Play your didgeridoo, Blue,
    Play your didgeridoo.
    Keep playing till I shoot through, Blue,
    Play your didgeridoo. All together now!
    Refrain

184

I Write the Songs

Words and Music by Bruce Johnston
Arranged by Buryl Red

Study the score. Which parts of this arrangement can you sing most comfortably? Work with others and plan a vocal performance.

I've been a - live for - ev - er,

and I wrote the ver - y first song.

I put the words and the mel - o - dies to - geth - er, I am

mu - sic, and I write the songs.

I write the songs that make the whole world sing;

I write the songs of love and spe - cial things.

I write the songs that make the young girls cry;

I write the songs, I write the songs.

I am mu - sic, and I write the songs.

185

Lesson Focus
Harmony: Two or more musical lines may occur simultaneously. *(P–I)*

Materials
o **Piano Accompaniment:** page 222
o **Record Information:**
 • I Write the Songs
  Record 1 Side A Band 1
  Voices: mixed chorus
  Accompaniment: piano, electric guitar, electric bass, percussion
o **Instrument:** suspended cymbal and mallet
o **Teacher's Resource Binder:**
 • Optional —
  Kodaly Activity 10, page K14

The Lesson

1. Before the students enter the room, write the following song phrases on the chalkboard:

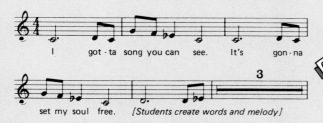

I gotta song you can see. It's gon - na

set my soul free. *[Students create words and melody]*

OPTIONAL

Guide the students to sight-read this incomplete song; then create a melody with words for the remaining measures.

2. Ask the students to follow the instructions at the top of page 185 and decide which part each voice group should sing. (In this song the harmony is written above the melody.) Changing Voices and Baritones should sing an octave below the written pitch. The harmonization in thirds above the melody is a very common musical device, particularly in country-western arrangements.

3. Before learning the melody and harmony, study the rhythm. Establish the eighth note as the short sound. As one student maintains the short sound by tapping lightly on a suspended cymbal, ask the class to chant the rhythm on "ch."

4. Examine the melody and the harmony. Play the recording of "I Write the Songs" as the students follow the score. Play the recording again, asking the students to softly hum their parts. Challenge them to sing the song independently. After the errors have been corrected, perform with the recorded accompaniment alone by adjusting the balance on the record player.

Lesson Focus

Form: A musical whole is a combination of smaller segments. *(P–I)*

Materials

o **Piano Accompaniment:** page 236
o **Record Information:**
  • Ease On Down the Road
    Record 1 Side B Band 1
    Voices: mixed chorus
    Accompaniment: piano, electric guitar, electric bass, percussion

The Lesson

1. Help the students understand the expressive nature of "Ease On Down the Road." Play the recording as the students follow the notation on pages 186–187; then sing with the recording. Some Treble II voices may be able to sing the refrain with the Changing Voices.

2. *(OPTIONAL)* Use the questions on page 186 to trigger a discussion about the expressive nature of the music. The students may find that during the refrain, the melody centers around D and F; the verse centers around G and B, or B♭. The lowered third in each section gives a blues quality to the melody. Ask students to offer ideas as to differences in feeling between the two sections. (They may suggest that the rising melodic line during the refrain provides a more positive feeling, while the narrower range and increased emphasis on descending patterns of the verse are less positive.)

3. Encourage the singers to listen carefully and sing the altered pitches with precise intonation to stress the differences.

4. Notice the sections where there are two vocal parts. Decide which group will sing the harmony and which should continue to sing the melody. Then perform the entire song.

steps you've ta - ken leave you three, four steps be - hind. __ Just you
legs, keep mov - in', don't you lose __ no ground, ___ 'cause the

keep on keep - in' on the road that you choose and don't
road you're walk - in' might be long some - time, but just

give up walk - in' 'cause you gave up __ shoes. __ 2. Pick your
keep on step - pin' and you'll

Refrain

C.V.
only   *D.S.*

be just __ fine. __

Come on,

187

Lesson Focus

Time and Place: The way musical elements are combined into a whole reflects the origin of the music. *(P–I)*

Materials

o **Piano Accompaniment:** page 254
o **Record Information:**
   • Delta Dawn (Choral)
   Record 2 Side A Band 3b
   Voices: mixed chorus
   Accompaniment: piano, electric guitar, electric bass, percussion
o **Teacher's Resource Binder:**
   • Optional —
   Enrichment Activity 13, page E19
   Instrumental Arrangement 7, page 120

Delta Dawn

Words and Music by Alex Harvey and Larry Collins
Arranged by Lowell Rogers

Can you identify one or two popular music styles that have influenced this song?

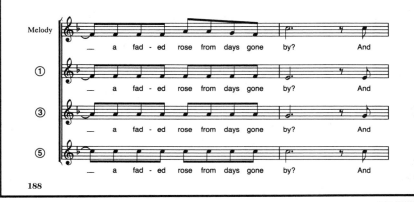

188

The Lesson

1. If the students have not had an opportunity to learn "Delta Dawn" by following the ikonic representation found on pages 26–27, return to those pages and complete that lesson. After the melody and harmonization have been learned, ask the students to pair off. Tell every other student to open his or her book to pages 188–189 while the others keep their books open to pages 26–27.

   Ask the students to share their books while they compare the parts written in ikons to the traditionally notated parts. They will discover that the up-and-down direction of the parts is the same in both versions. **Which version provides more accurate musical information?** (The traditionally notated score on pages 188–189 has precise information about pitches and shows rhythmic relationships.)

2. Sing this song following the notated score. Point out that any of the voice parts may be sung at the pitch shown or an octave lower, according to the voice range of the singer. Invite the students to experiment with different combinations of voice parts.

3. In response to the question on page 188, conclude that the harmony and melody are in a country-gospel style while the slow, heavy rhythm is derived from rock. Stress the rock feeling by emphasizing the second and fourth beats in the accompaniment.

   Although the meter signature indicates groups of four, suggest that the students count groups of eight short sounds. This will help them sense the way in which the underlying short sound often controls the rhythmic pulse in rock music.

189

Lesson Focus

Time and Place: The way musical elements are combined into a whole reflects the origin of the music. *(P–S)*

Materials

o **Piano Accompaniment:** page 370
o **Record Information:**
  • *La Bamba*
    Record 11 Side A Band 4
    Voices: mixed chorus
    Accompaniment: trumpets, double bass, harp, accordian, guitar, percussion

La Bamba

Mexican Folk Song

190

The Lesson

1. Introduce the lesson by explaining that *"La Bamba"* is a popular Mexican folk song. Play the recording to give the students an overview of the style. Play the recording again and focus their attention on the chord sequence. Explain that there are only three different chords used: A (I), D (IV), and E7 (V7). The changes occur in the same order in each measure of the song except the last.

2. Discuss the Latin-American mariachi style. (See **For Your Information.**) Explain that the melody and the harmony parts both outline the I, IV, and V7 chords and frequently contain passing tones that add interest to the repeated chord sequence.

3. Invite the students to learn the harmony part. Decide which groups can most easily sing this part (Treble II's and Baritones). Draw attention to the fact that this part uses a limited set of pitches that are frequently repeated.

4. Select a group to learn the melody (Treble I's and Changing Voices). Perform the piece in harmony.

5. Adjust the balance control of the stereo to eliminate the vocal track, and add the live vocal parts to the accompaniment on the recording.

6. Have the students sing the English translation as follows:

   OPTIONAL

   When you're dancing the *Bamba*,
   When you're dancing the *Bamba*,
   Your troubles fly with the rhythm that's swaying,
   Yes the rhythm is swaying, your heart feels gay!

190

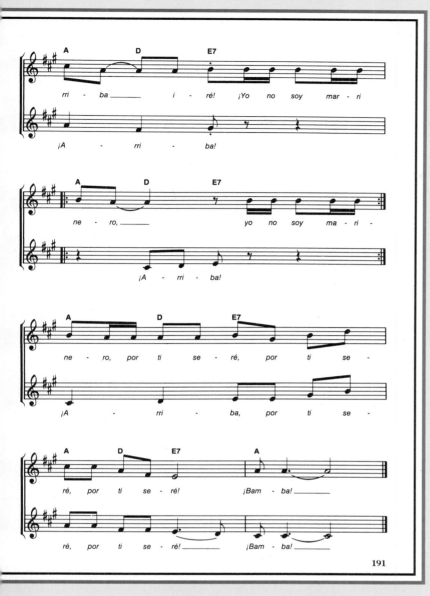

For Your Information

The song *"La Bamba,"* originally from Veracruz, is popular today in all parts of Latin America. Popular Latin bands have made various recordings of *"La Bamba."* This recording is done by a mariachi band. Mariachi bands, which are Mexican in origin, typically consist of two trumpets, two violins, two guitars, and a bass guitar. Dancers often contribute percussive sounds to mariachi bands by rapid movement of their feet against the ground or wooden platforms.

The phonetic pronunciation for *"La Bamba"* is:

Bahm-bah, **bahm**-bah! Ah-**ree**-bah!
Pah-rah bie-**lahr** lah **Bahm**-bah,
Pah-rah bie-**lahr** lah **Bahm**-bah
Say neh-seh-**see**-too **ah**-nah
Poe-kah day **grah**-see-ah,
Oo-nah **poe**-kah day **grah**-see-ah
Ee **oe**-trah Koe-**see**-tah!
Ee ah-**ree**-bah, ah-**ree**-bah,
Ee ah-**ree**-bah, ah-**ree**-bah,
Ee ah-**ree**-bah, ah-**ree**-bah,
   ee-**ray**!
Yoh noh **soy** mah-ree-**nay**-roh,
Yoh noh **soy** mah-ree-**nay**-roh,
Pawr tee seh-**ray**, pawr tee seh-**ray**, pawr
   tee seh-**ray**!
Bahm-bah!

191

Sing *arriba, arriba,*
Sing *arriba, arriba,*
Sing *arriba, arriba iré!*
Yes, you're dancing the *Bamba,*
Yes, you're dancing the *Bamba,*
When you're dancing the *Bamba,* you
can't go wrong, you can't go wrong,
you can't go wrong!
Bam-ba!

English Words by Elena Paz

Lesson Focus

Expression: Musical elements are combined into a whole to express a musical or extra-musical idea. *(P–S)*

Materials

o **Piano Accompaniment:** page 374
o **Record Information:**
  • The Home Road
  Record 11   Side A   Band 5
  Voices: mixed chorus
  Accompaniment: oboe, French horn, cello, harp, percussion

The Home Road

Words and Music by John Alden Carpenter
Arranged by B.A.

1. Sing a hymn of free-dom, Fling the ban-ner high!
2. In the qui-et hours ____ of the star-ry night,

Sing the songs of li-ber-ty, Songs that shall not die,
Dream the dreams of far-a-way, Home fires burn-ing bright,
For the

Sing the songs of li-ber-ty, Songs that shall not die, not die,
Dream the dreams of far-a-way, Home fires burn-ing bright, so bright,

long, long road to Tip-pe-ra-ry is the road that leads me home, O'er

long road leads me road that leads home, yes home, O'er

192

The Lesson

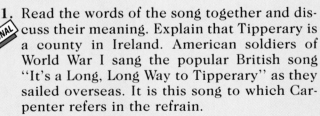

1. Read the words of the song together and discuss their meaning. Explain that Tipperary is a county in Ireland. American soldiers of World War I sang the popular British song "It's a Long, Long Way to Tipperary" as they sailed overseas. It is this song to which Carpenter refers in the refrain.

2. As the class listens to the recording, discuss the expressive contributions of the music to the poem. **What is the musical climax of this song? What helps you to know?** Guide the students to conclude that the musical climax occurs in the last phrase of the refrain. The contrast in rhythm, which now contains longer, weightier note values, and the leap upward to the high E♭ ("My cornfields!") contribute to the importance of this final phrase.

3. Suggest that the students read or hum along with their vocal part as the recording is played. Point out that when the Baritones and Changing Voices are not singing in unison or octaves with the Trebles, they are performing a contrasting part.

4. Invite the Treble Voices, then the Changing Voices and Baritones to individually sing their part with the recording. When each group is familiar with its part, ask the class to sing the song in two-part harmony.

hills and plains, By lakes and lanes, My wood-lands! My corn-fields! My

hills and plains, lakes, lanes, wood-lands, My corn-fields! My

1. coun - try! My home!
2. home! My coun - try! My home!

1. coun - try! My home!
2. home! My coun - try! My home!

193

The Bagpipers' Carol

Arranged by Hartley Snyder

Sicilian Carol

194

CHORAL 13

Lesson Focus

Texture: Musical quality is affected by the number of musical lines occurring simultaneously. *(P–S)*

Materials

o **Piano Accompaniment:** page 367

o **Record Information:**
  • The Bagpipers' Carol
  Record 11 Side A Band 6
  Voices: mixed chorus
  Accompaniment: recorders, krumhorns, lute, viola da gamba, bagpipe, percussion

o **Instruments:** cello or double bass and bow

o **Other:** Scale Strip prepared for Choral 4, page 177

The Lesson

1. Guide students to warm up by following your signals as you point to scale steps on the Scale Strip. (See **Materials**.) Begin with all the students singing in unison; then split up the class, asking the Treble I's and Changing Voices to sing the upper numbers while Treble II's and Baritones sing the lower numbers. Point to numbers that are thirds, fifths, sixths, and octaves apart.

2. Ask the students to turn to pages 194–195 and examine their part in relation to the other parts on the same staff. Treble Voices should observe that they will most frequently be singing in thirds, with larger intervals (especially the sixth) occurring occasionally, most frequently at the ends of sections. **What do the Changing Voices and Baritones notice about their parts?** Guide them to realize that their part is a type of drone. In the first

section, they begin at the interval of a fifth, then shift to the octave and return to the fifth. They sing either in unison or at the octave for most of the final phrase.

3. Set a moderate tempo by tapping short sounds in groups of six. Challenge the Changing Voices and Baritones to perform their part for the first eight measures while you support them on the autoharp. Explain to the students that this part imitates the sound of the bagpipes. It is an instrument that originated in the Orient but has been very popular throughout Scottish and Irish history. Sound on the bagpipe is produced by pressing air through a bellows. In addition to a melody created on the chanter (the reed pipe section), a continuous drone is produced on pipes called drones. If a cello or double bass is available, a student performer might also reinforce the drone pitches.

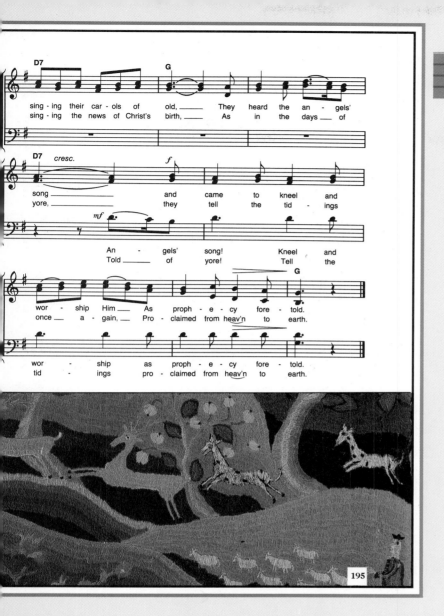

sing - ing their car - ols of old, _____ They heard the an - gels'
sing - ing the news of Christ's birth, _____ As in the days _____ of

song _____ and came to kneel and
yore, _____ they tell the tid - ings

An - gels' song! Kneel and
Told _____ of yore! Tell the

wor - ship Him _____ As proph - e - cy fore - told.
once _____ a - gain, Pro - claimed from heav'n to earth.

wor - ship as proph - e - cy fore - told.
tid - ings pro - claimed from heav'n to earth.

195

4. When the Changing Voices and Baritones can perform their parts, ask them to continue singing while the Treble Voices practice theirs. **Listen carefully to be sure you are maintaining the correct intervals.** As the students rehearse, call attention to the accent marks above the Changing Voice–Baritone parts. **What information do these accents give us about how to sing this part?** (Each tone should be stressed.) Guide the singers to begin each point with a strong accent. **How should the upper voices sing?** (in a smoother, more legato manner, to provide contrast)

5. Ask the students to examine Section 2 of the song (beginning on page 194 in the last bar of the third line). Guide the Treble Voices to discover that the last six measures of Section 2 are the same as the last six measures of Section 1. After their entrance, the lower voices continue a drone, now in unison. Help the students practice this section, then perform the entire composition.

6. When the students can perform comfortably, draw attention to the dynamic markings. Challenge the students to recall what they have learned about enunciation, phrasing, and breath support as they prepare an expressive performance of this carol.

CHORAL 14

Lesson Focus

Harmony: Two or more musical lines may occur simultaneously. *(P–S)*

Materials

o **Piano Accompaniment:** page 343

o **Record Information:**
  • Go Down, Moses and Joshua Fought the Battle of Jericho
  Record 11 Side A Band 7
  Voices: mixed chorus
  Accompaniment: percussion

o **Instruments:** snare drums and sticks; electric keyboard or piano; double bass or guitar; one instrument for each student if possible

o **Other:** overhead projector

o **Teacher's Resource Binder:**

Activity Sheets
  • **Activity Sheet 49,** page A67 (Prepare as a transparency.)
  • Optional —
  Mainstreaming Activity 16, page M25

The Lesson

1. Ask the students to determine the key of "Go Down, Moses" on page 196. If they are unsure, ask them to name the pitches used in the unison melody, which makes up the first section of this arrangement. Write them on a staff starting with the pitch that ends this section: E.

After singing the pitch pattern thus created, identify it as a minor scale. Discuss the effect of the raised seventh. This creates a form of the minor scale known as the harmonic minor—it borrows the seventh step from its parallel major scale to give the movement from 7 to 1' a feeling of coming to rest. To help the students sense the difference, have them sing the natural minor scale (with D natural), then repeat the harmonic minor scale.

2. Challenge the students to sight-read the melody for "Go Down, Moses" as you provide a chordal accompaniment. (All Trebles and Changing Voices should sing the entire melody; Baritones should sing only where indicated.) After singing as written, play or sing the melody in E natural minor; discuss the difference that results when the seventh step is not raised.

3. Guide the students to learn the melody of "Joshua Fought the Battle of Jericho" (upper staffs beginning at the bottom of page 196). Sing it in unison after chanting the words in rhythm while tapping the shortest sound until the students have a sense of the recurring syncopation.

4. Help the students discover that harmony is created by combining these two songs as "partner songs." Assign parts as shown on

196

197

the score. Draw attention to the fact that, beginning with the third pair of staffs on page 197, the Treble Voices sing a one-pitch pattern while the Changing Voices and Baritones continue to sing the melody for "Go Down, Moses" (an octave lower). The coda (last four measures) includes new material which the students will need to practice before putting the entire song together.

5. Divide the class into three groups: 1) drums, 2) basses or guitars, 3) keyboards. Project the transparency of Activity Sheet 49 (Play an Accompaniment). Each group should practice its part until it is mastered.

6. Choose several players to continue to perform each of the three accompaniment parts as the rest of the class sings the vocal arrangement. Repeat, giving other students the opportunity to play the instrumental accom-

paniment. Allow as many students to play as time permits.

The Woodchuck

Music by Pat Shaw

How much wood would a wood-chuck chuck if a
wood-chuck could ____ chuck wood? Oh,
just as much wood as a wood-chuck could chuck if a
wood-chuck could chuck wood. Now tell me . . .

Vocal Ostinato Accompaniment

C.V. wood-chuck chuck

Bar. wood-chuck chuck

199

Lesson Focus

Form: A musical whole is a combination of smaller segments. *(P–I)*

Materials

o **Piano Accompaniment:** page 377
o **Record Information:**
  • The Woodchuck
    Record 11 Side A Band 8
    Voices: mixed chorus
    Accompaniment: 2 clarinets, 2 bass clarinets, percussion
o **Teacher's Resource Binder:**
    • Optional —
    Evaluation | **Checkpoint 4,** page Ev21
    Mainstreaming Activity 18, page M25

The Lesson

1. To begin, ask each student to count to ten and back in one breath. Gradually increase the difficulty of the game by having them count to eleven and so on. Students remain in the game until they can no longer perform the count in one breath.

2. Ask the students to read the lyrics on page 199 aloud, breathing only on the rests. Have the students gradually speed up the tempo.

3. Have the Changing Voices and Baritones sight-read the ostinato at the bottom of the page. Guide the Treble Voices to sight-read the melody. Then combine the parts.

4. While the Changing Voices and Baritones remain silent, Treble Voices may sing the song as a two- or four-part round.

Lesson Focus

Expression: The expressiveness of music is affected by the way dynamics contribute to the musical whole. *(P–S)*

Materials

o **Piano Accompaniment:** page 382
o **Record Information:**
  • Scarborough Fair
    Record 11 Side A Band 9
    Voices: mixed chorus
    Accompaniment: piano

The Lesson

1. Begin the class by writing the following dynamic symbols on the board in order from softest to loudest:

ppp pp p mp mf f

Play an E minor chord on the guitar or piano. Ask the students to find a tone within the chord on which to sing the syllable "loo." Practice changing the dynamic level. Begin by moving through the sequence of dynamics given above. Then randomly point from one dynamic level to another. Stress the importance of using breath support to avoid throat tension when changing the dynamic level. Insert *crescendo* or *decrescendo* marks between any two dynamic indications. Practice gradual changes.

2. Ask the students to open their books to page 200. The song, "Scarborough Fair," has been arranged to highlight the expressive contour of the melody as well as the rich sounds of the words. Discuss the selective use of dynamics. Draw attention to the way the loudest dynamics emphasize the high point in both the melodic contour and the lyrics, "Remember me to one who lives there."

3. Guide the students to examine the song. Note that it begins with the melody in the Treble I with the other voices singing lines that provide harmonic support. **What happens between the voices in Section II?** (The melody alternates between the Treble Voices and the Baritone–Changing Voices.) **How does the melody usually move, by steps or by skips?** (usually by steps)

Guide the students to begin learning the song by performing Section II. Each group should sing only when they have the melody. Provide

a simple harmonic accompaniment. When the melody for this section has been learned, return to the bottom of page 201 and challenge the harmonizing voices to read their parts as the Treble I voices continue to softly sing the melody.

4. Return to Section I. Challenge the students to sight-read in four-part harmony. Practice individual parts as needed.

5. When the students have demonstrated they can perform the song with reasonable accuracy, recall the discussion of the ways that the dynamics indicated in the score support the expressive intent of the words (Step 2). Play the recording so that the students may hear a model of an expressive performance. On the second playing, invite the students to sing along, making sure to observe the dynamic changes.

6. After repeated practice of the song, continue to help the students understand how to more musically express the word meanings. Explain that it is important to sustain primary vowel sounds for the full duration of the note; they should pronounce the consonant only at the moment of release.

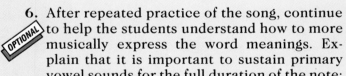

Primary Vowel: Maintain "eh" for "Fair" and "there"; "ah" for "thyme" and "mine."
Release: Be careful not to elongate the ending "r" sound in "Fair" and "there." Quickly add the "i" sound (secondary vowel) before singing the "m" in "thyme" or the "n" in "mine." The voiced consonants "m" and "n" may be stressed here to add clarity to diction. Be sure the "m's" and "n's" are voiced on the correct pitch; make sure that there is no sliding between pitches.

202

Ging Gong Gooli

Folk Song from Guyana

Rhythmically, in moderate 2

Tr. I
Tr. II

mf

Ging gong

C.V.
Bar.

mf pah, pah, pah, pah,

mf Um - pah, um - pah, um - pah, um - pah,

goo - li, goo - li, goo - li, goo - li, wat - cha, ging gong

pah, pah, pah, pah,

um - pah, um - pah, um - pah, um - pah,

goo, ging gong goo. [1.] Ging gong goo. [2.]

pah, pah, pah, pah, pah,

um - pah, um - pah, um - pah, um - pah, um - pah, um.

203

Lesson Focus

Form: A musical whole may be made up of same, varied, or contrasting segments. *(P–S)*

Materials

o **Piano Accompaniment:** page 378
o **Record Information:**
  • *Ging Gong Gooli*
    Record 11 Side B Band 1
    Voices: mixed chorus
    Accompaniment: tin whistle, electric guitar, electric bass, steel drums, percussion
o **Instrument:** autoharp
o **Other:** Chromatic Scale Ruler prepared for Traditions 21, pages 46–47 (Activity Sheet 13a) and Chord Finders prepared for Traditions 25, pages 54–55 (Activity Sheet 13d)

The Lesson

1. Begin the class by asking the students to listen to chords that you play on the piano or guitar. Have them find a pitch in the first chord that is comfortably within their range to sing on the syllable, "doo." **When I change chords, try to find a tone within that chord that is close to the one you just sang.** Play the following chord sequence in root position:

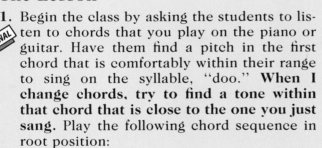

I–V7–I–IV–I–V7–I
(F–C7–F–B♭–F–C7–F)

I began with a I chord. (Play it.) Think the scale pitches from the lowest tone in this chord to the lowest tone in the next. (Play I again and move to V7.) Can you name this chord? Continue to help the students identify the chords until the entire sequence has been named.

2. Ask the students to determine the key of the song *"Ging Gong Gooli,"* on page 203. (F major) Guide them to identify the pitches that belong to each chord in the sequence they've just sung. Write the pitches for each chord on the chalkboard. Ask one student to use the Chromatic Scale Ruler (see **Materials**) and Chord Finders to make sure that the class has correctly named the pitches for each chord.

Look at Section A of this song. Can you determine the chord sequence on which the arrangement is based? Proceed measure by measure starting with the Changing Voices–Baritones part. Examine the notes for each measure and compare them with the chord pitches identified in Step 2: **F–F–F–F–C7–F** (repeated). Ask one student to play this chord sequence on the autoharp as the class experiments with reading their parts while

203

For Your Information

The students may create hand jives—any kind of action that moves with the feeling of the beat. Two simple illustrations are shown below:

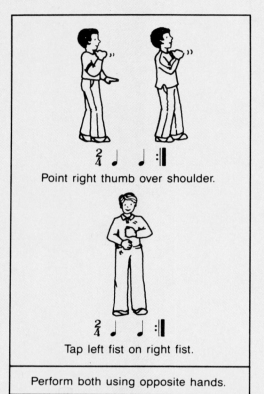

Point right thumb over shoulder.

Tap left fist on right fist.

Perform both using opposite hands.

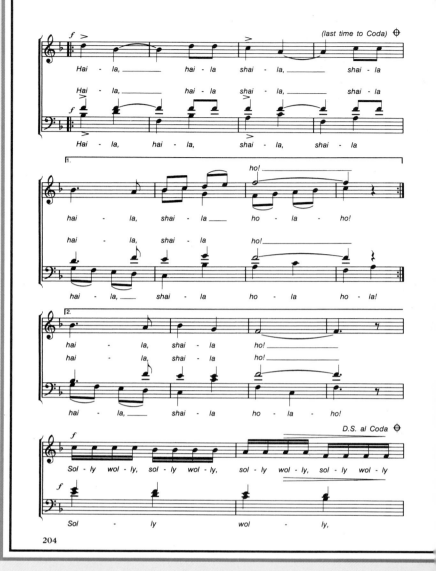

204

tapping the underlying short sound (the eighth note).

3. Proceed with a similar process in the other sections. After the students have worked through the entire composition, play the recording and ask them to evaluate the accuracy of their own performance.

4. As the students listen to the recording again, suggest that they respond to the rhythms by devising hand-jive patterns. Demonstrate some ideas such as those shown in **For Your Information**. Guide the students to identify the form of the composition (**Introduction, A, A, B, B, Interlude, A, A, Coda**) and plan a different hand-jive motion for each section. They may want to use similar hand jives for the Introduction, Interlude, and Coda.

5. Perform the composition in four parts, adding the hand jives.

Lesson Focus

Texture: Musical quality is affected by the degree of contrast between musical lines occurring simultaneously. *(P–S)*

Materials

o **Piano Accompaniment:** page 275
o **Record Information:**
  • Five Hundred Miles
    Record 3 Side B Band 1
    Voices: mixed chorus
    Accompaniment: dobro guitar, rhythm guitar, double bass, percussion

Five Hundred Miles

Words and Music by Hedy West
Arranged by Buryl Red

Locate the passages where the melody and harmonizing parts

• have the same words and rhythm
• have the contrasting words and rhythm

"Word painting" is a musical device used by composers to add interest to their compositions. The musical sounds specifically suggest the word's meaning. Locate examples of word painting in the following arrangement.

206

The Lesson

1. Begin the class by reviewing the arrangement of "Five Hundred Miles" found in Lesson 25, page 54. Discuss the relationship of the voices in this arrangement: one sings the melody while the others provide a harmonic accompaniment. Identify this style as homophonic.

   Recall the two canons on pages 181 and 199 where each part had an independent melody of its own. Identify this as polyphonic. Explain that the two terms come from the Latin derivation of the prefix *homo-*, meaning one, and *poly-*, meaning many. **What do you suppose the suffix *-phone* means?** (voice)

2. Ask the students to open their books to page 206 and examine the arrangement of "Five Hundred Miles." **Is this song homophonic or polyphonic?** Help them realize that it alter-

nates between the two styles. Like many compositions, it cannot be placed exclusively in one category or the other because it bears characteristics of both. The song begins with the voices moving together homophonically (Measures 1–4), followed by a four-measure section in which the lower voices move in contrast to the melody. This alternation of styles occurs throughout the composition, unifying the form by providing balance between repetition and contrast.

3. Play the recording of "Five Hundred Miles" as the students follow their parts. Ask them to listen for ways the music supports the word meaning. Draw attention to Measures 5–6 ("Blow, whistle blow") where the voices suggest the sound of a train whistle. **This is an example of "word painting," a musical device used by composers for hundreds of years. This term means to create sounds**

which suggest specific ideas. Notice that the coda is derived from ideas introduced in the last phrase of Verse 1.

4. After listening to the recording again to get a sense of the way the parts relate to each other, have the students practice their parts while you provide a simple chordal accompaniment. Practice by having the voice that sings the melody sing its part, while the other voices each take turns singing theirs in relation to the melody.

   The song may be performed in four parts as shown on the pupil page, or in three parts by asking the Baritones and Changing Voices to sing the Changing Voice part and deleting the Baritone line.

5. Adjust the balance on the record player so that only the accompaniment is heard and perform the piece.

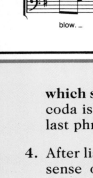

three, ___ Lord, I'm four, Lord, I'm five ___ hun - dred

three, ___ Lord, I'm four, five ___ hun - dred

miles ___ a - way from home. ___

miles ___ 'way from

miles ___ 'way from

Refrain
A - way from home, a - way from home, a - way from

home. ___ A - way from home, a - way from home, a - way from

home, a - way from home, Lord, I'm five ___ hun - dred

five hun - dred

home, a - way from home, five hun - dred

209

Lesson Focus

Texture: Musical quality is affected by the distance between the musical lines. *(P–S)*

Materials

o **Piano Accompaniment:** page 389
o **Record Information:**
  • Everything Is Beautiful
  Record 11 Side B Band 2
  Voices: mixed chorus
  Accompaniment: piano, rhythm guitar, electric guitar, bass drums, percussion
o **Instruments:** drum and brushes

Everything Is Beautiful

Arranged by Fred Bock

Words and Music by Ray Stevens

Ev-ery-thing is beau-ti-ful _____ in its own way, _____

Like a star-ry sum-mer night, or a snow-cov-ered win-ter's day.

Ev-ery-bod-y's beau-ti-ful _____ in their own way:

Un-der God's heav-en, the world's gon-na find ___ a way.

way, find ___ a

2nd time to Coda

There is none so blind ___ as he who will not

way.

210

The Lesson

1. Before the class begins, write these patterns on the chalkboard:

Invite the students to tap Pattern A on their palm with two fingers. One student may play the pattern on the drum using brushes. Discuss the difference between Pattern A and Pattern B (Pattern B could be thought of as Pattern A with the first two eighth notes in each triplet tied). Play Pattern B in a similar fashion.

Ask the students to read the words for the upper voice parts in "Everything Is Beautiful" up to the double bar at the bottom of page 210. As they read they should continue

to tap Pattern A in order to create a feeling for the underlying shuffle style and to assure that all dotted eighth-sixteenth patterns will be performed as triplets.

2. As Changing Voices and Baritones continue to tap Pattern A, the Treble Voices should sing their part up to the double bar. Examine the Changing Voice–Baritone part for this section of the song. **Do the voices ever sing in unison?** (yes, at the beginning of the first staff) **How far apart are the voices when they sing in harmony?** (usually a sixth apart; much of the harmony is parallel; frequently at the cadence points, the voices move in opposite directions) Help the Changing Voices and Baritones learn their part in this section.

3. Examine the remainder of the song. **Are the parts still moving in unison or sixths?** (Most of the time each part is heard indepen-

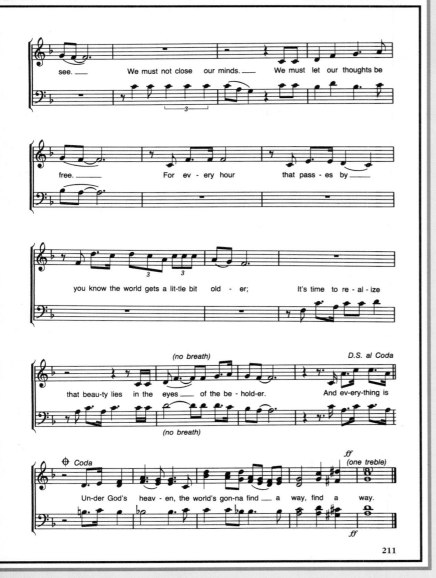

For Your Information

The basic style of this contemporary song is a country shuffle. This is exemplified by the notated rhythmic pattern, which should be performed as a triplet pattern:

Notated: ♩. ♪ and ♪ ♪

Performed: ⌐3⌐ ♩ ♪

Perform this piece with a minimum of vibrato and sing with a natural, conversational pronunciation. A clearly focused sound is needed for accurate intonation of the jazz-style chords found in the last two measures.

dently. On occasion, the lower voices sing in harmony with the upper voices.) Review the use of the direction, *D.S. al Coda.* Help the students determine the order in which the sections of the song are to be performed. Learn the middle section of the song, then the coda. Sing the entire song adding Pattern A to help maintain the shuffle feeling.

4. Sing with the instrumental accompaniment found on the recording of "Everything Is Beautiful."

OPTIONAL

Lesson Focus

Texture: Musical quality is affected by the number and contrast of musical lines occurring simultaneously. **(P–S)**

Materials

○ **Record Information:**
  • Which Is the Properest Day to Sing?
    Record 11 Side B Band 3
    Voices: mixed chorus
    Accompaniment: oboes, clarinets, bassoon, French horn, harpsichord
○ **Teacher's Resource Binder:**
  • Optional —
    Biography 8, page B15

Which Is the Properest Day to Sing?

by Thomas A. Arne

212

The Lesson

1. Ask the students to open their books to page 212 and chant the first phrase of the song "Which Is the Properest Day to Sing?" in rhythm, focusing on crisp enunciation. Have the class then sing the phrase on C. Repeat the phrase several times, each time singing one step higher.

2. Ask the students to rhythmically chant the words for the entire melody in unison. (When the song goes into harmony, the melody is found in the following voice parts: Treble I—Measures 9–12; Changing Voice and Baritone—Measures 13–20; Treble I—Measures 21–24; Baritone—Measures 25–28; and Treble I—Measures 29–32.) Then divide the class into parts and ask them to chant their parts together, observing how some voices speak together while others have contrasting rhythms.

3. Challenge the Treble Voices to a "sight-reading duel" with the Baritones and Changing Voices. Establish the key by playing the chord sequence **I–IV–V7–I**. Treble I's and II's should then sing Phrase I (Measures 1–4), answered by Changing Voices and Baritones (Measures 5–8). Students should decide who "won the duel."

4. For the remainder of the song, ask the group that has the melody to perform its part. Then help each of the other voices to practice their parts in relation to the melody. As the students learn their parts, remind them to continue to perform with crisp enunciation.

5. Explain that this kind of song, written in eighteenth century England, is known as a part song. Part songs were popular songs of that time. People would gather in each other's homes to enjoy singing the latest

OPTIONAL

CHORAL 20

213

"hits." Play the recording, drawing attention to the interlude that is performed by instruments of the time.

Lesson Focus
Timbre: The total sound is affected by the number and qualities of sounds occurring at the same time. *(P–S)*

Materials
o **Piano Accompaniment:** page 393
o **Record Information:**
• Route 66 (Medley)
by Bobby Troup, 1918–
Record 11   Side B   Band 4
Mel Tormé Live at the Maisonette
• Bourrée for Bach
Record 11   Side B   Band 5
Voices: mixed chorus
Accompaniment: electric piano, double bass, percussion

Bourrée for Bach

from *English Suite No. 2*

Music by Johann Sebastian Bach
Arranged by Bennett Williams

214

The Lesson

1. Play the recording of "Route 66." **What is different about this singing?** (Some of the words are nonsense syllables, with no literal meaning.) Play the recording again and ask the students to list the syllables that were used. The students should discover syllables such as these: "dee," "bo," "shu," and "dot." They occur in a variety of combinations throughout the piece. **What timbres were heard?** (male voice, trumpets, trombones, saxophones, drum set, and double bass) Discuss scat singing with the students as described in **For Your Information.**

2. Play the recording of "Bourrée for Bach" as the students follow their part in the score on page 214. **What did you notice?** ("Bourrée for Bach" has syllables similar to those in "Route 66.") This time the syllables used are "du," "bee," and "la."

3. Help the students learn their parts. Alternate between listening to the recording as the students follow the score and having the students practice the song, section by section, without the aid of the recording. Be especially aware of the dynamic change that occurs as each section is repeated. Perform "Bourrée for Bach" with the recorded instrumental accompaniment alone by adjusting the balance on the record player.

215

For Your Information

Scat singing is a jazz style that evolved as the result of instrumentalists attempting to imitate the sound of various instruments with their voices. Today it is considered a basic vocal jazz style.

Bell Gloria

Words and Music by Buryl Red

Perform this composition in a random manner to suggest the sound of carillon bells. Each part should establish its own underlying beat and need not attempt to perform in exact rhythmic relationship with the other parts. Begin with Bell Pattern A followed by Bell Pattern B, then Bell Pattern C. Vocal Parts then enter one by one, in any order. Repeat indefinitely!

Bell Pattern A

Bell Pattern B

Bell Pattern C

Play these pitches at random in any octave.

Voices

1. Glo - ri-a, Glo - ri-a.
2. Glo - ri-a, Glo - ri-a.
3. Glo - ri-a, Glo - ri-a.
4. Glo - ri-a, Glo - ri-a.
5. Glo - ri-a, Glo - ri-a.

Improvise other parts using pitches of the pentatonic scale.

217

CHORAL 22

Lesson Focus

Rhythm: Music may move in relation to the underlying steady beat. *(P–S)*

Materials

○ **Record Information:**
 • Bell Gloria
   Record 11 Side B Band 6
   Voices: mixed chrous
   Accompaniment: bells, chimes

○ **Instruments:** barred or keyboard instruments such as glockenspiels, xylophones, metallophones, resonator bells or piano, each set up with pitches D, E, F#, A, and B; mallets; hand bells or string instrument

○ **Teacher's Resource Binder:**
 • Optional —
   Instrumental Arrangement 8, page 122

The Lesson

1. Begin the class by guiding the students to study "Bell Gloria" on page 217. Ask each student to examine each of the five vocal parts and identify those that are appropriate for his or her voice range. Allow the students to organize into five equal groups.

2. Have each group work together in a different part of the room. Give each a pitched instrument to establish the key and to check accuracy. Each group should set its own tempo, counting in relation to the underlying short sound (eighth note). Allow the groups five minutes to learn their parts.

3. Follow the instructions on pupil page 217. Each part enters as it chooses, maintaining its own underlying pulse, without regard for any rhythmic relationship among parts.

4. Use any barred or keyboard instruments, such as the glockenspiel, xylophone, metallophone, resonator bells, and/or piano for the bell parts. If handbells are not available for Bell Pattern C, play it on the bass metallophone or a string instrument, using D and A open strings *(pizzicato).*

5. Guide the students to improvise their own parts as suggested on page 217; any pitches of the pentatonic scale shown may be used. Draw attention to the fact that each of the five vocal parts is a different length.

Suggest that the students might make their own patterns equivalent to 12 or 14 eighth notes to add another rhythmic dimension to the composition.

217

Lesson Focus

Evaluation: Review concepts and skills studied in the fourth unit.

Materials

o **Piano Accompaniment:** page 397

o **Record Information:**
  • Rain
    Record 11 Side B Band 7a
    Instrument: synthesizer
    Band 7b:
    Voices: mixed chorus
    Accompaniment: synthesizer

o **Teacher's Resource Binder:**

  Evaluation • **Review 4,** pages Ev21–Ev24
    (Prepare pages Ev23–Ev24 as a transparency.)
  • **Musical Progress Report 4,** page Ev25

The Lesson

1. Do not tell the students the name of the song. Play a short portion of Band 7a of "Rain." Invite the students to discover the shortest sound and begin tapping it on the palm of one hand.

2. Distribute copies of Review 4, pages Ev21–Ev22, and display the transparency of Ev23 and Ev24. Play the recording as often as needed for the students to answer the questions. When the students have completed their work, collect the papers.

3. Discuss Question 8 to get student input about a possible title for the song. When the students have had a chance to share their opinions, have them turn to page 218 of their books. Listen to Band 7b of "Rain" to hear the relationship between the text and the ac-

companiment. Encourage the students to suggest reasons for the composer's musical decisions made to describe a text about rain.

4. Help the students learn the song in four parts. When the parts are secure, sing with either the recorded accompaniment or the piano accompaniment.

5. Use the information gained in this lesson and other lessons in Unit 4 to complete a copy of Musical Progress Report 4 for each student.

For Your Information

The correct answers for Review 4, pages Ev21–Ev22, are:

1. _____ Introduction
   _a_ A
   _b_ B
   _a_ A'
   _b_ B'
   _____ Interlude
   _a_ A''

2. _a_ Introduction
   _a_ A
   _b_ B
   _a_ A'
   _b_ B'
   _a_ Interlude
   _a_ A''

3. homophonic
4. legato
5. steps
6. *andante*—indicates a steady walking tempo
   rit.—indicates slowing music down
   a tempo—indicates that the original tempo *(andante)* should be resumed
7. e
8. Answers will vary. Accept any that give logical reasons for the student's choice of title.

219

Glossary

Accelerando: becoming faster

Accent: a sound in a musical line that is performed with more emphasis than other sounds

Aerophone: an instrument whose sound is produced by air blowing against either a mouthpiece, a mouthpiece and a reed, or a double reed

Adagio: moderately slow speed

Allegro: fast speed

Andante: medium (walking) speed

Articulation: how sounds begin and end when they are performed

Baritone (Bar.): the male voice between tenor and bass

Beat: the steady pulse that underlies most music

Brass Family: instruments made of brass or other metal whose sound is produced by vibrations resulting from air blowing into a mouthpiece; includes the trumpet, French horn, trombone, and tuba

Central Pitch: scale step 1

Changing Voice (C.V.): the transitional stage of the male voice

Chord: three or more pitches occurring at the same time

Chordophone: an instrument whose sound is produced by the vibration of stretched strings

D.C. (Da Capo): a direction to go back to the beginning of a piece of music

Descant: a harmony part that is played or sung at a higher pitch than the melody

Dynamics: the degrees of loudness and softness in music

Fermata: a sign indicating that a note is to be held longer than its written value

Fine: the end

Flat: a sign (♭) that indicates the pitch is to be lowered a half step

Form: the shape of an entire piece of music in which individual sections may be the same, similar, or different

Forte (*f*): loud

Fortissimo (*ff*): very loud

Gamelan: a general term for an Indonesian orchestra

Harmony: a series of chords in a given piece of music

Homophony: music in which a melody is accompanied by other voices; these voices generally move in the same rhythm

Idiophone: an instrument whose sound is produced by the vibration of a solid material; the sound is initiated by striking, scraping, or rattling

Interlude: a section of a musical work that is inserted between two larger sections

Introduction: a section of music that comes before the main part of the composition

Jazz: a style of American music developed from ragtime and blues

Key signature: the sharps or flats at the beginning of each staff that indicate the key of a composition

Largo: very slow speed

Legato: a smooth, connected articulation

Marcato: a heavy, deliberate articulation

Melody: a series of tones arranged rhythmically to create a musical line

Membranophone: an instrument whose sound is produced by vibration of a stretched skin or membrane

Meter signature: the two numbers, one above the other, at the beginning of a composition; the upper number shows the number of beats per measure and the lower shows the value of the beat

Mezzo forte (*mf*): moderately loud

Mezzo piano (*mp*): moderately soft

Moderato: moderate speed

Movement: a complete and independent section of a musical composition

Note: a sign that shows the pitch and the length of a tone

Ostinato: a musical pattern or figure repeated over and over

Percussion Family: instruments played by striking or shaking; includes the xylophone, celesta, chimes, orchestra bells, timpani and other drums, gongs and cymbals, temple blocks, claves, tambourines, and maracas

Phrase: a grouping of notes that forms a musical sentence

Pianissimo (*pp*): very soft

Piano (*p*): soft

220

Pitch: the highness or lowness of a musical tone

Polyphony: music in which two or more independent melody lines occur at the same time

Presto: very fast speed

Rest: a sign that shows the length of a silence

Ritardando: a gradual slowing of the tempo

Scale: a series of tones arranged by pitch and separated by a specific ordering of whole steps and half steps

Sharp: a sign (♯) that indicates the pitch is to be raised a half step

Skiffle band: an informal musical group that performs on homemade and store-bought instruments

Staccato: a short, separated articulation

Staff: the five horizontal lines and four spaces on which notes are placed to indicate pitch

String Family: instruments played by plucking or bowing strings; includes the violin, viola, cello, and double bass

Symphony: a piece of music, typically of three or four movements, usually performed by an orchestra

Syncopation: a shift of accent from the strong beat to the weak beat in music

Synthesizer: an electronic instrument used to produce and organize musical sounds

Tablature: a system of musical notation that indicates the string, fret, or fingers to be used instead of the pitches on the staff

Tempo: the speed at which the beat moves in music

Theme: a melody or phrase used as a basic building block for a musical composition

Tie: a sign used to join two or more notes of the same pitch; they become a single note equal to the length of both notes

Timbre: the quality or color of a tone

Tonal center: usually the central pitch in a given key

Treble (Tr.): the highest voice in a choral composition

Variation: a musical idea that is repeated with some change

Woodwind Family: instruments usually made of wood or metal on which sound is produced by vibrations resulting from air blowing into or across a mouthpiece or reed; includes the flute, oboe, clarinet, and bassoon

Acknowledgments

Grateful acknowledgment is made to the following copyright owners and agents for their permission to reprint the following copyrighted material. Every effort has been made to locate all copyright owners; any errors or omissions in copyright notice are inadvertent and will be corrected as they are discovered.

"Alla en el rancho grande," English words by Bartley Costello, music by Silvano R. Ramos. Copyright © 1935 by Edward B. Marks Music Company. Copyright Renewed. International Copyright Secured ALL RIGHTS RESERVED. Reprinted by permission of Hal Leonard Publishing Corporation. Recording licensed through the Harry Fox Agency.

"America," from "West Side Story," music by Leonard Bernstein, lyrics by Stephen Sondheim. Copyright © 1957 by Leonard Bernstein and Stephen Sondheim. Copyright Renewed. International Copyright Secured. All Rights Reserved. Reprinted by permission of Hal Leonard Publishing Corporation. Recording licensed through the Harry Fox Agency.

The Armour Hot Dog Song," copyright © 1968 by Armour and Company, Omaha, NB. Reprinted and recorded by permission.

"As Tears Go By," words and music by Mick Jagger, Keith Richard and Andrew Loog Oldham. © Copyright 1961 Forward Music Ltd., London, England. TRO—Essex Music, Inc., New York, controls all publication rights for the USA and Canada. Reprinted by Permission. Recording rights licensed through the Harry Fox Agency.

"Baby, Please Don't Go," words and music by Big Bill Broonzy, from Jerry Silverman's Folk Song Encyclopedia, Volume 2, edited and designed by Beverly Tillett. Copyright © 1975 by Chappell & Co., Inc. International Copyright Secured. ALL RIGHTS RESERVED. Reprinted by permission of Hal Leonard Publishing Corporation. Recording licensed through the Harry Fox Agency.

"The Bagpiper's Carol," words adapted and arranged by Hartley Snyder. From Birchard Music Series 7. Copyright © 1959 Birch Tree Group Ltd. All rights reserved. Reprinted by permission. Recording licensed through the Harry Fox Agency.

"Bamboo," by Dave Van Ronk. Copyright © 1962 WARNER BROS. INC. All Rights Reserved. Reprinted by Permission. Recording licensed through the Harry Fox Agency.

"Bell Gloria," music by Buryl Red. Copyright © 1970 by Generic Music. Reprinted and recorded by permission.

"Bo Diddley," words and music by Ellas McDaniel. Copyright © 1955 (Renewed) by Arc Music Corp. All Rights Reserved. Reprinted by Permission of The Goodman Group, Music Publishers. Recording licensed through the Harry Fox Agency.

"Bo Weevil," words and music by Antoine Domino and Dave Bartholomew. Copyright © 1956 by UNART MUSIC CORPORATION. Reprinted by permission of Columbia Pictures Publications. Recording licensed through the Harry Fox Agency.

"Bourree for Bach," by J.S. Bach, Transcribed by Bennett Williams. Copyright © 1965 by Sam Fox Publishing Company, Inc., New York, NY. This arrangement Copyright 1987 by Sam Fox Publishing Company, Inc., Santa Maria, CA. Reprinted and recorded by Holt Rinehart Winston, Publishers by permission. Made in USA. International Copyright secured. All Rights Reserved.

"Brethren in Peace Together," from We Sing of Life. Permission to reprint and record was granted by the American Ethical Union. Copyright 1955: The American Ethical Union Library Catalog number 54:11625.

"The Cruel War," by Paul Stookey and Peter Yarrow. Copyright © 1962 PEPAMAR MUSIC CORP. All Rights Reserved. Reprinted by permission of Warner Bros. Music. Recording licensed through the Harry Fox Agency.

221

7. and 185. I Write the Songs

Words and Music by Bruce Johnston
Arranged by Buryl Red

I've been a - live for - ev - er,___ and I wrote the ver - y first song.___

I put the words and the mel - o - dies to - geth - er, I am

mu - sic, and I write the songs.___

I write the songs___ that make the

whole world sing; I write the songs— of love and spe - cial things.—

I write the songs— that make the young girls cry;—

I write the songs,— I write the songs.—

I am mu - sic, and I write the songs.—

6. Ring, Ring the Banjo

Traditional

1. The time is nev-er drear-y   if a fel-low nev-er groans.   The
2. Oh nev-er count the bub-bles   while there's wa-ter in the spring.   A

la-dies nev-er wear-y   with the rat-tle of the bones.
fel-low has no trou-bles   when he's got this song to sing.

1. Ring, ring the ban-jo.   I like that good old song.

2. Ring, ring ban - jo,   I like that good old song. So won't you

8. Lonesome Traveler

Words and Music by Lee Hays

1. I am a lone - ly and a lone - some trav - el - er;
2. I trav - eled here and then I trav - eled yon - der, well;
3. One of these days I'm gon - na stop all my trav - el - in';
4. Gon-na keep on a-trav' - lin' on the road to free - dom;

I've been a trav - el - in' on.___
I've been a trav - el - in' on.___
I've been a trav - el - in' on.___
keep right on a trav - el - in' home.___

10. Bo Diddley

Words and Music by Ellas McDaniel

Bo Did-dley-'ll buy Ba-by a dia-mond ring.

If that dia-mond ring don't shine,___
If that pri-vate eye can't see,___

He's gon-na take it to a pri-vate eye.
He bet-ter not ___ take that ring from me.

Bo Did-dl-ey caught a nan-ny goat ___
Bo Did-dl-ey caught a bear ___ cat ___

To make his pret-ty ba-by a Sun-day coat.____
To make his pret-ty ba-by a Sun-day hat.____

Won't you come to my house and rack that bone?____
Look at that____ Bo-do. Oh where's he been?____

Take my ba - by all the way from home.
Up to your___ house and gone a - gain.

Bo Did-dl-ey, Bo Did-dl-ey have you heard?

My___ pret-ty ba-by said she was a bird.

Repeat and fade

12. I Walk the Line

Words and Music by Johnny Cash

I keep a close watch on this heart of mine. I keep my

eyes wide o-pen all the time. I keep the ends out for the tie that

binds. Be-cause you're mine, I walk the line.

I find it ver-y, ver-y eas-y to be true. I find my-

self a - lone when each day is through. Yes, I'll ad - mit that I'm a fool for

you. Be - cause you're mine, Be - cause you're mine.

As sure as night is dark and day is light. I keep you

on my mind both day and night; And hap - pi - ness I've known proves that it's

I keep a close watch on this heart of mine! I keep my eyes wide o-pen all the time. I keep the ends out for the tie that binds. Be-cause you're mine, I walk the line.

13. and 186. Ease on Down the Road

from *The Wiz*

Words and Music by Charlie Smalls
Arranged by Buryl Red

Lyrics:

Come on,

ease on down, ease on down the road. _____ Come on,

ease on down, ease on down the road._____ Don't you

car - ry noth - in' that might be a load.___ Come on,

1. *Last time, repeat and fade*

ease on down, ease on down the road._____ Come on,

238

road   that   you choose   and   don't   give   up   walk - in' 'cause you
long   some - time,   but   just   keep   on   step - in' and you'll

1. gave up__ shoes.__ 2. Pick your

2. be just__ fine.__

Refrain
C.V. only *D. S.*

Come on,

14. and 154. Mama Don't 'Low

Traditional

1. Ma - ma don't 'low   no   gui - tar   pick - in' 'round   here. _____
2. Ma - ma don't 'low   no   ban - jo   play - in' 'round   here. _____
3. Ma - ma don't 'low   no   mid - night   ram - blin' 'round   here. _____

Ma - ma don't 'low   no   gui - tar   pick - in' 'round   here. _____
Ma - ma don't 'low   no   ban - jo   play - in' 'round   here. _____
Ma - ma don't 'low   no   mid - night   ram - blin' 'round   here. _____

I   don't care what   Ma - ma don't 'low;   Gon - na   pick   my   gui - tar   an - y - how.
I   don't care what   Ma - ma don't 'low;   Gon - na   play   my   ban - jo   an - y - how.
I   don't care what   Ma - ma don't 'low;   Gon - na   ram - ble   at   mid - night   an - y - how.

Ma - ma don't 'low   no   gui - tar   pick - in' 'round   here. _____
Ma - ma don't 'low   no   ban - jo   play - in' 'round   here. _____
Ma - ma don't 'low   no   mid - night   ram - blin' 'round   here. _____

240

16. Know Where I'm Goin'

Irish Folk Song

1. I know where I'm go-in', and I know who'll go with me.
2. I have stock-ings of silk____ and shoes of fine green leath-er,
3. Feath-er beds are soft,____ And paint-ed rooms are bon-ny; But
4. Some____ say he's dark,____ But I_____ say he's bon-ny;

I know who I love, but who knows who I'll mar-ry.
Combs to buck-le my hair, a ring for ev-ery fin-ger.
I would trade them all For hand-some, win-some John-ny.
Fair-est of them all Is hand-some, win-some John-ny.

17. Memphis, Tennessee

Words and Music by Chuck Berry

Long dis - tance in - for - ma - tion, give me Mem - phis, Ten - nes - see;
Help me, in - for - ma - tion, get in touch with my Ma - rie;

Help me find the par - ty try-ing to get in touch with me. She
She's the on - ly one who'd phone me here from Mem - phis, Ten - nes - see. Her

could not leave her num - ber, but I know who placed the call 'cause my
home is on the south___ side,___ high up on a ridge,

un - cle took the mes - sage, and he wrote it on the wall.
just a half a mile___ from the Mis - sis - sip - pi Bridge.

18. You Are My Sunshine

Words and Music by Davis and Mitchell

You are my sun - shine, ___ my on - ly sun - shine; ___ You make me hap - py ___ when skies are gray; _____ You'll nev - er know, dear, ___ how much I love you. ___ Please don't take my sun - shine a - way. _____

18. As Tears Go By

Words and Music by Mick Jagger,
Keith Richard, and Andrew Loog Oldham

1. It is the eve-ning of the day;_____
2. My rich-es can't buy ev-ery-thing;_____

I sit and watch the chil-dren play._____
I want to hear the chil-dren sing._____

Smil-ing fac-es I can see,_____ but not for
All I hear_____ is the sound_____

me._____ I sit and watch as tears go

by._____ of rain__ fall -ing

on the ground.__ I sit and watch as tears go

by._____ 3. It is the eve - ning of the

day;_____ I sit and watch the chil - dren

play.＿＿＿＿＿＿＿＿＿＿ Do - in' things I

used to do＿ they think are new.＿＿＿＿

I sit and watch as tears go by.＿＿＿＿

Mm＿＿＿＿＿＿＿＿

20. A Place in the Sun

Lyrics by Ronald Miller

Music by Brian Wells

249

21. Ramblin' Boy

Words and Music by Tom Paxton

1. He was a man_____ and a friend al - ways._____ He stuck with
2. In Tul-sa town_____ we__ chanced to stray._____ We thought we'd
3. Late__ one night_____ in a jun-gle camp,_____ The weath-er
4. He left me here_____ to__ ram-ble on._____ My ram-blin'

me_____ in the hard old days._____ He nev-er cared_____ if I had no
try_____ to__ work one day._____ The boss said he_____ had__room for
it_____ was__cold and damp._____ He got the chills,_____ and he got 'em
pal_____ is__dead and gone._____ If when we die_____ we__ go some-

dough._____ We ram-bled 'round_____ in the rain and snow.
one._____ Says my old pal,_____ "We'd__ rath-er bum."
bad._____ They took the on - ly__ friend I had.
where._____ I'll bet you a dol - lar he's a-ram-blin' there.

Refrain

And here's to you＿＿＿＿ my ram - blin' boy;＿＿＿＿ May all your

ram ＿ blin' bring you joy. And here's to you＿＿＿＿ my ram - blin'

boy; **May** all your ram ＿ blin' bring you joy.

22. Leaving of Liverpool

Words and Music by Will Schmid

fare thee well, my own true love, And when I re-turn, u-ni-ted we will be. It's not the leav-ing of Liv-er-pool that's griev-ing me, But my dar-ling, when I think of thee.

26. and 188. Delta Dawn

Words and Music by Alex Harvey
and Larry Collins

Arranged by Lowell Rogers

Del - ta___ Dawn, what's that flow - er you have on? Could it be___

Del - ta Dawn, what's that flow - er you have on? Could it be___

Del - ta Dawn, what's that flow - er you have on? Could it be___

Del - ta Dawn, what's that flow - er you have on? Could it be___

254

a fad - ed rose from days gone by?   And

a fad - ed rose from days gone by?   And

a fad - ed rose from days gone by?   And

a fad - ed rose from days gone by?   And

33. You Just Can't Make It by Yourself

Words and Music by Barbara Dane

No, you just can't make it by your-self.

No, you just can't make it by your-self._____ Fa-ther,

moth-er, sis-ter, broth-er, you know you're go-in' to need each oth-er.

30. Fiddler on the Roof

Words and Music by Jerry Bock
and Sheldon Harnick

1. A - way a - bove my head   I   see the strang - est sight,   A
   un - ex - pec - ted breeze   could blow him to the   ground;   Yet

fid - dler on the roof,   who's up there day and night.   He
af - ter ev - ery storm,   I   see he's still a - round.   What-

fid - dles when it rains;   He fid - dles when it snows.   I've
ev - er each day brings,   This odd, out - land - ish man;   He

nev - er seen him rest,   Yet on and on he goes.
plays his sim - ple tune,   As sweet - ly as he can.

34. Bamboo

Words and Music by David Van Ronk

260

36. Brethren in Peace Together

Paraphrase of Psalm 133:1

Jewish Folk Song

38. Goin' Down to Town

American Folk Song

1. I used to have an old gray horse; He weighed ten thou - sand
2. That horse he had a hol - ler tooth; He could eat ten bush-els of

pounds.   Ev - ery tooth in his head was
corn.   Ev - ery time he o - pened his mouth, Two

eight - een in - ches a - round.
bush-els and a half were gone.

Chorus

I'm go - in' down to

town;   I'm go - in' down to town;   I'm go - in' down to

Lynch - burg town, To car - ry my to - bac - co down.

*Where there are two parts in the R.H., the upper part matches the melody in the pupil's book.

264

42. Sixty-Six Highway Blues

Words and Music by Pete Seeger,
Woody Guthrie, and Jerry Silverman

1. There is a road from the coast to the coast,
been to the East and I've been to the West,
look - in' for the wo - man that'd love me the best,
try - in' to make an hon - est dol - lar a day,
ain't got no home in this world an - y - more,

New York to Los An - ge - les. I'm a go-in' down that

road with wor-ries on my mind; I've got those Six - ty - six high - way

blues.

blues.

2. I've
3. I've been
4. Been
5. I

44. America

from *West Side Story*
Lyrics by Stephen Sondheim

Music by Leonard Bernstein

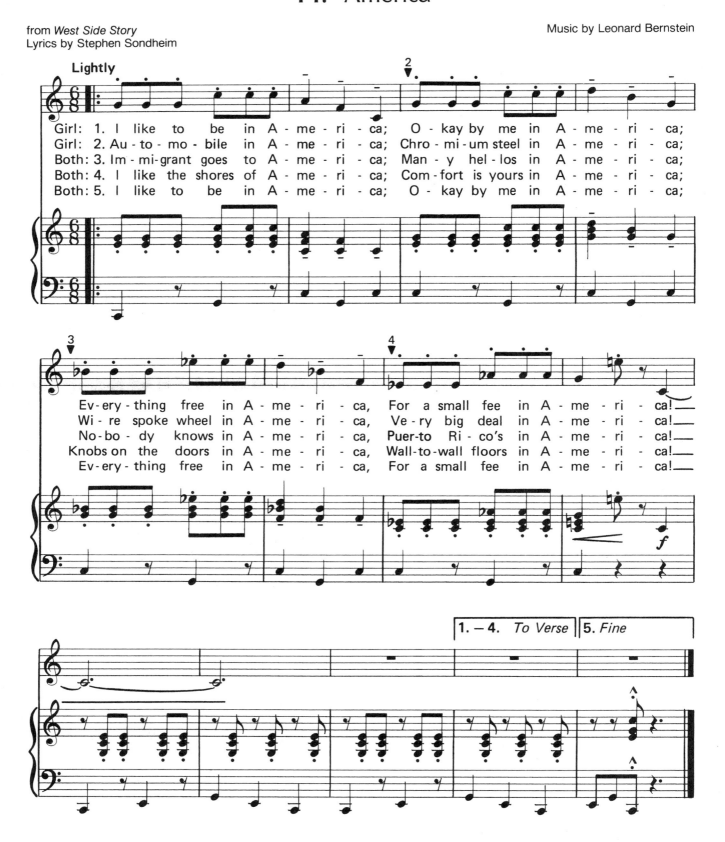

Girl: 1. I like the ci-ty of San Juan.__ Boy: I know a boat you can
Girl: 2. I'll drive a Bu-ick through San Juan.__ Boy: If there's a road you can
Girl: 3. When I will go back to San Juan,__ Boy: When you will shut up and
Girl: 4. I'll bring a T – V to San Juan.__ Boy: If there's a cur-rent to

get on.___ Girl: Hund-reds of flow-ers in
drive on.___ Girl: I'll give my cous-ins a
get gone?__ Girl: I'll give them new wash-ing
turn on.____ Girl: Ev - ery-one there will give

full bloom.__ Boy: Hund-reds of peo-ple in each room!__
free ride.__ Boy: How you fit all of them in - side?__
ma - chine.__ Boy: What have they got there to keep clean?__
big cheer.__ Boy: Ev - ery-one there will have moved here!__

47. Jacob's Ladder

American Folk Song

We are_ climb-ing_ Ja-cob's_ lad-der;_ We are_
climb-ing_ Ja-cob's_ lad-der;_ We are_ climb-ing_
Ja-cob's_ lad-der;_ Bro-thers_ in our_ land.

48. The Cruel War

Words and Music by Paul Stookey
and Peter Yarrow

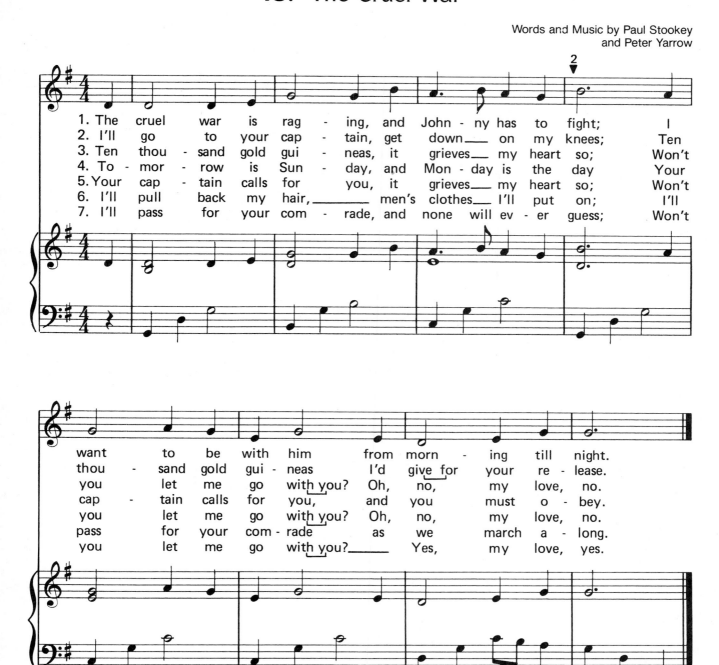

1. The cruel war is rag - ing, and John - ny has to fight; I want to be with him from morn - ing till night.
2. I'll go to your cap - tain, get down on my knees; Ten thou - sand gold gui - neas I'd give for your re - lease.
3. Ten thou - sand gold gui - neas, it grieves my heart so; Won't you let me go with you? Oh, no, my love, no.
4. To - mor - row is Sun - day, and Mon - day is the day Your cap - tain calls for you, and you must o - bey.
5. Your cap - tain calls for you, it grieves my heart so; Won't you let me go with you? Oh, no, my love, no.
6. I'll pull back my hair, men's clothes I'll put on; I'll pass for your com - rade as we march a - long.
7. I'll pass for your com - rade, and none will ev - er guess; Won't you let me go with you? Yes, my love, yes.

49. Get Thy Bearings

Words and Music by Donovan Leitch

1. Get your bear-ings,   know your time,__   Don't you wor-ry,
2. Get to-geth-er,   work it out,__   Sim - pli - ci - ty

weath-er's fine.__
is what it's   a-bout.__   (1. & 2.) All the world knows   what I'm say-ing;

All the world knows   what I'm say-ing;   The world knows fine well.

50. Oh Be Joyful

from *Gaudeamus Hodie (Let Us Rejoice Today)*

Words and Music by Natalie Sleeth

52. It's a Long Road to Freedom

Words and Music by Sr. Miriam Therese Winter, SCMM

It's a long___ road to free - dom, a - wind - ing steep and high. But when you walk in love with the moon on your wing and cov - er the earth with the songs you sing, the miles fly by.___

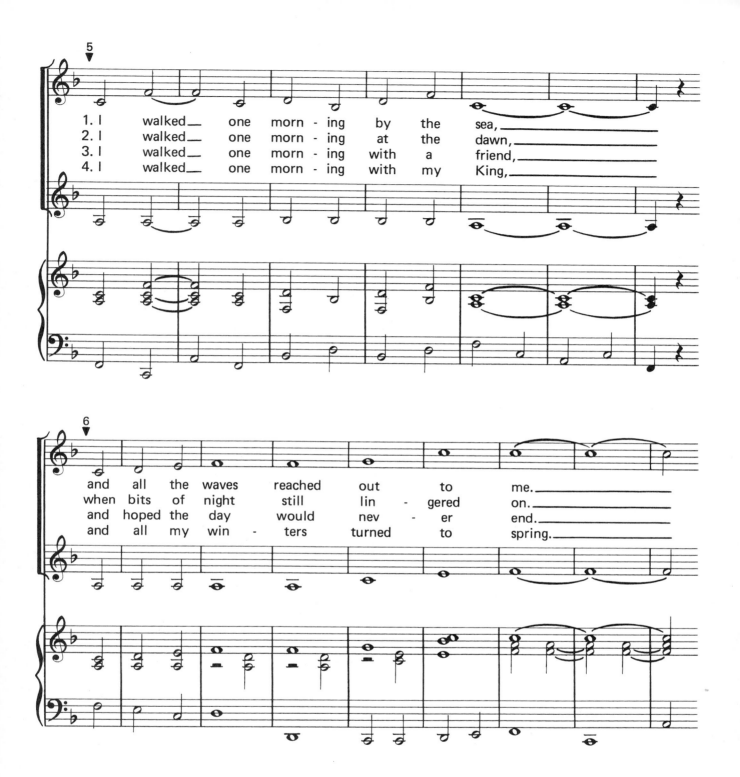

1. I walked___ one morn - ing by the sea,___
2. I walked___ one morn - ing at the dawn,___
3. I walked___ one morn - ing with a friend,___
4. I walked___ one morn - ing with my King,___

and all the waves reached out to me.___
when bits of night still lin - gered on.___
and hoped the day would nev - er end.___
and all my win - ters turned to spring.___

54. and 206. Five Hundred Miles

Words and Music by Hedy West
Arranged by Buryl Red

miles, a hun-dred miles, a hun-dred miles, a hun-dred miles, you can

miles, a hun-dred miles, a hun-dred miles, a hun-dred miles,

2nd time to Coda ⊕ 7   Verse

{ hear the whis-tle blow____ a hun-dred miles.____
{ Blow, whis-tle blow,   whis-tle blow._ }

Blow, whis-tle blow,____   whis-tle blow._ 2. Lord, I'm

mp

home, a-way from home, a-way from home, a-way from home,   Lord, I'm

home, a-way from home, a-way from home, a-way from home,

D. S. al Coda
mf

five___ hun-dred miles_____ a-way from home._____
five hun-dred miles 'way from home.__   If you
five hun-dred miles_____ 'way from home.   If you

56. Kid Stuff

Arranged by Emily Bedient

Traditional Song

Have you ev - er seen a Las - sie, a

Chomp   chomp

Boom chick chick,   Boom chick chick,

Boom chick - a chick - a, Boom chick - a chick - a,

(For rehearsal only)

Las - sie, a Las - sie? Have you ev - er seen a

chomp   chomp   chomp

Boom chick chick, Boom chick chick, Boom chick chick,

Boom chick - a chick - a, Boom chick - a chick - a, Boom chick - a chick - a,

57. William Goat

Words Anonymous

American Folk Melody

Tr. II — Mar - y had a Will - iam Goat, Will - iam Goat, Will - iam Goat;

Tr. I — Nay nay nay nay nay nay nay nay

C. V. — Nay nay nay nay nay nay nay nay

Bar. — Nay nay nay nay nay nay nay nay

(For rehearsal only)

Mar - y had a Will - iam Goat and he was lined with zinc.____

nay   nay   nay   nay   nay   nay   nay.____

nay   nay   nay   nay   nay   nay   nay.____

nay   nay   nay   nay   nay   nay   nay.____

283

63. Dundai

Composer Unknown

Dun - dai, dun - dai, dun - dai, dun - dai. E - rets Yis - ra - ël b' -

Dun - dai, dun - dai,

li To - rah Hi k' - guf____ b' - li n' - sha - ma.

dun - dai, dun - dai, dun - dai, dun - dai, dun - dai - dai.

Dun - dai,   dun - dai, dun - dai, dun - dai - dai

dun - dai,   dun - dai, dun - dai   dun - dai - dai.   dun - dai - dai.

63. Follow the Drinkin' Gourd

Traditional Black-American Song

Fol-low___ the drink-in' gourd.___ Fol-low___ the drink-in' gourd,___ For the

Fol - low, Fol - low, Fol - low, Fol - low,

old man is a wait-in' for to car-ry you to free-dom; Fol-low the drink-in' gourd.

Fol - low, Fol - low, Fol-low the drink-in' gourd.

1. When the
2. Now the
3. Now the

286

sun comes up and the first quail calls;___ Fol - low the drink - in' gourd.___ The
riv - er bank'll make a **mighty good** road;___ The dead trees will **show you** the way.___
riv - er ends be - tween two hills;___ Fol - low the drink - in' gourd.___

old man is a wait-in' for to car-ry you to free-dom;
Left___ foot___ peg___ foot___ trav-el - in'___ on;___ Fol-low the drink-in' gourd.
There's an-oth-er riv-er on the oth - er___ side;___

Fol - low, Fol - low,

74. The Wreck of the Edmund Fitzgerald

Words and Music by Gordon Lightfoot

The leg-end lives on from the Chip-pe-wa on down of the big lake they called "Git-che Gu-mee." The
wind in the wires made a tat-tle-tale sound, and a wave___ broke o-ver the rail-ing. And
an-y-one know where the love___ of God goes when the waves turn the min-utes to hours?___ The

lake, it is said, nev-er___ gives up her dead when the skies of No-vem-ber turn gloom-y. With a
ev-ery man knew as the___ cap-tain did too 'twas the witch of No-vem-ber come steal-in'. The___
search-ers all say they'd have___ made White-fish Bay if they'd put fif-teen more miles be-hind 'er. They___

load of i-ron ore twen-ty-six thou-sand tons more than the Ed-mund Fitz-
dawn___ came late, and___ the break-fast had__ to wait when the Gales of No-
might have split up or___ they might have cap-sized; they__ may have broke

ger-ald weighed emp-ty,
vem-ber came slash-in'.
deep and took wat-er.

That
When
And

good ship and___ true was a bone to be___ chewed when the Gales of No-
af-ter-noon___ came, it was freez-in' rain___ in the face of a
all that re-mains is the fac-es and the names of the wives and the

vem-ber came ear-ly.___
hur-ri-cane west wind.___
sons and the daugh-ters.___

The
When
When

ship was the pride of the A-mer-i-can side___ com-ing
sup-per-time came, the old cook___ came on deck say-in',
Lake Hu-ron rolls,___ Su-pe-ri-or sings___ in the
mus-ty old hall in De-tro-it they prayed, in the

back from some mill in Wis - con - sin. As the
"Fel - las, it's too rough t' feed ya." At ___
rooms of her ice - wa - ter man - sion. Old ___
"Mar - i - time Sail - ors' Ca - the - dral." The ___

big freight - ers ___ go it was big - ger than most with a
sev - en P. ___ M. a main hatch - way caved in; he said,
Mich - i - gan ___ steams like a young man's ___ dreams; the
church bell chimed ___ 'til it rang twen - ty - nine times for each

crew and good cap - tain well sea - soned, con -
"Fel - las, it's been good t' know ya!" The
is - lands and bays are for sports - men. And
man on the Ed - mund Fitz - ger - ald. The

clud - ing some terms with a cou - ple of steel firms when they
cap - tain wired in he had wa - ter com - in' in, and the
far - ther be - low Lake On - tar - i - o ___ takes ___
leg - end lives on from the Chip - pe - wa on down of the

left ful - ly_____ load - ed for Cleve - land. And
good ship and_____ crew was in per - il. And
in what Lake___ E - rie can send her, and the
big lake they___ call "Git - che Gu - mee." "Su -

lat - er that night when the ship's bell rang,_____ could it
lat - er that night when 'is lights went out - ta sight came the
i - ron boats go as the mar - i - ners all know with the
pe - rior," they said, "nev - er gives up her dead when the

To Coda ⊕

be the north wind they'd been feel - in'?_____
wreck of the Ed - mund Fitz - ger - ald._____
Gales of No - vem - ber re - mem-bered._____
Gales of No - vem - ber come ear - ly!"_____

1. & 2. | **3.** *D. S. al Coda* | ⊕ *Coda*

The   In a
Does

76. Goin' Up Yonder

Words and Music by Walter Hawkins

1. If you wan-na know_____ where__ I'm__ go - ing,_____
2. I can take the pain,_____ the heart-aches they__ bring,_____

Where__ I'm__ go - ing_____ I'll soon be
The com - fort's there in know-ing_____ I'll soon be

soon._____ If an - y - bod - y asks you_____
gone._____ As God__ gives me grace,_____

goin' up yon - der___ to be with my Lord!___

80. Alla en el Rancho Grande

Translated by Bartley Costello

Music by Silvano R. Ramos

Refrain

1. I love to roam out yon - der, Out where the buf - f'lo wan - der,___
2. A - llá en el ran - cho gran - de, A - llá don - de vi - ví - a,___

___ Free as the eag - le fly - ing, I'm rop - ing and a -
___ Ha - bia u - na ran - che - ri - ta, Que a - le - gre me de -

ty - ing, I'm rop-ing and a - ty - ing.____ Give me my ranch
ci - a, Que a le - gre me de - ci - a.____ Te voy ha - cer

and my cat - tle,____ Far from the great cit - y's
tus cal - zo - nes,____ Co - mo los u - sal el ran -

rat - tle;____ Give me a big herd to bat - tle,____
che - ro;____ Te los co - mien - zo de la - na,

____ For I just love herd - ing cat - tle.____
____ Te los a - ca - bo de cue - ro.____

69. The Miracle

Words by William Shakespeare

Music by Malvina Reynolds

Oh, what a piece of work is man, How mar-vel-ous-ly wrought, The quick con-triv-ance of his hand, The won-der of his thought.

95. Shady Grove

American Folk Song

Refrain: Shad - y Grove, my lit - tle love,
1. Wish I was in Shad - y Grove,
2. Had a ban - jo made of gold,
3. When I was in Shad - y Grove,

Shad - y Grove, I say,
Sit-tin' in a rock - in' chair,
Ev - ery string would shine;
Heard them pret-ty birds sing;

Shad - y Grove,
And if those blues would
The on - ly song that
The next time I go to

my lit - tle love, Bound for Shad - y Grove.
both - er me, I'd rock a - way from there. *(to Refrain)*
it would play was Wish that gal was mine. *(to Refrain)*
Shad - y Grove, take a - long a dia - mond ring. *(to Refrain)*

106. Good News

Spiritual

* The Refrain can be found on page 106.

** The Verse can be found on page 108.

hind. There'll be peace and free-dom in this world, I know;

Peace and free-dom in this world, I know; Peace and free-dom in this

world, I know, and I don't want it to leave a-me be-hind.

125. Jungle

Words and Music by Jeff Lynne

Choo-ka choo-ka hoo la ley.___ Look-a look-a koo la ley.___ A

hun-dred an-i-mals were gath-ered 'round this night,___ mm___ hmm, mm___

hmm. And they were sing-in' out___ a love-ly song un-der the pale___ moon-light, mm___

hmm, mm___ hmm. I stood and stared___ for quite a while,___ then a

li-on sang___ to me and smiled: "Come and join us___ if you so de-sire."

Choo-ka choo-ka hoo la ley.____ Look-a look-a koo la ley.____

Choo-ka choo-ka hoo la ley.____

Look-a look-a koo la ley.____ I said, "Now please ex-plain the mean-ing

of this song you sing," mm__ hmm, mm__ hmm.

"Won-drous is our great blue ship that sails a-round__ the might-y sun and

joy to ev - ery - one that rides a - long."___

Choo-ka choo-ka hoo la ley.___ Look-a look-a koo la ley.___ (Do

you know the an - swer? Have you heard the word?)

Pret-ty soon___ I knew the tune___ and we sat and sang un-der the moon___ and the

jun - gle rang in joy - ful har - mo - ny.___

Fine

Interlude

D. S. and fade

129. Bile Them Cabbage Down

American Folk Song

Bile them cab-bage down, down, turn them hoe cakes 'round. The on-ly song that I could sing was bile them cab-bage down.

Went up on the moun-tain just to give my horn a blow,

Thought I heard my true love say, "Yon-der comes my beau."

131. Red River Valley

American Folk Song

1. From this val - ley, they say you are go - ing,_____ We will

Refrain: Come and sit by my side if you love me,_____ Do not

2. Won't you think of the val - ley you're leav - ing?_____ Oh, how

Spoons (rhythm throughout)

miss your bright eyes and sweet smile, For they say you are tak - ing the

has - ten to bid me a - dieu, But re - mem - ber the Red Riv - er

lone - ly, how sad it will be. Oh,___ think of the fond heart you're

sun - shine That bright - ens our path - way a - while._____

Val - ley And the girl that has loved you so true._____

break - ing And the grief you are giv - ing to me._____

132. Worried Man Blues

American Folk Song

It takes a wor - ried man to sing a wor - ried song. It
takes a wor - ried man to sing a wor - ried song. It
takes a wor - ried man to sing a wor - ried song. I'm wor - ried
now, _____ but I won't be wor - ried long.

135. Old Joe Clarke

American Folk Song

Verse

1. Old Joe Clarke he had a house, Fif - teen stor - ies high, And
2. Old Joe Clarke he had a mule, It's name was Mor - gan Brown, And
3. Old Joe had a yel - low cat, She'd nei - ther sing nor pray,
4. I went down to Old Joe's house, Nev - er been there be - fore,

ev - ery stor - y in that house Was filled with chick - en pie.
ev - ery tooth in that mule's head Was six - teen in - ches 'round.
Stuck her head in the but - ter - milk jar To work her sins a - way.
He slept on a feath - er bed And I slept on the floor.

Refrain

Fare ye well, Old Joe Clarke, Fare ye well, I say.

Fare ye well, Old Joe Clarke, I'm a - goin' a - way.

133. She Wore a Yellow Ribbon

Traditional

Moderately

'Round her neck she wore a yel - low rib - bon. She

wore it in the spring-time and in the month of May. And

if you asked her why the heck she wore it, she'd

say, "It's for my lov - er who is far, far a - way." Far a-

way, _____ far a - way, _____ She

wore it for her lov - er far a - way. _____

'Round her neck she wore a yel - low rib - bon. She

wore it for her lov - er who is far, far a - way.

136. The M.T.A. Song

Words and music by Jacqueline Steiner
and Bess Hawes

1. Well let me tell you of the sto - ry of the man named
2. hand - ed in his dime____ at the Ken-dall Square
3. Now____ all night long____ Char - lie rides through the
4. Char - lie's wife goes down____ to the Scol-lay Square

Char - lie, on a trag - ic and fate - ful day.____ He put
Sta - tion, and he changed for Ja - mai - ca Plain.____ When he
tun - nel say - ing, "What will be - come of me?____ How can
Sta - tion, ev - ery day____ at quar-ter past two.____ And

ten cents in his pock - et, kissed his wife and fam - 'ly, went to
got there the con - duc - tor told him one more nick - el, Char - lie
I af - ford to see my sis - ter in Chel - sea, or my
through the o - pen win - dow she hands Char-lie a sand - wich, as the

Refrain

ride on the M. T. A. Well, did he
could - n't get off that train. But did he
cous - in in Rox - bur - y?" But did he
train____ comes rum - blin' through. Well, did he

ev - er re - turn,___ No he nev - er re - turned___ And his

fate is still un - learned.___ He may ride for -

ev - er 'neath the streets of Bos - ton, He's the man who

1. – 3.

nev - er re - turned. 2. Char - lie

4.

turned.___

139. Sixteen Tons

Words and Music by Merle Travis

Some peo-ple say a man is made out of mud.__ A I
born__ one__ morn-in' when the sun did-n't shine.__

poor man's made out of mus-cle and blood, Mus-cle and blood and
picked up my shov-el and I walked to the mine. I load-ed six-teen tons of

skin and bones,__ A mind that's_ weak and a back that's strong. You load
num-ber nine coal,__ And the straw-boss_ said, "Well-a bless my soul." You load

314

six - teen tons, what do you get?__ An - oth - er day old - er and

deep - er in debt.__ Saint Pe - ter, don't you call me 'cause

I can't go,__ I owe__ my soul to the com - pa - ny store.__

1.

2.

I was

141. Baby, Please Don't Go

Words and Music by Big Bill Broonzy

Melody in pupil edition is an octave lower.

1. Ba - by, please don't go.
2. Ba - by, please don't go.

Ba - by, please don't go. _____ Ba - by, please don't
Ba - by, please don't go. _____ Ba - by, please don't

go back to New Or - leans, _____ You know it hurts _ me so. _____
go _____ and leave me here, _____ You know it's cold _ down here. _____

143. Alabama Bound

Traditional

(Leader) (Answer) 2 (Leader)

1. I'm Al - a - bam - a bound,__ I'm Al - a - bam - a bound,__ I'm Al - a -
2. Oh don't you leave me here,__ Oh don't you leave me here,__ Oh don't you
3. Oh, well your hair don't curl,__ And your__ eyes ain't blue,__ Oh, well your

(Answer) 3

bam - a bound,__ I'm Al - a - bam - a bound,__ And if the train don't stop and
leave me here,__ Oh don't you leave me here,__ But if you train must go __
hair don't curl,__ And your__ eyes ain't blue.__ Well if you don't want me, sweet

4 (Leader) (Answer)

turn a - round__ I'm Al - a - bam - a bound,__ I'm Al - a - bam - a bound.__
an - y - how,__ Don't let me see a tear.__ Don't let me see a tear.__
Pol - ly Ann,__ Well I__ don't want you.__ Well I__ don't want you.__

145. Clementine

Traditional

Slowly

In a cav - ern, in a can - yon, Ex - ca - vat - ing for a mine, Lived a

min - er for - ty nin - er And his daugh - ter Clem - en - tine. Oh my

dar - ling, oh my dar - ling, oh my dar - ling Clem - en - tine! You are

lost and gone for - ev - er, Dread - ful sor - ry Clem - en - tine!

150. Rocka My Soul

Traditional

Oh, a rock-a my soul__ in the bos-om of A - bra-ham, A

rock - a my soul__ in the bos-om of A - bra-ham, A

rock-a my soul__ in the bos-om of A - bra-ham; Oh rock-a my

soul. So high, you can't get o - ver it;

So low, you can't get un - der it; So wide, you

can't get a - round_ it; You must go in at the door.

153. Put Your Hand in the Hand

Words and Music by Gene MacLellan

Put your hand in the hand of the man who stilled_ the

wa - ter.____ Put your hand in the hand of the

man   who   calmed____   the   sea.   Take   a

look   at   your-self   and-a   you   can____   look   at   oth   -   ers____   dif-f'rent-

ly____   By   put-tin'   your   hand   in   the   hand   of   the

man   from-a   Gal   i   -   lee.____

146. Putting On the Style

Traditional

1. Young man in a car - riage, driv - ing like he's mad,
Refrain: Put - ting on the ag - o-ny, put - ting on the style,
2. Young wom-an just from col - lege makes a big dis - play,

With a pair of hors - es he's bor - rowed from his dad. He
That's what all the young folks are do - ing all the while. And
With a great big jaw - break which she can hard - ly say. It

cracks his whip so live - ly just to make the peo - ple smile. To
as I look a - round me I'm __ ver - y apt to smile, But
can't be found in Web - ster's and __ won't be for a while, But

But they know he's on - ly put-ting on __ the style.
see so man - y peo - ple put-ting on __ the style.
ev - ery - bod - y knows she's on - ly put-ting on __ the style.

322

151. He's Got the Whole World in His Hands

Spiritual

1. He's got the whole world___ in His hands,___ He's got the
2. He's got the wind and rain___ in His hands,___ He's got the
3. He's got both you and me___ in His hands,___ He's got both

whole world___ in His hands,___ He's got the whole world___
wind and rain___ in His hands,___ He's got the wind and rain___
you and me___ in His hands,___ He's got both you and me___

in His hands,___ He's got the whole world in His hands.___
in His hands,___ He's got the whole world in His hands.___
in His hands,___ He's got the whole world in His hands.___

147. Guantanamera

Words and Music by José Fernandez Dias

Moderato

Introduction not accounted for in Student's Book

Guan - ta - na - mer - a,   gua - ji - ra

Guan - ta - na - mer - a.   Guan - ta - na - mer - a,   gua - ji - ra

last time to

Guan - ta - na - mer - a.

1. Yo soy un hom - bre sin-ce - ro,   De don-de
2. Mi ver-so es de un ver-de cla-ro,   Y de un
3. Con los___ pob-res de la tie-rra,   Quie-ro yo

325

148. The 59th Street Bridge Song

Words and Music by Paul Simon

Slow down,— you move too fast,— You got to make the morn

-ing last.— Just kick-in' down the cob-ble - stones,—

look-in' for fun and feel - in' groov - y.———

Hel-lo lamp-post, what-cha know-in', I've come to watch your flow - ers grow - in'.

Ain't'cha got no rhymes___ for me? Doot-in' doo-doo, feel-in' groov - y.___

___ Got no deeds to do, no prom-i-ses to keep. I'm

dap-pled and drow-sy and read-y to sleep. Let the morn-ing-time drop all its

pet-als on me. Life, I love you, All is groov - y._____

156. On Top of Old Smoky

Kentucky Folk Song

156. I'm Going Down the Road

American Folk Song

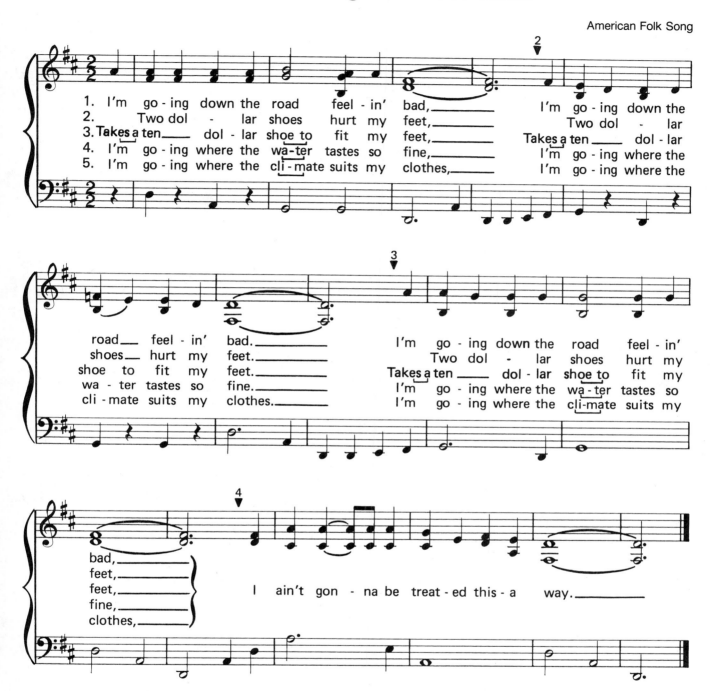

157. Deep Fork River Blues

Words and Music by Tom Paxton

1. Now the Deep Fork is a mud-dy
2. Now the Deep Fork is in Ok-la-
3. Well I don't have to stay a-way for-

riv - er near my home, near my
hom - a near my home, near my
ev - er I can go home, I can go

home.
home. Yes, the Deep Fork
home. Yes, the Deep Fork
No, I don't have

is   a   mud - dy   riv -   er_____   near   my
is   in   Ok - la - hom - a_____   near   my
to   stay a-way for - ev - er_____   I can   go

home,   near   my   home._____
home,   near   my   home._____
home,   I can   go   home._____

158. Hold the Wind

Collected by Alan Lomax

Collected adapted and arranged by John A. Lomax and Alan Lomax   Publisher:
Alan Lomax (BMI)

All   Leader

Hold   the wind, don't let it   blow,

I'm gon-na talk a-bout   you   on the
Three__ bright an-gels go__
Me and   my   God   gon-na
Tell um 'bout the world   I__

All

bend-in' of my   knees.__
ring__ them__ bells.__
do as we__ please.__
just__ come__ from.__

Hold   the wind, don't   let it   blow.

159. Bo Weevil

Words and Music by A. Domino
and D. Bartholomew

On Sat-ur-day night, where I was born,___ down on the farm,___ Gui - tar plink - ing and we start - ed sing - ing 'til the break of dawn. A - bout twelve o' - clock ev - ery - thing gets hot, up steps old Jones.___

We start-ed clap-pin' and he start-ed sing-in' a sweet lit-tle coun-try song. Bo Wee-vil, Bo Wee-vil,

where've you been all day?_____ Your mom-ma's been look-in',
where did you go and stay?_____ You'll_____ get a lick-in' as

has-n't stopped look-in' since you went a-way. Bo
sure as I'm sit-tin' on this bale of hay.

1.
2.

166. Oh, Lonesome Me

Words and Music by Don Gibson

Ev - ery - bod - y's go - in' out and hav - in' fun;_____ I'm
bad mis - take I'm mak - in' by just hang - in' 'round;_____ I

just a fool for stay - in' home and hav - in' none._____ I can't get o - ver
know that I should have some fun and paint the town._____ A love - sick fool that's

how she set me free,_____ Oh,_____ lone-some
blind and just can't see,_____ Oh,_____ lone-some

me._____ A me._____ I'll bet she's not like

me, she's out and fan-cy free, Flirt-ing with the boys with all her

charms._____ But I still love her so and, broth-er, don't you

know I'd wel-come her right back here in my arms._____ Well, there

must be some way I can lose these lone-some blues,_____ For-

get a-bout the past and find some-bod-y new._____ I've

thought of ev-ery-thing from A to Z,_____ Oh,____

____ lone-some me._____

170. Lord, Lord, I've Got Some Singing to Do

Words and Music by Robert Schertz

1. – 3. The Lord made all the world in just six days, __ And on the sev-enth day we

1. sing His praise. __
2. shout His praise. __
3. won-der at His ways. __

For land so green and sky so blue,

Lord, Lord, __ I've got some
{ sing - in' }
{ shout - in' }
{ won - derin' }
to do.

196. Go Down, Moses and
Joshua Fought the Battle of Jericho

Spirituals

Expressively
C.V.

mf

When Is - rael was in E - gypt's land, Let my peo-ple go, Op -

2

pressed so hard they could not stand, Let my peo-ple go.

3 Bar. *(an octave lower)*

f

Go down, Mo - ses, 'Way down in E - gypt's land,—

4

Tell__ old Pha - roah,_____ *pp* Let my peo - ple

344

Jer - i - cho,__ And the walls came tum - bling down.

could not stand, Let my peo - ple go.

C.V.

Josh-ua fought the bat - tle of Jer - i - cho,__ Jer - i - cho,__

Go down, Mo - ses, 'Way down in

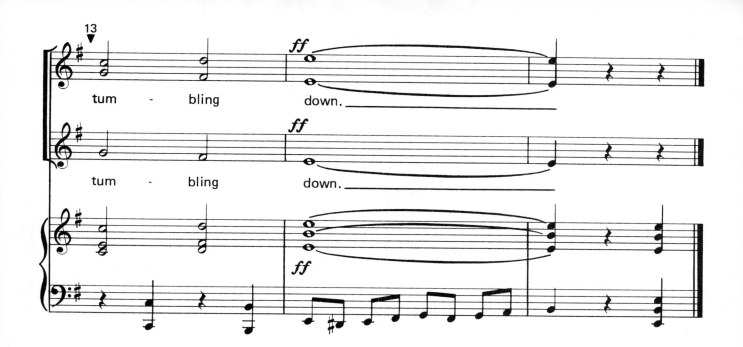

tum - bling   down._____

tum - bling   down._____

172. Song Sung Blue

Words and Music by Neil Diamond

Me and you___ are sub - ject to___ the
Fun - ny thing___ but you can sing___ it with a

(2nd verse)

blues now and then,___
cry in your voice,___

Tr. II and C. V.

but

when you take the blues and make a song,___ you sing them

out a - gain.___ (out a - gain.)___ Sing them

out a - gain.___ (out a - gain.)___

2. Tr. II and C.V.

(cry in your voice.)___ And be - fore you know it start to feel-in' good___

174. Getting to Know You

Lyrics by Oscar Hammerstein II

Music by Richard Rodgers

say. _____

Have-n't you no - ticed

So much now for Val-en-tine's Day, we'll just be friends, What da ya say?

Tr. I
Tr. II

sud-den-ly I'm bright and breez - y _____ Be - cause of

C. V.
Bar.
8va lower

sud-den-ly I'm bright and breez - y Well

all the beau-ti-ful and new things I'm learn-ing a-bout you,

All the new things I learn of you,

day by day.

Mon - day, Tues - day, Wednes-day, Thurs - day, Fri - day, Sat-ur-day, Sun - day.

177. There's a Meetin' Here Tonight

Words and Music by Bob Gibson

Brightly

There's a meet-in' here to - night, There's a meet-in' here to - night, I

know you by your friend-ly face, There's a meet-in' here to-night. There's a

meet-in' here to-night, There's a meet-in' here to-night, I

Fine

know you by your friend-ly face, There's a meet-in' here to-night.

5 *Verse*

There's a meet-in' here to-night, Good Lord, I'm glad you came a-long, I

D. C. al Fine

hope all my broth-ers and my sis-ters here will help me sing this song.

178. Encouragement

Arranged by Buryl Red

Words and Music by Jack Noble White

I will give it back to you.___ In ev-ery-thing that we do.___

1. When some-thing has___ you down and out,___
2. When some-thing seems___ to be too hard,___

don't give up hope,___ just stand and shout___ It can't keep you down___ 'cause
don't hang it up,___ just stay on guard___ I pro-mise it's true___ that

I will be a - round   with some en - cour - age - ment.
I will come to you   with some en - cour - age - ment.

In ev - ery-thing that we do,   In ev - ery-thing that we do,

From those who real - ly love you,   En - cour - age - ment__

is some-thing ev-ery-bod-y needs, en-cour-age-ment_ from those who love you. You

give it to me_ and I will give it back to you_

in ev-ery-thing that we do, En-cour-age-ment_ in ev-ery-thing that you do,

En - cour - age - ment __ from those who real - ly love you. En - cour - age - ment __

in all that we do! _____

182. Tie Me Kangaroo Down

Words and Music by Rolf Harris
Arranged by Buryl Red

194. The Bagpipers' Carol

Arranged by Hartley Snyder

Sicilian Carol

1. From dis-tant hills a-far____ they saw a shin-ing
2. From dis-tant hills to-day____ the shep-herd bag-pipes

Ding dong ding dong ding dong

star,____ To lead them to the in-fant child____ who
play.____ Through-out the neigh-b'ring, sleep-ing town____ mel-

ding dong ding dong ding dong

lay in sta - ble mild. With bag - pipes play - ing and sheep a -
o - dious songs re - sound. With bag - pipes play - ing and sheep a -

ding   dong   ding.

stray - ing, dron - ing and sing - ing their car - ols of old, _____ They
stray - ing, dron - ing and sing - ing the news of Christ's birth, _____ As

heard the an - gels' song _____ and came to kneel and
in the days _____ of yore, _____ they tell the tid - ings

An - gels' song! Kneel and
Told _____ of yore! Tell and the

wor - ship Him _____ As proph - e - cy fore - told.
once _____ a - gain, _____ Pro - claimed from heav'n to earth.

wor - ship as proph - e - cy fore - told.
tid - ings pro - claimed from heav'n to earth.

190. La Bamba

Mexican Folk Song

Very fast

¡Bam-ba, bam-ba!___ ¡A-rri-ba! ¡Pa-ra bai-lar la Bam-ba___ Pa-ra bai-lar la

¡Bam-ba, bam-ba!___ ¡Bam-ba, bam-ba!___ ¡Bam-ba, bam-ba!___

Bam-ba se ne-ce-si-tu a-na po-ca de gra-cia,___ u-na po-ca de

¡Bam-ba, bam-ba!___ ¡Bam-ba, bam-ba!___

ne - ro, por ti se - ré, por ti se - ré, por ti se - ré!　　　¡Bam - ba!_____

¡A - rri - ba, por ti se - ré, por ti se - ré!_____　¡Bam - ba!_____

192. The Home Road

Words and Music by John Alden Carpenter
Arranged by B.A.

1. Sing a hymn of free - dom, Fling the ban - ner
2. In the qui - et hours Of the star - ry

1. Sing a hymn of free - dom, Fling the ban - ner
2. In the qui - et hours Of the star - ry

high! Sing the songs of lib - er - ty,
night, Dream the dreams of far - a - way,

high! Sing the songs of lib - er - ty,
night, Dream the dreams of far - a - way,

199. The Woodchuck

Music by Pat Shaw

How much wood would a wood-chuck chuck if a wood-chuck could chuck wood? Oh, just as much wood as a wood-chuck could chuck if a wood-chuck could chuck wood. Now tell me...

203. Ging Gong Gooli

Folk Song from Guyana

380

200. Scarborough Fair

Arranged by Fred Bock

English Folk Song

mar - y, {and thyme;____ Re - mem-ber me to
{and thyme, rose - mar - y, and thyme;____

one who lives there,____ {For he once was a true love of

Are you go-in'___ to Scar-bor-ough Fair?_____ Pars-ley, sage, rose-

mar-y, and thyme;_____ Re-mem-ber

me to the one who lives there,⸺

For

he once was   a   true love of mine,⸺

For she once was   } a

210. Everything Is Beautiful

Arranged by Fred Bock

Words and Music by Ray Stevens

Ev-ery-thing is beau - ti - ful ____ in its own way, ____

Like a star-ry sum - mer night, or a snow-cov-ered win - ter's day. ____

214. Bourrée for Bach

from *English Suite No. 2*

Music by Johann Sebastian Bach
Arranged by Bennett Williams

218. Rain

Words by Loretta Spatz

Music by Ronald LoPresti

but   I   love   the   rain_____

but   I   love   the   rain_____

but   I   love   the   rain_____

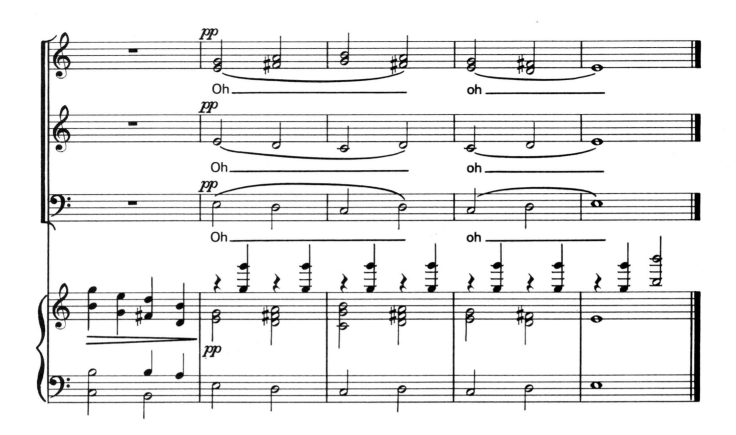

Arpeggio SEE *BROKEN CHORD*.

Arrangement The adaptation of an existing piece of music for another instrument or group of instruments.

Beat The basic unit of time in music, usually organized within a certain meter into groups of two or three. Also referred to as the underlying beat, or pulse.

Bluegrass A type of country music originating in the Appalachian mountains that features free improvisation and the use of acoustical string instruments (such as guitar, banjo, and fiddle).

Blues A style of popular music emerging from Afro-American work songs and spirituals in the first decade of the twentieth century. Usually follows a 12-bar chord progression.

Broken chord The pattern produced by the successive execution of the notes of a chord. Also referred to as an arpeggio.

Calypso style A type of music originating in Trinidad that usually employs vocal improvisation about current events. The music is highly syncopated and uses repetitious melodic patterns.

Cadence A melodic line or chord sequence moving to a point of rest.

Canon A textural device whereby two or more voices imitate the melody at different times, though not always at the same pitch or in the same rhythm.

Carol A traditional piece associated with the celebration of Christmas.

Chord root The note of a triad that dictates the remaining tones regardless of their relative position. Each of the seven scale degrees can function as the chord root.

Chord sequence A given succession of harmony in a piece of music.

Chord symbol The symbol giving the name of a chord and often its inversion (the relative position of the lowest note in that chord).

Country-Western A style of American popular music derived from the folk music of the southern states and western cowboys.

Diminuendo Getting softer (same as decrescendo).

Dixieland style A type of jazz originating in New Orleans featuring acoustical instruments in small ensembles.

Dominant-seventh chord The chord built on the fifth scale degree with an added seventh. In the key of C, the dominant-seventh chord would be spelled g–b–d–f.

Drone A deep, continuous sound often used as an accompaniment.

Gospel music A style of American music associated with evangelism and popular devotion. Includes elements of spiritual, jazz, and folk music.

Half step The smallest interval in traditional Western music. It is equivalent to the interval between any two adjacent keys on a keyboard.

Ikon A pictorial depiction of musical notation.

Imitation A repetition of all or part of the melody closely following its last statement.

Improvisation The spontaneous performance or creation of music, often with the aid of a preexisting harmonic structure.

Interval The distance between any two musical pitches.

Intonation The accurate relationship of pitches to each other.

Mode A specific arrangement of pitches to form a scale. Usually refers to the pitch systems of the medieval church.

Monophony A single, unaccompanied musical line.

Motive A recurrent figure or short phrase that is often developed or fragmented throughout the course of a musical composition.

Open strings The unstopped strings of any string instrument.

Orchestration The arrangement of a piece of music for an orchestra. Usually refers to instrumentation.

Ornament The embellishment of a note or musical line.

Parallel major or minor Refers to keys or scales with similar letter names. For example, the parallel major of C minor is C major, and the parallel minor of C major is C minor.

Passing tone A nonharmonic tone providing for ascending or descending stepwise motion between two chord tones.

Pizzicato A term indicating that the string (on a violin, viola, etc.) should be plucked instead of bowed.

Refrain A phrase or a group of phrases that occurs after each verse of a poem or song.

Relative major or minor Refers to keys or scales with corresponding key signatures. For example, the relative major of A minor is C major, and the relative minor of C major is A minor.

Rhythmic pulse The underlying beat in music.

Rondo form A classical form that includes two or more episodes (B and C) and a recurring refrain (A) so that the resulting scheme might be ABACA.

Scale An ascending or descending series of musical tones arranged in order of pitch according to a specified scheme. Because scales represent the basic tonal materials of music and so many different styles and periods of music exist, there are a very large number of scales. European music is based on the diatonic (major) scale, which is arranged c, d, e, f, g, a, b, c′ in the key of C major. Other important Western scales include the natural minor (c, d, e♭, f, g, a♭, b♭, c′); melodic minor (ascending: c, d, e♭, f, g, a, b, c′ and descending: c′, b♭, a♭, g, f, e♭, d, c); harmonic minor (c, d, e♭, f, g, a♭, b, c′); and whole tone (c, d, e, f♯, g♯, a♯, c′).

Scat singing A style of jazz singing with vocal syllables that often imitate instruments. Introduced by Louis Armstrong and Cab Calloway in the 1920s.

Score A notation illustrating the instruments or voices of an ensemble and their particular parts.

Semitones SEE *HALF STEP.*

Shuffle A rhythmic style that groups quarter notes into four groups of three, creating a $\frac{12}{8}$ feel.

Tessitura The normal range of a voice part.

Triad A three-note chord consisting of the root, third, and fifth. The four types of triads are major (consisting of a major and a minor third); minor (a minor and a major third); diminished (two minor thirds); and augmented (two major thirds). Consequently, the C major triad would be spelled c–e–g; C minor: c–e♭–g; C diminished: c–e♭–g♭; and C augmented: c–e–g♯.

Vibrato A slight trembling or fluctuation of the pitch produced by vocalists or instrumentalists to increase the expressiveness of the tone.

Walking bass A bass pattern, usually in $\frac{4}{4}$ meter, consisting primarily of stepwise motion.

Suggested Recordings for Student Listening

MEDIEVAL AND RENAISSANCE (c. 1000–1600)

ANTHOLOGIES

Vocal & and Instrumental:	*Music of the Gothic Era* (with illustrated 52-page book), Early Music Consort of London, David Munrow	*3 DG ARC-2710019 DG ARC-415292-2AH (excerpts)*
Plainchant:	*Gregorian Chant,* Deller Consort	*Harmoni Mundi 234*

COMPOSERS

Josquin Des Prez:	*Chansons of Josquin Des Prez,* Hilliard Ensemble	*Angel S-38040(D)*
Morley:	*Madrigals of Thomas Morley,* Deller Consort	*Vanguard HM-4*
Palestrina:	*Motets* (with Veni Spousa Christi — Mass, Motet, and Antiphon), St. Johns College Choir of Cambridge, Guest	*Argo ZK-69 PSI*

BAROQUE (1600–1750)

Bach:	*Six Brandenburg Concerti,* English Chamber Orchestra, Leppard	*2-Phil 6747166*
	Cantata 140, "Wachet auf" (with *Cantata 80, "Ein Feste Burg"*), Munich Bach Orchestra and Chorus, Richter	*DG ARC 2533495*
Corelli:	*Christmas Concerto* (with Op. 6, Nos. 5–7), La Petite Bande, Kujiken	*D Har Mon H-99613(Q)*
Handel:	*Water Music* (with *Music for the Royal Fireworks*), Academy of St. Martin's in the Fields, Marriner	*Argo ZRG-697*
Monteverdi:	*Incoronazione di Poppea,* Concentus Musicus, Harnoncourt	*5-Teldec 5635247 Teldec 641974 (excerpts)*
Purcell:	*King Arthur, Dido and Aeneas, Dioclesian, Fairy Queen, Abdelazer,* City of London Chamber Orchestra, McIntosh	*Vox C 9005(D)*
Scarlatti:	*Harpsichord Sonatas,* Kirkpatrick	*DG-ARC-2533072 (Vol. 1)*
Vivaldi:	*Concerto for Two Violins,* St. Paul Chamber Orchestra, Stern, Zuckerman	*CBS IM/MK 37278 (D)*

CLASSICAL (1750–1825)

Haydn:	*Symphony No. 104 in D* (with *Symphony No. 100*), New Philharmonia, Klemperer	*Angel AE-34464*
	String Quartets, Op. 77, Nos. 1 & 2, Guarneri Quartet	*AGL1—4898*
	Piano Trios 14 & 15, Beaux Arts Trio	*Phillips 9500034 PSI*
	Mass in Time of War, Academy of St. Martin's in the Fields, Marriner	*Argo ZRG 0 634 PSI*
Mozart:	*Symphony Nos. 40, 41, & 39,* Israel Philharmonic, Mehta	*Lon 410277-4*
	Magic Flute, K. 620, Vienna Philharmonic, Levine	*CRC4-4586 (D) ARC1-4621 (excerpts)*
	String Quartet in F, K. 590, No. 23 (with Nos. 17 & 19, and Beethoven: Nos. 2, 3, & 10), Budapest Quartet	*3 Odys Y3-35240*
	Piano Concerto No. 21 in C, K. 467, Cleveland Orchestra, Casadesus, Szell	*CBS MY-38523*
	Oboe Quartet, K. 370 (with J. C. Bach, Stamitz, & Vanhal Oboe Quartets), Still, Perlman, Zuckerman, Harrell	*Angel S-37756*
	Mass in C Minor, K. 427, Vienna Singverein, Berlin Philharmonic, Karajan	*DG 2532028 (D)*

ROMANTIC (1825–1900)

Beethoven:	*Symphony No. 5,* NBC Symphony Orchestra, Toscanini	*RCA-VICS-1648E*
	String Quartet Op. 59, No. 1 in F, "Rasumovsky" (with *Op. 59, Nos. 2 & 3; Ops. 74 & 95),* Guarneri Quartet	*4 RCA VCS 6415*
Berlioz:	*Symphonie Fantastique,* Boston Symphony Orchestra, Munch	*RCA-AGL1-5203*
Brahms:	*Clarinet Quintet in B Minor, Op. 115,* Leister, Vermeer Quartet	*S 068831*
	Symphony No. 3, Cleveland Orchestra, Szell	*CBS-MY-37777*
Mahler:	*Symphony No. 5* (with *Kindertotenlieder)* New York Philharmonic, Walter	*2 Odys 32260016 E*
Mendelssohn:	*Violin Concerto, Op. 64* (with Bruch: *Violin Concerto),* Perlman, Concertgebouw Orchestra, Haitink	*Angel DS 38150 (D)*
Schubert:	*Die Schöne Müllerin,* Fischer-Diskau, Gerald Moore	*DG 415186-2GH*
	Symphony No. 8, "Unfinished," Concertgebouw Orchestra, Haitink	*Phil. Seq. 412370-1PS*
Strauss:	*Don Quixote, Op. 35* (with Schönberg: *Cello Concerto),* Yo-yo Ma, Boston Symphony Orchestra, Ozawa,	*IM 39863 (D)*
Tchaikovsky:	*Symphony No. 5,* Cleveland Orchestra, Szell	*CBS MY 37767*
Verdi:	*La Traviata,* National Philharmonic, Bonynge	*Lon LDR 73002 (D)* *Lon LDR 71062 (D)* *(excerpts)*
Wagner:	*Tristan and Isolde,* Dresden State Opera, Kleiber	*5 DG 2741006 (D)*
	Die Meistersinger von Nürnburg (excerpts), New York Philharmonic, Bernstein	*CBS MS–7141*

TWENTIETH CENTURY (1900–PRESENT)

Armstrong:	*The Genius of Louis Armstrong* (Vol. 1)	*Col CG 30416*
Bartók:	*Concerto for Orchestra,* Chicago Symphony, Reiner	*RCA AGL1-2909*
	Music for Strings, Percussion, and Celesta (with Berio: *Sinfonia),* New York Philharmonic Orchestra, Bernstein	*CBS MP 38779*
Beatles, The:	*Sgt. Pepper's Lonely Hearts Club Band*	*Cap SMAS 02653*
Berg:	*Violin Concerto,* London Symphony Orchestra, Zuckerman, Boulez	*IM 39741*
Davis:	*Kind of Blue*	*PC 8163*
Debussy:	*Le Mer* (with Ravel: *Daphnis et Chloé & Pavane),* Cleveland Orchestra, Szell	*Odys YT 31928*
Dylan:	*Times They Are A-Changin'*	*Col PC 8905*
Ives:	*The Unanswered Question* (with *Central Park in the Dark),* New York Philharmonic, Bernstein	*MP 38777*
Schönberg:	*Serenade, Op. 24* (with "Song of the Wood Dove" from *Gurrelieder; Ode to Napoleon Bonaparte),* Ensemble InterContemporain, Boulez	*M-36735*
Stravinsky:	*The Rite of Spring,* London Symphony Orchestra, Bernstein	*CBS M-31520*
	Petrouchka (with *Firebird Suite),* New York Philharmonic, Bernstein	*CBS MY-37221*
Varèse:	*Poème Electronique* (with *Density 21.5, Hyperprism, Intégrales, Ionisation, Octandre),* Columbia Symphony, Craft	*MP 38873*
Webern:	*Complete Works* (Volume 1), Boulez (Op. 1–31)	*MA 35193*

Acknowledgments and Credits

ACKNOWLEDGMENTS

Grateful acknowledgment is made to the following copyright owners and agents for their permission to reprint the following copyrighted material. All effort has been made to locate all copyright owners; any errors or omissions in copyright notice are inadvertent and will be corrected as they are discovered.

"Alla en el rancho grande," English words by Bartley Costello, music by Silvano R. Ramos. Copyright © 1935 by Edward B. Marks Music Company. Copyright Renewed. International Copyright Secured ALL RIGHTS RESERVED Reprinted by permission of Hal Leonard Publishing Corporation. Recording licensed through the Harry Fox Agency.

"America," from *West Side Story*, music by Leonard Bernstein, lyrics by Stephen Sondheim. Copyright © 1957 by Leonard Bernstein and Stephen Sondheim. Copyright Renewed. International Copyright Secured. All Rights Reserved. Reprinted by permission of Hal Leonard Publishing Corporation. Recording licensed through the Harry Fox Agency.

"The Armour Hot Dog Song," copyright © 1968 by Armour and Company, Omaha, NB. Reprinted and recorded by permission.

"As Tears Go By," words and music by Mick Jagger, Keith Richards and Andrew Loog Oldham. © Copyright 1961 Forward Music Ltd., London, England. TRO—Essex Music, Inc., New York, controls all publication rights for the USA and Canada. Reprinted by Permission. Recording rights licensed through the Harry Fox Agency.

"Baby, Please Don't Go," words and music by Big Bill Broonzy. Copyright © 1975 by Chappell & Co., Inc. Reprinted in the United States and Canada by permission of Hal Leonard Publishing Corporation. Recording licensed through the Harry Fox Agency.

"The Bagpipers' Carol," words adapted and arranged by Hartley Snyder. From *Birchard Music Series 7*. Copyright © 1959 Birch Tree Group Ltd. All rights reserved. Reprinted by permission. Recording licensed through the Harry Fox Agency.

"Bamboo," by Dave Van Ronk. Copyright © 1962 WARNER BROS. INC. All Rights Reserved. Reprinted by Permission. Recording licensed through the Harry Fox Agency.

"Bell Gloria," music by Buryl Red. Copyright © 1970 by Generic Music. Reprinted and recorded by permission.

"Bo Diddley," words and music by Ellas McDaniel. Copyright © 1955 (Renewed) by Arc Music Corp. All Rights Reserved. Reprinted by Permission of The Goodman Group, Music Publishers. Recording licensed through the Harry Fox Agency.

"Bo Weevil," words and music by Antoine Domino and Dave Bartholomew. Copyright © 1956 by UNART MUSIC CORPORATION. Reprinted by permission of Columbia Pictures Publications. Recording licensed through the Harry Fox Agency.

"Bourrée for Bach," by J. S. Bach, Transcribed by Bennett Williams. Copyright © 1965 by Sam Fox Publishing Company, Inc., New York, NY. This arrangement Copyright 1987 by Sam Fox Publishing Company, Inc., Santa Maria, CA. Reprinted and recorded by Holt, Rinehart and Winston, Publishers by permission. Made in USA. International Copyright Secured. All Rights Reserved.

"Brethren in Peace Together," from *We Sing of Life*. Permission to reprint and record was granted by the American Ethical Union. Copyright 1955: The American Ethical Union Library Catalog number 54:11625.

"The Cruel War," by Paul Stookey and Peter Yarrow. Copyright © 1962 PEPAMAR MUSIC CORP. All Rights Reserved. Reprinted by permission of Warner Bros. Music. Recording licensed through the Harry Fox Agency.

"Deep Fork River Blues," by Tom Paxton. © Copyright 1962 Cherry Lane Music Publishing Co., Inc. This arrangement © Copyright 1987 Cherry Lane Music Publishing Co., Inc. International Copyright Secured. All Rights Reserved. Reprinted By Permission. Recording licensed through the Harry Fox Agency.

"Delta Dawn," words and music by Alex Harvey and Larry Collins, arranged by Lowell Rogers. Copyright © 1972 United Artists Music Co., Inc. and Big Ax Music. All rights administered by Columbia Pictures Publications. Reprinted by permission. Recording licensed through the Harry Fox Agency.

"Donkey Kong," music copyright by Nintendo, Inc. Reprinted and recorded by permission.

"Ease on Down the Road," words and music by Charlie Smalls. Copyright © 1974 WARNER-TAMERLANE PUBLISHING CORP. All Rights Reserved. Reprinted by permission of Warner Bros. Music. Recording licensed through the Harry Fox Agency.

"Encouragement," words and music by Jack Noble White, arranged by Buryl Red. Copyright © 1984 by Kesco Enterprises, Inc. Reprinted and recorded by permission.

"Everything Is Beautiful," words and music by Ray Stevens, arranged by Fred Bock. Copyright © 1970 by Ahab Music Company, Inc. Reprinted by Permission. Recording rights licensed through the Harry Fox Agency.

"Fiddler on the Roof," words by Sheldon Harnick, music by Jerry Bock. Copyright © 1964 by Alley Music Corporation and Trio Music Co., Inc. All rights administered by Hudson Bay Music, Inc. International Copyright Secured ALL RIGHTS RESERVED Reprinted by permission of Hal Leonard Publishing Corporation. Recording licensed through the Harry Fox Agency.

"The 59th Street Bridge Song (Feelin' Groovy)," Words and Music by Paul Simon. Copyright © 1966 Paul Simon. Used by permission. Recording rights licensed through the American Mechanical Rights Agency, Inc.

"Five Hundred Miles," words and music by Hedy West. Copyright © 1961 & 1962 by Friendship Music Corp. All rights controlled by Unichappell Music, Inc. (Rightsong Music, Publisher). International Copyright Secured. ALL RIGHTS RESERVED. Reprinted by permission of Hal Leonard Publishing Corporation. Recording licensed through the Harry Fox Agency.

"Get Thy Bearings," WORDS AND MUSIC BY DONOVAN (MUSIC) LTD. SOLE SELLING AGENT PEER INTERNATIONAL CORPORATION. COPYRIGHT © 1968 by Donovan (Music) Ltd. Sole Selling Agent Peer International Corporation. Reprinted by permission of Columbia Pictures Publications. Recording licensed through the Harry Fox Agency.

"Getting to Know You," words by Oscar Hammerstein II, music by Richard Rodgers. Copyright © 1951 by Richard Rodgers and Oscar Hammerstein II. Copyright Renewed. Williamson Music Co., owner of publication and allied rights throughout the Western Hemisphere and Japan. All Rights Administered by Chappell & Co., Inc. International Copyright Secured ALL RIGHTS RESERVED Reprinted by Permission of Hal Leonard Publishing Corporation. Recording licensed through the Harry Fox Agency.

"Go Down, Moses and Joshua Fought the Battle of Jericho," from *More Partner Songs* selected and arranged by Frederick Beckman, © Copyright, 1962, by Silver, Burdett & Ginn, Inc. Reprinted and recorded with permission.

"Goin' Down to Town," copyright © 1975 by Chappell Music Co. International Copyright Secured. All Rights Reserved. Reprinted by permission of Hal Leonard Publishing Corporation. Recording licensed through the Harry Fox Agency.

"Goin' to a Place," by Walter Hawkins, © Copyright 1981 by LIBRIS MUSIC/HAWKINS MUSIC, BMI. All rights reserved. International copyright secured. Used by permission.

"Guantanamera," original music and lyrics by José Fernandez Dias, music adapted by Peter Seeger, lyrics adapted by Hector Angulo, based on a poem by José Martí. © Copyright 1963, 1965 by FALL RIVER MUSIC INC. All Rights Reserved. Used by Permission. Recording licensed through the Harry Fox Agency.

"Hold the Wind," Collected, adapted and arranged by John A. Lomax and Alan Lomax. Publisher: Alan Lomax (BMI). Reprinted and recorded by permission.

"There's a Meetin' Here Tonight," new words and new music adaptation by Bob Gibson. TRO—© Copyright 1960 and 1964 Melody Trails, Inc., New York, NY. Reprinted by Permission. Recording rights licensed through the Harry Fox Agency.

"Tie Me Kangaroo Down, Sport," words and music by Rolf Harris. © 1960 by Castle Music Pty., Ltd. All Rights for the US and Canada controlled by Beechwood Music Corp., 6920 Sunset Blvd., Hollywood, CA 90028. All Rights Reserved. Reprinted by Permission of Warner Bros. Music. Recording licensed through the Harry Fox Agency.

"The Wreck of the Edmund Fitzgerald," words and music by Gordon Lightfoot. Copyright © 1976 by Moose Music Ltd. (CAPAC). Reprinted and recorded by permission.

"You Are My Sunshine," WORDS AND MUSIC BY JIMMIE DAVIS AND CHARLES MITCHELL. COPYRIGHT © 1940 PEER INTERNATIONAL CORPORATION. COPYRIGHT renewed by Peer International Corporation. Reprinted by permission of Columbia Pictures Publications. Recording licensed through the Harry Fox Agency.

"You Just Can't Make It by Yourself," words and music by Barbara Dane. © Copyright 1964 by Stormking Music Inc. All Rights Reserved. Reprinted and recorded by permission.

"Zenizenabo," from *The World of African Song* by Miriam Makeba, copyright © 1971 by Quadrangle Books, Inc. Reprinted and recorded by permission of Sanford Ross Management, Nashville, TN.

PHOTO CREDITS

Pupil Book:

HRW photos by Bruce Buck on pp. 7, 149, 162, 172, 175; Russell Dian pp. 85, 86, 92, 93; Henry Groskinsky p. 57; Elizabeth Hathon pp. 5, 29; Richard Haynes pp. 68, 69, 82, 84, 86, 93, 95, 96, 117, 130, 131, 140, 144, 145, 150, 152, 161, 169, 170; Don Huntstein p. 112; Ken Karp pp. 39, 84, 85, 86, 87, 90, 91, 92, 93, 128, 132, 134, 137, 138, 139, 181; John Kelly p. 79; Ken Lax pp. 90, 92, 93; John Lei pp. 26–27, 163, 189; Greg Schaler p. 118.

p. 13 Martha Swope; 20 Jim Brandenburg/Bruce Coleman; 24 Ernst Haas/Magnum Photos; 25 Oak Ridge Boys, P.R.; 25 Les Friedlander, CBS Records; 28 Kunsthistorisches Museum, Vienna © Archive/Photo Researchers; 44 © 1985 Martha Swope; 54 Robert Semeniuk/The Stock Market; 61 Museum of Modern Art, N.Y., Mrs. Simon Guggenheim Fund; 66 Adam Wolfitt, Juha Jormanainen/Woodfin Camp Agency; Ric Ergenbright, Mary Ergenbright; Enrique Shore/Woodfin Camp Agency; 67 © 1986 Jack Vartoogian Agency; © 1982 Thomas Nebbia, Michael S. Yamashita/Woodfin Camp Agency; Nawrocki Stock Photo, © 1985 Jack Vartoogian; 68 Dan J. McCoy, Neal Preston/Camera 5; 81 Rosalie La Rue Faubion/Bruce Coleman; 84 Xylophone, Indonesia; 85 Crescent, Turkey; 91 Harp, Burma; 92 Sheng, China, The Metropolitan Museum of Art, The Crosby Brown Collection of Musical Instruments, 1889; 84 Sistrum, Egypt, The Metropolitan Museum of Art, Gift of C. and E. Canessa; 85 Rattle, Africa, U.C.L.A. Ethnomusicology Program; 87 Kaganu, Africa, Professor J. H. Nketia, U.C.L.A. Ethnomusicology Program; 90 Sarangi, India, The Metropolitan Museum of Art, Gift of Mrs. Harold Krechmer in memory of her husband, 1982; 92 Bone Flute, Venezuela, P. Hollembeak, The American Museum of Natural History; 101 © 1980 Alon Reininger/Woodfin Camp Agency; 102 Curt Gunther/Camera 5; 105 © 1985 Jack Vartoogian; 106 John Anderson/Click Chicago; Rod Planck, Gary Milburn/Tom Stack Agency; Pete Rosendale, William Meyer, Paul Roberts/Click Chicago Agency; 109 © Catherine Noren; 112 Robert Lightfoot III, Nawrocki Stock Photo; 118 Bettmann Archive, Jook Leung/Stereo Review, Sony Corporation of America, Culver Pictures; 119 Oil on Canvas by Adolph von Menzel, Granger Collection; 121 Hoagy Carmichael Jr.; 124 Wolfgang Bayer/Bruce Coleman; 124 Kenneth W. Fink/Photo Researchers; 124 Richard Blair; 158 Marc Solomon/Image Bank; 160 The Mansell Collection; 187 Martha Swope; 192 Chuck O'Rear/Woodfin Camp Agency; 195 Detail of Needlework on Wing Chair, The Metropolitan Museum of Art, Gift of Mrs. J. Insley Blair, 1950; 198 Walking Lions, Babylonian Ceramics, Period of Nebuchadnezzar II, The Metropolitan Museum of Art, Fletcher Fund, 1931; 203 Lawrence Fried/Image Bank; 205 Gerhard Gscheidle/Image Bank; 216 Museum of Modern Art, N.Y.

Teacher's Edition:

HRW Photos by Elizabeth Hathon appear on pp. ii–iii (top), xvi–xxi.
HRW Photos by Richard Haynes appear on pp. ii–iii (bottom).

ART CREDITS

Pupil Book:

pp. 9, 21, 218 Thomas Thorspecken; pp. 12, 143 Steven Cieslawski; p. 30 Robin Moore; pp. 52, 199 Debbie Dieneman; pp. 63, 64 Linda Miyamoto; pp. 70, 71 Arthur Walsh; p. 159 Arthur Thompson; p. 202 Curtis Woodbridge/Represented by Mulvey Associates, Inc.; p. 10 Les Gray; p. 43 Tom Powers; p. 136 Bill Colrus/Represented by Publisher's Graphics, Inc.; p. 14 Paul Harvey; pp. 58, 164, 165 Patti Boyd; p. 206 James Watling/Represented by Philip M. Veloric; p. 57 Lane Yerkes/Represented by Lou Gullatt; p. 75 Guy Kingsbery/Represented by Bookmakers, Inc.; pp. 125, 126, 127 Susan Miller/Represented by Ascuitto Art Representatives, Inc.; pp. 129, 167, 179, 180, 216 Sal Murdocca; p. 175 Jan Pyk; pp. 183, 184 Fred Winkowsky/Represented by Carol Bancroft and Friends, Inc.; p. 181 Susan Dodge.

All technical art prepared by Jimmie Hudson and Bud Musso. All black and white instrument art prepared by Jimmie Hudson, Brian Molloy and Bud Musso. All cartography prepared by Paul Pugliese.

Teacher's Edition:

All technical art prepared by Vantage Art.

All illustrative art prepared by Jody Wheeler/Represented by Publisher's Graphics, Inc.

Classified Index of Music, Art, and Poetry

*Topics of special interest to teachers who use the Kodaly and Orff methods are indicated with a **K** and an **O**.*

ART REPRODUCTIONS
Simultaneous Contrasts: Sun and Moon (1913) *(Robert Delaunay)*, 59
Detail depicting a scribe from St. Gregory statue *(Middle Ages)*, 28
Ivory-relief book cover *(Tenth Century)*, 28
Ranashringa (Indian Trumpet), 65
Bone flute from Venezuela *(Hoti Indians)*, 92
Detail of needlework upholstery on wing chair *(Queen Anne Type)*, 195
Walking lions in relief (Panel One of pair) *(Mesopotamian, Babylonian Ceramics)* 198

COMPOSED SONGS
Alla en el Rancho Grande *(S. Ramos)*, 80
America *(L. Bernstein)*, 44
As Tears Go By *(M. Jagger, K. Richards, and A.L. Oldham)*, 18
Baby, Please Don't Go *(B. Broonzy)*, 141
Bamboo *(D. Van Ronk)*, 34
Bell Gloria *(B. Red)*, 217
Bo Diddley *(E. McDaniel)*, 10
Bo Weevil *(A. Domino and D. Bartholomew)*, 159
Bourrée for Bach *(J.S. Bach)*, 214
Cruel War, The *(P. Stookey and P. Yarrow)*, 48
Deep Fork River Blues *(T. Paxton)*, 157
Delta Dawn *(A. Harvey and L. Collins)*, 26
Dundai *(Composer unknown)*, 63
Ease on Down the Road *(C. Smalls)*, 13
Encouragement *(J.N. White)*, 178
Everything Is Beautiful *(R. Stevens)*, 210
Fiddler on the Roof *(J. Bock)*, 30
59th Street Bridge Song, The *(P. Simon)*, 148
Five Hundred Miles *(H. West)*, 54
Get Thy Bearings *(D. Leitch)*, 49
Getting to Know You *(R. Rodgers)*, 174
Goin' Up Yonder *(W. Hawkins)*, 76
Guantanamera *(J.F. Dias)*, 147
Home Road, The *(J.A. Carpenter)*, 192
I Am Falling Off a Mountain *(B. Andress)*, 58
I Walk the Line *(J. Cash)*, 12
I Write the Songs *(B. Johnston)*, 185
It's a Long Road to Freedom *(Sr. M.T. Winter, SCMM)*, 52
Jungle *(J. Lynne)*, 125
Leaving of Liverpool *(W. Schmid)*, 22
Lonesome Traveler *(L. Hays)*, 8
Lord, Lord, I've Got Some Singing to Do *(R. Schertz)*, 170
M.T.A. Song, The *(J. Steiner and B. Hawes)*, 136
Memphis, Tennessee *(C. Berry)*, 17
Miracle, The *(M. Reynolds)*, 69
Oh Be Joyful *(N. Sleeth)*, 50
Oh, Lonesome Me *(D. Gibson)*, 166
Place in the Sun, A *(B. Wells)*, 20
Put Your Hand in the Hand *(G. MacLellan)*, 153
Rain *(R. LoPresti)*, 218
Ramblin' Boy *(T. Paxton)*, 21
Sixteen Tons *(M. Travis)*, 139
Sixty-Six Highway Blues *(P. Seeger, W. Guthrie, and J. Silverman)*, 42
Song Sung Blue *(N. Diamond)*, 172
Summer Morning *(W.S. Haynie)*, 181
There's a Meetin' Here Tonight *(B. Gibson)*, 177
Tie Me Kangaroo Down *(R. Harris)*, 182
Which Is the Properest Day to Sing? *(T. Arne)*, 212
Woodchuck, The *(P. Shaw)*, 199
Wreck of the Edmund Fitzgerald, The *(G. Lightfoot)*, 74
You Just Can't Make It by Yourself *(B. Dane)*, 33

CONTEMPORARY
Circles *(L. Berio)*, 59
Color Him Folky *(H. Roberts)*, 155
Composition for Synthesizer *(M. Babbitt)*, 97
Duelin' Banjos *(E. Weissberg)*, 7
Fanfare for the Common Man *(A. Copland)*, 122
Gymnopédie No. 3 (excerpt) *(E. Satie)*, 41
Microtimbre I for Amplified Tam-Tam *(R. O'Donnell)*, 60
Monkey Chant *(J. Field and T. Duhig)*, 116
Piece for Tape Recorder, A *(V. Ussachevsky)*, 97
Raga Puriya Dhanashri *(R. Shankar)*, 70
Reelin' and Rockin' *(C. Berry)*, 153
Silver Apples of the Moon *(M. Subotnick)*, 97
Spinning Wheel *(D.C. Thomas)*, 149
Stardust *(H. Carmichael)*, 120
Talking Guitar Blues *(E. Tubbs)*, 151
Wolf Eyes *(P. Winter)*, 124

COWBOY SONGS
Alla en el Rancho Grande, 80

FOLK SONGS—K, O
African
Mwatye, 101
Zenizenabo, 72

American
Bile Them Cabbage Down, 129
Down in the Valley, 142
Follow the Drinkin' Gourd, 63
Go Down, Moses and Joshua Fought the Battle of Jericho, 196
Goin' Down to Town, 38
Good News, 108
He's Got the Whole World in His Hands, 151
I'm Going Down the Road, 156
Jacob's Ladder, 47
Old Joe Clarke, 135
On Top of Old Smoky, 156
Red River Valley, 131
Shady Grove, 95
William Goat, 57
Worried Man Blues, 132

English
Scarborough Fair, 200

Guyanese
Ging Gong Gooli, 203

Irish
Know Where I'm Goin', 16

Italian
The Bagpipers' Carol, 194

Jewish
Brethren in Peace Together, 36
Dundai, 63

Mexican
La Bamba, 190

FOREIGN-LANGUAGE SONGS
African
Mwatye *(Zimbabwe)*, 101
Zenizenabo, 72

Hebrew
Dundai, 63

Spanish
Alla en el Rancho Grande, 80
La Bamba, 190

HOLIDAYS AND SPECIAL DAYS
Christmas
The Bagpipers' Carol, 194

Patriotic
Cruel War, The, 48
Home Road, The, 192
Lakota National Anthem, 79

Valentine's Day
Getting to Know You, 174

LISTENING LESSONS
Atsia, 88
Badinerie (W. Carlos), 116
Badinerie from Orchestra Suite in B Minor (J.S. Bach), 110
Bile Them Cabbage Down, 168
Circles (L. Berio), 59
Color Him Folky (H. Roberts), 155
Colorado Trail, The, 140
Composition for Synthesizer (M. Babbitt), 97
Concerto in G Major for Two Mandolins, Strings, and Organ (A. Vivaldi), 119
Conversation With Milton Babbitt, 96
De Natura Sonoris (K. Penderecki), 110
Donkey Kong Theme, 164
Duelin' Banjos (E. Weissberg), 6
Fanfare for the Common Man (A. Copland), 122
Fiddler on the Roof (J. Bock), 16
First Movement of Symphony No. 40 in G Minor (W.A. Mozart), 114
Gymnopédie No. 3 (excerpt) (E. Satie), 40
Hudan Mas (excerpt), 89
I Walk the Line, 118
Just a Closer Walk With Thee (Jackson), 118
Kalagala Ebwembe from Africanus Brasilerias Americanus (excerpt), 116
Kalamtianos, 90
Kele'a, 92
''Ketjak'' Chorus from The Ramayana, 70
Magic Fire Music from Die Walküre (R. Wagner), 110
Menuetto II from String Quartet in F Major (attributed to B. Franklin), 16
Microtimbre I for Amplified Tam-Tam (R. O'Donnell), 60
Minuet from Symphony No. 40 in G Minor (W.A. Mozart), 110
Monkey Chant (J. Field and T. Duhig), 116
No Reaction Recording, 10

Oldest Rabbit Song, 86
Piece for Tape Recorder, A (V. Ussachevsky), 97
Raga Puriya Dhanashri, 102
Rakish Paddy, 92
Reelin' and Rockin' (C. Berry), 153
Sematimba ne Kikwabanga, 84
Silver Apples of the Moon (M. Subotnick), 97
Spinning Wheel (D.C. Thomas), 149
Stardust (H. Carmichael), 118
Symphony No. 40 in G Minor, First Movement (W.A. Mozart), 114
Talking Guitar Blues (E. Tubbs), 151
This Train, 152
Trouble in Mind, 84
Waltz from Les Patineurs (excerpt) (G. Meyerbeer), 40
Wedding March from A Midsummer Night's Dream (F. Mendelssohn), 40
What Makes My Baby Cry?, 92
Wolf Eyes (P. Winter), 124
You Are My Sunshine (A. Franklin), 18
Zenizenabo, 72

MINOR, MODAL, AND PENTATONIC SONGS— K, O
Minor
Deep Fork River Blues, 157
Dundai, 63
Get Thy Bearings, 49
Lonesome Traveler, 8
Lord, Lord, I've Got Some Singing to Do, 170
Miracle, The, 69
Shady Grove, 95

Modes
Aeolian
Brethren in Peace Together, 36
Follow the Drinkin' Gourd, 63
Rain, 218

Dorian
Scarborough Fair, 200
When You're Gone, 23

Mixolydian
Alabama Bound, 143
Wreck of the Edmund Fitzgerald, The, 74

Pentatonic
Bell Gloria, 217
Cruel War, The, 48
Five Hundred Miles, 54

PARTNER SONGS
Go Down, Moses and Joshua Fought the Battle of Jericho, 196

PART SINGING
Two-Part
As Tears Go By, 18
Bo Diddley, 10
Dundai, 63
Ease on Down the Road, 186
Encouragement, 178
Follow the Drinkin' Gourd, 63
Go Down, Moses and Joshua Fought the Battle of Jericho, 196
Good News, 108
Home Road, The, 192
I Write the Songs, 185
It's a Long Road to Freedom, 52
La Bamba, 190
Lord, Lord, I've Got Some Singing to Do, 170
Ring, Ring the Banjo, 6
Song Sung Blue, 172
Woodchuck, The 199
You Just Can't Make It by Yourself, 33

Three-Part
Alla en el Rancho Grande, 80
Everything Is Beautiful, 210
Getting to Know You, 174
Goin' Up Yonder, 76
Good News, 107
Home Road, The, 192
I Am Falling Off a Mountain, 58
Scarborough Fair, 200
Zenizenabo, 72

Four-Part
Bagpipers' Carol, The, 194
Bourrée for Bach, 214
Delta Dawn, 188
Five Hundred Miles, 206
Ging Gong Gooli, 203
Kid Stuff, 56
Oh Be Joyful, 50
Place in the Sun, A, 20
Rain, 218
Which Is the Properest Day to Sing?, 212
William Goat, 57

Five-Part
Bell Gloria, 217
Tie Me Kangaroo Down, 182

PATRIOTIC SONGS (SEE HOLIDAYS AND SPECIAL DAYS)

PENTATONIC (SEE MINOR, MODAL, AND PENTATONIC SONGS)

POETRY AND CHANTS—O
Song of the Wandering Aengus, The (W.B. Yeats), 97
stinging gold swarms (e.e. cummings), 59

POPULAR SONGS
As Tears Go By, 18

Cruel War, The, 48
Delta Dawn, 188
Ease on Down the Road, 186
Everything Is Beautiful, 210
59th Street Bridge Song, The, 148
I Write the Songs, 185
Oh, Lonesome Me, 166
Put Your Hand in the Hand, 153
Song Sung Blue, 172
Wreck of the Edmund Fitzgerald, The, 74

ROUNDS AND CANONS
Summer Morning, 181
Teens, 99
Woodchuck, The, 199

SINGING GAMES, PLAY-PARTY SONGS, AND DANCES
Ring, Ring the Banjo, 6

SONGS IN $\frac{6}{8}$, $\frac{3}{8}$, $\frac{3}{4}$, $\frac{12}{8}$, AND CHANGING METER— O
Six-Eight
America, 44
Bagpipers' Carol, The, 194
Brethren in Peace Together, 36
Which Is the Properest Day to Sing?, 212

Three-Eight
Lakota National Anthem, 79

Three-Four
Clementine, 145

Jacob's Ladder, 47
Kid Stuff, 56
Scarborough Fair, 200
Summer Morning, 181
William Goat, 57
Wreck of the Edmund Fitzgerald, The, 74

Twelve-Eight
Song Sung Blue, 172

SONGS WITH THREE TONES—K, O
Good News, 106

THREE-CHORD SONGS
Alla en el Rancho Grande, 80
Bile Them Cabbage Down, 129
Bo Diddley, 10
Bo Weevil, 159
Deep Fork River Blues, 157
59th Street Bridge Song, The, 148
Go Down, Moses, 196
Goin' Down to Town, 38
Guantanamera, 147
I'm Going Down the Road, 156
It's a Long Road to Freedom, 52
Joshua Fought the Battle of Jericho, 196
La Bamba, 190
Leaving of Liverpool, 22
Lonesome Traveler, 8
Mama Don't 'Low, 154
Old Joe Clarke, 135
On Top of Old Smoky, 156
Put Your Hand in the Hand, 153
Ring, Ring the Banjo, 6

Shady Grove, 95
Sixteen Tons, 139
There's a Meetin' Here Tonight, 177
Worried Man Blues, 132
You Just Can't Make It by Yourself, 33

TRADITIONAL
Alabama Bound, 143
Clementine, 145
Down in the Valley, 142
Hold the Wind, 158
Just a Closer Walk With Thee, 24
Kid Stuff, 56
London Bridge, 57
Mama Don't 'Low, 154
Paw-Paw Patch, 57
Putting on the Style, 146
Ring, Ring the Banjo, 6
Rocka My Soul, 150
She Wore a Yellow Ribbon, 133

TWO-CHORD SONGS
Alabama Bound, 143
Bagpipers' Carol, The, 194
Clementine, 145
Good News, 106
He's Got the Whole World in His Hands, 151
Jacob's Ladder, 47
London Bridge, 57
Paw-Paw Patch, 57
Putting on the Style, 146
Rocka My Soul, 150

WORK SONGS
Sixteen Tons, 139

Classified Index of Activities and Skills

*Topics of special interest to teachers who use the Kodaly and Orff methods are indicated with a **K** and an **O**.*

ACTIVITY PAGES IN THE PUPIL BOOK

Accompany Your Song, 53
Aerophones, 92–93
Bottleneck Guitar, 152
Categories of Musical Style, 168
Chordophones, 90–91
Create a Choral Piece, 59
Electrophones, 96
Harmonica, The, 140
Idiophones, 84–85
Instrumental Combos, 161
Interpreting Notation, 40
Jug, The, 132
Language and Music of the Wolves, 124
Learn to Read Melody, 33
Learn to Read Rhythm, 32
Make Your Own Aerophones and Chordophones, 94
Melodies Around the World, 100–101
Membranophones, 86–87
Message: Music, The, 20
Message Transmitted: Performer, The, 24–25
Message: Words, The, 21
Modern Symphony Orchestra, The, 110–113
More Help From the Meter Signature, 42
More Skiffle Instruments, 134
Mouthbow, The, 137
Organizing Music in Time and Space, 104
Read Melodies Based on Different Scales, 49
Read Melody in a Major Key, 46
Sounds Exist in Space, 37
Sounds Exist in Time, 36
Spoons, The, 130
Vocal Sound Prints, 68–69
Washtub Bass, The, 138
Whole Earth Sings, The, 70–71
You, the Composer of Video-Game Music, 164–165
You, the Record Collector, 118
Your Own Message, 23
Your Singing Voice, 8, 9

CAREERS, 112, 163–165

CREATIVE ACTIVITIES—O

constructing instruments, 82, 88, 94, 137–139
improvising accompaniments, 22, 35, 39, 53–59, 82, 156, 159, 217
improvising melodies, 11, 22, 58–59, 77, 82, 100, 105, 185
improvising movements, 179, 204

improvising rhythm patterns, 82, 131, 138
sound exploration and composing, 23, 59, 82, 162–165

CURRICULUM CORRELATION

Language Arts
American Indian language (Lakota Tribe), 79
ballad history, 74
language and music similarities, 12, 16
Latin terms, 206

Nursery Rhymes
London Bridge, 57
Paw-Paw Patch, 57

Poems
A Place in the Sun, 20, 22
Ramblin' Boy, 20, 22
Song of the Wandering Aengus, The, 96
stinging gold swarms, 59
Wreck of the Edmund Fitzgerald, The, 74–75

Spanish Language, 80, 147, 190

Stories
Ramayana ("Story of Rama"), 73

Textual Idea, 20, 23–24, 206

Physical Education
movement and pantomime, 8, 9, 31, 73

Science
acoustical properties of instruments, 60–61, 82–95
electronic instruments, 96–97, 116
wolves, 124

Social Studies
American history, 114
American Indians, 79
Australia, 183
commercial music, 162–165
encouraging others, 179
Oral Tradition, The, 12–13

World Cultures, 65–93, 98–105
Africa, 72, 88, 101, 104–105
Bali, 73
British Isles, 74
India, 102–103

ELECTRONIC MUSIC, 60–61, 96–97

EXPRESSION
articulation, 69, 172, 175, 195
overall expressive quality, 12, 20–25, 36–37, 58–59, 68–69, 76, 77, 79, 82, 84, 89, 90, 92, 122–123, 156, 158–159, 162, 165, 179, 186, 206–207
tempo, 73, 77, 98, 100, 170
volume, 69, 73, 77, 105, 120, 170, 173, 195, 200–201, 214

EVALUATIONS, 63–64, 116, 168, 218–219

FORM—K, O
call-response form, 124, 143
concerto principles, 119
interludes, 9, 125
introduction, 75, 125
ostinato, 106, 199
part songs, 212–213
same–different, 7, 30–31, 41, 101, 104–105, 122, 124–126, 148, 154, 162, 164, 177
sections, 104–105, 204, 211
sonata allegro, 114–115
theme and variation, 105
two- and three-part, 20, 74–75, 114–115
verse–refrain, 9, 52, 77

HARMONY
chords, 14, 15, 21, 26, 30, 52–57, 77, 80, 126, 137, 138, 145, 150–152, 158, 172–173, 203
harmonic lines, 6, 7, 13, 18, 19, 21, 52, 55, 104, 106–108, 124, 126, 138, 144–146, 148, 150, 152–155, 160–161, 181–182, 185, 196–197, 200, 210–211
major chords, 37, 54
ostinato, 59, 199
seventh chords, 54–55, 57, 145, 150, 152
tonality, 56, 114, 196, 203

INSTRUMENTAL ACTIVITIES—O
autoharp, 20, 137, 203–204
bass viol, 42, 52
claves, 34–35, 125–126
comb, 134–135
cowbell, 125–126
cymbals, 60–61, 89, 185
double bass, 183, 196–197
drums of all kinds, 22–23, 34–35, 44, 52, 73, 79, 89, 125–126, 196–197, 210
electric keyboard, 196–197
environmental sound sources and

invented instruments, 82, 88, 94

glockenspiel, 30–31, 89, 125–126, 160–161, 217

gong, 60–61, 89

guitar, 20, 42, 52, 144–156, 160–161, 196–197

handbells, 217

harmonica, 140–141

jug, 132–133

kazoo, 134–135

keyboard, 46, 48–49, 59

limberjack, 138–139

maracas, 34–35, 44, 125–126

metallophone, 89, 156, 160–161, 217

mouthbow, 136–137

piano, 34–35, 156, 158–159, 182, 217

resonator bells, 30–31, 46, 48–49, 59, 89, 158–165, 217

sleigh bells, 125–126

spoons, 130–131

students' string and wind instruments, 82, 160–161

synthesizer, 125–126

tambourine, 22–23, 30–31, 63–64

unspecified pitch instruments, 22–23, 217

unspecified unpitched instruments, 32–33

vibraslap, 125–126

washboard, 134–135

washtub bass, 138–139

woodblock, 22–23

Xylophone, 59, 158–159, 217
alto, 156
bass, 30, 31, 42, 125–126, 182

INSTRUMENTAL SKILLS
playing accompaniments, 22, 30, 34–35, 39, 42, 44, 53, 73, 79, 94, 125–126, 133–135, 142, 145, 146, 148–156
playing by ear, 140, 153
playing in parts, 33

INSTRUMENTS FEATURED IN LISTENING LESSONS

Bagpipes
Bagpipers' Carol, The, 194–195
Rakish Paddy, 92–93, 106–107

Band, Dixieland
Just a Closer Walk With Thee, 24–25

Band, Jazz
Route 66, 214–216

Band, Rock
Jungle (J. Lynne, The Electric Light Orchestra), 125–127

Banjo
Duelin' Banjos (E. Weissberg), 6

Brass ensemble
Fanfare for the Common Man (A. Copland), 122–123

Conch shells
Kele'a, 92–93, 106–107

Gamelan
Hudan Mas, 84–85, 89

Guitar
Duelin' Banjos (E. Weissberg), 6
Talkin' Guitar Blues (E. Tubbs), 151

Mandolin
Concerto in G Major for Two Mandolins, Strings, and Organ (A. Vivaldi), 118–119

Orchestra
Badinerie from Orchestra Suite in B Minor (J. S. Bach), 110–113
Circles (L. Berio), 59
De Natura Sonoris (K. Penderecki), 110–113
First Movement from Symphony No. 40 in G minor (W. A. Mozart), 114–115
Gymnopédie No. 3 (E. Satie), 40–41, 50
Magic Fire Music from Die Walküre (R. Wagner), 110, 113
Minuet from Symphony No. 40 in G minor (W. A. Mozart), 110–115
Waltz from Les Patineurs (G. Meyerbeer), 40–41, 50
Wedding March from A Midsummer's Night Dream (F. Mendelssohn), 40–41, 50

Percussion
Atsia, 88

Saxophone
Duet (P. Winter), 124–125
Wolf Eyes (P. Winter), 124–125

String Quartet
Menuetto II (attr. to B. Franklin), 160–161

Synthesizer
Badinerie (J. S. Bach, performed by W. Carlos), 116
Composition for Synthesizer (M. Babbitt), 96–97

Tam-Tam
Microtimbre I for Amplified Tam-Tam (R. O'Donnell), 60–61

Xylophone (amadina)
Sematimba ne Kikwabanga, 84–85, 104–105

LISTENING SKILLS
following a call chart, 122, 125–126, 154
following ikons, 26–27, 188–189

following music notation, 6, 34, 40, 60, 72, 75, 79, 120, 122, 125, 126, 148, 188–189
listening warm-ups, 10, 12, 14, 16
recognizing chords, 203
recognizing instruments, 6, 25, 84–87, 91, 93, 125, 128–130
recognizing a melody, 6, 12, 13
recognizing rhythms, 34
recognizing sounds, 14
recognizing words, 18

MELODY—K
chromatic scale, 164
major scale, 37–39, 46, 47, 49, 125, 154
melodic contour, 14, 36–37, 101, 124, 186, 200
melodic direction (up-down-same), 8, 10, 11, 14, 16, 100–101
melodic patterns, 20, 30, 34, 72, 76, 100, 101, 164, 175, 177
minor scale, 37, 68, 154, 170, 196
modal scales, 48, 74
pentatonic scale, 49, 54
scale organization, 33, 46–49, 51, 56
sequence, 122
step-skip-same, 6, 16, 22, 32, 47, 100–101, 140–141, 200
tonal center, 33–35, 38–39, 46, 47, 50–51, 100, 186
transposition, 100
whole-tone scale, 59

MOVEMENT (SEE ALSO *CREATIVE ACTIVITIES*)
body as percussion instrument, 44
patterned dance, 8, 9, 31

response to music elements
rhythmic, 44

NOTATING MUSIC
on computer, 165
with notation, 23, 33, 34, 51, 59–61, 88, 165

READING MUSIC
bass clef, 6, 42, 55
grand staff, 51
harmonic elements, 49, 112
melodic ikons, 16, 26–27, 94, 125, 140–142, 188–189
musical notation, 14, 17, 28–33, 36, 37, 40, 42, 46, 48, 49, 51, 52, 53, 58, 68, 72, 74, 76, 77, 80, 94, 100, 101, 119, 125, 132, 136, 138, 158, 160–161, 162–163
rhythmic ikons, 40, 98, 125, 178
scale numbers, 137
score, 88, 89, 185, 188–189, 196–197, 214

RHYTHM—K
beat and accent, 20, 32–33, 36, 40–42, 44, 50–51, 56–57,

98–100
even–uneven, 38
longer–shorter–same, 34–35, 38, 120
meter, 17, 36, 38, 40, 42, 44, 50, 56, 98–99
mixed meter, 23
rhythmic patterns, 13, 22, 23, 33–35, 38, 42, 56–57, 63, 73, 88, 126, 130–131, 178, 181, 210
shortest sounds, 17, 32, 34, 36, 40, 54, 63, 99, 136, 173, 182, 218
stressed sound, 32–33, 40–42, 44, 50–51, 56–57, 188
syncopation, 50, 67, 76
underlying pulse, 34–36, 38–39, 50, 98–99, 130–131, 177, 185, 188, 204

SINGING SKILLS—K

antiphonal singing, 30, 32, 105
breath control, 199–201
chanting, 11, 17, 77, 99, 174–175, 210, 212
choral speaking, 58
diction, 201, 212
echoing, 11, 16, 158, 174
singing in parts, 15, 19, 21, 26, 49, 58, 63, 72, 77, 80, 100, 178–179, 181–183, 185–186, 194, 196–197, 200–201, 207, 210–212, 218
singing with scale numbers, 50, 178, 181, 194
vibrato, 69
vocal accompaniments, 15, 19, 21, 26, 49, 52, 55, 106, 154
vocal ranges, 8, 11, 69

STYLES, 18, 24–27, 34, 70–77, 79–81, 84–94, 96–101, 104–107, 110–116, 118–123, 128–129, 137, 140–141, 156, 212–215

TEXTURE, 18–19, 98–99, 106–109, 181, 194–195, 206, 210, 212

TIMBRE, 60–61, 68–73, 79, 82, 84–88, 90–94, 96–97, 128, 132–142, 154, 214

TIME AND PLACE, 28, 66–67, 70–77, 79, 80, 84–87, 90–94, 96–101, 104–116, 118–121, 128–129, 136–137, 156–157, 188, 194

Alabama Bound, 143
Alla en el Rancho Grande, 80
America, 44
Anduve (Brazil), 66
Are You Sleeping?, 28
Armour Hot Dog Song, The, 163
As Tears Go By, 18
Atsia (Africa), 88
Azuma Jishi (Japan), 66

Baby, Please Don't Go, 141
Badinerie (W. Carlos), 116
Badinerie (J. S. Bach), 110
Bagpipers' Carol, The, 194
Bamboo, 34
Banuwa, 104
Bell Gloria, 217
Bile Them Cabbage Down, 129
Bo Diddley, 10
Bo Weevil, 159
Bourrée for Bach, 214
Brethren in Peace Together, 36

Circles (L. Berio), 59
Clementine, 145
Color Him Folky (H. Roberts), 155
Colorado Trail, The (harmonica demonstration), 140
Composition for Synthesizer (M. Babbitt), 97
Concerto in G Major (A. Vivaldi), 119
Conversation With Milton Babbitt (monologue), 96
Cruel War, The, 48

Dance Song (Eskimo), 66
De Natura Sonoris (K. Penderecki), 110
Deep Fork River Blues, 157
Delta Dawn, 26, 188
Donkey Kong (video game), 165
Down in the Valley, 142
Duelin' Banjos (E. Weissberg), 7
Duet (P. Winter), 124
Dundai, 63

Ease on Down the Road, 13, 186
Encouragement, 178
Everything Is Beautiful, 210

Fanfare for the Common Man (A. Copland), 122
Fiddler on the Roof, 30
59th Street Bridge Song, The, 148
Five Hundred Miles, 54, 206
Follow the Drinkin' Gourd, 64

Get Thy Bearings, 49
Getting to Know You, 174
Ging Gong Gooli, 203
Go Down, Moses and Joshua Fought the Battle of Jericho, 196
Goin' Down to Town, 38
Goin' Up Yonder, 76
Good News, 106
Guantanamera, 147

Gymnopédie No. 3 (E. Satie), 41
He's Got the Whole World in His Hands, 151
Hold the Wind, 158
Home Road, The, 192
Hudan Mas (Javanese), 89

I Am Falling Off a Mountain, 58
I Walk the Line, 12
I Write the Songs, 7, 185
I'm Going Down the Road, 156
It's a Long Road to Freedom, 52

Jacob's Ladder, 47
Jungle, 125
Just a Closer Walk With Thee, 24

Kalagala Ebwembe (arr. P. Winter), 116
Kalamtianos (Greece), 90
Kele'a (Tonga), 92
"Ketjak" Chorus (Bali), 73
Kid Stuff, 56
Know Where I'm Goin', 16

La Bamba, 190
La Huichola (Mexico), 70
Lakota National Anthem, 79
Leaving of Liverpool, 22
London Bridge, 56
Lonesome Traveler, 8
Lord, Lord, I've Got Some Singing to Do, 170

Magic Fire Music (R. Wagner), 110
Mama Don't 'Low, 14, 154
Memphis, Tennessee, 17
Menuetto II (B. Franklin), 160
Microtimbre I for Amplified Tam-Tam (R. O'Donnell), 60
Miracle, The, 69
Monkey Chant (J. Field and T. Duhig), 116
M.T.A. Song, The, 136
Mwatye, 101

Oh Be Joyful, 50
Oh, Lonesome Me, 166
Old Joe Clarke, 135
Oldest Rabbit Song (American Indian), 86
On Top of Old Smoky, 141, 156
Oscar Mayer Wiener Song, The, 162

Paw-Paw Patch, 56
Piece for Tape Recorder, A (V. Ussachevsky), 97
Place in the Sun, A, 20
Put Your Hand in the Hand, 153
Putting On the Style, 146
Rabbit Dance (American Indian), 70
Raga Puriya Dhanashri (R. Shankar), 102
Rain, 218
Rakish Paddy (Scotland), 92

Ramblin' Boy, 21
Red River Valley, 131
Reelin' and Rockin' (C. Berry), 153
Ring, Ring the Banjo, 6
Robot Basketball Theme (arr. F. Willman), 164
Rocka My Soul, 150
Route 66 (B. Troup), 214

Saeta (Spain), 70
Scarborough Fair, 200
Sematimba ne Kikwabanga (Uganda), 84
Shady Grove, 95
She Wore a Yellow Ribbon, 133
Silver Apples of the Moon (M. Subotnick), 97
Sixteen Tons, 139
Sixty-Six Highway Blues, 42
Soldier's Joy (spoons demonstration), 130
Song Sung Blue, 172
Spinning Wheel (D. C. Thomas), 149
Spoons, The (demonstration), 130
Stardust (H. Carmichael), 120
Summer Morning, 181
Symphony No. 40 (W. Mozart), 114

Talking Guitar Blues (E. Tubbs), 151
Teens, 98
There's a Meetin' Here Tonight, 177
This Train (United States), 152
Tie Me Kangaroo Down, 182
Trouble in Mind (United States), 84

Waltz (G. Meyerbeer), 41
Wedding March (F. Mendelssohn), 40
What Makes My Baby Cry? (United States), 92
Which Is the Properest Day to Sing?, 213
William Goat, 57
Wolf Eyes (P. Winter), 124
Wolf Howls (authentic nature sounds), 124
Woodchuck, The, 199
Worried Man Blues, 132
Wreck of the Edmund Fitzgerald, The, 74

You Are My Sunshine (Davis and Mitchell), 18
You Just Can't Make It by Yourself, 32

Zenizenabo (Black South Africa), 72

TEACHER'S NOTES

TEACHER'S NOTES

TEACHER'S NOTES

TEACHER'S NOTES

TEACHER'S NOTES

TEACHER'S NOTES